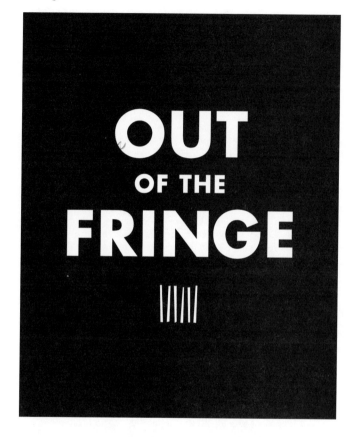

OUT
OF THE
FRINGE

CONTEMPORARY LATINA/LATINO
THEATRE AND PERFORMANCE

**Caridad Svich and
María Teresa Marrero,**
EDITORS

THEATRE COMMUNICATIONS GROUP

Out of the Fringe: Contemporary Latina/Latino Theatre and Performance
is published by Theatre Communications Group, Inc.,
355 Lexington Ave., New York, NY 10017–6603.

This publication is made possible in part with public funds from
the New York State Council on the Arts, a State Agency.

Theatre Communications Group wishes to acknowledge the Jerome Foundation
for helping to make this publication possible.

TCG books are exclusively distributed to the book trade by
Consortium Book Sales and Distribution, 1045 Westgate Dr., St. Paul, MN 55114.

Library of Congress Cataloging-in-Publication Data

Out of the fringe : contemporary Latina/o theatre and performance / edited by
Caridad Svich and María Teresa Marrero. — 1st ed.
p. cm.
ISBN 1-55936-171-9 (paper : alk. paper)
American drama—Hispanic American authors. 2. Hispanic American gays—Drama.
3. American drama—20th century. 4. Hispanic Americans—Drama. I. Svich,
Caridad. II. Marrero, María Teresa.
PS628.H57 O78 1999
812'.54080868—dc21   99-044193

Book design and typography by Lisa Govan
Cover design by Cynthia Krupat
Cover art by Nereida García-Ferraz

First edition, February 2000

We dedicate this anthology to
the many Latina/o playwrights, actors, directors,
dramaturgs and the various theatre artists
who continue to energize Latina/o theatre
in the United States and abroad.

CONTENTS

OUT OF THE FRINGE: IN DEFENSE OF BEAUTY

In the margins, in the black boxes, clubs, art galleries, performance spaces, garages, basements, universities, cabarets, poetry slams and other alternative spaces, a new kind of Latina/o theatre and performance aesthetic has been forged over the last ten years: a bold, frank, uncompromising, lyrical, private, metaphorical kind of work that re-visions what it is to be a Latina/o dramatist in the U.S. Created outside the mainstream of "official" culture (both Latina/o and Anglo), this new generation of theatrical writing seeks to deconstruct and reconstruct not only theatrical forms but also the boundaries by which those forms have been created. Drawing, in part, from the rich and varied exploration of a generation of novelists and visual artists from Spain and Latin America, these young dramatists have discovered new ways of shaping text, addressing the audience, working with language, and exploring and decoding the encoded taboos of the Latina/o culture. Feminist, proto-feminist, gay, lesbian, bisexual, transgressive, pagan, spiritual and reinvented Americans, these dramatists have slowly taken their work beyond the expected and established tropes made available to them by "official" culture, and in so doing have moved out of the fringe and into the virtual center of contemporary American performance.

In the 1970s and 1980s, Latina/o dramatists were encouraged by the bold experiments of master playwright and teacher Maria Irene Fornes, activist and storyteller Luis Valdez, maverick playwright and pioneering publisher of Latino/a work Pedro Monge-Rafuls, and a handful of other brave writers who were testing the uncharted, previously forbidden waters of American theatrical writing. An interest in old world versus new world issues—the border experience, multiculturalism and the postmodern hold of "magic realism" on the audience's imagination—led to the support and development of new work by mostly U.S.-born Latina/o writers. Theatres actively began seeking funding for work that would specifically address issues of ethnicity and gender in the hope of discovering new voices and serving a necessary political end. No longer could the generation upon generation of Latinos in this country be ignored. These were artists to be nurtured, and a growing visible audience among them as well.

However, support for development of such work, despite so many good intentions, bred a conservative expectation of the kind of work to be written. Although Fornes, Valdez, Miguel Piñero and others were breaking structural and emotive ground in their work, regional theatres, which receive the bulk of the funding for development, favored work that dealt with the Latina/o experience in the United States as "exotic," or imitative of other "immigrant" experiences. "Magic realism" became the convenient code word to describe a variety of theatrical work with little thought as to the term's origin or meaning, and with little regard to the diversity of subject matter and points of view emerging from the labs, workshops and festivals sponsored by the same theatres and organizations committed to their existence.

At the same time, solo artists, poets and self-styled wordsmiths were creating quick, furious works as part of the burgeoning performance art scene in cities across America. Aligned to the visual arts, creating pieces "against theatre," these artists were nonetheless influencing playwrights and students of playwriting in universities where performance studies served as the litmus test for the avant-garde. The Nuyorican Poets' Cafe, the WOW Cafe, Dixon Place, Sushi Gallery in San Diego, Highways in Los Angeles and a host of other venues spoke directly and imaginatively to an audience interested in the direct expression of the artist in space, whether through autobiographical texts, nonlinear word-image collages, installations, ritualized acts or other means. Though the work presented in these spaces did not always have verbal texts, a growing number did, and their nontraditional qualities, their very "anti-theatrical-ness," created not only a new audience but managed to filter into works made expressly for the theatre. Certainly, the works of individual artists and companies like John Jesurun, and Reza Abdoh and established companies like The Wooster Group and Mabou Mines owed a reciprocal debt to the performance art/storytelling artists that were staking new ground.

As funding in both the theatre and performance-art worlds dwindled in the mid-1980s and 1990s, the dividing line between these two worlds became less distinct, as performance artists began writing "plays," and playwrights began to adopt performance techniques. This was most evident in the works written by a new generation of Latina/o dramatists, who already had been investigating different methods of shaping texts in reaction to the extraordinary literary output of Latin American and Iberian fiction and its availability in translation, as well as the explosive nature of works by Latina/o visual artists, whose experiments with found materials, color, the ritualized body and scale were already sanctioned by and incorporated into the "official" culture. In addition, there was the reaction "against" notions of "Latino-ness" established by both the Anglo and the Latino culture, especially in the worlds of Spanish-language tabloid television and community theatre.

Bilingualism and biculturalism engenders not only a double view of society and one's place in it but also an outside perspective on one's own identity within the cultures of which one is part. If the U.S. Anglo world had its expectations and perceptions of who/what a Latino is, the U.S. Latino commercial world also created its own set of expectations. At issue was not only the language or languages one spoke, but how one presented oneself in society, down to what clothes one wore and what one thought about a given political situation. Celebrations of "Latinidad," while certainly valid, begged for a homogenized view of Latinos, reinforcing old world taboos and structures, whether the old world in each individual case was Mexico, Cuba, Puerto Rico or elsewhere.

The few theatres that presented Latino work tended to follow the established models of boulevard comedy, the educational/historical play, melodrama and works that specifically addressed the immigrant experience. Although "forbidden" territory was occasionally explored, it was a rarity to find expressions of the Latina/o gay or lesbian experience, or works by Latina/o dramatists that viewed America through a different lens besides (1) the established "exotic" lens, expected by the mostly white regional theatre community or (2) the "correctly ethnic" one expected by the Latino theatres. While one generation of playwrights' work was being produced and cast to the fate of public opinion, another was being left on the fringe, not necessarily abandoned, but certainly not allowed to be seen.

At the intersection of theatre and performance, this work developed in excitingly contrary ways, and was nurtured by an audience that was looking for expressions that reflected a wider range of reality (within and out of the Latino community) than the one represented by the various strands of the mainstream.

· · ·

In New York, a wave of playwrights stirred the significant waters of American theatre under the mentorship of master writer, Maria Irene Fornes. From all over the country, Latino writers came to work and study at her famed Lab housed at Intar Hispanic American Arts Center (New York City), and later at other venues. Graduate school refugees, self-taught writers, actors, performers, storytellers and sometimes the simply curious worked intensively at the Lab, producing a wealth of imaginative work determined to break with established and, therefore limiting, Western narrative structures.

At the Lab, performance artists from the Kitchen and Dixon Place shared a space with theatre-trained and -oriented writers. Although acknowledgment was made of the difference in sensibilities, at the Lab the writers were treated equally and experienced their work as such. The dividing line that was drawn outside the Lab's doors—uptown versus downtown—was erased inside, as work was developed under Fornes's demanding eye, and an atmosphere of rigorous, playful innovation and competition was created. Nothing was forbidden at the Lab. The personal, political and the outrageous, the gender and ethnically specific, the fictive and emotive all had a place where they could be voiced, be it through the vehicle of the well-made play, the traditions of the avant-garde, or more often an authorially created hybrid form.

Breaking ground in the early years of the Lab were Eduardo Machado, Cherríe Moraga and Milcha Sanchez Scott. Their works as well as that of others, such as José Rivera who trained outside of the Lab, could be deemed the "first wave" of Latina/o playwriting in the United States, following the singular presences of Fornes, Piñero and Valdez. Exploring issues of coming-of-age, assimilation, and incorporating elements of myth and history, they sought (and continue to do so) a new way to understand Latino identity. The success of Sanchez-Scott's *Roosters* and the critical notice of Machado's *The Modern Ladies of Guanabacoa*, Moraga's *Shadow of a Man*, and Rivera's *The House of Ramon Iglesia* focused national attention on not only the promise of these new voices in the American theatre but also on the prospect of discovering the riches of a heretofore ignored (by the mainstream culture) theatrical sensibility.

Government and corporate funding began to be aimed toward the development of Latina/o voices. Monies and interest were also invested in the translation of Spanish-language classic and modern plays into English. Acknowledgment and validation, which were for so long denied Latina/o artists, particularly in the theatre, were beginning to take place. Articles in *Time*, *Newsweek* and other popular national publications claimed that the time of the "Latino" in the United States had come. But the waters would not be sweet for long.

Spurred by the acclaim given to the "first wave" of playwrights, a younger school of writers decided to take the initial experiments set forth by Sanchez-Scott, Moraga and Machado and push them further to create a looser, more diverse, less paradigm-ridden work that would rock society's notion of what Latino theatre could be. Inspired in part by a wave of mostly New York-based wordsmiths who called themselves "language playwrights" (including Mac Wellman, Len Jenkin and Eric Overmyer), as well as the growing influence of imagistic theatre and performance art, this "second "wave" sought both a more realistic and more metaphorical kind of presentation, one that could exist outside the imposed "ghetto" of "Latino" theatre and sit in all its complexity at the "American" table.

Writers and performers like Migdalia Cruz, Coco Fusco, Nao Bustamante and Carmelita Tropicana went beyond issues of coming-of-age and assimilation to question the very fabric of both the Latino and Anglo cultures of which they were a part. Exploring taboos with the abandon granted to them by their forebears, they pushed the venerable envelope of what was "acceptable" representation. In acknowledging the gay and lesbian sensibility in Latina/o culture, the socially transgressive, the feminist and post-feminist, this second wave of dramatists upended all expectations at a time when such boldness was only tentatively encouraged, for the country was about to enter an era of "political correctness" as the fallout of the Reagan years diminished the initial spark of funding and general perceived societal interest.

Caught in between a still-burgeoning movement of writing, which had already produced two distinct waves of theatrical thought, of writers who were still in the midst of actively developing their craft, was a "third wave" of dramatists, storytellers and poets who were not so much interested in breaking taboos as creating work that was intensely personal and idiosyncratic—expressions of "Latinidad" without the word "Latino/a" necessarily attached. Eerie and lyrical, metaphysical and emotive, this third group of writers began to flourish in the margins of what was an already marginalized theatrical environment. Aligning themselves in part with the resurgent poetry and spoken-word movement, and alternative music and literature scenes, their work was bred on the economics of poverty, of presenting and/or nurturing work outside official venues. As national cultural wars raged over the NEA, appropriateness and the "elitism" of art, writers like Nilo Cruz, Luis Alfaro and Naomi Iizuka sought a purposeful elitism: politically engaged yet defiantly hard-won beauty.

Such defiance inspired in turn the work of the first and second wave, as José Rivera produced *Marisol*, Migdalia Cruz *Fur* and Cherríe Moraga *The Hungry Woman: Mexican Medea*. Challenging and provocative, elusive and strange, Latina/o writing in this country has traveled a great distance over the last ten years and it is of no small significance that this work—our work—is still considered new.

In a country where theatre is an almost invisible presence, save for the commercial theatre's musicals and British imports, Latina/o theatre is practically nonexistent in terms of the general populace's perception. *Zoot Suit* remains one of the few landmark pieces that an average educated audience is able to recognize, if only for the arresting image of Edward James Olmos's "Pachuco" character. For example, an artist of Maria Irene Fornes's caliber, who has been producing work for over forty years both here and abroad, is still virtually unknown in this country outside academic and theatrical circles, whereas Sam Shepard, who began his career at about the same time as Fornes, is widely known, despite his movie stardom.

This invisibility is due in part to mainstream culture's marginalization of the Latina/o population in this country even though it remains its fastest-growing "minority," as well as a history of neglect in the U.S.' relationship with South and Latin America. Although "Latin" music and art have been appropriated by and incorporated into the mainstream, Latina/o theatre, by virtue of its already marginal status, has been ignored, whereas other "minority" voices have been afforded a visible forum.

The provocative nature of Latina/o work is perhaps one reason the mainstream refuses to fully acknowledge its presence. Sensual, frank, disruptive and often centered around the body in relation to issues of cultural scarring and trauma, the strongest Latina/o writing for theatre and performance confronts audiences and critics alike with visions that do not sit comfortably with what the mainstream will *tolerate* from its "colorful" citizens. It is also work that by its very nature calls into question old world versus new world tensions, still alive as the "problems" of the border, and Latin and South America attest.

The various waves of Latina/o spectacle also confound conventional expectations. Although some of the work deals directly and explicitly with issues of ethnicity, a majority of it does not. What to do with a Latina/o writer that does not use "Spanglish," "sombreros," "salsa" or other *expected* cultural signs? How is one to "read" a text by a Latina/o dramatist if it does not fit the established mode? Why is this question not asked of a Russian-Jewish-American writer like David Mamet, or Irish-American writer like John Patrick Shanley?

Syncretic by nature, Latina/o theatre fuses images from American pop culture or myth with those from ancient or modern images from the Americas, while simultaneously offering an abstract, purely fictive reality. In Luis Alfaro's work, for example, concrete images from the Latino community coexist with pop references from American advertising and more personal symbols of Alfaro's making. The intersection of identities in such work is representative of a distinctly hybrid sensibility, which is at the core of Latina/o dramatic writing in the United Sates.

What makes the work different from other hybrid sensibilities is its refusal to fully integrate its syncretic strands. Instead, cultural allusions, mythic images and symbols of the writer's personal iconic vocabulary coexist on the same playing field, moving freely within the demands of a given text, with a fluidity which lays bare the very nature of being a hybrid-American, thus questioning the notion of "assimilated text."

If assimilation was one of the central issues debated in the plays of early Latina/o theatre and performance, where most of the work focused on coming-of-age and the immigrant experience, the spectacles that haunt our performing spaces today, and which give so many producers and critics discomfort, speak to the incorporated bodies of artists who are both inside and outside the American experience, artists who are willing to use the theatrical canvas as a way to reinvent and/or reimagine their history. When Oliver Mayer, for instance, addresses the American nomadic tradition in his text *Ragged Time*, his deliberate play with language fractured by slang and cultural idioms of another era addresses the difficulty of communication across time and indirectly across cultures. Although the piece is not identifiably "Latino" from a conventional, standardized perspective, Mayer's point of view as a writer directly bound to the Latino experience, allows him an opportunity to redefine the issue of how text is assimilated, and therefore how a text becomes an assimilated text vis-à-vis the culture of the mainstream.

Uncomfortable and demanding, Latina/o theatre and performance as evidenced in the work of Monica Palacios and others who
have come of age in the dawn of an incipient Latina/o theatrical revolution is both of the Americas and fits its own particular illusory
world. Creating texts of resonance and beauty at a time when the
mechanics of "yuppie" realism or the severely ironic, often coolly
nihilistic, stance of the postmoderns are in vogue, the courage to
stand outside, on the fringe—a position imposed by economics, politics and artistic bias—has allowed our writers to create an alternative dramatic language that speaks with power and grace about the
body politic, transitional identities and the complex workings of the
human heart, defending the concept of beauty at a time when it has
ceased to be fashionable. The work of the first, second, third and
future waves of Latina/o playwrights and performers, through its
concerns styles and subject matter, offers not only an alternative
legacy of dramatic writing in the Unites States, but a celebratorily
diverse record of what it means to be Latina/o in this country. As the
doors of mainstream theatres open to include the voices of Octavio
Solis, Edwin Sanchez, Carmen Rivera and less "identifiably
Hispanic" playwrights like Lisa Loomer and Lillian Garrett-Groag,
the possibilities for rewriting a dramatic vocabulary increase and
broaden the still-emerging portrait of Latina/o theatre. In so doing,
it speaks with imaginative fierceness of the possibilities that exist
outside artistically and culturally imposed borders and of the unex-
pected truths to be found out of the fringe.

Caridad Svich
Mark Taper Forum
Los Angeles, CA
December 1999

MANIFESTATIONS OF DESIRES:
A CRITICAL INTRODUCTION

In this anthology, ten of the most prolific Latina/o artists working in the late twentieth century find a temporary "home." (I place home in quotation marks due to the lack of overall homogeneity found among the pieces.) Some, like Caridad Svich's *Alchemy of Desire/Dead-Man's Blues* (1997) and *Fur* (1995) by Migdalia Cruz are set within an internal terrain, which the plays themselves construct, making no allusions to identifiable, specific, geographic locations (be they Hispanic or Anglo). Theirs is a self-contained world set within what could be termed the deliberations of language, the psychological, and the theatrical. Other plays: Luis Alfaro's *Straight as a Line* (1997), *Greetings from a Queer Señorita* (1995) by Monica Palacios, *Trash* (1995) by Pedro Monge-Rafuls, *Stuff* (1997) by Nao Bustamante and Coco Fusco, *Hungry Woman: Mexican Medea* (1997) by Cherríe Moraga and *Skin* (1995) by Naomi Iizuka clearly take a stance at the junction between the sexual, sexual preference, AIDS, postcolonial discourse and identity politics. However, Oliver Mayer's *Ragged Time* (1994) and Nilo Cruz's *Night Train to Bolina* (1993) do not fit into these categories. *Ragged Time* is constructed along the lines of the turn-of-the-century American vaudevillian tradition; *Night Train* fuses an absurdist sensibility to an implicit Latin American context.

The heterogeneous space of these texts is marked by a number of characteristics, the most prominent and innovative of which is the foregrounding of sexual identities that defy both Latino and Anglo cultural stereotypes. The contemplating of the central role of the physical body and its multiplicity of desires/states, serves as the temporary space for the performance of theatrical, cultural and gender expressions. In these works, notions of love, beauty, the beastly, death, the economy of desire among unequal "trade partners" and the unabashedly homoerotic often engage in the tension that Homi

Bhabha describes as the ambivalence of the stereotype in colonialist discourse. It is as if the generation of authors here have already digested/processed/expiated themselves of the repetitions of stereotypical "Latinidad" historically imposed upon their predecessors. Not only do they generally reject alluding to them, they seek the ambiguity of the gaps, of the poetic, of the theatrical. It is a space hard won by fifteen years of individual productions. Some of the works are contestatory in nature, in what I see as a conscious move away from the types "allowed" by Latino and non-Latino producing organizations. Therefore, I propose the concept of *re-formation* as a sort of re-grouping that has taken place in Latino theatre in the late 1990s, in which performance artists and playwrights have assumed a mature, self-confident, position within U.S. artistic communities. This is not to suggest that Latino plays circulate widely, though they may be produced with some regularity (if not certainty), and the authors in this book have achieved an admirable level of success.

Because a number of the works included in this volume deal with Latina/Latino gay and lesbian sensibilities, and because the open display of this sensibility indeed represents a breakthrough in Latina/o performing identities, I will begin by considering these plays first.

In Chon A. Noriega and Ana M. López's anthology, *The Ethnic Eye, Latino Media Arts* (Minneapolis: University of Minnesota Press, 1996), Frances Negrón-Muntaner, using Raymond William's concept of structure of feeling, offers six basic elements as characteristics of the gay and lesbian films she considers in her article "Drama Queens: Gay and Lesbian Independent Film/Video": formal hybridity (mixing of diverse genres and modes of address); self reflexivity; the construction of an artist persona often involved in a journey of self-discovery and confrontation; the representation of geographical dislocation; the contextualization of the subject's drama within the immediate and/or symbolic family; and the selfconscious use of media to construct an alternative reality for the speaking subject/subject of representation. While not all of the performances or plays display all of the aforementioned characteristics, they provide a useful initial framework for considering these plays.

Although Negrón-Muntaner's research focuses upon film and video, I find these constructs useful in discussing the work of Latino gay and lesbian performance. However, within the specificity of the work about to be considered, I feel the need to expand the categories to include: the notion of constructing a performance persona through the incorporation of playful, consciously irreverent humor, a humor which does not self-deprecate in any way; an inclination toward demonstrating a subtle, inferred awareness of gender stereotyping paralleled by the refusal to yield to dominant sexual and cultural taboos (particularly those raised by Latino Catholicism and the "sanctity" of the family); and the performance of sexual and cultural identities as a form of pleasure clearly coded within the female physical body. This playfulness in performing identities certainly plays a key role in some of the works; it is often the construction of a multiplicity of identities that stridently keeps taking the place of any "fixed" notion of either gender (homo or heterosexual), ethnic, cultural, political or artistic boundaries.

Thus, a one-woman performance like *Greetings from a Queer Señorita*, by Monica Palacios, initially carved in the battleground of standup comedy, simply picks up at that space already gained by Palacios and other lesbian standup comedians (such as television's Ellen De Generes), beyond the struggle and homophobia of the night club scene. *Greetings* takes on the direct pleasure felt by the lesbian character upon fantasizing on refreshingly new images, such as that of the Surfer Chola and Miss Sabrosita at the *taquería* (taco stand):

> Yes, I watched her eat her *carne asada tacos* from afar . . .
> She was a *Chicana*, brown woman, dark eyes, dark thick
> Mexican girl hair . . . athletic built and she was, *hungry!*
> Didn't just wolf down her two *tacos* and *Corona* with two
> limes. She consumed her meal creatively, slowly, tenderly—
> *Con pasión*—she closed her eyes after every bite . . . as if she
> was becoming one with the *carne asada*. OOOOMMME!
> Peaceful and beautiful she looked as her full *Chicana* lips
> produced *kisses* as she mas-ti-ca-ted!

Not only does Palacios tell us earlier in the text that she is a "lezbo—dyke—queer—homo—butch—*muff diver!*" but she lets us in on a secret: while lesbian sex is good, Chicana lesbian "brown" sex is better. By creating a Chicana/lesbian sexual nationalism, Palacios suggests the positive values of loving an Other who is like her Self. Gender and cultural identities blend in a seamless way. By signifying lesbian Chicana desire within the ambience of a self-confidence about being "out," and by describing the pleasure she emotionally and physically experiences from her sexuality, Palacios precludes the possibility of suggesting any anomaly.

Palacios includes a family scene in which she describes what happens when she brings her "wife" home to a Mexican family dinner. She announces: "My family—*mi familia, this is my wife!*" The polyphony of her family's reaction, after the initial "thick, intense silence" starts off with her mother's response: "Come on, everybody, let's eat. Food is getting cold . . ." To which Palacios retorts, addressing the audience: "You see they know, but they don't want to talk about it. What for? Why ruin a good meal?" In a one-woman act, Palacios plays all of the roles, multiplying herself into a family of seven characters.

Her family's reaction to her open lesbianism gives voice to a wide range of heterosexual as well as cultural biases. The mother wants to ignore it; the father demonstrates an unstereotypical (un-macho) helplessness, the older sister's comments about the girl-friend's "prettiness" make allusions to the unacceptability of a *mari-macho* (vulgar expression in Spanish meaning "butch") female, implying relief that the "wife" is not a butch-type; her two brothers are mainly concerned with protecting their macho privileges from the "corruption" (subversion) introduced by the acceptance of female/female desire; the young niece displays a brutal, child-like honesty by giving voice to the unspeakable: "L-word." The Latino notion of close family ties, however, requires that her family accept her in spite of their homophobia.

In *Straight as a Line*, Luis Alfaro's second nonperformance-art piece (the first was *Bitter Homes and Gardens*), Paulie and his Mum (both British) live out his days with AIDS in an absurdist thirteen-scene play set in the glitter of Las Vegas. Mum, a former prostitute, matter-of-factly acknowledges Paulie as a "chip off the old block" (it is implied that they both love "hard living"). The opening scene begins with them rehearsing Paulie's suicide in New York City:

> PAULIE: I should make it good. Need to jump in front of the *right* train. An express, don't you think?
> MUM: Good thinking . . . For the sake of cashing in on a considerable amount of frequent flyer miles, I would like to know if you are going to jump or not, dear?
> PAULIE: When I do, you should say something like, "My son, my son Paul . . ."
> MUM: *Paulie.* I want to say *Paulie.* A little less formal I think.

When his suicide attempt fails, she takes him home with her to Las Vegas, where she, a woman in her sixties, thrives, while he, a young man, withers. But first the text explores the relationship between two unconventional characters whose maternal/filial relationship subverts Catholic notions of self-sacrifice, and where his deteriorating physical condition serves as the centerpiece for the action.

Alfaro clearly positions himself as a gay rights activist in his work; his theatre and performance work arises from his deep political commitment. As in his other work, Alfaro offers a glimpse of gay male identity that is sometimes, but not always, encased within a Chicano framework. In *Straight as a Line* he experiments with a fictional voice other than that of the self-referential Chicano gay activist (as *in Cuerpo Politizado/Politicized Body*). In doing so, he moves us closer to a growing body of dramatic work that focuses on AIDS with humor and pathos.

Moving still further toward the male centered body, Pedro Monge-Raful's monologue, *Trash*, posits a painful look at the male body as locus of the U.S. stereotypical social construct of the Cuban Marielito immigrant as human "trash." Jesús, a young, athletic mulatto man who took advantage of the massive exodus allowed through the Peruvian embassy and the Havana port of Mariel in 1980, leaves Cuba and ends up in New York. The monologue exposes negative, circulating concepts of Marielitos as homosexuals, thieves and social deviants. Simultaneously Monge-Raful strips the Cuban immigrant's illusion of the U.S. as an imagined safe haven.

Although we don't know it until the end, Jesús is speaking from inside a jail cell. Jesús is a victim of appearances and circumstance. In need of money, he agrees to allow a stranger to give him fellatio. Although Jesús finds pleasure in the exchange, same-sex relations is not his primary preference. A struggle ensues after the sex when the man wants more than agreed. A gun Jesús is carrying accidentally goes off and the man is killed. The stranger happens to be a Catholic priest, and according to newspaper accounts he is a "pillar of the community." Jesús becomes incarcerated. By the end of the monologue, the audience feels his entrapment by circumstance; his subordinate and expendable position in U.S. society. He is presumed to be a gay "deviant" from Cuba. The cards of fate are stacked against him, regardless of his innocence or his "true" sexual orientation. What began as a simple economic exchange ends as a statement of homophobia and xenophobia.

Stuff, a comedic piece by Chicana performance artist Nao Bustamante and Cuban-American Coco Fusco, expands the imaginary horizon to discuss Latin women within the context of world-wide postcolonialist, neoliberal economies. Using the trope of a global tourist service, E. E. Jones (the only male in the performance piece) speaks to the audience from a TV monitor:

> Have you thought about what are you going to do on your next vacation? Would you like to try something . . . different? Most of my clients . . . long to bask in the sensual beauty and ancient wonders that my part of the world offers up so willingly. Then . . . they come back irritated by all of the tropical storms, masked bandits, parasites and poverty . . . I have devised a service that will bring you heat without sweat, ritual without revolution, and delicacies without dysentery.

Tapping upon key elements of the so-called First World's hunger for touristy tropicalizations of the "primitive" Third World, yet unable to move beyond its own fixation upon the clinical, the antiseptic, the virtual aspect of reality, *Stuff* places its fictional reality within the sexual and economic structures of the global, neoliberal marketplace.

Through the postspatial travel service, members of the audience are invited on stage to participate as Travel Tasters. One segment that illustrates the benefits of the hot international guide comes with translations for love and sex in seven different languages. Blanca (Fusco) engages a male Travel Taster in a "how to" seduction lesson in Spanish with the mediation of Rosa (Bustamante):

> BLANCA: ¡Me estás usando!
> ROSA: She thinks you're using her. Say it isn't true. That you're looking for love. "No es cierto—busco amor!
> TRAVEL TASTER: ¡No es cierto—busco amor!
> BLANCA: Y yo estoy buscando apoyo financiero (But I am looking for financial support.)

Disproportionate relations of economic power strip the amorous context of its possible seductive allure, grounding it within the realm of economic disparity. This is brilliantly illustrated by the character of Judy (Fusco), the Cuban transvesti who works within the Havana tourist economy commonly known as *jineterismo*. (From the word "jinete": a jockey, one who mounts. It is used to describe men and women who offer their services, sexual or otherwise, to dollar-spending European, Canadian and Mexican tourists in, the often called, "Cuban sex tourism" of the post-Soviet 1990s.)

> JUDY: When I tell the guys that I'm doing this to buy a
> pound of ground beef, they feel better about giving me
> money, and they leave me more.

Ever aware of the manipulations of sentiment, Judy will use her choice of prostitution to her advantage, without the usual connotations of sexual servitude associated in Latin American sexual politics of aggressive and receptive sexual exchanges.

> JUDY: . . . Depressed? Sure I get depressed. But it's a job,
> honey. What can I do? Nobody chooses to be born in
> the middle of a mess like this one.

While she may not have chosen to be born during a particularly difficult economic time, how she views what she does with her body *is* her own construction. A "mess like this one" evidently refers to Cuba's current economic situation—the 1990s "special" period of adjustment after the disintegration of the Soviet Block as Cuba's primary trade partner. The exchange of sex for U.S. dollars is presented as an economic necessity of the times, stripped of moral judgments. Her identity construction as a transvesti is framed just as matter-of-factly.

In *Stuff* the truly erotic is coded within the aesthetic of same-sex relations among women, and it's enacted by Bustamante while she sits at a dinner table and picks her teeth with gusto, suggesting an after-dinner discussion. An overtly pro-woman voice-over about the taste of women accompanies her actions:

> . . . Those who enjoy eating women must enjoy the flavor
> and scent and juice of seriously potent fruit . . . I've eaten
> both, and it takes more raw talent . . . to eat a woman.

The overt sexual-genital reference refers not only to the allusion of "forbidden fruit," but the description functions matter-of-factly, in lieu of a culinary description one might read in a tourist restaurant guide. The conjugation of sex, women and food, brings the audience to the "obvious" and even "logical" conclusion: women's genitalia makes for a more delectable taste experience. The male body, its relative delicacy in the marketplace of desire, is relegated to a secondary status. There is no male desire expressed in *Stuff*. The only male presence is encased (contained?) within the TV/video monitor: the virtual image of the postindustrial marketer, the flat image whose function is to sell a product, who sells pleasure of the virtual, antiseptic variety.

Migdalia Cruz's play, *Fur*, on the other hand, also raises questions about the nature of desire within the tropes of a dramatic structure. Citrona, Nena and Michael make up a trilogy of displaced desire where what is questioned is the heterosexual as the standard or norm. Citrona is, in the author's words, "A hirsute woman who has been sexually mutilated by her mother and sold [to Michael] like a dog." Michael's desire is provoked by the anomaly, by "her otherness, her exoticness, her Latina-ness," by a woman whose entire face and body are covered with hair. For Michael:

> The more different it is—the more beautiful it can be. The potential for beauty increases proportionate to the oddity of the substance.

The male fixation upon "the different" can be read as a move toward the exotic, which, in this case, is tied to the freakish, reminiscent of Coco Fusco's research in her book, *English Is Broken Here* (New York: The New York Press, 1995), of the European colonial power's spectacles by introducing the colonized as "freaks." The first documented example, according to Fusco was in 1493 when Columbus brought an Arawak to Spain from the Caribbean, who was "left on display for two years in the Spanish Court until he died of sadness."

Fur identifies power with the masculine (as coded in gender) and with the masculine power to purchase and cage (as coded in economic terms). Benevolent though this junction may want to initially pose itself (Michael buys the biggest cage possible as "proof" of his love for Citrona), the unfolding of the dramatic action takes care of *naming* and *disarming* this double-edged power play. This is accomplished through the sheer strength of Citrona's will and desire.

Citrona rejects Michael's notions of heterosexual romantic love; instead, she is aroused by Nena, the girl-woman whom Michael hires to catch the live rabbits that Citrona eats. Michael's role is limited to that of the voyeur, who watches the two women. He is deeply disappointed when he discovers while eavesdropping that the two women do *not* talk about him. Thus the notion of what women "do," what we contemplate beyond the gaze of men's desire, is deconstructed and reconstructed in self-referential, homoerotic terms: Citrona wants Nena.

Nena, on the other hand, wants Michael. Her desire, however, is self-generated, since Michael does not respond to her sexually. Therefore Nena's self-construction of her desire is seen in a masturbatory monologue where she fondles herself as she speaks about the object of her desire. *Fur* suggests that even while Nena's preference is heterosexual, the female desiring subject can do without the physical presence of a man to satisfy her. As in *Stuff*, the heterosexual male desire is never experienced. Michael's realm is that of unfulfilled longing: he speaks of love, describes it, circumvents it, but it is never represented on stage, nor are there any textual hints that imply Michael's erotic nature, *in itself*. In terms of gender relations, *Fur* posits female desire as primary, palpable and complex (in Citrona the beast is both desiring and desirable, she is both beauty and ugliness); Nena's desire, while it is not fulfilled, is represented as self-generated and physical. On the other hand, Michael's desire is simply discursive, words stripped of a deeply felt eroticism. Eroticism, then, is constructed within the realm of the homoerotic between the women and *not* within the societal standard of heterosexuality.

In Naomi Iizuka's one-act play *Skin* (an adaptation of Büchner's *Woyzeck*) physical desire resides also in the domain of the woman (Mary) which is as hard-edged as that of the testosterone-driven Navy Men, while "love" is (mis)placed as discursive longing (through her one-time lover, Jones). The play is staged in a postapocalyptic setting, in which time is both now and a long time ago, before memory: ". . . that happened like a thousand years ago, before I was born, before I even remember." Mary's drive for physical pleasure sets itself as an even match within a dangerous game of night club pick-ups. By contrast, Jones, the father of Mary's child, longs to construct a virginal Mary that does not exist. In an attempt to penetrate beyond the boundaries of her being, *her skin*, he consummates his desire in an ultimate act of possession, eradicating the object of his eros through thanatos.

The Hungry Woman: A Mexican Medea by Chicana lesbian playwright Cherríe Moraga constructs a complex set of sexual and political relations among the predominantly lesbian cast of characters. Moraga sets *The Hungry Woman* in a postapocalyptic, "*Blade Runner*esque" world in which gender identity and irreconcilable cultural differences are radicalized on different sides of "the border." As the play describes, it is set in:

> the near future of a fictional past—one only dreamed in the Chicana imagination. An ethnic civil war has "balcanized" the United States. Medea, her lover Luna, and Medea's child

Chac-Mool have been exiled to what remains of Phoenix, Arizona. Located in the border region between Gringolandia (white Amerika) and Aztlán (Chicano country), Phoenix is now a city-in-ruin, the dumping site of every kind of poison and person unwanted by its neighbors.

In this liminal space outside both the white and Chicano "straight" culture is where lesbians (there is no reference to gay men) are allowed to reside. This transcultural space is the topography of non-heterosexual desire, set within three generations of Mexicana/Chicana women: Medea's elderly mother, Medea (middle-aged) and Luna (younger). It is also a stigmatized place where neither psychological nor physical mobility from one space to the other is possible. By radically separating cultural locations from gender identities, and by creating a geographic locus for lesbian identity, Moraga shifts the focus toward the complexity of woman-on-woman same-sex relations. Within this complexity, one's age and how late in life one arrives at one's lesbianism create a point of contention between the older Medea and her younger lover, Luna. Because of her previous heterosexuality, Medea's ex-husband doubts her relatively recent lesbianism:

> JASÓN: You're not a lesbian, Medea, for chrissake. This is a
>   masquerade.
> MEDEA: A seven-year-old one?
> JASÓN: . . . you're not a Luna.
> MEDEA *(Sadly)*: No, I'm not.

Medea's response acknowledges that she is not like Luna, a younger lesbian woman who has never had sex with men, who is a stonemason and clay sculptor; someone who has and is capable of constructing her own identity entirely outside of the male hegemony. Medea, in her mid-forties, had a life of privilege as a heterosexual woman and mother, something she "lost" upon transgressing the Chicano social order of Aztlán.

In a subsequent scene Medea surprises Luna, who is using a mirror to gaze at her own genitalia. Luna sees it not as an object of beauty but as "a battleground. I see struggle there before I see beauty." A concept Medea rejects by "kiss[ing] her . . . first on the mouth, then grabs Luna by the hips, and goes down on her." This erotic scene is quickly interrupted by the entrance of the Border Guard who demands that Luna confess to being a lesbian. This complex scene moves from the evident longing for a self-centered identity, Luna's desire of herself for herself as seen through Medea's mirror, to a mutual woman-centered desire focused on each other (through each other?) to the disruption of this desire by the phallic male figure of the Law, the Border Police agent. The economy of desire here moves from the deeply intimate (Luna is contemplating her own genitalia), to the reflection of that desire through Medea, to its disruption by the symbolic phallic Law (the Border Guard).

Moraga's Medea came to her lesbianism after having had a child with her Chicano former husband. Trespassing the symbolic, also phallic Law of Aztlán, Medea is exiled for loving Luna and rejecting her heterosexuality. Years later, the father returns to claim their son, Chac-Mool, who is approaching the age of initiation into maleness. Prioritizing her son over her female lover places Medea on the edge of madness; the play predominately takes place in the insane asylum/prison/border area, where she is being held. Rather than losing him to the symbolic patriarchal Father, she takes drastic action which, in a sense, kills at least two parts of herself: the mother and the lesbian. The play seems to suggest, however, that her Mexicana/Chicana self is indelible and therefore not subject to erasures. *The Hungry Woman: A Mexican Medea* suggests the problematic junction of the lesbian motherhood of a male son, lesbian desire and cultural exile. It creates an overwhelming sense of the inescapability of the symbolic order of the Father within Chicano culture.

Caridad Svich's full-length play, *Alchemy of Desire, Dead-Man's Blues*, in many ways posits a different vision from the plays so far discussed here. *Alchemy* has no reference to anything Latino/a; it is not overly political. It is not representational, but as Svich herself says, "It is presentational." She considers herself a "true" hybrid culturally as well as aesthetically. She likes to push notions of creative identity beyond gender and culturally bound codes, and appeals to a sense of beauty and creativity as justifiable in themselves. Her work is often elusive, poetic and musical. She writes the accompanying scores. The play was originally conceived for radio, its strong sense of rhythm and musicality punctuates the women's speech, whose function is analogous to that of a Greek chorus.

Alchemy of Desire starts with Simone lamenting her husband Jamie's death in a war in "some little country somewhere [she] couldn't even find on a map." Again, the male is constructed as missing (here he is literally "missing in action"). They had been married less than a month. The setting is a nonspecific, Southern U.S. town, reminiscent of Louisiana's Bayou. The characters speak with a Southern accent, and, although it is full-length, the play is deceptively simple: it revolves around Simone's desire which plays itself out in the liminal emotional space where sorrow meets longing. As a counterpart, Jamie, now dead, is glimpsed in the play as a lost soul, wondering about looking for the limbs that were severed from his body in the war. In a ritualistic rite of passage, four women neighbors function as the chorus and help Simone exorcise the house and herself.

The women in *Alchemy* are as physical in their expressions as those in *Stuff* and *Fur*, although they navigate through the consequences of a larger, external world of which they seem to know little. They are the alchemists, the knowers of rituals and of the invisible. Food does not feed these characters: ritual, music, fire and water do. Svich works on the lyrical qualities of the words much as a lyricist does, sonoric and beautiful:

SIMONE:

> I am gonna find the breath.
> I'm gonna trespass on the night.
> I'm gonna swallow the stars until I find you.

> 'Cause I am comin to you—yeh—
> don't know where I'll find you, but I can feel you in my skin—
> oh—like tinder.

In *A Lover's Discourse, Fragments*, Roland Barthes makes the following observation, which aptly describes the function of language and desire in *Alchemy of Desire*:

> Language is skin: I rub my language against the other . . .
> my language trembles with desire. The emotion derives
> from a double contact: on the one hand, a whole activity of
> discourse discreetly, indirectly focuses upon a single signi-
> fied, which, "I desire you," and releases, nourishes, ramifies
> it to the point of explosion (language experiences orgasm
> upon touching itself): on the other hand, I enwrap the other
> in my words, caress, brush against . . . extend myself to
> make the commentary to which I submit . . .

Desire, as a quality of spirit projected onto the flesh through language is transformed into an act of possession of self and an inter-

nalization of the Other. Desire, loss and longing push Simone past her own pain toward the freedom she may have not known before: the option to carve herself a pair of shoes—a path—toward herself. Beyond marriage and its promise of fulfillment, the ritual accomplishes its goal: to lead her back into the well from which all desire springs, the depth of her own being.

Nilo Cruz's *Night Train to Bolina* is the only play in *Out of the Fringe* set in a Latin American context. The nonspecific geographic setting and generalized fear of the military, however, suggest our continent's turbulent twentieth-century history. A play in two acts, the dramatic action revolves exclusively around two young characters, Clara and Mateo. Mateo's body is the ledger of bruises inflicted upon him by his mother, who is obsessed with a lack of food. In an absurdist vein, she coerces every one in the family to contribute something to each meal, be it a shoe, a finger or a body part. The suggested entropy of this cannibalism alludes to the unsurmountable socioeconomic restraints (poverty) apparent in numerous Latin American countries historically. As a theatrical trope it spurs Mateo's impetus to rebel in the only way available to him, by running away.

Clara, Mateo's only friend, cares for him by tending his bruises and feeding him; they eventually run away together. Their love is prepubescent and innocent, nevertheless it encompasses the urgency of any adult passion. By running away from their respective families, Clara and Mateo encounter an institutionalized world (a hospital for runaway children) that is even less hospitable. The hospital introduces into their lives the tinged sense of Catholic guilt, one which brings into question the purity and innocence of their attachment.

In *Ragged Time*, Oliver Mayer masterfully recreates a turn-of-the-century U.S. "Deep South of the mind" in which two, black, blind minstrels mix with a "light-skinned colored lady of the evening," a Jewish boxer newspaper "boy," Ignacio an orphaned "Messican" boy and two newspaper cartoon characters, the Yellow Kid and the Sanctimonious Kid. In two acts this unlikely cast sets up a fast-paced vaudevillian show laced with subtlety with interwoven comments on race, politics and the power of the Hearst newspaper empire. *Ragged Time* asserts that the historical present, with our obsession on race relations, the political and marketing is nothing new. Two distinct historical moments (the late nineteen and twentieth centuries) are set up in parallel fashion, thus turning one's awareness to the entertaining ways in which we, as a society, redress the same old issues. The point of view of this play is "American," as in the mosaic paradigm in which all of the characters are deeply aware of their place in society: constructing a national identity based on social, economic, racial and ethnic difference.

While not all of the texts in this anthology deal with gender related issues, a significant number of Latina and Latino playwrights and performers have chosen the arena of sexual/cultural identity as a (momentary) expression of their creativity. The foregrounding of women's desires holds special significance within the context of this anthology. Whether represented as Lesbian, heterosexual or ambivalent, women's physical as well as spiritual longings overwhelmingly shape the dramatic action, at the expense of male desire, which is relayed as peripheral and discursive rather than as central and emotive. This shift points toward a new Latina/o thematic boldness evidenced in the plays selected for this anthology.

Transgression, as Coco Fusco states in *Stuff*, is not only the act of crossing, it is the what and the how, the historical specificity of a particular crossing that embeds it with particular significance. In the past two decades a significant amount of ground has been gained by Latina and Latino performers and playwrights—a ground they have fought for in the political and cultural arts arenas. The works of this anthology energetically move beyond what Homi Bhabha describes in his *The Location of Culture* (London/New York: Routledge Press, 1997) as the colonizing constructs of a stereotypical identity, whose excess is never objectively verifiable, but which paradoxically generates an ambiguity that emerges between the fixed image and its repetition. Rather, these texts disrupt fixed notions of sexual and cultural identities to re-form them as fluidly as their art, temporary yet aspiring toward longevity, intense and passionate. Urgent. Visible. Out of the closet.

María Teresa Marrero
University of North Texas
December 1999

A version of this introduction was presented in April 1998, at the conference: State of Latino Theater and Other Hispanic Voices of the Diaspora, held at the University of Minnesota, sponsored and organized by Dr. Luis A. Ramos-Garcia and his Department of Spanish. Subsequently, a version of this essay was published in Latin American Theatre Review, *Spring 1999: 87–103.*

STRAIGHT AS
A LINE

Luis Alfaro

THE WRITER SPEAKS
Luis Alfaro

I am an activist who became an artist. I mean that I have always felt that art picked me to use my work to create social change. My work as an administrator in the AIDS field and the time that I spent working in a labor union were some of the most creative artistic times in my life. These experiences were both inspiring and upsetting to the way that I lived.

I started working at a factory in Vernon, California, when I was thirteen. I stayed until I was twenty-one. My first writings were based on the people that I knew there and that I grew to love and admire. Everything from immigrant culture to blue-collar working environments show up in my first writings. Being immersed in this community of workers informed my art as much as the years that I spent at the Wallenboyd Theater or the Inner City Cultural Center.

The other interesting thing that has happened to me as an artist is being connected to teaching on various levels. I have worked with gang teens, gay and lesbian high schoolers, boys in prison, HIV-positive performers, etc. Each one of these experiences has brought me into a new level of not only creating work, but understanding how I can impact and make change.

As a community-based artist, I like the social and/or political responsibility of art. Of course, when I make art I work with the idea that I have no social responsibility whatsoever. But in the presentation of my work I am *conscious*. I have a desire to inspire, provoke, entertain and to move community in new ways forward, whether in thought or action. I am beginning to think that this is my life's work. My notion of community is more fluid than the current discourse. Sometimes it is Latino, sometimes it is gay and sometimes it is gay Latino. The last few years I have been working in the community of artists. One of my roles in this community has been to create opportunities for other artists. I think of this as essential to my art-making process.

I primarily work as a writer who sometimes performs his work. This work takes the form of a play, a spoken-word recording, a video or a submission to an anthology. Each text is a performance that is in the process of discovering its medium. For instance, sometimes when I think that I am writing a short story and the text starts to move toward a certain kind of theatrical dialogue, I realize that what I'm really writing is a play. I am always surprised at the fact that what I intended to do changes so much in the writing process. Mostly I try to stay out of the way of my own writing.

One of my goals as a writer has been to make our profession a little less lonely. A few years ago I produced a literary festival called Fierce Tongues. I brought together over sixty Latina writers from throughout the Southwest. Mostly I did it because I wanted to meet more Latina writers. A year later I produced a gay Latino performance festival called Homeboy Beautiful.

In the end I work in the theatre because I want to learn to be a better person. Art and community have always made me try harder.

Production History

Straight as a Line was commissioned by Mark Taper Forum in Los Angeles. It received its world premiere at Chicago's Goodman Studio Theater. Henry Godinez was the director. The cast was:

PAULIE	Guy Adkins
MUM	Linda Kimbrough

The play received a production at Minneapolis's 3 Legged Race @ Hennepin Center for the Arts. Laurie Carlos was the director. The cast was:

PAULIE	Joe Wilson, Jr.
MUM	Kathryn Guignon

It received a production at Playwrights Arena in Los Angeles. Jon Rivera was the director. The cast was:

PAULIE	James Sie
MUM	Emily Kuroda

Straight as a Line has received readings and workshops at Mark Taper Forum, A.S.K. Theater Projects in Los Angeles; South Coast Repertory in Costa Mesa, CA; Playwrights' Center Playlabs Festival in Minneapolis; New Dramatists in New York City; and SoHo Repertory Theatre in New York City.

Characters

PAULIE, good-looking man in his thirties, British, in black jeans,
black T-shirt, cowboy boots and a suit jacket.

MUM, woman in her sixties, mother to Paulie, British,
in a winter coat over a casino outfit, mini-skirt, pumps, panty hose,
with a bandana around neck, wearing a cowboy hat,
a holster with fake gun and a quarter-change belt.

Time

Present.

Set

Bare white stage. Projections on three sides. Two chairs.

a long, long time ago, mother was not a dirty word

—ANA CASTILLO

last chance lost in the tyranny of a long goodbye

—JONI MITCHELL

and these are the dangers;
the jackknife, the mouth
the wing-shaped muscles of the back,
the sudden loss of weight
till nothing is holding me down,
just bones and leather,
the scars of being eaten alive

—GIL CUADROS

Vacation

House lights out. The sound of a subway platform in New York. The sound of rap music. A bare white stage. Lights fade to black. The rap music continues with the sound of a slow hissing noise coming up from the ground and the sound of people talking. Every few minutes, the sound of a subway train approaching, stopping and leaving. Slide comes up on upstage wall: "Vacation." Slide fades. The set is designated by full-length slides on three sides that make up the subway station. Sound lowers. Entering and standing at a platform are Paulie and Mum. They talk to unseen persons on the platform.

PAULIE: Went to church this morning.

A fat queen in black robes, was telling us all about his *vacation* in the *Bahamas* and how we needed to give more money to the Jamaicans.

It seems the Jamaicans live at the beach and sell trinkets to people from religious orders on holiday.

Well, I was thinking to meself, Why walk the streets of New York risking life and limb, holding up tourists, when you can hang out on the beach, smoking *ganja*, selling key chains?

I wanted to scream, Shut up, fat arse. You've got us confused with St. Patrick's again. This is the Bronx! None of us can *afford* a *vacation* and we're all feeling a bit overworked just listening to you.

But I couldn't say anything, because me mum was with me. Say allo Mum.

(Beat.)

MUM: Allo.

PAULIE: I love me mum. Flew in from the desert to be with me today. What is that dear, four hours?

MUM: Yes, that's right, dear. Although with the current airline regulations, metal gun detectors and bomb detonators, it takes a few more minutes. But if it guarantees you won't blow up in the sky, it makes it all worth it, I say.

PAULIE: We went to get me *nipple pierced*, and now we're down here because I've decided to jump in front of a train and kill meself.

I wanted Mum to be with me on this special day and she came. Didn't you sweetie?

MUM: Yes. That's right.

PAULIE: Tell them about me *nipple piercing* Mum.

MUM: What about it?

PAULIE: Talk to them about *scarification*.

MUM: Well, it's a *tribal* thing, really.

Much like the football clubs we had back in England. I said to me son Paul, I said, "Paulie, why'd you want to belong to a *club* so badly, if you're going to jump in front of a train later?"

"And besides, it's *antisocial*. People with lots of metal objects sticking out of their bodies, make the gun detectors go off at the airport. It sets them apart from the rest of us, *frequent flyers*. Makes no sense, lad. Save your money," I say.

PAULIE: Me mum was a prostitute once.

MUM: Aw, Paulie boy, you mustn't run around telling family secrets, lad. It's not like I was having so much fun *down there*.

PAULIE: Mum's here because I got the shingles and these little purple spots on me back.

MUM: He's fine really. Just needs a little bit of that desert air.

PAULIE: Mum hates New York.

MUM: Nothing *new* about *New York*.

PAULIE: I used to be a prostitute. Just like me mum. But, I quit last year because I got these *lesions* on my back. Small really, but they turn people off.

MUM: They're quite pretty, I say. If you've got to have them, at least they're a pretty purple color. In fact, I wouldn't even call them purple, Paulie. I would call them *lavender*. So much nicer, *lavender*.

PAULIE: Mum sees the good in everything.

Last year on holiday, I was standing in this very subway station, and four men ran up and knifed a man in the back. They took his money and ran. And me mum says . . .

MUM: What's he carrying so much money on the tube for? Deserved it, really. Well, not the death part. Nobody deserves the death part.

Except, of course, the Queen of England.

PAULIE: That's not very nice.

MUM: But really, what's he carrying so much money on the tube for? This is New York. Murder is culture.

What is that channel, *MTV*?

PAULIE: Yes.

MUM: *Murder TeleVision*. That's what it is. *Murder TeleVision*.

PAULIE: Six months ago I told me mum I was positive.

MUM: Well, that doesn't sound so bad. Negative sounds worse, doesn't it?

Death's around every corner, Paulie boy. Nothing to be afraid of.

PAULIE: I've lost some weight, but all me medications seem to be working.

MUM: Paulie's always been a bit vain about his looks.

PAULIE: It's true. I wouldn't normally jump in front of a train. We're not that kind of people. *Train Jumpers*. Leave something like that to the Irish.

MUM: Now that's a reason to want to kill yourself.

PAULIE: Why go fall apart in front of people, clients and otherwise, when you can come down to the belly of New York and be done away with?

MUM: I wish there were more people who thought like you, dear.

I've seen quite a number of women, women in my age category, women who have let themselves, quite frankly, fall apart. It's embarrassing.

PAULIE: Right you are, Mum.

MUM: Well, that's what comes from *easy living* and *buffet lifestyles*. Paulie and I love *hard living*. Don't we dear?

PAULIE: Yes, that's right.

MUM: Other than that, *this* is a lovely country.

(Beat.)

PAULIE: All about *beauty*, isn't it?

MUM: Yes, dear. I'm afraid so.

PAULIE: Do you suppose that there are ugly people standing on this platform right now who disagree with us?

(She looks around.)

MUM: Oh, I'm sure of it. There always are. And bad postured too.

PAULIE: Bad postured?

MUM: Yes. Ugly *bad postured* people.

PAULIE: Do you think these ugly, *bad postured*, people are angry with us?

MUM: Stands to reason. In fact, I see an ugly person right now. *(Discreetly, rolls her eyes to indicate person)* But, I won't point him out. Because we are not *those* kinds of people. The kind who point out the ugly things in life. We only see nice, or *ignore* it.

PAULIE: A cycle you could have broken.

MUM: Don't hold grudges, dear. It's bad for your posture.

I'm here now, that's what counts.

PAULIE: *Yes, right.*

MUM: Besides, none of these people want to hear that dreadful story. They want to know whether or not you're going to jump.

PAULIE: Well, this is a once in a lifetime opportunity, isn't it?

MUM: Right.

PAULIE: I should make it good. Need to jump in front of the *right* train. An express, don't you think?

MUM: Good thinking.

PAULIE: Drama. That's what I need.

MUM: The only reason I came back to this *big rotten apple*, was because Paulie promised that if he did *not* kill himself, he would come to the oasis in the desert and live with me.

PAULIE: *Not.*

MUM: And you know, I am a *mother.* We always hold out one last bit of hope that our children's suicides will somehow *fail.*

Such *awkward* positions we're put into, us mothers. All *worry and pain.* Makes you wonder why one does it.

PAULIE: Right. I wonder.

MUM: For the sake of cashing in on a considerable amount of frequent flyer miles, I would like to know if you are going to jump or not, dear?

PAULIE: When I do, you should say something like, "My son, my son Paul . . ."

MUM: *Paulie.* I want to say *Paulie.* A little less formal I think.

PAULIE: Right. Okay. "My son *Paulie* has just jumped in front of a train. He's killed himself, I think." Make sure you say, *"I think."* Don't implicate yourself if you don't have to.

MUM: How sweet of you. Think of your dear old Mum, did you?

PAULIE: Well, that's suicide for you. No need in complicating anyone's life.

MUM: That's right.

PAULIE: *Especially yours.*

MUM: As you can tell from our accents, Paulie and I are British.

You see, we Brits have the most difficult time *explaining*, much less, *showing* anger. That is why we have football clubs in every part of England, and lots of people with no teeth.

PAULIE: What are you going on about now?

MUM: Historical context, dear.

PAULIE: Whose?

MUM: Ours.

(Beat.)

My son Paulie is a *homosexual.*

PAULIE: *Oh please*, Mum.

MUM: You are.

He is.

An unhappy one, but a homosexual never the less. I was going to mention it earlier, but I wanted his suicide to stand on it's own merits. Wasn't that nice of me, dear?

PAULIE: *Terribly* nice.

MUM: Paulie has trouble talking to people.

PAULIE: I talk through my body.

MUM: Yes, right.

PAULIE: A clinic in Frankfurt, Germany, is going to change Mum's life.

MUM: Right . . . the pain will not bother me. I have been married numerous times!

That is why Paulie distresses me so. Never as a woman with an imperfect back, did I think of killing meself.

Has Mr. Wayne Newton killed himself? Has Ms. Ann Margaret killed herself? Have Siegfried and Roy killed themselves? Of course not. These are pillars of the entertainment industry. And, believe me, they have *lots* of reasons for wanting to kill themselves.

PAULIE: Train should be here any minute.

MUM: Don't jump just yet, dear.

PAULIE: Christ! I thought this was about *me?*

MUM: I am a woman who has struggled with *imperfect posture* all of her years. All me life I've slept on flat wooden boards in me effort to have a perfect posture. In hopes, that one day, at the height of my *desirability*, I could becomes a *hostess.* All I ever wanted to be was a *hostess.* But I became a *feminist.*

One of the joys of being a *feminist* is that I don't have to talk about anything that I do not want to talk about. Isn't that right, Paulie?

PAULIE: That's right, Mum.

MUM: Paulie taught me everything there is to know about *feminism*. One day these lessons will pay off for himself as well, because he will either become an activist, or a drag queen.

PAULIE: Christ!

MUM: Me own mum used to say that I paid more attention to me back than to me ex-husbands. Rubbish! These are the issues that women face in a modern world. When is me life and back mine and when is it me husbands?

All I know is that the *vertebrae* is a very special gift. A series of bones that god puts together very carefully and distinctly.

I was born imperfectly. God—like most surgeons—falls asleep at the wheel every once in a while. Missing fingers, toes and hairlips are all due to god's *sleepiness*.

(Beat.)

Look at my back. Look. The *vertebrae*. A delicate little gift inching up from our bottoms.

I have *always* been poised for perfection.

PAULIE: It's time.

MUM: Nervous are you?

PAULIE: No. Not at all.

MUM: Well, that's good. No sense in getting nervous now.

PAULIE: Right.

MUM: No need in letting anyone down.

PAULIE: Any last thoughts?

MUM: None.

PAULIE: Have anything to say to me?

MUM: Do you?

PAULIE: No.
　　　　Wish me well?

MUM: I could.

PAULIE: Never mind. I'm ready.

MUM: All right, then.

(Beat.)

PAULIE: Bloody mess we're about to make.

MUM: Blood is right. *Paulie's blood.*

It's different now. *Tainted.*

No one ever lies to us anymore. No one tells us it's going to be different. That our children won't die before us. No one. Not even *Oprah.*

But Paulie, why must he . . . so young . . . Isn't that right, dear?

Paulie? Paulie? *Paulie . . .*

(Lights out. The sound of a subway train racing by. Sound out.)

Las Vegas

Slide comes up on upstage wall: "Las Vegas." Slide goes out. The sound of a television. The sound of someone switching channels on a remote. Every channel is a talk show. Lights up. The full-length slides on all three sides reveal a Las Vegas living room with a picture window. Paulie sits on a recliner with a remote control in his hand and a phone on his lap. He is channel cruising. The sound a door slam. Footsteps. Mum enters dressed in a Frontier Casino outfit: mini-skirt, pumps, panty hose, cowboy hat, holster with fake gun, quarter-change belt.

MUM: Oh dear. Not again. Another day, Paulie? You haven't moved since I left Pauline, that's right. What is wrong with you, lad? You sit here *all day* with that telephone in your lap, as if it was a cat, or a piece of china or something.

PAULIE: It is.

MUM: You're a foolish boy, Paulie. Don't be an *unhappy homosexual.*

PAULIE: I'm an indoor person.

MUM: Look out that window. Look.

PAULIE: What?

MUM: What do you see out there?

PAULIE: Desert.

MUM: Desert? Oh dear.

What is the desert?

PAULIE: Dirt. Dirty.

MUM: The desert, *my dear*, is cacti, sand, little lizards, stranded motorists gasping their last breath. *That's* the desert. Full of life. Breathing—with difficulty of course—but breathing. Living. Life!

PAULIE: *Dirty desert.*

MUM: Beautiful downtown Las Vegas. The oasis in the desert.

PAULIE: Ugh.

MUM: You can go visit Mr. Liberace's museum or ride horses on Mr. Wayne Newton's ranch.

For god's sake, do *something* Paulie. You sit here all day, *fading*. In a *recliner*. How boring. Maybe if you got caught in the crossfire of a casino robbery, but a *recliner*?

PAULIE: Can't leave the house.

MUM: Why not?

PAULIE: It's too hot.

MUM: Well, you shouldn't wear black.

PAULIE: I am depressed. It's a *disability*.

MUM: *Well*, you are not surprising me in the least. Who would not feel depressed sitting in this house all day with Mr. Benjamin Britton on the phono? And the telly! All talk show and vomiting of emotion. Sitting here watching people embarrass and ridicule each other. Why, you can do that yourself, if you just get out for a few minutes each day.

PAULIE: Don't want to.

MUM: Little Paulie. All alone. All by his cynical self.

PAULIE: That's right.

MUM: And that phone on your lap. Christ, do you ever call someone?

PAULIE: Yes, sometimes.

MUM: You mustn't lie.

PAULIE: Am not.

MUM: I've never as much as seen a tourist talk to you. You don't know a *single soul* in Las Vegas. The drag queen capital of the world, and you do not know a single one. You must *disappoint* your people so.

PAULIE: I am not disappointing anyone. The *slot machine hungry* are not my people.

MUM: You know Paulie, we are the largest convention capital in the world. *In the world*.

PAULIE: Oh stop.

MUM: How many hotel rooms are there on the strip?

PAULIE: I don't bloody well care!

MUM: You know, in my casino alone, there are . . .

PAULIE: I don't care about your casino! I couldn't care less about your silly job, miniature hot dogs or any other matter of minor trivia. You *bore* me.

(Beat.)

MUM: So bitter.

PAULIE: Sod off!

MUM: *Bitter, bitter, bitter.*

PAULIE: You know, if you really loved me, you'd work overtime, start saving a little goddamn money for my impending doctor bills.

MUM: I wish I could, but it is my duty as a mother and a *healthy optimistic individual* to help you live out the last of your days in a respectful and dignified manner.

PAULIE: Oh dignity! Yes.

MUM: I said to meself, after you chickened out of that fruitless suicide attempt in the *big rotten apple*, that I would take care of you. Take care of you until you lost all your faculties. *Like a baby*, I would bring you back to the womb. Like a *Benetton* ad. But it has been nothing of the sort. All *hostility* and *grudge holding* with you.

If I get screamed at one more time, I am going to file a complaint with a government agency! Mothers have rights too, you know.

PAULIE: Oh hush up. What do you know about motherhood anyway?

MUM: Enough.

PAULIE: Not a thing.

MUM: I saw a movie on the telly the other day. An *AIDS* film with *Ms. Elizabeth Taylor*. Ms. Elizabeth Taylor, who has raised millions of dollars, from the proceeds of an extravagant perfume, for *layabouts* such as yourself. Her son was played by a charming young man from a soap opera. A young man who got his start in the *Las Vegas* production of *Cats, might I add.* Not half as good looking as you, but *he* was pleasant right up to his last gasp. Without kicking and screaming, he took all of his medications. In a tender and touching moment, he thanked his dear old mum for making all of his funeral arrangements.

PAULIE: Like hell I will.

MUM: He died a wonderful death with his family at his bedside. That family included Mrs. Jessica Tandy, Mr. Hume Cronyn and a *Labrador* I have seen in many a children's film. And I thought to meself, Now, that's the kind of death Paulie should be having.

PAULIE: Don't even think about it.

MUM: Instead, you mock me, spite me and ridicule me for trying to improve the quality of your *much shortened* life.

(Beat.)

You're not angry at me are you?

PAULIE: Angry? Why would I be angry at *you*?

MUM: All children feel they are unbalanced and undeserved. It's called *adolescence*!

I should start a support group for *Mothers of Children Who Do Not Want to Die Nice Deaths Like in the Movies.*

PAULIE: Yes, why don't you do that?

MUM: Kicking and screaming. Always kicking and screaming with you. What more can I do?

PAULIE: Well, I'll tell you one thing. I wouldn't *mind* a goddamn Labrador and an evening with Siegfried and Roy, if *I* had Elizabeth Taylor as my mother.

(Lights out.)

Telecommunications

Slide comes up on upstage wall: "Telecommunications." Slide goes out. The sound of the ocean. Paulie is still sitting on the recliner. He has a cordless phone on his lap. Mum sits opposite Paulie, watching him. She is still dressed in her Las Vegas quarter-change outfit.

PAULIE: Stop it.

MUM: Can't help it. I'm a single woman and you are my only child. If I'm not looking after you every waking minute, I can't imagine I'm being a *decent* mother.

PAULIE: There's no such thing as a *decent* mother. And besides, you're not looking after me every waking minute.

MUM: Well, I'm trying.

PAULIE: Don't worry about your maternal habits. You haven't got any.

MUM: So nice the way you talk to your mother. Must be *Mother's Day.*

PAULIE: You shouldn't come home on your break. This is my *quiet time.*

MUM: *Quiet time?* You've got the telly on and a phone on your lap! Who do you talk to on that phone?

PAULIE: None of your business.

MUM: I'm just trying to show an active interest in a life that might not be here tomorrow.

PAULIE: You make me sound like some pet, some goldfish, you'll look after, until I wake up one morning, belly up, at the top of a bowl.

MUM: Yes, and I'll flush you down the toilet . . .

Oh, indulge me, dear.

PAULIE: If you must know, I talk to *people*.

MUM: What kind of people?

PAULIE: People. Anyone that calls.

MUM: Anyone?

PAULIE: They do, you know.

MUM: People talk to you on the phone?

PAULIE: *Chat*.

MUM: People *chat* with you on the phone?

PAULIE: Yes.

MUM: Who calls?

PAULIE: Friends.

MUM: Friends? You've got friends. That's marvelous!

PAULIE: Friends on a phone line.

I pay a flat fee of twelve dollars to talk to anyone in the Continental United States.

MUM: Anyone?

PAULIE: People like me.

MUM: Self-obsessed recluses?

PAULIE: No, people like me. *Gay* people. My own kind.

MUM: You *chat* with gay people. *How sweet* . . .

PAULIE: It's a Gay Chat Line.

MUM: How curious. What do you talk about?

PAULIE: Lots of things.

MUM: Sex?

PAULIE: Well, to start off with, always, of course.

MUM: Are you a phone prostitute?

PAULIE: Of course not. I *chat*.

MUM: It's quite all right if you are, you know. I was a prostitute once myself.

PAULIE: Yes, I know.

MUM: *You* are the product of a business transaction.

PAULIE: Yes, I know.

MUM: Well, what do you say in these chats?

PAULIE: It's a private matter.

MUM: It's a private matter what you say to *strangers* on a chat line?

PAULIE: Private, about personal issues.

MUM: You talk to strangers about your personal life?

PAULIE: Yes.

MUM: You can talk to me.

PAULIE: It's not the same.

MUM: What do you mean?

PAULIE: You wouldn't understand. It's a *sensibility*. *Besides*, a lot of it is about you.

MUM: About me?

PAULIE: Your ill regard of me.

MUM: Ill regard? Well, I'll admit to a great number of things, but ill regard? I doubt that very much.

PAULIE: It's a help line. I ask for help.

MUM: Help with what?

PAULIE: Living.

MUM: Twelve dollars seems an awful lot of money to ask strangers in the Continental United States for help with living.

PAULIE: Well, I'm dying.

MUM: You are not dying, dear.

PAULIE: Yes, I am. My body talks to me.

MUM: Well, it's lying. You look better than I've seen you in years.

PAULIE: You haven't seen me in years.

MUM: *Oh, right.*

(Beat.)

PAULIE: I tell them I live in Las Vegas and they understand.

MUM: They do, do they? Where do *they* live, these *Gay Chat Liners?* Probably near large bodies of water. They have no idea what it means to live in the desert.

PAULIE: This isn't the desert. It's a *re-creation* of the desert. You wouldn't be making change if we lived in the desert.

MUM: Jealous.

PAULIE: That's right. Every morning I wake up and watch you put on that shiny panty hose and that Frontier Casino mini-skirt for that jackpot of a hell job you enjoy so much. You make change, for Christ's sake!

And I think to myself, how very *old* you are. Much older than that skirt and hose. And you know what? I know that fake smile and that stupid skirt and that hat and holster should be on me. Yes, me. That casino hostess smile should be dripping off of my face. I'm the one with the great face. I'm the one with the great ass. I'm the one who's supposed to have the *big future*. You should be on your way out. Not me.

(Starts choking on an inhale. Coughs loudly. Spits out.)

This isn't the way it's supposed to be. *You* die first. *I* die last.
    I hate the fucking modern world.

(Beat.)

Yes, that's pretty much what I say to them. And if they haven't hung up on me by then, I beg them to take me away from here.

MUM: Oh dear. I guess it is worth the twelve dollars.

PAULIE: Don't make fun.

MUM: I'm not.

PAULIE: There's more.

MUM: No need.

PAULIE: Yes, need. I have lots of needs.

MUM: Maybe so, but all I can see is a selfish homosexual with no drag queen friends. I think that's unheard of these days . . .

PAULIE: You haven't listened to a thing I've said.

MUM: I come home on my lunch break for a little chance at some *civilization*. For a *tea time*. I come home from my job at a world famous casino to give you a purse full of miniature hot dogs, on baby buns, that I have stolen for you. *For you*. And you call me *old*.

PAULIE: I called you *worse*.

MUM: Well, that's all I remember!

PAULIE: Well, your memory must be going.

(Beat.)

MUM: Oh Paulie, look at you. Stress, stress, stress. You're getting yourself all worked up and eating up all those precious little cells of yours.

PAULIE: T-cells, T-cells, T-cells!! You make them sound like sea horses!

MUM: I don't understand what it is you want, dear. *Revenge of some sort?*

PAULIE: If I am stressed in any way, it's because you come home on your lunch break to nag me into going out into that miserable world that made me sick in the first place.
    I want you to give me back the time that was taken from me.

MUM: I've taken nothing from you.

PAULIE: It's because of you that I am sick.

MUM: Rubbish! You're a *blamer*.

PAULIE: I'm not blaming. I just *want*.

MUM: I see millions of jackpot *lives* like yours everyday in the casino.
You placed the bet, pulled down on the slot machine handle of life and lost.

PAULIE: What do I know about the world?
You lied to me with cheap corner pub tales about the adventure of it all. It hasn't been an adventure.

MUM: The school of hard knocks! I haven't lied about a thing. You're just afraid to live. I've done a lot better than the Queen of England. I'll say that much for meself.

PAULIE: And you refuse to take responsibility.

MUM: This speech has been given before by Mr. Mickey Rooney in a *Boys Town* movie. And better, *might I add*.
I'm a mother, not Jesus Christ!

PAULIE: You lied.

MUM: Haven't lied about a thing.

PAULIE: You lied about this place. I want to go home.

MUM: Home? This is home.

PAULIE: This isn't home. This is the desert. A fake desert. There isn't anything here.

MUM: Look at where we are. An oasis. A new frontier. Look at this city. You can go from Egypt to New York to Monte Carlo. The world. The world on one corner. No better place to reinvent yourself. And you, more than anyone, should welcome the chance to reinvent yourself.

PAULIE: I don't want to reinvent myself. I want to *remember* myself.

MUM: What for? Don't you want a future?

PAULIE: A real world.

MUM: The world isn't any more real than this is, dear.
What would you say to people in a real world?

PAULIE: I, I don't know.

MUM: See?

PAULIE: I just want to talk. About the real places I'll never see. Paris . . .

MUM: Oh Paris, yes. Lots of ill-content men in *berets* who piss in rivers. A whole country that refuses to bathe. *Eau de Toilette*. That should give you a clue.

(Beat.)

If you want to talk, you can talk to me.

PAULIE: It's not the same.
MUM: It's not?

(Phone rings. They both look at it.)

PAULIE: There it goes. The information superhighway.
You'll have to leave now.
MUM: *Not* if you're going to talk about me.
PAULIE: Don't you understand? It might be a faraway place.
MUM: This is the place to see.

(Phone keeps ringing. They both keep looking at it.)

PAULIE: Oh, Mum. Please. Leave.
MUM: Can't. I've got a run in me stockings.

*(Phone stops ringing. They both look at each other.
Lights out.)*

Tea Time

*Slide comes up on upstage wall: "Tea Time." Slide goes out. The
sound of a ticking clock. A loud knock on the door. Lights up. The
full-length slides on all three sides reveal the living room in Las
Vegas. Paulie sits on recliner with phone in hand.*

MUM: Paulie? Paulie? Open the door! Hurry for Christ's sake! Open
the door, lad.

*(Paulie opens the door. Mum enters carrying a large industrial-
sized white container with a very large medical label on it.)*

PAULIE: What is that?
MUM: Medicine.
PAULIE: What sort of medicine?
MUM: AZT.
PAULIE: AZT?
MUM: It's for you. A gift.
PAULIE: What do you mean for me?
MUM: You take AZT don't you?
PAULIE: Where did you get it?
MUM: I found it.
PAULIE: Found it?

MUM: Yes. I found it.

PAULIE: Where did you find it?

MUM: In a lab at the hospital.

PAULIE: At the hospital?

MUM: Where I was having my checkup today.

PAULIE: Did you buy it?

MUM: I *looted* it.

PAULIE: You *looted* it?

MUM: It's the new thing. You just pick it up and run. Those security guards. *Fat, fat, fat.* Can't run a block most of them.

PAULIE: You looted AZT?

MUM: A *lifetime* supply.

PAULIE: Well, you'll have to take it back.

MUM: Like hell I will. I looted this AZT fair and square.

PAULIE: You can be arrested for that.

MUM: I doubt very much that one can be arrested for trying to save her son's life.

PAULIE: But it's stolen.

MUM: It's *looted*. I *looted* it. Big difference.

PAULIE: I beg your pardon? There is no difference.

MUM: One of them is, of course, stealing. Yes, I see that. But I've *looted*. I've committed a political action. I've *acted up*.

PAULIE: I can understand your concern, but stealing people's medication? You've just broken the law.

MUM: Nonsense.

PAULIE: It's a fragile balance, and you've gone and tipped the scales. I don't suppose you shot a guard on your way out?

MUM: Don't forget your stress, dear. Let your mum make you some tea.

PAULIE: Am I dreaming this?

MUM: Maybe it's your *dementia* starting to settle in.

PAULIE: *Yes, right.* Enjoy your lawlessness.

MUM: I got this for *you*. You should be grateful. I don't know of any other mother who goes out of her way like I have. I could have just walked right out of that hospital. Instead, I had to break into lots of cabinets to find this bucket of *life saving* drugs for you.

PAULIE: Shameless.

MUM: Yes, that's right, dear. And why not? I've been betrayed. Every morning I wake up, look down there and say to meself, "Oh dear, once again, another day without a penis." It's a struggle.

PAULIE: Let me tell you a little bit about how this world works . . .

MUM: To hell with how it works!

I've brought you a gift. The least you can say is *thank you*.

I am getting tired of playing the *selfless* mother. It's starting to show in my lower back.

PAULIE: Yes, think of yourself.

MUM: Yes, that's right, dear. Nobody else does.

PAULIE: You're wrong about the world.

MUM: Am not.

PAULIE: The world I talk to is much kinder than the one you've led me to believe.

MUM: Do you think anybody out there gives a damn whether you live or not?

Do you think anybody notices your *T-cells* like I notice them? No one.

(Beat.)

PAULIE: I'm done with AZT.

MUM: Don't be silly.

PAULIE: I've stopped taking me medications, Mum.

MUM: You're playing with your life, Paulie.

PAULIE: No more AZT. No more DDI. It's all chemicals in me system. Don't want my body to become a sewage plant.

MUM: Don't be foolish, boy.

PAULIE: Nothing foolish about it.

MUM: Might I offer a reason as to why it's good to take your medication? It helps you keep *breathing*, dear. Remember *breathing*?

PAULIE: I'm tired, Mum.

MUM: Yes, I know. But who isn't tired?

The whole world is chemically imbalanced. But you don't see millions of people throwing out their AZT.

We don't give up. That's not our nature.

PAULIE: You don't know my nature.

MUM: Like hell, I don't!

The other day at The Mirage, I saw a drag queen trip and break her ankle. I thought they were going to have to put her out to pasture. But, do you know what she did? She stood up, tightened the strap on that twelve-inch heel, and walked right into that casino showroom and gave the performance of her life.

PAULIE: I'm not a drag queen!

MUM: Well, that's beside the point.

We all get tired. But we don't quit.

I often times think of bombing a building. Slashing me supervisor's throat. You see? I stay *active*. I stay active and alive.

PAULIE: I don't want anymore side effects. I'm done with the fatigue and the nausea. I want out.

(Beat.
Mum goes to Paulie and slaps him hard across the face.)

MUM: Foolish boy!

PAULIE: What did you do that for?

MUM: Because I felt like it. One of the gifts of the active person.

(Beat.)

I hate quitters. Especially *life quitters*.

The world awaits you, Paulie, and you turn your back on it. You can do what you want, but you can't die. Sorry.

PAULIE: Damnit.

MUM: If you don't like what I've just done, then do something about it. Do something. I don't care what it is you do. Slap me back for Christ's sake. Break me *Michael Crawford* records. Just stay in the present.

I can't keep looking back for you.

(Beat.)

PAULIE: Don't you ever touch me again, goddamnit. Because I swear, I'll beat the living daylights out of you.

(Coughs. Spits.)

Do you hear me? Don't you hit me again.

(Beat.)

I need a little bit of self decency.

MUM: Yes dear.

(Smiles.)

Thank you dear.

(Lights out. Paulie exits.)

Motherhood

Slide comes up on upstage wall: "Motherhood." Slide goes out. The sound of a Las Vegas casino. The constant ringing of slot machines and people talking in the background. Lights up. The full-length slides on all three sides reveal the middle of a large casino in Las Vegas. Paulie is laying on the floor. He is in the middle of a seizure. Mum is standing over him.

MUM: There are things you let go of when you get older. Or, as you can see, in Paulie's case, sicker. Little gripes you have about the world.
Oh dear.
Everyone has gripes, don't they? I know I do.
Now, let's see. He's already on the floor. That's a good thing, Isn't it?
Is it, *on his side*, or *on his back*? Anybody have an idea about this?

(Beat.)

It's just awful isn't it? These terrible and embarrassing positions us mothers are put into.
When you're working in a casino all day, *customers* just run to the restroom for these sort of things. More often than not, they tend to die in the buffet lines.

(Beat.)

His first trip out of the house, and now this.
Full of *revenge* he is. Just likes to get even, that's all.
Nothing to worry about. A *seizure*. Millions of people in the world have *seizures* every day. I wouldn't be surprised if somebody was having the same kind of *seizure* in China, right this second.
Oh dear.
I guess I should stick a wallet in his mouth.
I guess a *change purse* is kind of like a wallet. Yes, I would say it is. Let's see.

(She pulls a change purse from her outfit. She sticks wallet in his mouth.)

Should I hold him, you think?

I think it's best *not* to hold him. I'll just stand here and watch him. Yes, that's what I'll do. I'll stand here. I'll make sure he doesn't hurt himself. That's the best. I'll watch him. Yes. No need to hold him. No.

It's a gift you know, these diseases. Second chances. Second chances to make up for the mistakes you made in your life. I haven't made too many, I don't think. But, I'm not Jesus Christ. Mothers are close, but they are *not* Jesus Christ.

(Beat.)

I never really knew what mothers did until my sweet Paulie boy begin to disappear.

Now, I will be an *angel*. Thanks to me little Paulie boy.

(Lights out.)

Transition

Slide comes up on upstage wall: "Transition." Slide goes out. The sound of a heartbeat. Lights up. The full-length slides on all three sides are gray. Paulie and Mum are both standing, facing the audience.

PAULIE: Great news.

MUM: What is it, dear?

PAULIE: The doctor was here today. He said that my T-cells have doubled.

MUM: Oh really. From what? One to two?

(Paulie looks at Mum horrified. Then he begins to laugh. Mum begins to laugh with Paulie. Paulie begins to cry. Mum continues laughing. Lights slowly fade on Paulie crying and Mum keeled over in laughter.
Lights out.)

Baptism

Slide comes up on upstage wall: "Baptism." Slide goes out. The sound of water in a bathtub. First through a faucet. Then some splashing and some giggling. Lights up. The full-length slides on all three sides reveal images of water. Mum is bathing Paulie.

MUM: There. How does that feel?

PAULIE: Umm. Fine.

MUM: Are you happy?

PAULIE: Not that *un*happy.

MUM: Oh good.

How are your legs today?

PAULIE: I'm afraid I can't feel a thing. *(Laughs)*

MUM: You'll get them back. All temporary it is.

PAULIE: I'm not so sure.

MUM: Mr. Frank Sinatra once *lost his voice.* It came back.

PAULIE: And if it doesn't?

MUM: Kiss it good-bye.

It's all dead weight after a while. If you don't need it, get rid of it, I say. That's the trouble with marriages.

(Beat.)

PAULIE: You embarrassed?

MUM: Not at all. I'm your mum.

PAULIE: So? What about *Oedipus?*

MUM: Oedipus was Greek. The Greeks are always up to something *funny.*

When I look at you, I don't see a man. I see a little boy.

PAULIE: Even more perverse.

MUM: *Funny.*

A baby. I see a little baby. Just arms and legs and skin.

PAULIE: Doesn't it make you feel strange?

MUM: Oh, no. I don't feel a thing.

Who needs a pair of useless legs when you've got a mum to take care after you? A mum to watch your every move. A mum to make all your decisions. A mum to be a mum.

PAULIE: Oh dear.

Lower your hand a bit.

(She places her hand near his mouth. He reaches over and bites it.)

MUM: Ow! Christ, you bit me.

PAULIE: I may not have my legs, but don't even think about messing with me.

MUM: Not very nice, Paulie.

PAULIE: Wasn't meant to be nice.

MUM: You're not going to bite me again are you?

PAULIE: Might.

MUM: Don't.

PAULIE: Okay.

(Beat.)

I like these quiet moments between us, Mum.

MUM: Me, too. Wish we had a large tub like the ones on the strip. I'd jump right in with you, dear.

(Beat.)

I saw what you did in the kitchen, Paulie.

PAULIE: All my fault now, is it?

MUM: No. We just can't keep ignoring those little lesions of yours.

PAULIE: Christ.

MUM: You can't cook if your *synapses* are not *synapsing*, dear. If you get hungry, you can just call me and I will bring you some *healthy and nutritious* cocktail franks.

PAULIE: They are neither *healthy* nor *nutritious*.

MUM: They're *turkey* franks, dear. A whole new concept in healthy casino eating.

PAULIE: I can't help it, you know.

MUM: Yes, right.

Water warm enough?

PAULIE: Yes, thank you.

MUM: Promise you won't cook again.

PAULIE: No.

MUM: Well, then you've got to let me know when you are. I am not *Liza Minnelli*. I don't just punch in whenever I feel like it. It doesn't work that way.

PAULIE: I know.

MUM: Oh, you do now, don't you? And how, might I ask, would Paulie *the unemployable* know that?

PAULIE: Saw it on the telly.

MUM: Ha ha. I am a hostess at a world famous casino! Do you know how many people can say that?

PAULIE: Everybody you work with?

MUM: Yes, go ahead and make fun. *Sour boy.* Just like your father.

PAULIE: I thought you didn't know my father?

MUM: Sure I knew him. I just didn't know him that long. I was a prostitute. My job was to make money, not socialize. You know that.

PAULIE: Yes, I do.

MUM: Knew him about fifteen minutes actually.

PAULIE: Generous with your time were you?

MUM: *Funny.* Nowadays, you have to practically perform a gymnastics routine.

PAULIE: And counseling.

MUM: Back then, things were different.

PAULIE: I'll say. Funny how things change. Used to be quite fun. A great sport.

(Beat.)

MUM: Did you work a day shift or a night?

PAULIE: Night. What about you?

MUM: Lunch hour in the business district.

PAULIE: Ooh. Big tips.

MUM: Did all right for meself.

PAULIE: Did you talk much?

MUM: Oh no. Kept me mind on the job. It used to be a *service industry*, dear. It was about the customer, not about me.

PAULIE: But the chatting helps, don't you think?

MUM: Killed time a bit, I suppose.

PAULIE: Did you like it?

MUM: No. Of course not.

PAULIE: I rather liked it.

MUM: Oh dear, married your job, did you?

(Beat.)

PAULIE: What about my father?

MUM: What about him?

PAULIE: Was he nice?

MUM: Quick.

PAULIE: Well . . .

MUM: Well, who knows. Lunch time crowd. Punch in, punch out.

PAULIE: Good-looking?

MUM: Don't remember. All pretty fast. You know.

PAULIE: Yes.

MUM: It's best to forget him.

PAULIE: Yes. Right.

(Beat. She considers.)

MUM: It was nice.
PAULIE: What was nice?
MUM: He was.
PAULIE: I thought you didn't remember?
MUM: Some you do.
PAULIE: Some you do.
MUM: Yes, right.

(Beat.)

What is this dreary music?
PAULIE: Opera.
MUM: Oh dear, *opera*. If you were happy, you'd be listening to show
tunes.

(Beat.)

PAULIE: Were you ever scared?
MUM: Scared?
PAULIE: Prostituting.
MUM: Never scared. I mean, uh, I had no choice.
PAULIE: It's not choice, Mum. It's destiny.
MUM: Not when it comes to work.
PAULIE: Yes, even that.
Mine is being sick right now.
MUM: Don't say that.
PAULIE: Go away now. The water's getting cold and I want to prac-
tice drowning.

(Lights out.)

Redemption

*Slide comes up on upstage wall: "Redemption." Slide goes out. The
sound of a drip, drip, drip. Paulie is seated in a chair. He begins to
suggestively pull off his shirt to reveal his chest. On the upper right
side of his chest, a catheter is attached. Mum appears, rolling out an
IV drip and begins to administer medicine.*

PAULIE: In New York, I worked in a *go-go* house.
MUM: A *go-go* house?
PAULIE: A male burlesque.

MUM: Really. Did you tell jokes?

PAULIE: *Ha. Ha.*

I would stand at the edge of a little stage, on Broadway, *might I add*, and wave my dick . . .

MUM: Vulgar.

PAULIE: . . . Sorry, *my penis*, in people's faces.

MUM: That doesn't sound so bad.

PAULIE: People would pay to see me wave my body parts.

MUM: What kind of people?

PAULIE: Oh, I don't know. Businessmen. Pizza delivery boys. Executive assistants. Probably big Broadway stars. But I couldn't see them all very well, on account of the lights directly on my pelvis.

MUM: Well, then, how could you tell?

PAULIE: Tips. How much they tipped. The way they folded or crumpled up their money into my cowboy boots. I was a *cowboy*.

MUM: See? *You are* interested in exploring new frontiers. I knew it.

PAULIE: That was just the audition. The real job was afterward. Walking around, with an imaginary sandwich board around me neck, selling the *private show*.

MUM: I see . . . Make a decent sort of money?

PAULIE: Decent enough.

(Beat.)

It wasn't about the money.

MUM: Oh dear, you *do* marry your jobs don't you?

PAULIE: It was the hands.

MUM: Hands?

Huh, I forgot that feeling.

PAULIE: New York is a very *cool* place.

MUM: Right.

PAULIE: *Cool* as in cold.

MUM: Just call it *York*.

PAULIE: I would have preferred yours.

MUM: Mine?

PAULIE: But, those were the ones that kept me warm.

(Beat.)

MUM: I'm sorry, Paulie.

PAULIE: Now, I've got the permanent warmness of this catheter.

(Beat.
   Mum places her hands on Paulie's face. He begins to cry.)

Heal me mum?

MUM: I wish I could.

PAULIE: Please.

MUM: I am in a limited occupation. Motherhood is a very limited field. It's destiny. You're the one who said it. And your job is to fight it.

PAULIE: I'm sorry, dear, but I don't like the hours or the duties.

MUM: I've been fighting destiny since I first noticed my posture. It's the good fight, Paulie boy. In the end, it's just the *resistance*. The push and the pull.

PAULIE: Pull it out, Mum.

MUM: Pull what out?

PAULIE: This stupid catheter.

MUM: Absolutely not.

PAULIE: It's doing nothing but making me want to *try*.

MUM: Good. It's the reminder of the *living* in you. It's a sign post of the *good fight* still left in you.

PAULIE: Do it because you love me.

(Beat.)

MUM: Well, there, that proves it. I'll leave it in because *I don't*. I don't love you at all. I don't love you. So there. I don't.

(She places her hands on his chest, over the catheter.)

I don't love you.

(Lights out.)

Reckoning

Slide comes up on upstage wall: "Reckoning." Slide goes out. The sound of a heartbeat. Lights up. The full-length slides on all three sides are red. Paulie and Mum are both standing, facing the audience.

PAULIE: Bad news.

MUM: What is it, dear?

PAULIE: The doctor was here today. He said I haven't got much longer.

MUM: Oh really. How much? A week?

(Paulie looks at Mum. Then he begins to laugh. Mum begins to laugh with Paulie. They both continue laughing. Lights slowly fade on Paulie and Mum keeled over in laughter.
  Lights out.)

Fencing

Slide comes up on upstage wall: "Fencing." Slide goes out. The sound of two people fencing. Lights up. The entire space is white. Slowly, throughout the scene, the full-length slides on all three sides reveal a bedroom with lots of medical equipment. Paulie lays on a bed. Mum enters in a white fencing outfit. She is carrying fencing equipment. She stands over Paulie on the bed.

PAULIE: Oh dear! I thought you were a ghost. What are you wearing?

MUM: A fencing outfit.

PAULIE: When did you learn how to fence?

MUM: I'm starting today. I've brought you one too.

PAULIE: For me?

MUM: And look at these blades. If you want, we can even take the safety caps off.

PAULIE: *Fencing*, Mum?

MUM: For exercise. The doctor says you need your exercise. I've chosen an indoor sport.

PAULIE: But, it's so . . . *violent.*

MUM: Right. I thought you might enjoy that.

PAULIE: I don't want to play a *violent sport* with you.

MUM: Sure you do. This is your mum you're talking to. All young men want to play a violent sport with their mums.

PAULIE: Not me.

MUM: You can't wait to jab me one. It's all Shakespeare and Greek dramas. *All* children want to kill their parents.

PAULIE: Do you want me to kill you?

MUM: Of course not. But *all* children need to try at least once. If you are going to have any sort of decent relationship with me, you've got to give it a go.

PAULIE: It's a bit late for that, don't you think?

MUM: My job as *mother* has been to control your desires. That's my role, and you *hate* me for it.

PAULIE: But you haven't controlled my desires.

MUM: You see, I've *failed* you!

PAULIE: A minor failure in the scheme of things.

MUM: Well, maybe you're right, but you need your exercise. Now, get up and jab me one. For your generation.

(She jabs him.)

PAULIE: Ow! That hurts! Cut it out, damnit.

(Beat.)

I'm too weak, Mum. Go exercise with someone your own age.

MUM: Paulie, you've held a million grudges against me. Think of one and *on guard*!

PAULIE: I'm a bit tired for *grudge holding*.

MUM: Oh dear, we're never going to get a decent exercise.
Hate me for this!

(She jabs him.)

PAULIE: Cut it out, for Christ's sake!

MUM: Stand up you coward.

(She jabs him again.)

PAULIE: Stop it. I forgive you.

(She jabs him and then she kicks him.)

MUM: Oh no, you don't!

PAULIE: There's no more fight left in me, Mum.

MUM: Lies.

PAULIE: Face it.

MUM: Fight back for once.

(Mum continues to jab and kick him.)

We're not those kinds of people. Quitters. You are not.
Fight me, Paulie. Fight me for the neglect.
Get up. Fight me for ignoring you all those years. Yes, you can. Yes, you can.
Don't you dare.
Fight me. Fight back. Active. Stay active. Get up. Get up. Get up! GODDAMNIT! GET UP!!

(She realizes that he isn't moving. Beat.)

PAULIE: Are you done with your exercise?

MUM: I thought . . . I thought . . .

There must be *something* you truly hate me for?

PAULIE: I can't think of a thing at the moment.

(She rationalizes.)

MUM: It must be the *dementia*. I'll *loot* you a morphine drip today.

(Lights out.)

Reversal

Slide comes up on upstage wall: "Reversal." Slide goes out. The sound of a heartbeat. Lights up. The full-length slides on all three sides are white. Paulie and Mum are both standing, facing the audience.

PAULIE: Terrible news.

MUM: What is it, dear?

PAULIE: The doctor was here today. He said my time is up.

MUM: Oh really.

(Paulie looks at Mum. Then he begins to laugh. Mum begins to laugh with Paulie. Mum begins to cry. Paulie continues laughing. Lights slowly fade on Mum crying and Paulie keeled over in laughter.

Lights out.)

Dementia

Slide comes up on upstage wall, "Dementia." Slide goes out. The sound of labored breathing. Sound out. Lights up. The full-length slides reveal a ticket counter. Paulie is attempting to stand up. Mum is present, but in the dark. The sound of continuous rain.

PAULIE:

Is it raining at Victoria Station?

Two tickets, please.

One for me, and one for . . .

She can come if she wants.
I'm not going to force her anymore.

Surprised to see me here?
So am I, dear.

I have decided to forego *reinvention* for a little *remembrance.*

(He looks at himself.)

How do I look?
What about these legs?
What about this ass?
How much you got?
I could cut you a deal.
A *going-away* special.

Is it cold? How hard is it raining?
    I'm sure I can make it? Do you think I can make it, Mum?
MUM: Sure you can make it.
PAULIE: Tell them. Will you tell them for me?
    Tell them there's no need for another benefit.

Tell them they can save
those pills
that drip
that bed
at the hospice.

Save it for a *quitter.* Ain't that right, Mum?
MUM: What dear?
PAULIE: Ain't that right, Mum?
MUM: That's right, dear.
PAULIE: Damn right.

I've seen people.
People without legs.
Legless people.
Fight the good fight.

Ain't that right?
MUM: That's right.
PAULIE: You can beat it. Yes, you can.
    Yes, I can.

He said it was in my blood.
I said, drain my goddamn blood.

He said it was in my T-cells?
I said, to hell with my T-cells.

My legs?
Cut them off.
MUM: That's right. Get rid of them, dear.
PAULIE:
My eyesight?
I've seen enough.
I don't care.
I don't need 'em.

I'm here.
Yes, I am.
I'm here.

So, tell them to stop the pills.
Stop the chemo.
Stop the benefits.
Stop the last rites.

Tell Liza.
Tell Barbara.
Tell Pia.
Tell all of those *bitches* to stop singing those goddamn *show tunes.*

Will you please?

Save the fundraiser for someone else.

'Cause, *I'm buying a ticket.*
Yes, I am.

I've seen the curves.
I've seen the lines.
I've seen the bodies.
The bodies . . .

(He starts to laugh.)

Yes, I am.

Yes, I am.

Mum?

I've bought the ticket.

(He's laughing harder.)

Yes, I am.

*(Laughing out loud.
    Lights out.)*

● ● ●

Slide comes up on upstage wall: missing the mark. *Slide goes out. The
sound of a heartbeat. Lights up. The full-length slides on all three sides
are white. Paulie and Mum are both standing, facing the audience.
    Beat.
    Beat.*

MUM: What is it dear?

(Beat.)

Doctor was here today?

(Beat.)

Oh, really?

*(They both look out.
    Lights out.)*

Love for Sale

*Slide comes up on upstage wall: "Love for Sale." Slide goes out. The
sound of a morphine drip. Lights up dimly. The full-length slides on
all three sides reveal a darkened bedroom with lots of medical equipment. Paulie is lying down on the bed. Mum is standing.*

MUM: Time waits for no one, Paulie.
PAULIE: Not asking for anymore time.
MUM: Yes. I know. But, it's nice to have it, even though you're not
    asking for it. Don't you think?

(Beat.)

PAULIE: Hmm.
MUM: Comfortable.
PAULIE: Somewhat.
MUM: How about a double dose of morphine.
PAULIE: Absolutely not.
MUM: What am I going to do without you, Paulie boy?
Who will I *loot* medication for?
PAULIE: For you. You'll need it.
MUM: *Funny.*

(Beat.)

Like a little telly?

(Paulie grunts no.)

We could listen to my ocean tape for a while . . .
PAULIE: I forgive you, Mum.
MUM: Forgive me for what?
PAULIE: Everything.
MUM: Everything?
PAULIE: Yes.
MUM: Motherhood too?
PAULIE: Motherhood. The world. All of it.
MUM: There's nothing left after you, dear.
PAULIE: *History.*
MUM: Don't like *histories*. That's why I came to the desert.
PAULIE: Right.
MUM: So, you see, you can't leave. There's lots of casinos to be built.
Jackpots to win. Slot machine handles to pull down.
PAULIE: If you don't like histories, how will you remember me?
MUM: Silly boy. you're right here.
PAULIE: Where?
MUM: Would you like to see yourself in the map of me history book?
PAULIE: Yes.
MUM: Let go for a moment, dear. Lie still now.

(Mum turns her back to the audience, unzips her dress from the neck down to waist and reveals her imperfect back.)

Look at this. Can you see it?

(Paulie lays dying. Eyes closed. Blind.)

PAULIE: Straight as a line.
MUM: Like the edge of a knife.
PAULIE: A life.
MUM: Our life.
    All the hard work. All the *hard living.*
PAULIE: And me.
MUM: Yes, dear.

(Paulie mumbles. Mum begins to zipper up.
    Beat.)

I'm starting to like this, Paulie. These quiet little moments between us. The way you sit there and listen to me all day. The way you are so agreeable. I like these moments. Yes, I do.
    And I thank Ms. Elizabeth Taylor for the lessons learned.

(Beat.)

And I thank you, dear. I thank you for . . . *(Looks at him)* Paulie? Paulie?

(Paulie is dead. Mum starts to cry.)

Paulie? My Paulie boy. My dear sweet Paulie boy.

(Beat. Devastated. Trying to compose herself.)

A life. A whole life. I saw it.

(Beat.)

Paulie?
    Oh my, it's so quiet, isn't it?

(Space.)

Paulie?
    Thank you. Thank you for the gift of motherhood.

(Beat. Looks out into the audience. Desperate and devastated.)

Oh dear.

(Looks back.)

Paulie. Please.

Would you like to see me back, dear?
You heard him. Straight as a line, it is.

(Walks into the audience.)

How about a cup of tea? Stay for a little tea time?

(Talks to someone else.)

Could show you around beautiful downtown Las Vegas.
The oasis.

(Lights slowly dim.)

The oasis in the desert.

(Lights out.)

END OF PLAY

LUIS ALFARO is a writer/performer who works in poetry, plays, short stories, film, performance and journalism. A multidisciplined artist, he also works as a director, curator, producer and community organizer. He is a Chicano, born and raised in the Pico-Union district of downtown Los Angeles.

Mr. Alfaro is the recipient of a MacArthur Fellowship, a 1999 NEA/TCG Theatre Residency Program for Playwrights grant and a 1999 Los Angeles Treasure. He is the winner of the 1998 National Hispanic Playwriting Competition. He was selected for the 1997 Midwest PlayLabs for *Straight as a Line,* which was named by the *Los Angeles Times* as one of the top ten productions of the year (Playwrights Arena in Los Angeles).

His work has often been anthologized, and this year it will be featured in the collections *Extreme Exposure: An Anthology of Solo Performance Texts from the Twentieth Century* (Theatre Communications Group), *Latino Heretics* (FC2 Press), *Urban Latino Cultures* (Sage Publications), *O Solo Homo* (Grove Press), *Twelve Shades Read* (Graphically Speaking LTD) and *Corpus Delecti* (Routledge).

He is a resident artist at Mark Taper Forum in Los Angeles, where he has been co-director of the Latino Theatre Initiative since 1995. Recently he was a visiting artist at The Kennedy Center in Washington D.C.

He has toured his solo performance work throughout the United States, England, Mexico, and recently presented a new piece, *Cuerpo Politizado/Politicized Body*, to a sold-out audience at The Getty Center. He currently has commissions with Deaf West Theater (*52 Mexicans*) and South Coast Repertory (*Mojave Medicine*).

He teaches throughout the country including five years in the Writer's Program of UCLA Extension. He is a member of New Dramatists and The Dramatists Guild.

STUFF

Coco Fusco and
Nao Bustamante

THE WRITERS SPEAK
Coco Fusco and Nao Bustamante

We decided to create a performance that dealt with Latin women, food and sex. We started from our own stories. Nao is from an immigrant farm-worker family that was involved in the Chicano political struggles of the 1960s and 1970s. She grew up in the San Joaquin Valley of California, a region that at one time produced more fruit and vegetables than any other area in the world. Coco's family is from Cuba, a country that gained a reputation in the 1950s as an international whorehouse, and which in response to its present economic crisis, has reverted to sex tourism as a strategy for survival. In the course of writing *Stuff*, Coco traveled to Cuba to interview women in this burgeoning industry. Then we both went to Chiapas, the center of indigenous-culture tourism in Mexico, and the site of the 1994 Zapatista insurrection. We spent several weeks in conversation with women and children whose livelihoods are linked to their daily contact with foreigners.

Stuff is our look at the cultural myths that link Latin women and food to the erotic in the Western popular imagination. We weave our way through multilingual sex guides, fast food menus, bawdy border humor and much more. In the course of the performance, we mingle with audience members, treating them to a meal, a host of rituals and exotic legends, an occasional rumba and at least one Spanish lesson as part of our satirical look at relations between North and South. Our spoof, however, is not without its serious side. Latin American literature is full of references to cannibalism—as the European colonial's fear of the indigenous "other" as cannibal, as a trope for Europe and America's ravaging of Latin America's resources and, finally, as a symbolic revenge of the colonized who feed off the colonial. If food here serves as a metaphor for sex, then eating represents consumption in its crudest form. We are dealing with how cultural consumption in our current moment involves the trafficking of that which is most dear to us all—our identities, our myths and our bodies. *Stuff* is our commentary on how globalization and its accompanying versions of "cultural tourism" are actually affecting women of color both in the Third World, and in Europe and North America, where hundred of thousands of Latin women are currently migrating to satisfy consumer desires for "a bit of *the other*."

A version of this essay was published in The Drama Review *41, 4 (T156), Winter 1997, and is copyright © 1997 by New York University and the Massachusetts Institute of Technology. Reprinted by permission.*

Production History

Stuff premiered at the National Review of Live Art in Glasgow in November 1996. Subsequently, it has been performed at London's ICA, Highways in Santa Monica, PICA in Portland, The Brady Street Theatre in San Francisco, Stockholm's Backstege, Artspace in Auckland, Otego Polytechnic in Dunedin (New Zealand), ASU West in Phoenix, University of Iowa and the Ex-centrics Festival in Vordinborg, Denmark.

BLANCA	Coco Fusco
ROSA	Nao Bustamante
EEE JONES (on video)	Adam Bresnick
TRAVEL TASTERS	variable

Preshow

Before the show the audience receives with their tickets a colored slip of paper. There are four colors—red, blue, yellow and green—and an equal number of audience members have received stubs of each color.

Top of show lights and music fade-out. Coco and Nao take their places onstage at small dressing tables, stage left and right. Lights up over the two tables. Coco and Nao are sitting at the table in their street clothes, writing postcards.

COCO *(Picks up a postcard and reads from it)*:
March 15, New York
Dear Liz,
I finally had that meeting about my piece on Cuban hookers. First, the editor was disappointed that I didn't want to say that Cuban women turned tricks because of the U.S. blockade. Then the editor says to me, "You know, if I go to a bar here to pick up a guy, it's for my enjoyment, but if a girl there does it, she has to give the guy what he wants." Imagine a bunch of overeducated women sitting in an office on Madison Avenue, saying things to me like, "I mean, if a guy says put my cock in your mouth, those girls just have to do it. How could that possibly be pleasurable?"
NAO *(Reading from a postcard)*:
April 4th, Copenhagen
Dearest D. L.,
Last night I was walking home at 3:00 A.M. when a young guy started following me. He asked me to go home with him and said he just wanted to make me feel good. At one point he noticed that I had dark hair sticking out from under my cap, and that made him very excited. He wanted to know if I was Mexican. When we got to the house where I was staying and I started to go inside, he made one last attempt to win my affec-

tions. And then he said, with a smile on his face as if it were some big turn-on, "I have chips and salsa at my place and you can have some if you come home with me." That asshole thought I was some little chihuahua or something, desperate for mama's home cooking.

COCO *(Picks up another postcard)*:

November 20, Toronto

Dear Kim,

I really ticked off some people at the film festival when I joked about how the documentary on Zapatista women looked like a rerun of films about Sandinistas, Salvadoran guerrilleras and Cuban milicianas. It's not that I don't agree with the Zapatistas. I mean, come on, those woman are saying they want to marry the men they choose, and they're enjoying getting free condoms when they're in combat. Who wouldn't sympathize with someone who says they'd rather wash clothes in a machine than on a riverbank? It's just that I'm not that crazy about seeing yet another movie about women getting off on guns.

NAO *(Picks up another postcard)*:

May 10, Hamburg

Hello my sweet Suzy,

I just can't seem to get away from sex! I'm staying in St. Pauli, the bizarre sex district of this city. The working girls here dress like aerobics instructors. I guess it's more practical than the usual puta-wear. Well, the locals and the tourists are eating it up. They are really crazy about the Brazilian girls. Ooh-la-la, the Brazilenias are beautiful, and I guess it's cheaper for the men to have them here than to go to Brazil. Dark-skinned women drive the Germans wild! Everywhere I go there is a lingerie ad staring me in the face that features a gorgeous black girl with huge breasts. I see the ad all over the place, but I can't seem to remember which company I'm supposed to buy from. The girl is oh oh oh-so-distracting.

COCO *(Picks up another postcard)*:

July 14, San Cristobal de las Casas, Chiapas

Dear Consuelo,

Last night we had dinner with Marieta. She told us about how the fighting between the mestizos and Indians here goes way way back. The Indians don't really believe that anyone else has the right to live on this land, and the mestizos are afraid of the prophecies that say they'll have to leave one day. Marieta said that one thing people don't talk much about is that the mestizos in San Cristobal rape Indian women from the countryside all the time. She told us about one Indian woman from the market who was raped and got pregnant. When the baby was born the guy went and took it away from her. That woman went mad. From then on, she would only go out with her face covered with mud so that no one would ever go near her again.

(Lights fade-out on stage left table. Nao exits. Jorge Reyes music plays, starting at a high level and lowering as speaking begins. A large video screen—or TV set—is lowered in front of a platform with dim lights and, if possible, drawn curtains. Weird, New Age music tunes in and then out, slowly. A man's face fills the screen. He is wearing a conservative dark-colored suit. His hair is slicked back, and he has a mustache. He smiles in a geekish way and holds his smile a little too long.)

Scene One

EEE JONES: Good evening and welcome. I am your host, Elizardo Eduardo Encarnación Jones (also known as Triple E). I am the director of the Institute for Southern Hemispheric Wholeness. Please allow me to ask you this: have you thought about what are you going to do on your next vacation? Would you like to try something . . . different?

Most of my clients have endured the pain of waiting all year long for their holiday trip to someplace warm and inviting. They long to bask in the sensual beauty and ancient wonders that my part of the world offers up so willingly. Then, much to their chagrin, they come back irritated by all the tropical storms, masked bandits, parasites and poverty. They find themselves saying, "Why not stay home, get some of that spicy take-out food and fondle some crystals instead?"

To them, and to you, I say, "Objects are not enough." You need complete nutrition for the spirit, and only people can provide that. Why not have the best without suffering the worst? I have devised a service that will bring you heat without sweat, ritual without revolution and delicacies without dysentery. And you don't have to go anywhere—we deliver it to you. In just a few moments you'll begin to sample the delights of postspacial travel as we approach the third millennium. *(Music fades out)*

For our first session, we will need four members of our audience. *(House lights up. He anticipates Blanca's entrance)*

My agency representative, Blanca, *(Pause; Blanca stops abruptly and poses like a stewardess)* will escort each postspacial traveler into our studio. *(Lights up on dining table and entire stage)*

Would all those with red tickets please raise your hand? *(Pause)* Blanquita, please escort a male with a red ticket onstage. *(Video pauses. Blanca picks male and escorts him onstage. Video plays)* For this evening's first event, you are going to be an economist in search of authentic pre-Colombian food and music. Your name is François. *(Male sits down at table)* Good.

Now would all those with yellow tickets please raise your hand? *(Pause)* Blanquita, please escort a woman with a yellow ticket onstage. *(Video pauses. Blanca picks woman and escorts her onstage. Video plays)* You were orphaned at birth and you just found out that you're Cher's cousin. You want to train as a medicine woman. Your name is Wanda Desert Flower. *(Woman sits at table)* Wonderful.

Now would all those with blue tickets please raise your hand? *(Pause)* Blanquita, be a dear and find a man with a blue ticket, please. *(Video pauses. Blanca picks male and escorts him onstage. Video plays)* You've been wanting to quit smoking for ages and are ready to try anything. Your name is . . . um, Bert. *(Man sits at table)* Marvelous. Only one more.

This time, those with green tickets please raise your hand. *(Pause)* You know what to do, Blanca darling. Female again. *(Video pauses. Blanca picks woman and escorts her onstage. Video plays)* You're a creative consultant for the Body Shop and you're eavesdropping on my seminar. Your name is Tippy O'Toole. *(Woman sits at table)*

I'm sure you're all comfortable. Please notice that you each have a spiritual guidebook in front of you, which you will be asked to read from occasionally. You have entered a new realm and will be known from now on as Travel Tasters. Are you ready?

BLANCA: All Travel Tasters nod your heads.

EEE JONES: Marvelous, marvelous. Let the program begin. Course number 1.

(EEE strikes a pose, then video fades to black. Lights reveal a large book being lowered from the ceiling. It stops at chest level. A different Jorge Reyes song plays. All the while, Blanca is playing the rainstick and praying to the heavens.)

BLANCA *(Going off at moments and not remembering she's onstage reading)*: A long, long time ago, before the times of our mothers, our grandmothers and our great-grandmothers, before credit-card debt, toxic waste and computer viruses, life was good. The sun shone, the rain was light and it was never cold. No one had to make decisions about anything because the gods decided everything. Adults and children alike frolicked all day long, since the land bore fruit without any need of human effort. Corn, yucca, potatoes, papaya, tomatoes, chile and cacao sprang forth from the soil in abundance. *(Pause)* Recognizing their extreme good fortune, the people occasionally ceased their playing to give thanks. Travel Tasters, you give thanks too. *(Music fades out)*

TRAVEL TASTERS *(In unison)*: We give thanks and praise that the dead once ate.

BLANCA: At the end of each lunar cycle, the people prepared an homage to their most revered goddess, Cuxtamali, keeper of the earth, the mother of all things; Travel Tasters, repeat—

TRAVEL TASTERS: The keeper of the earth, the mother of all things.

(Blanca moves rainstick as a downstage left floorlight comes up on Rosa. Rosa appears with a small food cart on wheels from stage right. She starts to dance toward downstage center, pounding her feet in a rhythm complementary to Blanca's reading. Rosa faces the audience, standing behind her cart. Front light comes up on Rosa, as the floorlight fades out.)

BLANCA: Cuxtamali not only provided for the world, but she was wise enough to provide for herself. Being somewhat insatiable, she kept three lovers. One of them was water *(Rosa spits to the side)*, the second one was the wind *(Rosa yawns)*, and the last one was fire. *(Rosa lights her cigarette and takes a drag)* Cuxtamali needed all three of them to fulfill her needs. When she took up with the wind, together they spread seeds *(From her apron pocket Rosa throws seeds at audience)*, when she embraced water, they increased the land's bounty *(Rosa serves drinks to tasters)* and when she fought with fire, the world shook and spat forth its insides. *(Rosa looks at Blanca and shrugs)* To satisfy herself, she rotated her sessions with her three lovers on a regular basis. Tasters—

TRAVEL TASTERS: The goddess is wise.

ROSA: You betcha she's wise.

BLANCA: In honor of this wise and lustful goddess, the people would make a feast at the end of each lunar cycle and would eat and eat and eat and eat . . .

ROSA *(Getting corn from cart)*: I've been serving up this corn mush for 3,000 years and, boy, am I fed up. *(Rosa moves around table, spooning corn mush or tamales onto each Taster's plate.)*

BLANCA: Oh, Priestess, please tell the Tasters what you are about to serve them.

ROSA *(Serving, speaking very casually)*: Oh . . . yeah. The feast would begin and end with corn, because corn is the beginning and end of all things.

BLANCA: Yes, this is true. Most of the people would be given corn to eat. Filling themselves with the wealth of the earth, they celebrated the generosity of their great goddess. When they had filled themselves with corn, they would begin to eat potatoes. And when there were no more potatoes, the people would eat papaya. Then tomatoes, and then avocados, and then chiles, which were, of course, seeded and finely chopped in advance. *(Meanwhile, Rosa takes each food off of cart and puts it on the table)*

ROSA: Don't look at me! I ain't no prep cook, and I'm not doing the dishes either! Tasters repeat after me: The goddess does not do dishes!

TRAVEL TASTERS: The goddess does not do dishes!

BLANCA: Let us continue. Between each course the people would commemorate the rise and fall of the great goddess's love affairs with the wind, water and fire. They sprinkled water on their food, burned incense and blew sanctified melodies with horns made of giant shells. Tasters, raise your horns and blow!

TRAVEL TASTERS: With this, we honor the goddess. *(They blow on paper horns)*

BLANCA: Then, the priestesses of the people would take corn, the potatoes, the papaya and tomatoes, the cacao and the avocado, and they would begin to make an offering to the great sensual goddess Cuxtamali with them. *(Rosa scrambles to pick up each fruit as it is being named)*

ROSA: Actually, the priestesses had the feeling at one point that the goddess was getting a little sick of her three boyfriends . . .

BLANCA: Excuse me?

ROSA: Yeah, over it. Cuxtamali had had enough. One day, she decided that she was going to make the perfect mate for herself and dump those machos.

BLANCA: Uh, well yes, let us praise the goddess for being an independent spirit! Tasters! Raise your cups! ¡Qué puta madre!

TRAVEL TASTERS *(They raise their cups)*: ¡Qué puta madre!

ROSA: She decided to make her mate out of the stuff she loved the most—food!

BLANCA: You must have gotten a revised version of the legend . . .

ROSA: She started with corn figuring that, since corn is the beginning and the end of all things, why not make it the middle too?

BLANCA: And so with that, she made the torso.

ROSA *(Piecing together the figure)*: Then she took the yucca and fashioned it into delectable arms and legs. The potato became the head. And from the tomato she created her lover's soft and tender heart. When that was done, she took a nice, big banana and—

BLANCA: Uh yes, well, and then the dancing to the goddess, mother of all things and keeper of the earth, would begin.

ROSA: The dance?

BLANCA: Yes, the dance of the blade. For on the occasion of the twelfth lunar cycle, the ceremonies included a knife dance that would be led by the priestesses. *(She pulls out a knife)*

ROSA: Could I have some ritual blade-dance music with drums, flutes and horns please?

(Tribu music starts high and fades down quickly. Rosa starts "The Dance.")

BLANCA: The dance was a particularly sacred element of the celebration of the great goddess. All the people would sway back and forth while the priestesses surrounded them. Tasters, please sway! *(The sculpture lies on the table. Rosa is circling the table sensually with the knife)* And then, the priestesses would reach the climax of their dance. At that point there would have to be a blood sacrifice—

ROSA *(Turns the knife on herself, then stops abruptly)*: Are you kidding or something?

BLANCA: No. No. Not at all. Blood sacrifice was needed to satisfy the great, lustful and all-powerful goddess. By order of the goddess, the priestess must self-sacrifice.

ROSA: Oh for Christ's sake! *(Music fades out)*

BLANCA: I beg your pardon, Priestess, there was no Christ in those times. Tasters, repeat after me: self-sacrifice!

TRAVEL TASTERS: Self-sacrifice! Self-sacrifice!

ROSA *(Staring at the knife)*: OK, OK, listen to this. The priestess did sacrifice a part of herself—

BLANCA: Oh really?

ROSA: Yes. The fruits they had used for their offerings were born of the earth, of the goddess herself. Hence it was flesh of her flesh.

BLANCA: Oh. I hadn't thought of that.

ROSA *(Turning her knife on her food sculpture)*: Die, Mr. Potato Head, die!

BLANCA: Tasters, please move back and give the priestess enough space for her to carry out her bloodletting ritual. And so, they would first baptize their creations and then begin to draw and quarter them, crying tears of blood as they completed their sacrifice.

(Rosa is tearing away at the food in a frenzy.)

Rosa, you'd better get a hold of yourself!

ROSA *(Ranting)*: The priestess cried tears of blood! Tears of blood!

BLANCA: Tasters, please don't worry, I'm sure the priestess will be finished shortly. And so, according to the legend left to us by our mothers, our grandmothers and our great-grandmothers, the priestesses would reach a state of ecstasy in the course of their sacrifice, while the people stood witness. Their wild state was said to symbolize the goddess's happiness at having a new lover who was more pleasing to her than those she had had before. And then, as night fell on them, and the people grew weary, they would begin their return to their cute little grass-roofed huts. *(Rosa is still pounding away at the sculpture)*

Tasters, please rise and return to your seats in the audience. I'm sure this has been an enriching experience for you. I thank you for your participation.

(Tasters rise and file offstage with Blanca assisting them. House lights are brought on until audience participants are seated. Book is lifted out. Colored lights shine on the screen. Rosa keeps on cutting up the sculpture and is now groaning. The video comes on with EEE's face on it, smiling.)

Rosa, the session is over. You can stop now. *(Rosa ignores her)*

EEE JONES: Well, my friends, wasn't this wonderful? The energy circulating in this room is so powerful it makes my soul jump for joy. I am so glad to see how well our first session with you has gone and how satiated and spiritually satisfied you all look.

BLANCA: OK Rosa. Do you realize that you've wrecked everything? First, you wrecked the ritual, then you go nuts on me and scare everyone at the table—what is your problem? *(Rosa ignores her)*

EEE JONES: Do you feel as cleansed and fortified as I feel that you are?

BLANCA: Rosa, are you listening to me? I can find somebody else to do this with, you know—

EEE JONES: Isn't it simply marvelous to move in and out of a distant time and place at the flick of a switch?

BLANCA: All right, let's stop things right here. *(Blanca points remote control toward screen. Video pauses)*

ROSA: What do you mean, I blew it? That was a great finale!

BLANCA: Come on Rosa, you're not supposed to make a mess of everything and groan like some weird extraterrestrial.

ROSA: I thought our ancestors were extraterrestrials and, besides, whose idea was this blood-spilling business?

(Rosa takes remote control and turns on video.)

BLANCA: Gimme that control!

(Blanca and Rosa start a cat fight for the control. Rosa wrestles it away and points it at screen; video resumes. Blanca pulls off Rosa's wig. Rosa turns to Blanca and pulls off her wig. They fight throughout Triple E's speech.)

EEE JONES: It is at this stage of our sessions that our guests feel so spiritually renewed that they are ready to embrace the world anew. But first they must embrace one another. So, now, turn and hold out your arms to your neighbor. Share with one another the richness you carry inside yourselves!

Thank you. And thank you, my beloved initiates, for being

part of this occasion. You have received a taste, only a taste, of
what we'll be offering to you via satellite in the very near future.
So keep tuned in and turned on.

(Triple E poses in a smile; video fades to black. Stagehand gives
Rosa her clipboard and begins to clean up mess.)

ROSA *(Approaches downstage)*: Hi. I'm Nao. I need to get some
information about your experience of our Travel Taster service
this evening. Some of the questions maybe a bit embarrassing, but
I'm not afraid to ask them. You see in my other life I also service
people's desires. I work as a mail-order sex educator and a sales
associate for women-owned sex toy cooperative. I help men and
women decide which dildos and vibrators work best for them.

As you can imagine, the most common question I get is,
"What size is right for me?" Not for me, I mean, for them.
Although a part of my mission is to truly help people, I can't tell
what sort of dildo a person needs just by looking at them. So I tell
customers to take a trip to the supermarket, and check out some
vegetables. Long, thin vegetables. Then they've gotta take them
home, and let them reach room temperature. Then put condoms
on them and try them out. Once they've figured out which ones
satisfy them the most, I tell them to measure them and come back
to me with this information, and then I can help them out.

Now talking to you about this has made me a little curious,
so before I get to our questionnaire, let me ask you this: let's say
you're in the supermarket, and you're in the cucumber section.
There are the smooth, short, waxy, fat ones, and then there are
the English kind, long with ridges. Or those yellow summer
squash with the curved tip—great for G-spot stimulation . . .
Which ones would you prefer? Can I see a show of hands for the
regular cucumbers? OK, I understand that this is a delicate question, and you may not want to reveal the information to your
neighbors . . . So everyone close your eyes. Come on, close your
eyes. Now you're with me and we are walking hand in hand at the
supermarket. You feel safe. You feel the cooling mist from the lettuce . . . You breathe in the refreshing scent of the citrus . . . and
there we stand in front of the cucumbers and the squash. You
reach to pick one out. Which one is it? Can I see a show of hands
for the English cucumber? Now we go to the dairy section for a
canister of whipped cream. You don't wait until you get home,

you begin to spray cream all over your body, and your fellow shoppers begin to lick and lick . . . and you feel moist and creamy and sticky . . .

(Lights dim out slowly as Nao walks backward offstage, leaving a spotlight on Coco's dressing table. Coco stands by her small table with the spotlight on her. She puts on nerd glasses.)

COCO *(Reads a postcard with date and place of performance)*:
Dear Audience,
I think it's time to explain why we are so interested in Latin women and food. Actually, this piece is about consumption—of our bodies and our myths—and food. Let's start with Antropofagia. That's what the Brazilians used to call it in the 1920s. Anthro-po-pha-gi-a. That was supposed to be our great, creative, cannibalistic revenge. Absorb our sacred enemies and transform them into totems, they said. Take everything that is thrown our way and have our way with it. That's how we were supposed to live up to our ancestors. So when you come charging in our direction, running from whatever it is you're running from, you may not think that we who serve you could be eating as well. But we do. Gently but efficiently, we devour you. The more visceral your desires, the more physical our labor.

(Lights out.)

Scene Two

Stage is dark. When Nao (Customer #1) is downstage center; a spotlight comes up on her. Her hair pulled back, she wears a ripped "Bahamas" T-shirt. She does yoga poses.

VOICE-OVER *(Airy voice)*: I hadn't really grasped why I felt so . . . empty. I just couldn't satisfy myself. Then, a true friend referred me to Triple E. I didn't know what to expect when I called. But everything was as promised, no surprises and no problems. I can tell I've made contact with the deepest parts of myself. My spiritual practice has grown, and I feel desirable again. I'm eternally grateful to the Institute and, of course, to the goddess.

(Voice pauses. Light out. Customer #1 leaves the stage. Table light comes up on Coco, wearing a black bathrobe, resetting the table.)

The first lesson I learned about gringos when I was little was that their food tastes gross. I thought I was supposed to learn how to cook decent food as a matter of cultural survival. I ended up as the only one in my crowd who doesn't live on takeout. I'm the one who makes the big dinners for everybody. I got so into it that I never even complained when guys never did shit to help. I even told one guy I wanted to cook for all his friends, no matter how many stopped by unannounced. I said I wanted to cook for his family, even though I was terrified they wouldn't like my food. Once, one of them showed up with a ham-and-cheese croissant that was oozing with mayonnaise, and I took it as a personal affront. When another one asked for a beer while I was cutting up the lasagna, and I knew there were no more in the fridge, I dropped the knife and ran out to the store and let my own food get cold. Every once in a while I would fall asleep at dinner while the guests were still around because I was so tired. And they say we use food to trap them.

(Voice pauses. Light out. Coco exits. Meanwhile, Customer #2—Nao—stands at stage left, in the book position. Lights up on her, in a baseball cap, with dreadlocks and a "human race" T-shirt.)

(Whiny voice) Well, it's not exactly what I expected. Kind of a hodgepodge of stories or, what do ya call 'em, ancient tales or something like that. I think it had to do with women and their sexual appetites, and well . . . I dunno. The corn was OK, nothing to write home about. The bit with the knife was cool. Did I say enough?

(Voice pauses. Light out. Customer #2 exits. Meanwhile Judy—Coco—is downstage center, wearing a black bathrobe and wild wig, as she begins to style her hair and primp "herself." Light comes up on her. An English translation slide is projected on the screen.)

(Spanish-speaking transvestite) Me puedes llamar Judy. ¿Me preguntas si me deprimo? Por su puesto que me deprimo. Pero esto es un trabajo, vieja. ¿Qué puedo hacer? Nadie escogió vivir en medio de esta mierda. Trato de no pensar mucho en estas cosas. Cuando me siento mal, pienso en un peinado nuevo. A los italianos les fascina el pelo rizado, así que me hice este permanente para estar más morena. ¿Qué te parece? Es que chica, ¿hay que comer, no?

¿Mi familia? Ya estan acostumbrados. Cuando traigo un gallego a la casa, mi familia no lo ve a él—ven un pollo, arroz, frijoles y plátanos, ven un refri lleno. Les digo a los pepes que estoy haciendo esto para comprarme una libra de picadillo, y así se sienten más culpables de mi situación y entonces me dan más plata. No digo que me gusta estar en un lugar con aire acondicionado. Yo pudiera estar en una oficina todo el día, como hacía cuando trabajaba en el banco. ¿Pero que saqué de eso? Ay mi cielo, absolutamente nada.

(Translation slide reads:
You can call me Judy. Depressed? Sure I get depressed. But it's a job, honey. What can I do? Nobody chooses to be born in the middle of a mess like this one. I try not to think about things too much. When I feel down, I start thinking about a new way to fix my hair. The Italians like wild hair, so I permed mine to look more morena, *what do you think? We have to eat, right?*

My family? Oh, they're used to it. When I bring a gallego *home, my family doesn't see him, they just see a chicken, rice, beans and* platanos—a full fridge. When I tell the guys that I'm doing it to buy a pound of ground beef, they feel better about giving me money, and they leave me more. I don't say I like to be in a nice room with air conditioning for a change. I could sit in an office all day—I did that when I was working in a bank. What did I get then? Oh darling, absolutely nothing.)*

(Voice pauses. Slide and light out. Judy exits. Meanwhile, Nao enters and sits at table. Light up over dining table. She begins to pick her teeth with a toothpick.)

I once asked an astronaut what he missed most about Earth, and he replied, "Food and sex." I can relate to that.

I am eating her and she tastes so tangy, a bit like a rusty papaya, unlike any other person I've tasted. Women taste strong, not like men. Men don't taste like anything if they are properly washed. Women always have a taste even if they are freshly bathed. When you consume a woman there is a taste and a smell left in your mouth and in your nose, which are connected by the way, as are your asshole and your mouth. But a woman's flavor changes depending on what she has eaten, how aroused she is, where she is in her cycle and who is in her vicinity. They say it's the same for men, with semen, but whatever, to me the taste of semen is repulsive. I think those who enjoy eating women must enjoy the flavor and scent and juice of seriously potent fruit . . . I've eaten both, and it takes more raw talent . . . to eat a woman.

(Voice pauses. Light out. Nao exits. Meanwhile Marta—Coco— enters wearing a braided wig and a rebozo. Lights up downstage center. Translation slide is projected on Marta as voice tape continues.)

(In Spanish. Marta lays out several dolls on top of a rebozo): Yo he trabajado aquí en el zócalo desde los siete años. Así que conozco bien como son los turistas que vienen a este lugar. Primero les ofresco mis muñecos. Mi mamá hace muy bonitos muñecos zapatistas, muy hermosos con pasamontañas de terciopelo. Nunca he visto a Marcos, pero tengo muñecos de Marcos, Ramona y Trini, Moisés y David. Yo digo siempre que el dinero es para mi tortilla. Algunos compran al tiro. Si eso no funciona les muestro mis pulseras. La gente que ya conozco a veces no quiere comprar, entonces les pido una coca. A veces hay otros que me llevan a cenar. Siempre trato de ver si mis amigos y mi mamá pueden venir también. Así nos sentamos en los restaurantes donde a veces nos echan, y los meseros no pueden decir nada. Mi amigo Alex de Alemania me regaló este traje. Lo uso para trabajar. El también me retrató y me pagó 20 pesos por haberme tomado la foto. Ahora les cobro 30 pesos a los gringos por cada foto.

(Translation slide reads:
I've been working here since I was seven, and I guess I've gotten to know what the tourists who come here are like. First, I offer them my dolls. My mother makes good Zapatista dolls, nice ones with velvet ski caps. I've never seen the real Marcos, but I have dolls of Marcos, Ramona, Trini, Moises and David. I tell people that the money is for my tortillas. Some people buy them right away. If that doesn't work I show them my bracelets. People I already know, though, sometimes they don't want to buy dolls or bracelets, so I ask them for a soda. Then sometimes there are people who will even buy me a meal, and then I always ask for chicken. I always try to see if my friends and my mother can come too. Then we can sit in the restaurants where we usu-

ally get thrown out and the waiters can't say anything. My friend Alex from Germany bought me my dress. This is what I work in. Alex also took my picture and paid me 20 pesos. Now I charge the gringos 30 pesos for one shot.)

(Voice pauses. Slide and light out. She picks up her dolls and puts the bundle on her back. Marta exits. Meanwhile Customer #3—Nao—enters. Book light comes up, stage left, on her. She wears sunglasses and a slick jacket.)

If you really wanna know, I think Triple E is a crackpot. I can't believe what I paid for this. I didn't feel a thing. They said the *camote* was an aphrodisiac, so I ate five and all they gave me was the runs. I was hoping to get a little more—you know what I mean. And those girls weren't exactly spring chickens. I thought it would be more like those kinds of places—it's like the way everybody moves, the way they let you know things with their hands. You don't need to speak the language even—you can just get into the music. The girls there, the way they . . . It's so . . . smooth, so . . . well, I'd like to see a little more of that.

(Voice-over ends. Light out. Customer #3 exits. Video of Triple E comes on. Lights come on over two dressing tables, where Coco and Nao are changing into new costumes throughout sequence.)

EEE JONES *(Video)*: I gather from your comments that our next intensive program will be more to your liking. Our aim is to please all sorts of tastes, and we recognize that serving you a meal is only one of the ways of heightening your experience of the senses and your connection to the spiritual. Many of you out there are demanding more of an immersion in another way of living—in, of course, the safest setting possible. In fact, our current research suggests that intercultural growth areas are the ones that offer the highest degree of, shall we say, intimate personal contact. *(Esquivel music starts)* Therefore, in order to attend to our increasingly diversified client base and, to satisfy your hunger for transformative physical encounters, we are upgrading our services to provide the most extensive and sophisticated multilingual intercourse you could imagine. Blanca, Rosa, would you like to give our studio audience tonight a preview?

BLANCA: Estoy lista, Triple E.

ROSA: Orale, jefito.

EEE JONES: Fine. Now, if a Travel Taster says, "Je veux t'offrir un verre," that means—

BLANCA: I would like to buy you a drink.

EEE JONES: And you say—

BLANCA: Je voudrais de l'eau minerale.

ROSA: No, je veux un martini.

EEE JONES: If a Travel Taster says, "Come ti chiami?" you say—

ROSA: Mi chiamo Lola.

EEE JONES: Now if a Travel Taster says, "Ist das dein Freund?" he means—

ROSA: Is that guy your boyfriend?

EEE JONES: And you say—

BLANCA: Das ist mein bruder.

EEE JONES: Which means?

BLANCA: He's my brother.

EEE JONES: When a Travel Taster says, "¿De qué signo eres?" what does that mean?

BLANCA: What's your sign? So we say—

ROSA: Soy virgo, soy virgen.

EEE JONES: Good. So if he says, "I'm married," you say—

BLANCA: Oh, do you have an open relationship? *(Music out)*

EEE JONES: Yes, and if he says, "Was magst du?" meaning—

BLANCA: What are you into?

EEE JONES: You'll answer—

ROSA: How do you want it? or, Wie willst du es? Right?

EEE JONES: Very good, ladies. I think you're ready. Can we have the lights up on our audience please?

(Video off. Audience lights up, general front, flashing colors from back. Music comes on—Herb Alpert and the Tijuana Brass. Blanca and Rosa go to get their microphones and then go out into the audience.)

BLANCA: Bienvenidos mis amigos, bienvenus mes amis, wilkommen mienen freunden, ahora queremos haceles algunas preguntas. So let's see who's the most ready to participate in our new program. Dale Rosa! *(Lights stop flashing, colored lights stay on)*

ROSA *(Standing in one of the aisles)*: Who knows how to say, "Bring me another Margarita" in another language?

   (If an audience member answers) Let's have a round of applause for this gentleman.

(If no one answers, Rosa goes to one audience member) Try saying: Tráeme otra margarita, por favor.

BLANCA: That was great! Does anyone know what this means: No puedo comer fritangas?

(If an audience member answers) Let's have a round of applause for our friend!

(If no one answers) It means: I can't eat fried food.

ROSA *(Standing next to a male audience member)*: OK, I have a feeling about you. Fuiste maestro de conga en tu vida anterior, ¿no es verdad? Know what that means?

(If the audience member answers) Well, I can't wait to get up and dance with you baby!

(If he doesn't answer) You may not know it but I can tell you were a bongo player in your past life.

BLANCA *(To a woman, doing a moño)*: ¿Quieres mover tu cintura como una mulata buena? Do you know what I said?

(If the woman answers yes; if not continue saying the phrase to other women until one says yes) Well, I think all of you have done marvelously! Rosa, could I see you onstage for a moment? *(Blanca and Rosa go back onstage. They whisper to each other briefly)*

ROSA *(Pointing to those in the audience who spoke)*: Would you please stand? Would you please stand? Would you, and you? Thank you! Congratulations, all of you have proven your multilingual potential. Please now join us onstage for an Afro-Frenetic extravaganza.

(Lights begin flashing! Four audience members go onstage. Lights stop flashing. Music fades out.)

BLANCA *(Pointing to guy marked as Congero)*: Ven acá Señor Congero. Música por favor.

("Afro-Frenetic" music plays. Rosa grabs the guy and sits him down, hangs mini bongos on him, a white cap and a cigar. She begins to show him the rhythm, and he starts drumming. Rosa signals for the audience to applaud. Meanwhile, Blanca puts the other three audience members on their marks. Blanca and Rosa take their positions in front of dancers. They begin to step and clap to the music.)

Soy Blanca—

ROSA: Soy Rosa—

ROSA AND BLANCA: —and we're going to teach you to rhumba!

BLANCA: Are you ready for an Afro-Frenetic dance extravaganza?

ROSA: Yeah, let's do it!

ROSA AND BLANCA: ¡Vámonos!

ROSA: This is the basic step you'll need *(Blanca and Rosa start moving their feet only)* We'll add the shoulders later. *(Blanca goes around behind the dancers and starts correcting their positions)* ¡Fantástico! OK, let's add the shoulders!

BLANCA: Everybody!

ROSA: OK! Try to keep control of your upper body!

BLANCA: Yeah, no window washing!

ROSA *(Demonstrating)*: And no funky chicken either!

BLANCA: Gimme a minute, I'm gonna check Maestro Bongo. *(Blanca goes over to Congero)* OK, OK. That was great. Now you're ready to learn how to moño.

ROSA AND BLANCA: ¡Moño! *(Quick music change to Eddie Palmieri. They start gyrating)* Do it! *(Dancers do moños. Rosa and Blanca motion for audience to applaud dancers)*

ROSA: And now, it's time for the frenetic part. Let's go freestyle!

(Music cranks up. Lights begin to flash, chaotic scene. Blanca, Rosa and dancers go bananas. After thirty seconds or so of unbridled dance, music fades out. Lights go back to general wash. Rosa and Blanca pull out fans and take dancers over to table.)

BLANCA: You guys deserve a rest. *(Rosa fans dancers)*

ROSA: And a drink! *(Rosa serves drinks)*

BLANCA: Well, that was just great. Now Travel Tasters, Rosa and I are just beginning to develop this part of our repertoire and would like to ask for your help. Would one of you be willing to volunteer for a test dialogue to get us going?

(A Travel Taster volunteers. Blanca, Rosa and Travel Taster move to downstage center. Blanca and Rosa set up to two chairs. A downstage center spot comes up from the front.)

OK, you're going to have a conversation with me, and Rosa will show you what you need to say. Now, let's take our little game down here, so the two of us can get to know each other better. *(Blanca and Travel Taster sit downstage center)*

ROSA: We've been working on our conversational abilities with our fantastic *Hot International* guide, which comes with translations for love and sex in seven different languages. Tonight though, we're going to work on our Spanish. Ready? Or should I say, listo? Now you've just come off the dance floor with Blanca, and you're going to ask her if she liked the dance. Say, "¿Te gustó el baile?"

TRAVEL TASTER: ¿Te gustó el baile?

BLANCA: ¡Sí! ¡Eres buenísimo!

ROSA: She's saying that you're really great—so you ask her if she wants to go to your place. Say, "¿Quieres ir a mi casa?"

TRAVEL TASTER: ¿Quieres ir a mi casa?

BLANCA: ¿Vamos a esperar a conocernos mejor, no?

ROSA: Oh, oh, she says you have to get to know each other better. So make small talk. Ask her what her name is— "¿Cómo te llamas?"

TRAVEL TASTER: ¿Cómo te llamas?

BLANCA: Me llamo Lola. ¿Y tú de donde eres?

ROSA: She wants to know where you're from. Tell her you're Nigel from England. "Soy Nigel de Inglaterra."

TRAVEL TASTER: Soy Nigel de Inglaterra.

BLANCA: Ya es tarde. Debo ir a mi casa.

ROSA: Oh, oh, She wants to go home. You better offer to take her. Say, "¿Te llevo?"

TRAVEL TASTER: ¿Te llevo?

BLANCA: Bueno, vámonos.

ROSA: Lucky guy. She said yes! OK, now you're home together, and you've gotten through the initial formalities. You've got to tell her to get on the bed. Say, "¡Echate en la cama!"

TRAVEL TASTER: ¡Echate en la cama!

BLANCA: OK.

ROSA: That was easy! Now, get her on her knees. "Ponte en rodillas."

TRAVEL TASTER: ¡Ponte en rodillas!

BLANCA: ¡Ya voy! Espérate, ¡eres muy grande!

ROSA: She thinks you're a little big. You tell her to try another way. "Vamos a probar otra cosa."

TRAVEL TASTER: Vamos a probar otra cosa.

BLANCA: ¡Qué rico es así!

ROSA: Great—she likes it.

BLANCA: ¡Me estás volviendo loca!

ROSA: You're driving her wild. Now you can tell her to get some rope. "Busca la cuerda."

TRAVEL TASTER: Busca la cuerda.

BLANCA: ¡No me ates, por favor!

ROSA: Oops, she doesn't want to be tied up. Tell her she's gotta be punished. "¡Hay que castigarte!"

TRAVEL TASTER: ¡Hay que castigarte!

BLANCA: ¡Eres un animal!

ROSA: You better tell her to calm down. Say, "¡Cálmate!"

TRAVEL TASTER: ¡Cálmate!

BLANCA: ¡Vete al carrajo!

ROSA: She's very angry. Tell her you lost control and that you're sorry. "Perdóname, perdí el control."

TRAVEL TASTER: Perdóname, perdí el control.

BLANCA: ¡Me estás usando!

ROSA: She thinks you're using her. Say it isn't true, that you're looking for love. "¡No es cierto—busco amor!"

TRAVEL TASTER: ¡No es cierto—busco amor!

BLANCA: Y yo estoy buscando apoyo financiero.

ROSA: And she's looking for financial support. Travel Taster, why don't you suggest that you could live together in your country? "Podemos ir a vivir en mi país."

TRAVEL TASTER: Podemos ir a vivir en mi país.

BLANCA: Vamos a conocernos un poquito mejor.

ROSA: She still wants to get to know you better. But I think it's going very well. The next morning, you offer to take her out for breakfast. Say, "¿Quieres ir a desayunar?"

TRAVEL TASTER: ¿Quieres ir a desayunar?

BLANCA: ¡Ay sí!

ROSA: She's game. Now, just to be sure, ask her for her name again. "¿Cómo era que te llamabas?"

TRAVEL TASTER: ¿Cómo era que te llamabas?

BLANCA: Me llamo Lola.

ROSA: Tell her you'll never forget her. "Nunca me olvidaré de tí."

TRAVEL TASTER: Nunca me olvidaré de tí.

ROSA AND BLANCA: Gracias guapo.

ROSA (To the audience): Aren't they fantastic? Let's give them a hand.

(Applause. Blanca and Rosa lead travel tasters back to audience. House lights up remain up until audience participants are seated.)

MALE VOICE: Un momento compañera. I saw you with that foreigner. (Lights change to flashlight at Blanca) ¿Cómo te llamas?

BLANCA (Walking back into the spotlight): Me llamo Lola.

MALE VOICE: Sure. Where do you live?

BLANCA: En Centro Habana.

MALE VOICE: Where do you work?

BLANCA: Wherever I can. *(She clasps her hands in prayer)* Todos seguimos al Señor. You know, the man in charge here? *(She makes a gesture to show a beard on a chin)* He's bending every which way to keep things going. And we're following him.

MALE VOICE: What did you say your name was again?

BLANCA *(Taking off her wig)*: Coco.

MALE VOICE: You know, that guy you talked to didn't seem like the kind of man who would take advantage of a Third World woman.

BLANCA: Not all the guys who come here are pigs you know.

MALE VOICE: Aren't you making light of a very serious situation?

BLANCA: What else can I do? Haven't you ever had sex with someone who had more than you?

MALE VOICE: More?

BLANCA: More. More power. More money. More food. More youth. More. *(Lights out. Rosa comes onstage with two microphones)*

ROSA: Did I hear more? It's time for our grand finale. But first I would like to introduce my wonderful partner in crime, the divine, the marvelous, Miss Blanca de la Blanquita!

BLANCA: Thanks, Rosa. You know, when we first wrote the song we're about to present to you, we thought we would sing it ourselves. But since then, we've decided it would be much better to turn it into a karaoke number so we can all share in the fun! *(Cabaret-style spotlight comes up on Rosa and Blanca, off to the side of back screen, where karaoke video is projected)*

ROSA AND BLANCA:
Señor John is a Malibu swinger
Who decided to take a trip south.
His friends said he should first learn some Spanish
But that John insists that he's learned enough.
I learned from my be-lov-ed maid
When I was a little muchacho
And then from the gardener, the butler,
The driver, the waiter and cook.

(Yell) And John started singin':

Que me des unos huevos rancheros
Yo quiero bananas and nuts

Tu quieres mi concha-biscocha
It's your pinche salchica I lust.

And with that he took off with his backpack.
Some days later he lands on our isle
And he stumbles right into our hangout,
A hip bar called the Crocodile's Smile.

There we two girls work hard for our money
Putting up with a whole lot of schmucks.
We dance and sing, and grind our hips nightly
To be sure we take home lots of bucks.

(Yell) And he says:

May I squeeze tu melón y papaya?
You can pinch my panocha if you want.
How I relish the zest of your chile.
That chamoya 'n' chorizo is enough.

Our poor John, he has never been sober.
But on holiday he gets much worse.
Married ladies must tolerate spouses
But drunk gringos are the island girls' curse.

(This last line is repeated over and over while curtained platform is wheeled off. Spot fades into general light that can catch the exit of the platform. Applause. Jorge Reyes music resumes. The video comes on.)

EEE JONES: Ladies and gentlemen, I am sure that you will agree with me that this has been an absolutely exceptional evening. I have no doubt that each and every one of you will go home transformed. Thank you for choosing our first-class Travel Tasters' service, brought to you by the Institute for Southern Hemispheric Wholeness. For complete tour information, please pick up one of our brochures located in the lobby of the theatre. We also offer a frequent travelers' card that will allow you to accumulate a host of exotic and lustful benefits. Adios and Bon appetit.

(Triple E smiles, as the video fades to black. All lights fade out with the video. Music fades out.)

END OF PLAY

COCO FUSCO is a New York-based interdisciplinary artist, who has lectured, performed, exhibited and curated programs throughout the U.S., Europe, Canada, South Africa and Latin America. Her collection of essays on art, media and cultural politics, *English Is Broken Here*, was published by The New Press in 1995. Her current solo work, *Better Yet When Dead*, was recently featured at the Bienal de Arte of Medellin. Fusco's work has been included in The Whitney Biennial, the Sydney Biennale, The Johannesburg Biennial, The London International Theatre Festival, the National Review of Live Art, The Los Angeles Festival, The Festival 2000 of San Francisco and other events. Her videos include *The Couple in the Cage, Pochonovela* and *Havana Postmodern: The New Cuban Art*, all of which have been broadcast on public television. Fusco's writings have appeared in the *Village Voice,* the *Los Angeles Times, Art in America,* the *Nation, Ms., Frieze, Third Text, Latina* and *Nka: Journal of African Art,* as well as a number of anthologies. She has also contributed to National Public Radio's Latino USA. She has received grants from The National Endowment for the Arts, The New York Council on the Arts, The New York Foundation for the Arts, The Los Angeles Department of Cultural Affairs and Arts International, and was a 1994 Mellon Fellow in Critical Studies at the California Institute for the Arts. Fusco currently teaches at the Tyler School of Art at Temple University.

NAO BUSTAMANTE is a performance artist pioneer who is originally from the San Joaquin Valley, central California. She has been living and developing her work for the past twelve years in San Francisco's Mission District. In addition to performing, Nao works as a writer and curator, and has also acted in film and video. Her performance work has been seen in Mexico, Asia, Europe, Canada and the United States.

FUR
A Play in
Nineteen Scenes

Migdalia Cruz

THE WRITER SPEAKS
Migdalia Cruz

beau•ty \byüt-e\ *n* 1 : loveliness; elegance; grace; a beautiful woman . . .

In my work, I define beauty as the transformation of women from sexual object to spiritual being. The protagonist in *Fur*, Citrona, though considered a disposable piece of human sideshow flesh, comes to realize her own power through the act and reaction of love. Citrona is both the beauty and the beast defining her own postapocalyptic fairy tale. The other two characters, Michael and Nena, also take turns being the ideal of physical beauty—but acting in "beastly" ways to get the object of their affections to love them. Until each character achieves her or his own spiritual enlightenment, true beauty is inaccessible to her or him. In *Fur*, true beauty is the goal of each of my characters—who each feels like a beast—either because of unrequited love or physical attributes outside the norm.

¹**body** \bäd-ē\ *n* 1 : the trunk of an animal; main part; matter; a person; a system; strength; reality; any solid figure. ²**body** *vt* 1 : to give a body to; to embody . . .

Women who inhabit my plays often use their bodies as their sole commodities. It is through their bodies that they feel power. And when the body is less than ideal anguish overcomes them. If the only thing society judges you on is your body, then the body becomes your only access to happiness, mental health and success. When Miriam of my play *Miriam's Flowers* becomes hypersexual, it is not because she loves sex, but because that is all she feels she has to offer anyone, and to replicate a bodily wound helps her to soothe her sorrow over her brother's accidental death. In *Fur*, each character lusts for the character most likely not to give them what they want or need. Physically ideal and seemingly angelic, Michael lusts for Citrona, a hirsute woman who has been sexually mutilated by her mother and sold to him like a dog. The beauty Michael sees in Citrona is about her otherness, her exoticness, her Latina-ness. Citrona lusts for Nena, another woman who could be her twin—if only Citrona were as hairless as she. The physically perfect Nena yearns for Michael —her male counterpart in physical terms. Each character in the play is at first repulsed by the one who loves them most, but in the end learns something about the true nature of love.

Production History

Fur was developed at the Padua Hills Playwriting Festival, INTAR's Playwrights Laboratory, under the direction of Maria Irene Fornes; at New Dramatists and at Latino Chicago Theater Company.

Fur was first produced in February 1995, at Latino Chicago Theater Company. The production was later remounted at Chicago's Steppenwolf Studio (Juan A. Ramirez, producer) in January 1997. It was directed by Ralph Flores and designed by Joel Klaff. The cast was as follows:

CITRONA	Marilyn Dodds Frank
MICHAEL	Mark Vann (1st production)
	Raul Esparza (remount)
NENA	Consuelo Allen

Fur was workshopped at SoHo Repertory Theatre in New York in May 1997. It was directed by Lisa Portes. It then opened in San Francisco on October 6, 1997 at Intersection for the Arts (Campo Santo, producer). It was directed by Roberto Gutierrez Varea. The production then moved to the Vortex Repertory Company in Austin, Texas, on October 10, 1997. It was produced at Kitchen Dog Theater in Dallas, Texas, in March 1999. Tina Parker was the director. The cast was as follows:

CITRONA	Shelley Tharp
MICHAEL	Chris Carlos
NENA	Leah Wysong

Characters

CITRONA, a hirsute young woman whose age is hard to tell;
a good sense of humor; a great sense of loneliness.

MICHAEL, a handsome man, older than he looks and acts,
who is searching for true love; the owner of Joe's,
a pet shop in the desert suburbs of Los Angeles, California.
Whenever Michael can, he watches and listens.

NENA, a woman that other people think is pretty, thirties,
an animal trapper; Michael's servant.

Time

Summer, in the near future.

Place

A desert suburb of Los Angeles.

Prologue: A carnival sideshow.

Scenes One through Nineteen: The basement room under Joe's
Pet Shop and its adjoining corridor and window. Also: No-Space, an
elevated space which represents the outside world and the passing of
time where a three-bladed fan spins until the characters begin to lose
hope. (A place conceived by Joel Klaff, Juan A. Ramirez and
Brendan McCarthy of Latino Chicago Theater Company during the
play's first production.)

As time goes on, a pile of fur pelts, thrown to one side of the
cage in the basement, piles higher and higher. Sand visible at the window also piles higher and higher as the play progresses.

"I shall not let you die!" cried Beauty.
"You shall live and I shall be your wife.
I know now that I love you and
I cannot bear to lose you."
Scarcely had she spoken than
there was a sudden flash of brilliant light;
and there before her
stood a handsome young prince.

—from *Beauty and the Beast*

Prologue

In a sideshow carnival tent. In front of a moving image of sideshow freaks, all mutations of humans with animals, such as a snakeskin man, a woman with the head of a pig, a dog-faced boy, etc. The sound of sand and wind compete with the human voices. Nena gazes at Michael who watches the images, enrapt in them.

NENA: Hey! Hi. You come to these things often?

(Michael stares at her. No response.)

Hey. Oh, hey. I'm sorry. Can't you—Oh, wow, are you one of them? Is that why I see you around all the time?

(Michael stares at her. No response.)

It must be really hard not to be able to talk . . .
MICHAEL: I talk only when I need to.
NENA: Oh . . .
MICHAEL: There's a new one today. I haven't seen her yet, but I bet she's a beauty.
NENA: There's some think I'm a beauty.
MICHAEL: Oh? People are so easily fooled, aren't they?

(He walks off into the images. She watches him go.)

NENA: So who was that? A vision or something! I looked into his heart and felt it throbbing between my legs. I was sexualized today . . . Maybe he'll be my Valentine . . . maybe not.

(Blackout. Lights up in the basement hallway of Joe's Pet Shop.)

Scene One

In the darkness, we hear the Beatles' song "Birthday." Lights come up on Michael, who speaks to a large, unseen animal in a sack. He is standing outside the entrance to the basement room.

MICHAEL: C'mon beauty. Let me stroke you. Let me rub my hands against your fur. I like furry things. They keep you warm. You could keep me warm.

(He takes out a vial with some water) Here you go . . . *(He pours it onto the ground)*

Clean water. Drink it. Go ahead, beauty. It's for you. It's fresh beautiful water. I collected it. It's rainwater. It'll make your fur shine and your eyes will go white if they're red when you drink this. All for you. All yours. It's straight from God. Now that you're home with me, you can be my lady friend. You are so pretty. You have soft eyes—soft brown eyes. You make me melt with eyes like that—when you look at me like that. You know things about me. You know how to make me feel better. We could get away, beauty. Go somewhere . . . I'm not letting anything stop me, if I'm with you. You don't have to be afraid. No one will touch you . . . no one but me. I won't let anyone harm you anymore. When you're at Joe's nobody can hurt you. Animals are the business of my inheritance. Joe left this shop to me. You'll make me happy. I know you will. I never would have guessed that love would cost so little . . . Your mother doesn't have a mind for business. She told me to keep you in a cage. "She's a wild one," she said. But if you'll love me—I'll set you free. Love me and I'll build you a palace.

(A scream from the sack. Lights cross to the basement window. Nena stands behind it and starts to speak.)

Scene Two

Nena outside the basement window. She holds a rabbit in a small cage.

NENA: I've been watching him. I see how he treats the bunnies I bring to him. He stares at them and pets them and he always knows just what to call them . . . I find them in the wild. I have a talent for finding them—they trust me. Because they are beasts and beasts are awed by me. I speak to them and they come right into my arms. And then I sell them . . . to him. He doesn't know my name—and I wonder what he thinks of me . . .

(Lights up on Dream Michael in the No-Space.)

DREAM MICHAEL: She's so good at bringing in the animals. She has a gift. I can never remember her name—but I remember the gift.

(Lights on Michael fade.)

NENA: He's like God to me . . . well, maybe not God, himself—I mean, really I'm not sure I believe in one person like that. I mean, really, too many friends have died for me to believe that—really. But he's a person surrounded by white light . . . Not like a clown or a mime—I mean, I hate mimes—but he's a different kind of white . . . like light, I mean. And I don't just mean the clothes. He wears white, of course, and so few people can, I mean and do it well—but he's light on the inside. I think it's because he cares about animals so much. And I attract animals—without traps or mechanical snares—I just look at them and they're mine . . . And I give them to him—I would do it for free except I don't think he'd respect me for that. So I put a price on it, and he appreciates that . . . I think. I think with a price he's assured of their value. Nothing wrong with that—I don't think . . . I think I love him.

(Lights cross to the basement room.)

Scene Three

Lights dimly reveal a cage in the basement room which has one small window in one corner. The cage is large enough for a person to stand in. It's top is solid, the sides are barred. The front of the cage is hinged at the top, so the front can fall straight down if opened. Citrona is squatting in one corner, her back to the audience. She shakes uncontrollably.

Michael enters. He sits next to the cage, mirroring Citrona. He is holding a framed photograph. He watches Citrona. He rocks with her.

She doesn't look at him. She whimpers and sighs. He whimpers and sighs . . . and slowly hands her the photo. It is a photo of him as a child.

MICHAEL: You see? I was alone too . . .

(*Citrona lays flat at the bottom of the cage, arms extended out through the bars. Michael mirrors her. When the tips of their fingers meet, Citrona pulls away in fear and makes herself as small as possible against the bars of the cage. It goes from night to day as Michael slowly exits. Sand begins to pour in through the window.*)

Scene Four

It goes from day to night. Citrona speaks from her cage, in the darkness.

CITRONA: People say you can't get used to some things—but you do. Like the smell of your own shit. You sit in it long enough and you want to feel it on your legs. You smear yourself. Because it keeps you warm. It's familiar. It's like your family. My shit and urine is my company. I check it all the time. I look for signs of life. I look for light. I sleep with my face toward the light. I keep track of myself. When I feel the light, I count my fingers. I count them out loud, because numbers are a comfort.

(*Long pause. Michael watches Citrona from the basement window.*)

You know what? Sounds get bigger when you're alone. Everything gets bigger. Everything is bigger than you. You know, I can hear the light coming in through that window up there. Before I can feel it. It sounds like the buzzing of a bee. It goes in and out at first. Buzz—nothing buzz—nothing. Then it's buzz-buzz—nothing. Then it's buzz-buzz-buzz—then it's a long screaming buzz. A "zzzz" that fills me up. It comes between my legs and it stays there until night. And in the night I wait for it to start again.

(*She listens in silence.*)

I'm waiting now. But you know, it's not so bad to wait. In the dark. When It's dark nobody can see me. I'm not ugly in the dark. I can touch myself then. I can stand to let my fingers part myself and touch my crown. You know what? That's the only thing I touch. I don't touch my arms or shoulders. And never my face. I can't stand to sneeze or yawn or belch. Or any of those things that make you put your hand to your face. If my fingers get too close to my mouth I will have to bite them off.

(Michael speaks from the window.)

MICHAEL: What do you want?

(Lights up revealing Citrona fully for the first time.)

CITRONA: Something pink.

(Lights cross-fade to No-Space as the fan goes on.)

Scene Five

In the threshold of No-Space. Michael interviews Nena for the job of caretaking Citrona.

MICHAEL: I need a trapper—I prefer women. A gentler touch. There's so few things one can trap anymore . . .

NENA: I know . . . I'm good at it though. I mean—so I've been told. I mean, I brought you catches before.

MICHAEL: But that's only one part of the job. I also need you to clean. Can you clean?

NENA *(To herself)*: He's looking for a wife—maybe. A wife figure anyway. Or a partner. I could be his partner.

MICHAEL *(Handing her a basin of water and a sponge)*: Clean something.

(Michael looks at his watch. Nena kneels in front of him.)

NENA: I saw this in a movie once.

(She takes off his sandals and washes his feet. She does one foot at a time, very meticulously, going between the toes last. When she's done, he checks his watch again, then holds out his wrist. She winds his watch. He speaks.)

MICHAEL: Good. You clean very well, uh, Nena. It's Nena, isn't it? If it isn't it should be.

NENA: Yes, Nena.

MICHAEL: You need certain skills for this job. It's not an easy job. Like you're used to. But I know you like to serve.

NENA: Yeah, sure. I'll serve. I can always serve. That's one thing I'm sure of—serving.

MICHAEL: Good. You gotta clean the cage and feed the animal. Do you like animals?

> (*He begins to play with her hair*) You don't have much hair—so I'm worried.

NENA: What do you mean?

MICHAEL: People who like animals usually have a lot of hair—you don't. I mean it's kind of thin.

NENA: I just washed it. That's what happens when I wash it. Usually it's very thick.

MICHAEL: Oh . . . so tell me how you feel about animals.

NENA: I like them. And they like me. I had two squirrels I trained once to dance to John Philip Sousa marches. Rodents like marches, I find . . .

MICHAEL: I hate marches. You won't bring any with you, will you? I don't want them in my house.

NENA (*She nods no*): Oh, no, no. I never travel with them . . .

MICHAEL: Good . . . Good. Well, okay. Nena . . . well, welcome aboard.

NENA: Oh! Gosh . . . Thank you for taking me on.

MICHAEL: I like to give people a chance. That's how I got Joe's Shop. He died. That gave me a chance to have a store. All important historical events happened by chance.

NENA: I wouldn't know about that . . . I don't know any history.

MICHAEL: You will. We need a rabbit by six o'clock. Think you can catch one?

NENA: I know I can. But—

MICHAEL: Yes?

NENA: Didn't I bring you enough last week?

MICHAEL: That was last week. This week I've got another mouth to feed. Okay?

NENA: Okay.

MICHAEL: What do you think of my suit?

NENA: It's ugly—but it looks good on you.

MICHAEL: Bring back a pretty one, okay? She likes pretty ones . . . all I want is to make her happy. I feel so lucky today. Today, I found my soul mate.

NENA: Oh . . .

MICHAEL: I wasn't looking for love. I wanted to see the sights. The ones I never saw before. That's what sideshows show you. Things, people, you'd never otherwise see.

NENA: I've seen things there too—you found an animal there?

MICHAEL: I found my wife. My woman. When she sang "I Wanna Hold Your Hand"—the world stopped moving on its axis. For a moment. For a moment, I felt her hand in mine and when I touched her I felt happy.

(Citrona sings "I Wanna Hold Your Hand" from her cage in the basement.)

I mean, I imagined I touched her. Other people laughed—looked at her and laughed. Her mother laughed the loudest. That's when I knew . . . I had to save her. Help me, Nena.

NENA: Sure . . . I can always help.

(Michael exits.)

When he moves away from me, I have memories.

(Pause.)

I wonder what it would mean to feel his lips on my stomach, in the folds of my lower back, behind my right knee. And then I wonder why he'll never love me. He's made his family—bought it. Bought the love of a freak. Maybe there is a woman under all that fur—but who has the time? Life is short—doesn't he know that? Doesn't he know it grows shorter now? I mean for all of us . . .

(Lights cross to the window light in the basement room.)

Scene Six

Michael watches from the window as Nena enters Citrona's room.

MICHAEL: I've always liked sideshows. And the ones we have now are truly the best ever—in my memory anyway. So many different things to see. I once saw a human baby born without eyes—in their place, he had small wings. He didn't fly or anything, but he had these feathers where his eyes should have been—these white pieces of fluff. I could see history through those feathers. We animals are all born with everything—with the possibility of everything—of being anything. Fish-fowl, man-woman . . . I like seeing those too, those man-womans . . . You see the separation is not complete in them. In them, the sex organs both develop— sometimes overdevelop—often dysfunctional. I'd like to see them . . . function. I've dreamt of that—of holding one. Kissing both a man and a woman through one set of lips. It's a strange dream, I think. I think it has to do with my father—even though I don't remember his face. When it got blown off I tried to save it. I wanted to sleep with it over my eyes, so I could have his dreams. But the pieces weren't big enough . . . so I let the animals eat them.

Scene Seven

Nena enters Citrona's room carrying a rabbit on a tray. Citrona sings the Beatles' "Yes It Is" to her as she puts down the tray and moves it to the cage with her foot.

CITRONA:

Please don't wear red tonight,
this is what I said tonight.
For red is the color that will make me blue,
In spite of you, it's true.
Yes it is, it's true,
yes it is, it's true . . .

(Citrona grabs her ankle.)

Fine bones. The bones of a well-bred lady. A sweet high-born beauty. Ankles of ivory. An elephant would kill for your tusks, baby. Hey, hey, I know I got a bad skin condition, but the hair covers it right up. Touch it. My face is smooth for something covered in thick, black fur . . . Hey, hey, wanna hear a joke? What do you call a woman without an asshole? Single! I like that one a lot.

(Nena breaks away and runs out the door.)

Hey, I'm sorry . . . I'm sorry you're so beautiful . . . Tell Michael I approve.

(Citrona sings the Beatles' "Yes It Is" to the animal she is tearing apart and eating. Her body gets soaked in its blood.)

Please don't wear red tonight,
this is what I said tonight.
For red is the color that will make me blue,
In spite of you, it's true.
Yes it is, it's true,
yes it is, it's true . . .

(She speaks in a rush) Look, I'm wet with you. It's too bad. It's too bad I don't have a cup. Then I could collect you and drink you. You know what? Then I'd drink you. I can only lick you now. And I don't like doing that, you know, because . . . You know, the hair thing. Listen, you were very tasty. I bet you're the tastiest thing ever. I bet you appreciate how I appreciate you.

(Long pause; as she continues to eat.)

I don't like the furry parts. The parts that still have fur. I mean, I do, the stuff right there next to it—that's the good stuff, but I'm too afraid to eat it. Because if I eat it I might find fur in my mouth. And I couldn't stand that. I would choke. I would choke and die. I don't feel like dying anymore.

(Pause.)

You know what this room needs? It needs a fan. Yeah, get air moving in here. Yeah, that would be good.

(Pause.)

And a view. It's so hard not to be able to look straight up. Like most persons. Most persons can lie on their backs and look straight up and see something. See the sky . . . I can't do that. All I see is concrete. But I don't know . . . You know what? It's getting prettier. I can change it. I can make it any color. I close my eyes and try to breathe and I can smell green or blue or pink. Pink's good because it's bubble-gum smell and I don't get much of that. You know what's best? Bazookas. With that cartoon and the fortune. I liked that guy with the turtleneck. He was funny. I remember all my fortunes. You know what? You know what's fun to do? When you get one of those fortunes—now I overheard this once—you take the fortune and you add "in bed" to the end of it and it's kind of amazing because it always works. Like, "You will be complimented by your peers—in bed." And,

"You will be a great success and make a lot of money—in bed."
And, "You will find the answers to your questions—in bed."
And, "You will receive a surprise visitor—in bed." You know?
See what I mean? See, see, see. See?

*(Long silence. Nena enters. She sees that Citrona is still eating
and turns to leave. Citrona grabs her arm with a bloody hand.)*

Hey, hey, baby. Talk to me today. You gotta talk or I won't let
go. And I'm strong.

*(Lights cross to Michael listening to them on the other side of
the door. He listens in silence for a moment, then he speaks.)*

MICHAEL: There was a time when I could only imagine what two
women did when they found themselves all alone, together. I
imagined first that they would talk about men. They would
yearn for men together. They would devise plans and systems on
how to catch and confine men, and how also to do it so carefully
that the men would never know they were caught . . . All each
man would know would be that he was in love with a beautiful
girl. That's what I imagined . . .

(Pause.)

I thought they would talk about me . . .

*(Lights fade. Nena jerks away from Citrona and runs out the
door that Michael is hiding behind. The Beatles' "For No One"
plays softly as Michael quietly enters the room. He watches
Citrona fall asleep, then climbs above her cage and sleeps in the
same position above her. Sand pours in through the window.
Lights cross to the hallway.)*

Scene Eight

*Nena in the hallway, her back against the wall. She has spread food
out around her. She sits waiting to catch small rodents.*

NENA: When you want to trap an animal, you feed it first. You watch
it and find out what it likes to eat and then you give it what it likes
. . . for a time. Slowly, the animal gets to know you. You get a little closer every day. You leave a trail of food which leads directly

to you. At first, it doesn't come that close. But as time goes on it comes closer and closer. One day, it's in your lap and you're stroking it and it is eating out of your hand. One day, as you are stroking it, you let your hand close tightly around its neck. You stroke its jugular until its heart slows down, until it's so calm that it falls faint—a deep sleep. Restful, trusting sleep. Then you kill it.

(Speaking to a small animal in a sack that she raises above her head) Do you think I'm beautiful? When you look in my eyes or smell my smell, do you think I have the look and smell of beauty?

(Nena takes the small rodent out of the bag and places it on a silver tray. She enters Citrona's room carrying the stunned animal on the tray. Citrona pretends to be sleeping. She watches Nena watch her in silence.)

CITRONA *(Jumping up)*: Yummy, yummy, yummy! Fresh food for my tummy! That's a beauty!

(She extends her arms, reaching for the animal on the tray) Ooooh, so soft. These kind are always so soft. Don't you think? Don't you think they're soft?

(Nena throws the tray down hard and exits.)

You really should get a hobby or something . . . Stress can kill you.

(Nena returns with a mop, a sponge and a bucket of water. She cleans the blood and organs of Citrona's meal from the floor and walls. The smell of blood and shit and urine make Nena gasp and gag.)

Hey . . . hey. Talk to me. Talk to me. Hey—you know what? You're beautiful. You smell good. You smell like rain. You bring rain with you when you come here. You bring cold, hard rain. I like that. You know what? I like that. You spray me when you come in. You spray me like grass. I'm grass that's not supposed to be alive. Like there's concrete covering me, so people think I'm dead. But I'm not because you get here and then I feel the blood in my arms again. It all starts to move. It moves and it feels like it's gonna come out through my fingertips. The tips get real hard and red. And I think I'm just gonna burst outta them—all of me reaching through myself and exploding. And you know what? It's not like this— *(She points at the pieces of animal on the floor)* I'm white inside. I'm a moon and I want to orbit you. Okay?

You know, orbit? Bit. Let me bite you. You're so beautiful. I could eat you right up. You know what? I get so wet when you come here. Because you're rain, right. Is that why? Is that why I keep hoping? I got too much hair on my arms probably . . . For you to love me.

(Michael enters carrying a brush. He sends Nena away. Citrona turns her back on him but doesn't move away.)

MICHAEL: You're still afraid of me. That's good for now, but soon you'll learn how not to be. Soon, you'll love me. I'm good to all my treasures. I'll be good to you because you are a treasure. You're a beautiful seed—someone should have buried you a long time ago . . . and then there'd be trees of you. Big ones. And branches would drop you, many yous like ripe, yellow fruit.

(He brushes the hair on her back.)

There. I'll touch you. You like to be touched. I can tell. You like me to run my fingers down your spine, around your neck.

(Citrona faints. Michael kisses her hand and exits. Lights cross to the hallway. Nena sits there waiting for Michael.)

NENA: You were in there a long time.

MICHAEL: No, I wasn't.

NENA: Yes, you were. A real long time. If I had a watch I would have broken it by now.

MICHAEL: You need a vacation.

NENA: But if I go, she'll stop eating.

MICHAEL: Just two weeks. In just two weeks no one could starve. I could bring her food.

NENA: If she dies, there's no job for me. She only wants young, beautiful girls to bring her flesh—

MICHAEL: You're not so young . . . but you are beautiful.

NENA: I don't want to go away. If I go away, I'll forget how to come back.

MICHAEL: I understand that.

NENA: Sit down with me.

MICHAEL: Can't. Linen. Wrinkles. *You* know.

NENA: Oh . . . you don't ever sit down?

MICHAEL: I lean.

(He pulls Nena to her feet and kisses her.)

That's enough. Leave your "vacation" address by the terrarium.

NENA: You'll come?

MICHAEL: There's a chance . . .

(He kisses her again.)

NENA: History . . .

(Citrona bangs on the bars of her cage. Nena exits. Lights cross to Citrona's room.)

Scene Nine

Michael enters Citrona's room. He carries a map of the pet shop building.

MICHAEL: I'm going to give you this map. It'll tell you where to find me. This building is big, so you'll need it if you're going to find me. Not that you can really ever find me, but you'll always know where I am by listening to the sound of my footsteps. Follow them on the map and then you'll know exactly where I am. And if you don't stop banging on your cage I'll cut your hands off. Okay?

CITRONA: Oh, I've always hated my hands. I have these great big knuckles—see?

(She shows her hands to him.)

See? The hands of a monster. You should be afraid of these hands.

MICHAEL: That cage is the biggest cage you've ever been in—doesn't that tell you a little something about my intentions? About how I feel?

CITRONA: When do I eat?

MICHAEL: You just ate.

CITRONA: That was yesterday . . . or maybe two days ago. I don't know. I lose track of time. It wasn't today though. I know that. I know how hungry I am . . .

MICHAEL: You're not the only one who gets hungry.

CITRONA: You want to fuck me, don't you? I don't know why. That's a sickness. To love an animal. I'm not clean inside. Inside I'm like rotted link sausages. Parks. Green and brown. Who'd want to poke into that? You must be crazy.

MICHAEL: Love's like that. You pick up your lover's vomit and treat it like a jewel. I'm going to call you . . . Beauty.

CITRONA: My name is Citrona. That's all I answer to. That's all I'll ever answer to.

MICHAEL: I brought you something else . . . *(He takes out ring)* Put out your hand.

(She does so, he puts the ring on her finger.)

When you take off that ring, you'll die. That ring is attached to your heart.

(He exits. Citrona stares at the ring in silence. Then she speaks to the pile of fur pelts she has accumulated by her cage.)

CITRONA: I wanted love and I used to dream about that. I had dreams where my mother would hold me. I had dreams all the time. I don't dream anymore. I don't remember how to sleep. I don't sleep because I'm a monster and monsters are hard to love. Look at Frankenstein's monster. The one thing that loved him—that innocent little girl—he goes and throws her down a well. Well, that's not gonna make life any easier. It's really not. Makes people afraid of us. They always expect us to kill the things we love. And there's some truth to that too. Because when I love someone I know she'll never love me back and so I want to kill her. Like those little girls who'd come to my mother's house and throw peanuts at the window—I loved them all and I wanted them dead. They made fun of my dresses—I liked pink dresses, pink satin. People said I should be on a TV show for gifted animals. I knew the words to every Beatles' song ever written and I could divide big numbers in my head—it was a gift. I was born with a caul—that's a sign of prophecy. People used to steal them to steal the power of the child and the mother. My mother kept mine in a glass case. It looked like a rotting cobweb. But it kept Mother from killing me—that's what she told me anyway. She knew I was here for a purpose—even though I was too ugly to love. That birth sac was my strength. My survival. Mother waited for me to tell her the future. I could only see what would happen after she died. She didn't like that.

She hit me so many times on the head that I lost my gift. I lost my hymen too. Mother thought it best. She pierced me with a letter opener made of wood, then she sold me.

(She touches the ring on her finger) I could never say no to a thing of beauty.

(Lights fade to the window light. The window light fades. Lights up on the doorway and the cage. Michael enters carrying a barbecued chicken on a tray. He hands it to Citrona. She pretends to be interested in it and then tosses it back at him.)

I don't eat barbecue.

MICHAEL: I thought it would be good for a change. A little change is good. It's very good chicken. I made it myself—my own special sauce. It's a sauce with an edge. A big, spicy edge. Don't you even want to try it? It'll wrap itself inside you like a snake.

CITRONA: The only thing I want wrapped inside me is gone. Where'd you send her? Where are you meeting her? I know you go to meet her. You go at night. You see her in a cheap motel and she puts on a wig and dances for you. She bends over and shows you her panties. She shows you her everything. She never bends here—she crawls and kneels. But I like her like that—then she's on my level. But with you, she could never be on your level. You give her things and that makes her love you . . . I can't believe you brought me barbecued chicken! Don't they sell live poultry anymore?

MICHAEL: Not around here. You can pick it out live, but then they kill it. They insist.

CITRONA: I hate when the world changes.

MICHAEL: It changes all the time.

CITRONA: I hate the world. When is she coming back?

MICHAEL: I don't know.

CITRONA: I liked the way she cleaned my room. I liked her on all fours. Her neck arches like rubber when she wipes my floor. I like the way she moves the air around her. Is she coming back?

MICHAEL: I don't know.

CITRONA: How does it feel to touch her? To press your body up against her? What does she taste like? Is it like paradise?

MICHAEL *(Picking up the scattered chicken)*: Paradise tastes like barbecued chicken. You should have eaten it.

(He begins to exit.)

CITRONA: I didn't memorize her face yet—I thought I had time.

MICHAEL *(Turning back)*: You always think that. And the next thing you know . . . somebody's dead.

(He closes the door and locks them both in.)

I worked in this pet shop. My first job. The guy who owned it— his name was Joe. I felt tender about his lips. I watched him talk. He especially talked to the rabbits. I don't know why. He liked rabbits, I guess. He liked the straw they lived in. He used to stick pieces of it up his nose. I laughed when he did that. Then he stuck the rabbit down his pants once. With some straw. I thought that was funny too. But it bit him. And he got some weird infection. And then he died. That's what I heard. That he died from this weird thing. But really what he died from was from being too close to a rabbit. People aren't supposed to be that close to rabbits. You see, working with Joey taught me a lot. About animals. We had a spider monkey once . . . she climbed all over me and gave me lots of kisses . . . and then she died too. She had that same weird disease. All the other animals started to drop, like dominoes, in a spiral. I got out of its way. I made it stop. I didn't want that disease on me . . . so I bought a wife. Will you marry me?

(Pause. Citrona stares at him in silence then begins to laugh.)

CITRONA: You bought a nothing.

MICHAEL: You could be my legacy, if only you would touch my face . . .

CITRONA: It's her face . . . I'll die soon . . . and in my dreams—she'll die first.

(He touches her head. We hear the Beatles' "Wait." Lights cross to the hallway.)

Scene Ten

Citrona's dream (to be performed in either English or Spanish, the author prefers Spanish).

Citrona is lying at the bottom of her cage, looking dead. Dream Nena is taking her pulse. Dream Michael enters.

DREAM MICHAEL: ¿Qué pasa?

(What's wrong?)

(No response.)

¿QUÉ SUCEDE?
(WHAT'S WRONG?)

(No response.)

¡Dime! ¿Que has hecho? La has envenenado. ¡Maldita! La has matado!
(Tell me! What did you do? You poisoned her. You bitch! You killed her!)

(He grabs Dream Nena and throws her against the wall.)

Yo la amaba . . .
(I loved her . . .)

DREAM NENA: Yo la amé más. Ella me amó más. Más que tú jamás hubieses podido.
(I loved her more. She loved me more. More than you ever could.)

(She takes out a gun and shoots him.)

¡Al fin Citrona querida! Está extinto.
(There. Citrona, honey. He's dead.)

CITRONA *(Getting up and shaking off the blood)*: No puedo creer que lo hiciste. Y por mí.
(I can't believe you did it. And for me.)

DREAM NENA: Claro, querida. ¡¿Qué más podría haber hecho?! Te Amó! *(Sure, honey. What else could I do? I love you!)*

(They embrace through the bars of the cage. Dream Nena slowly pulls away from Citrona into darkness.)

CITRONA: Dag . . . nice while it lasted, huh?! Is this what happens when you're going crazy?

(Dream Michael, isolated in a pool of light, speaks to Citrona. He stands over a smoldering pile of pink rags that was once Dream Nena.)

DREAM MICHAEL: La mate. Ahora podremos estar juntos para siempre. Ella no te merecia. Yo sabia que me amabas. Lo vi en tus ojos . . . no tuviste que decir ni una palabra . . .
(I killed her. Now we can be together forever. She didn't deserve you. I know you wanted me. It was in your eyes . . . you didn't have to say a word . . .)

CITRONA: I have nightmares too . . .

Scene Eleven

Nena enters the hallway. She looks disheveled. She's coated with sand. She's been crying. She's panting, out of breath.

Michael crosses from the room into the hallway and sees her, checks his watch.

MICHAEL: So . . . good weather?

NENA: Yes, for a while. For a while it was beautiful and then we had a sandstorm. I still have bits of sand in my eyes. They don't stop tearing. They're always red now . . .

MICHAEL: They're not too bad. If you rinsed them in clean water, they'd get better fast. Why don't you go rinse them?

NENA *(Holding up a sack)*: I brought dinner.

MICHAEL: Good.

NENA: She'll never love you . . .

MICHAEL: I'm patient, Nena. I've held a gun.

NENA: I know. I've seen you do it.

(Lights cross to the room and the cage. Citrona lies flat in her cage. She's facedown, her arm extended from the cage.)

CITRONA: Somebody's dead . . . that's me . . . Can't cry anymore. My tears are stones that pierce my skin. I'm tired of bleeding.

(Nena enters carrying the animal sack.)

Oh . . . I thought—where'd you go?

NENA *(Handing her an animal from the sack)*: Vacation.

CITRONA: Where to?

NENA: The beach. I like to burn.

CITRONA *(Moving into Nena's shadow)*: I like the shade.

NENA: I brought you a present.

(She takes a pink satin robe from the sack.)

I'm tired of seeing your naked butt.

CITRONA: This covers more than that.

NENA: Put it on.

(She does so.)

Looks . . . comfortable.

CITRONA: Oh, yes. It's delicious. But it'll get soaked in "you-know-what" now that it's dinnertime.

NENA: Take it off then.

(During the following monologue, Nena is mesmerized by Citrona, pulled physically closer and closer until a kiss is almost possible.)

CITRONA: If you were my girl, I'd treat you nice. You wouldn't have to wear lipstick for me. You could go natural. A natural girl. Been a long time since we seen one of those. I mean, besides myself, of course. I can't really wear makeup. It sticks to my beard, and when I cry or sweat it flakes off into my eyes and makes them screaming red . . . but you. I bet you could wear it all the time. I bet it even looks good when it melts off you onto white sheets. That's how I want you, baby. On white sheets, not off-white or gray-white, but white-white. Whiter than the hottest sun. Whiter than Caribbean sand. Whiter than the Holy Spirit—than the heart of Christ. Pure, simple . . . white. I'll stop being messy if you kiss me . . . If you kiss me, I'll eat cooked meat. You could cook it for me . . . you could make us happen, baby. Baby, baby . . .

(She sticks her lips and tongue outside the cage bars. This breaks the spell on Nena.)

Kiss, kiss, baby, kiss me. Let me kiss you.

NENA: You'd have to kill me first. It would kill me to kiss you. I'd throw up on myself, into your mouth. You'd make me so sick. You make me sick. I thought I could stand to come back here as long as you wear that robe sometimes. As long as a part of you wasn't showing. So long as I didn't have to see your nipples harden every time I walked into the room.

CITRONA: But that's the best part. The part where my nipples harden and you bend over in front of me, to clean my floor, to feed me warm animals, full of red life. I squeezed myself red for you while you were gone.

(She sings the second verse of the Beatles' "Girl" to Nena:)

When I think of all the times she *(Replacing "I" with "she")*
tried so hard to leave me *(Replacing "her" with "me")*
She will turn to me and start to cry.
And she promises the earth to me and I believe her.

After all this time I don't know why.

Ah, girl, girl, girl . . .

NENA: You can't love me.

CITRONA: Nena, will you marry me?

(Citrona reaches out her hand and Nena slaps it and runs out.)

Watch . . . I'll put it out again . . . It was good to feel your white skin beating against mine. Your skin is like Jersey corn—milk and honey. So sweet you can eat it raw. You take a kernel and put it between your teeth and chew it down to nothing but liquid that travels down your throat like an express train through the Swiss Alps. A long, fast ride into darkness.

(The recording of the Beatles' "Girl" comes up as the lights fade.)

Scene Twelve

Lights up on the hallway. Michael and Nena sit with their backs against the wall. They smoke cigarettes.

MICHAEL: You know what I hate? Those black cigarettes. So stuck-up.

NENA: And they taste like shit.

MICHAEL: You tasted them?

NENA: Yeah . . . Like shit.

MICHAEL: I could never actually smoke them.

(Lights up on the cage. Citrona speaks to the door, like she's engaging Michael and Nena in conversation.)

CITRONA *(Holding up a piece of her hair)*: Look! Come over here. I want you to look at something. See this?! I can't believe it!

MICHAEL: That kind of tobacco gives me a headache. But this stuff, I love . . .

CITRONA: A gray hair! I must have hundreds of them—in places I can't even see. Pull them out for me! Take them out. Take a pair of scissors and cut them and—

NENA: Me, too. Imported ones always taste better. Did you notice that? The farther they have to travel, the higher the quality.

CITRONA: And then take a match to the follicle and burn the fucking thing right out of my scalp! Quick, quick! They're taking over. Gray kinky hair. Shit. That's all I need . . . Shit . . .

MICHAEL: Well, I guess I'd agree with you. But that's true about everything—not just cigarettes. The more different it is—the more beautiful it can be. The potential for beauty increases proportionate to the oddity of the substance.

(Michael takes a Bazooka bubble gum out of his pocket.)

This for instance, is an unnatural product, based on a natural thing. It's color isn't found in nature—but gum is—the sap of certain trees becomes gum. It was chewed throughout history. Even while chasing bison, I think.

NENA: I love bison. I love things with heads as big as my body. It's something to count on.

CITRONA: Black and wavy was bad enough, but this I won't stand for. I will not let myself live long enough. I refuse to live long enough. I'll kill myself before I'm forty if this goes on.

I don't want to kill myself—I want to dance . . .

MICHAEL: Bison are the biggest-headed animals, I think. I wish I could buy one. They're protected, you know . . . Like the new saber-toothed tiger.

NENA: New?

MICHAEL: Yes, of course. Don't you read? That tiger has evolved four times. And each time, one part of it is different.

NENA: Wow! I guess some things just keep coming back.

CITRONA: Tell me about it.

MICHAEL: This time, it's bald.

CITRONA: I'd rather be bald than go gray. I've often prayed for baldness. Baldness would be bliss.

I wouldn't have been tied up in the gym for the boys to throw balls at, if I'd been bald. Boys like that hairlessness, especially as a girl gets older. No-hair-shows-all. Shaved pussy is always a turn-on.

NENA: I love protected things. They're always so beautiful.

MICHAEL: It has to do with their habitats. Their habitats are always so small. The smaller the habitat, the rarer the species. Those snakes that Marlon Perkins always had around his neck, those poor animals had the smallest habitats of all—the back of Marlon's van!

NENA: You're kidding!? That dirty old man!

MICHAEL: Yes . . . and then he almost always killed them after.

NENA: Wow . . . what a monster . . . Is that true?

MICHAEL: It's what I heard. How much of what you hear is ever true? People come to this pet shop to buy their pets. Especially at Christmas and Easter. People get pets then because they think it will help them be reborn. They think they'll get holier by buying an animal—that they'll be more like God, by feeding and stroking a little hunk of fur and flesh. And if they need to . . . a lot of stress can be relieved with a pet. Or through a pet. Or on a pet. They can relieve certain types of pain. But is that true for every type of pet? Or only the ones with fur? Like I said, how much of anything is ever really true?

(He exits handing Nena a piece of bubble gum. Both Nena and Citrona put a piece of gum in their mouths and begin to chew.)

CITRONA: I want to go to a dance. I wanna go to a dance and dance until midnight with the girl of my dreams . . .

NENA AND CITRONA: I have this fantasy sometimes. About my love . . . My love and I buy a trailer and watch sunsets all over these Americas.

NENA: We would buy as opposed to rent because we would decide to open our hearts and commit.

NENA AND CITRONA: He'd-she'd look exactly like me—

CITRONA: Except without the hair. None—smooth, hairless, except on her private part. That would be covered by a thick mat of soft down, like a feather pillow to rest on a while . . .

NENA AND CITRONA: And he-she has no ambitions—except to be with me . . . and watch the sunset.

NENA: He has very red lips.

CITRONA: And a very pink tongue . . . Of course, this is all a dream. There are computers out now that are better-looking than me. Probably kiss better too. Everyone betrays me—

NENA: I'd lay him on white linen sheets . . . His soul is white too.

(Nena plays with her breasts as Citrona continues to speak.)

CITRONA: When you're like me, no one thinks they can betray you because no one takes you seriously, because no one thinks you're human. I had a half-sister, Minda. She was very beautiful . . . Her beauty was dark though. Full of secrets. I found a birth certificate once . . . and a picture. It was all I could do to keep from crying. I hated knowing for sure that she was only a half-sister. I liked having a sister who looked like her. I told myself I could look like her, if I just shaved. I tried it once, but my hair was so thick, I had to peel away the skin to remove it. It hurt a lot and it made me look even worse because my purple-red flesh was exposed like a dead flower after a heavy rain.

NENA: I have no family. Michael is raising me now—but not like family. I have to do things for him. I turn his pages when he reads a book and I wind his watch. And in return, he taught me a skill—gave me a purpose. I have memories with him now . . . He was the one who taught me how to love the animals I trap . . . I build all my own cages. I know how much space every species needs. And how much water. It rains here sometimes. Sometimes there's so much rain, nobody goes out. And burrowing animals die because their holes get plugged up. You see them floating the next morning in the rancid water—blood on their teeth and in their pupils. I have a theory: I think they try to bite their own brains out. That's why their eyes fill with blood. Better to kill yourself than let nature drown you. Better to make a choice.

CITRONA (To Nena through the door): You could be my sister . . . She could've grown up to look just like you. You're beautiful.

You have long, thick fingers, like a man . . . What do you get up to with those fingers? I want to sit on those fingers and rotate. I bet you feel like me inside . . . I bet we're twins.

(Lights fade on Citrona. Michael enters with a bowl of water. He places it by the doorway, and kneels beside it, ignoring Nena, who tries to get his attention. She begins to masturbate as she speaks.)

NENA: I keep all my hot books in my closet in a plastic bag from Passport Foods. It used to be called Fancifoods, but it changed its name. I guess because it sounds more foreign with the passport in it. Anyway, I use these books to masturbate. I like the bondage ones—not that I want anybody doing that stuff to me, you understand, but I feel sort of like it's interesting to look at people looking for pain. Their nipples are always erect and their mounds do seem to glisten . . . And I wonder about my life, about my pain, and my come. And—are you listening to me? I could sit here with baby chicks coming out of my nose and you still wouldn't listen, would you? They could come flying right out of my nose and shit on my arm and still you wouldn't notice. You wouldn't notice because you don't love me . . . You're not my family.

(Nena exits.

Lights cross to a dimly lit cage. Michael enters, leaving the bowl of water within Citrona's reach. He quietly climbs the cage and rests above it. She plays with the water, sprinkling it on the floor. It makes her hands blood red.)

CITRONA *(Quietly)*: You shouldn't always listen to the sound of another's voice. Sometimes you should just store it, save it on the celluloid of your mind so you can play it back when you're most alone. That's when you appreciate that voice. You can't appreciate it when you fear it. When it bores a hole through your brain. When you look into that voice and see yourself there. You hear yourself falling. You hear yourself not being able to stop falling . . . Falling so fast.

(She begins to cry.)

MICHAEL: Don't do that . . . What do you want?
CITRONA: A love that smells of fire . . . and bubble gum.
MICHAEL: I'll find more gum for you. You know I'll always provide.
CITRONA: I know . . . and I also know it won't ever be enough.

(Nena is about to enter the room. Lights cross to tight spots on each one of them.)

Scene Thirteen

Nena is in the hallway. Michael and Citrona are in the basement. They each talk to themselves.

NENA: I begin to understand my own poison. I poison myself with love . . .
MICHAEL: Rat poison . . . Vitamin K—the "K" stands for kill. Anticoagulant. Bloodletting. Let the blood flow without stopping. It's a feeling that's a lot like love. I don't let myself love rodents.
CITRONA: I wish I knew how to let his love wash over me. The many mes I want to be . . . but the me I am won't let me. If her kisses were mine, I could be beautiful. I could feel inside, the way she looks—outside. I'd stop being a monster. I could sail on her love.
MICHAEL: I don't believe in poisons. Not the best way. There are other ways . . . I try to understand—but I don't. She's beautiful because she has nothing to hide. I hide all the time. I listen for the

heat. I have sand in my shoes that won't ever go away. Sand under my toenails, inside my ears. Hard, crusty bits of sand. Sand blows into my house. My footsteps are dry . . . Poisons can flow out through your eyes—but I keep mine inside. Inside my eyes don't stop crying. If I keep my poisons inside, then I don't need love to replace it. That's the only thing that takes away the poisons.

NENA: If he loves her . . . and she loves me . . . Then I know how to hurt him. I could let her love me. She understands love. She loves me like I want to be loved. From her heart to her tongue. I wonder if there's a difference between the tongues of men and women. I imagine his longer, of course, and deeper—an oddly welcome-invader, a tonsil-tickling tongue. Hers shallow, wide, flat like an island. Safe. Protected. Surrounded by water . . . I can never accept the love given me. I always want what I can't have. If it's good for me, I'm bored. You have to work at not being bored in this life . . . You have to find the time not to be. I need to find the time for love. He'll be so jealous . . . I think it's time.

(Nena enters Citrona's room as Michael exits. He pulls the door closed behind him and listens to Nena and Citrona through the door.)

Scene Fourteen

Nena and Citrona in Citrona's room. Dusk.

CITRONA: Chow time? So soon? I'm not complaining. You can come see me—
NENA: I want to ask you something.
CITRONA: Anything, baby. Ask a—
NENA: Do you really love me?
CITRONA: Oh, yes. Really. Truly. Forever. Why do you ask?
NENA: Just . . . asking.
CITRONA: Oh.

(They stare at each other a moment, in silence.)

NENA: If I fell down a hole, would you pull me out?
CITRONA: Yes.
NENA: If I was hungry, would you share your food?
CITRONA: You could have it all.

NENA: If my eyes went blind, would you see my thoughts?
CITRONA: I see them now.

(Citrona closes her eyes and play-swoons.)

NENA: I'd—I'd like to visit you . . . I mean, inside—there.
CITRONA: Why? Don't come in pity, dear heart. I've got enough of my own.
NENA: Not pity.
CITRONA: Not pity?
NENA: No.
CITRONA: When?
NENA: To . . . morrow—um, maybe. Maybe tomorrow. I might be . . . I could . . . come tomorrow.
CITRONA: Okeydokey.
NENA: At sunset.
CITRONA: How . . . romantic.

(Nena exits.)

What will I wear?

(Pause.)

Oh . . . no . . . only Michael can let her in. I'll just have to ask him. I'll beg him. Anything to touch her without metal between us . . . Michael! *(She pounds on the bars)* MICHAEL!

(Michael enters.)

You have to let me love her, for one day, let me have her.
MICHAEL: If I do this, you must promise. If this happens you'll love me or I'll die of a broken heart. I'll die and I'll take you with me. You wear my ring.
CITRONA: I haven't forgotten. My finger bleeds from that place.
MICHAEL: That's so you know you're alive.
CITRONA: I'd know that anyway. I know all about pain . . . It's a deal, then?
MICHAEL: Sure . . . one night—and then you're mine.
CITRONA: Sure . . . one night.

(They sing the Beatles' "Here, There and Everywhere" as the lights fade.)

To lead a better life, I need my love to be here.

MICHAEL AND CITRONA:
> Here, making each day of the year.
> Changing my life with the wave of her hands;
> Nobody can deny that there's something there . . .

MICHAEL *(In the darkness)*: Marry me . . .

Scene Fifteen

Lights first on the window, then on No-Space where Nena stands, wearing a beautiful pink dress. Citrona waits for her in the cage below.

NENA: I saw this movie once, about this girl, who was dying. She coughed a lot and looked so pretty—dying against her pink pillows . . . I mean, it was a black-and-white movie but I knew they were pink, because when I looked at her I thought about love . . .

(Pause.)

He'll see me now. *(Pause)* Although, when light travels it changes the colors it touches. The colors become a reflection of the light that is being beamed out like lasers at your eyes. I was born with brown eyes. But in the light my eyes could be violet. My pupils change with the light—everybody's does. But mine are especially violet. My name should be Violet when I'm in the light. But I never wear purple because it's such a dark color . . .

(Michael enters quietly behind her.)

And I don't appreciate darkness—not the way other people do. And Violet really is a black woman's name, a black woman especially from the Southern United States. So that's not even rational—as a name. Not at all. He would never love a girl named Violet . . .

(Michael picks Nena up and carries her off toward the cage. Lights fade. The sound of bubble gum popping.)

Scene Sixteen

Citrona readies her cage for Nena's visit. She piles all her animal pelts in one corner, very neatly and methodically. A basin of water and a sponge is at the foot of the cage.

CITRONA: I'm gonna weave a spell around her. I'll make a bed of fur for her. To lie on and dream . . . of me. *(She picks up two pelts with the heads still on and puts them on her own side of the cage)* Then she'll have to love me . . .

(Pause.)

It's times like these I wish I knew some Marvin Gaye songs.
   (Collecting the leftover bones) I could make her something. A chair, maybe. Ladies like to sit. *(She piles them up neatly)* There. Looks comfy. I think. A chair, a bed . . .

(She dips the sponge into the water and washes herself.)

I never thought I'd really want someone to smell my real smell. I thought if I covered it up, built a cloud of other animals' smells over me, then I could save the real me—the real smell of me— for someone I thought could love me . . . And could stand that smell—maybe even want it on her. Maybe even long for it . . .

Scene Seventeen

Lights up on Nena straining not to be put into the cage. Michael is holding her tightly. Citrona watches.

NENA *(To herself)*: I thought I could, but—I feel like I'm going to explode now. My teeth and gums and nose and eyes will fly all over the room. My smaller parts will slip through the bars and scar the walls. There won't be anyone to scrub me out with "Bon Ami." You'll have to tear down the walls to get me out. Or else you'll have to lick me off, because spit melts everything. Especially flesh. You'll help me disappear into the air, and then the air will be full of me. And my arms will attach to her chest. I'll make a new kind of monster out of her. My mouth will grow out of her stomach . . . it'll rest on her pelvic bone, and when I lick my lips—I'll lick hers too. Let's see how she likes that. *(Pause)* Oh . . . no . . . I bet she'll like that . . .

(Nena tries to rock in Michael's arms, but she can't.)

I'm locked in this space. I can feel the floor on the bones of my feet. She thinks she can love me, but she's wrong. My life is just beginning—I'm doing this for you. *(Kissing Michael)* I still love you.

(Lights out as the cage door opens.)

Scene Eighteen

Lights up on Nena and Citrona in the cage. Michael watches them from the window. Sand swirls around him. Citrona wears the pink robe.

CITRONA: Well . . . well, well, well. Welcome aboard. I mean, to my house.

NENA: Did Michael clean up?

CITRONA: I did it. Myself.

(Silence.)

I made you a place. Right here. On top of all these warm furs. Sit down. Please.

(Nena sits on the bone chair instead of the pelts.)

NENA *(To herself)*: It's not so bad in here. I thought her smell—so close on my skin—would kill me—but it didn't.

CITRONA: Are you hungry? I told Michael to bring us something nice, something—cooked.

NENA: What are you going to do to me?

CITRONA *(Avoiding the question)*: I wrote you a poem.

NENA: A what?

CITRONA: A poem.

(Pause.)

NENA: Oh . . .

CITRONA: Would you like to hear it?

NENA: I guess so . . . What's a poem?

CITRONA: Oh . . . It's a . . . well, it's a family of words you put together that says what's in your heart.

NENA: Oh.

CITRONA:
Before I met you, I dreamt of your face.
It was the face of love in an hourglass, pouring over me.
Sand filling me up, drawing out my darkness.
If I could rest my head between your legs—I could sleep.

(Silence. Michael disappears from view.)

Anyway . . . that's a poem.

NENA: Wow, well, I never knew words could be put together like that. It's beautiful, I think . . . Something new, every day . . .

CITRONA: Yep. Something new.

(Michael enters with some chicken on a tray, a lit candelabra, a bottle of wine and two glasses.)

MICHAEL: I thought a little romance was in order. A little mood modification.

(He puts down the tray. Pause. Pretending not to care:)

Okay. Don't ask me to stay. Please. I wouldn't let you even—

NENA: Michael, I—

MICHAEL: Don't. You say things I can't even hear.

(He exits, closing the door behind. Lights come up on him having a romantic dinner for one on the other side of the door, as the scene between Nena and Citrona continues.)

CITRONA: He's watching us. He listens. I know he does.

NENA: Really?

CITRONA: He watches everything I do.

NENA: Really?!

CITRONA: Yeah. Don't turn red for him, Nena. Not when you're with me.

NENA: At least, I'm here.

CITRONA: At least.

(Nena pulls the food through the bars. She fills up a plate for herself and then hands it to Citrona.)

I'm not very hungry.

NENA: No? It's delicious.

CITRONA: I'll pass.

NENA: You have to eat something.

CITRONA: Yes . . . I know . . . So did you like your poem?

NENA: Yes. Nobody ever wrote me one of those before.

CITRONA: You're happy then?

NENA: I'm not afraid anyway. I thought I'd be afraid, but I'm not.

CITRONA: Brush my hair?

NENA: Which hair?

CITRONA: On my back. Nothing kinky. Just a kind, gentle brushing . . .

NENA: Okay.

(Citrona hands her a brush. Their fingers touch, Nena exclaims:)

Ohh!

CITRONA: Electricity. Hard to keep it away with all this hair. I walk through clouds of static.

NENA: I never seen clouds.

CITRONA: Me neither. But I can imagine them. Like I can imagine a house. A little house for two. With a swing on the porch. And special wind chimes hanging from the ceiling to announce the arrival of all changes. All weather is recorded in those chimes. All life.

NENA: What are wind chimes?

CITRONA: Don't you read?

NENA: No. I was born in the desert. Our books would burn when we opened them. When we held them open too long, the pages would flame up. If we loved a book, we couldn't open it. If we read it, it would be destroyed. So I had many books. But I didn't read them. Except for the sex books. For some reason, they never burned.

CITRONA: Maybe it was the paper.

NENA: Maybe.

CITRONA: Kiss me.

NENA: Not—yet . . .

CITRONA: What's your favorite color?

NENA: Purple.

CITRONA: Oh . . . Purple and pink go good together.

NENA: Yes, I mean, I never thought about them together.

CITRONA: Yep. I'm good at that. Putting things together.

NENA: Yes.

CITRONA *(Patting the fur pile)*: Sit over here. On your bed.

NENA: Where are you going to sleep?

CITRONA: Over there.

NENA: Oh . . .

(They eat in silence as lights come up on Michael on the other side of the door.)

MICHAEL: I didn't think dinner could be so complicated. One night. One day. What does it matter? It's just animal instincts. Basic human needs.

(Pause.)

But I feel those poisons again, behind my eyes. I feel the blood pumping out of me. The poisons might escape now. I feel my eyes full and wet. I wish someone had taught me how to cry. I think it wouldn't hurt so much then. It wouldn't burn on the inside like this. Inside my skin and my bones. Inside my heart.

(Pause.)

They still don't ever talk about me . . . I'm nothing to her. I don't want the girl. I want the woman. The woman hidden behind long black hair. I think of it as hair. Others might say fur. But to me she's like Lady Godiva. A beauty covering her naked flesh in black tresses.

(Pause.)

Why does she love that—that pink thing? It makes no sense to me. She needs a darker color to love . . .

(Lights cross back to the women.)

CITRONA: Good?

NENA: Yes, I was hungry.

CITRONA: Me too. I mean, I wasn't. I mean, I can wait. Don't have to eat. Not at all.
    (Citrona's stomach growls. She clutches it in embarrassment) Oh, excuse me . . .

NENA: What do you usually do after dinner?

CITRONA: Talk to myself. Tell myself stories . . .

NENA: Oh . . .

CITRONA: Your eyes are very beautiful. You have a beautiful face.

NENA: Thank you.

CITRONA: I'm being good, aren't I?

NENA: Very.

CITRONA: Wanna sleep now?

NENA: I don't sleep very well.

CITRONA: Oh, I gotta cure for that. Go ahead and lie down.

(Nena lies down tentatively but defensively on the furs. Citrona pulls out two animal skins with the heads still attached and performs a puppet show, alternating voices to suit the characters. As she does this, a light comes up on Michael in the hallway, performing his own puppet show in silence.)

This is the story of Moo and Chew. This is Moo:

(A girlish voice) "Hello. I'm Moo."

(Back to regular voice) And this is Chew:

(In a low, spooky voice) "Yum, yum, yum. I'm Chew."

(Regular voice) Moo and Chew were enemies for many centuries. Moo wanted to wear nice clothes, eat at fancy restaurants and receive deliveries of flowers daily. Chew wanted to run naked, tear up her meat with her hands and dream about the death of her enemies. Moo avoided Chew like the plague:

"I hate that Chew. She's a pig-dog from Hell. She doesn't understand fashion or personal grooming."

And Chew followed Moo like a shadow:

"I say I hate her, but I really love that Moo. She could teach me things about the world. She could teach me how to feel beautiful. If I follow, maybe I'll become just like her."

Well, this following stuff really bothered Moo:

"Why don't you go home, you dumb freak midget?"

Chew said nothing. She just kept following Moo around, until one day, Moo came to a place that was burning. She knew that if she entered that place she would be consumed by flames. So she waited and waited and waited and waited . . . and waited . . .

(Nena falls asleep. Citrona continues in a whisper) And then she turns to Chew and says: "Marry me. Don't let me burn. I would stop breathing if I didn't have my shadow beside me."

And she took Chew's hand . . . and they walked together into the flames.

And you know what? You know what?

(She lies down opposite Nena, imitating her sleeping posture. She puts out her fingertips and touches Nena's hand.)

The fire went out.

(Citrona closes her eyes. We hear the Beatles' "Here, There and Everywhere" as they both sleep.

Michael enters quietly, climbs the cage and sleeps above them, also in the same posture.

Sand pours in through the window. It goes from night to day.

Michael moves to the hallway which is filling with sand, and closes the door behind him.)

MICHAEL: It's getting hard to walk. *(He kneels by the door)* The sand gets so thick when it's wet. And not just with blood—but with water. It's thicker when the water comes from behind your eyes . . .

(He cries silently as he listens at the door. The fan in No-Space stops spinning.)

Scene Nineteen

Lights up on the cage. Both Nena and Citrona are in the cage. Citrona is naked on top of Nena.

CITRONA: You look like summer in that dress. You remember summer? It's the season after next. Maybe we'll spend it together. Go to the beach. Maybe South . . . I want to turn brown with you and nest inside your browness. A pretty girl like you has been kissed by Apollo . . . Don't be afraid. Meet your destiny. I'll hold your hand. I'll take you there. I'll even lick your ass.

(Nena wakes up.)

I bet *you're* surprised.

NENA: I don't like you. I thought I could like you—but I can't. You rape me. All the time. You rape me with your eyes. With how much you want me. I thought it was love, but it's rape. Today, you smell bad to me. You smell like a slaughterhouse. You got the entrails of many different animals inside your blood and your skin sweats piss.

CITRONA: You got *me* pegged.

NENA: You're a beast . . . A beast will only harm you if you move. If you stay perfectly still, most wild animals will go away—

CITRONA: Unless you've got your period. More menstruating teenage girls have been lost to wild animals than any other single population group.

(She tries to kiss Nena.)

You're moving.

NENA: I can't help it. I don't want your lips on me. I don't want to feel the wetness of your mouth.

CITRONA: What you think will happen will—in bed.

(She kisses Nena who faints.)

That wasn't supposed to happen. Michael! Michael, you didn't tell me this would happen!

(Michael enters holding Citrona's mother's wooden letter opener.)

MICHAEL: Great restraint is called for—in bed.

CITRONA: This isn't working. She has to look at me. She has to let me kiss her sweetly. She has to kiss me back.

MICHAEL: I can't do that. I can't do miracles.

CITRONA: I thought you could. I trusted you.

MICHAEL *(Hands her a lipstick and a brush he takes from his pocket)*: Try these. A little M.U. never hurt anybody.

(Citrona puts on the lipstick and begins to brush her hair.)

Not like that. Let me. *(He gently brushes her hair and puts some lipstick on her cheeks like rouge)* There . . .

CITRONA: She won't ever love me, will she? I thought she could begin to love me . . .

MICHAEL: No. She'll submit. Most people do. But love? No. No love . . . Beauty-Girl.

CITRONA: You do . . . sometimes kill the thing you love the most. Look at Frankenstein's monster.

MICHAEL: He kills the girl by the well. His only friend—besides the old blind peasant who feeds him that soup. That soup didn't look very good either . . . Why did he kill the girl and not the bad cook? I never understood that.

CITRONA: Kill me, Michael.

MICHAEL: You shouldn't be so afraid. Don't you see? Love doesn't have to kill you.

(He tries to hand her the letter opener. She recoils from it.)

CITRONA: That was my mother's.

MICHAEL: Yes. Some things must be opened to be seen, don't you think?

(He holds the opener out to her again.)

You control your own heart.

(Citrona slowly takes the opener realizing that she must kill Nena in order to have her. She uses the letter opener like a stake and pounds it into Nena. Blood gushes from the wound. Nena dies.)

CITRONA: My mother's name was Ada. She was always cooking. She told me I could only cry if I was hungry. Nothing else should make me cry because nothing else was as important as food. She called me a bitch and sold me like a dog. I think she must live in Europe now. All those rude people move to Europe. Especially Switzerland. They all ski.

(She rips into Nena and eats a piece of her.)

MICHAEL: I told you. I told you you could have Nena if you really wanted her.

CITRONA: You told the truth.

MICHAEL: Of course. Angels always tell the truth.

CITRONA: Bring me to Paradise.

(She stands in the cage. Michael pulls the front of the cage open. It drops to the floor with a bang. Citrona steps out.)

I am the beast that was . . .

MICHAEL: I loved you as the beast . . . Marry me?

(He kisses her hand. She lifts his face to hers and moves to kiss him. Blackout.

Michael screams in the darkness. The Beatles' "Birthday" plays loudly.)

END OF PLAY

MIGDALIA CRUZ is the author of many plays, musicals and operas, produced in the U.S. and abroad in venues as diverse as Playwrights Horizons (New York City), Foro Sor Juana Ines de la Cruz (Mexico City), Old Red Lion (London), Latino Chicago Theater Company and Steppenwolf Studio (Chicago) and Houston Grand Opera (Houston). Among her plays are *Miriam's Flowers*, *Another Part of the House*, *The Have-Little*, *Frida: The Story of Frida Kahlo*, *Lolita de Lares* and *Cigarettes & Moby-Dick*. Her awards include: two NEA fellowships, a McKnight fellowship, a 1996 Kennedy Center Fund for New American Plays Award, a runner-up for the 1991 and 1997 Susan Smith Blackburn Prize, two residencies at Sundance Theatre Laboratory (Utah), a Connecticut Commission on the Arts award and a 1994 TCG/Pew National Theatre Artist Residency Program grant at Classic Stage Company (New York City). She was a 1996 member of Steppenwolf's New PlayLab (Chicago), and has been writer-in-residence at Latino Chicago Theater (Chicago) since September of 1996. Ms. Cruz has taught at NYU's Dramatic Writing Program, the University of Iowa's Playwrights' Workshop, Princeton University and Amherst College. An alumna of New Dramatists, she was born and raised in the Bronx.

Her recent projects and productions include, *Salt*, Actors' Studio/Raw Space (New York City), February 1998; University of Iowa, March 1998. *Mariluz's Thanksgiving* (part of the series "Mujer Positiva"/Latinas with Aids project for the Latino Experimental Fantastic Theater) at LaMama (New York City), April 1998. *Danger* (part of the series "Pieces of the Quilt III"), Solo Mio Festival/La Peña (California), October–November 1998. *Vishnu's Song/Featherless Angels*, ACT/Hedgebrook Women Playwrights Festival (Washington), May 1998; University of Connecticut/Storrs, June 1998, March 1999. Her Puerto Rican political history play was recently commissioned by The Joseph Papp Public Theater/New York Shakespeare Festival (New York City).

NIGHT TRAIN
TO BOLINA

Nilo Cruz

THE WRITER SPEAKS
Nilo Cruz

My plays are character oriented, and characters are people, and all the activities of men and women operate in the political realm. I believe the theatrical spectacle aims to inform, provoke, propose action and change. I'm in favor of Brecht's views on the use of character as an object of social forces—as a social being provoking thought.

The characters in my plays usually, if not always interrogate displacement, religion, postcolonial promises, sexuality, existential void and corruption of power. The political and social protest voiced in my texts is not always spelled out in dialogue, sometimes it streams out from under the surface of the writing and a presence, a tragic undercurrent at times swelling and rising above the plot and dramatic line.

Some critics view my plays in the vein of Magic Realism. But I prefer to exclude my work from the school of Magic Realism, because I always like to start from a raw, tangible reality and then have the characters of my plays transform their reality into something magical. I believe in the power of creativity and imagination, not in an existing magical reality. The children in my play *Night Train to Bolina* use the power of their imagination to transcend the poverties of their existence. I believe the function of art is to serve as a catalyst, as a means of transforming our lives, our society.

Beyond social responsibility, art more than anything aims for the soul, because it is there where it fully sheds its light, on the threshold of the spiritual, where we at times come close to finding out the meaning of our existence. But it is hard to make a statement of this sort in our modern times, in a world that views the spiritual as insignificant. Nevertheless, it is through the world of art, where we can feel profound contempt, the presence of the spiritual, the uncanny beauty which abounds in the paintings of the masters.

In my plays language functions in the same way that color operates in painting—creating contrast, hues and dimensions, but overall as a sense of composition and harmony. I firmly believe that in theatre language must be poetic, rhythmic and sensorial. I use lyrical language to dictate action. My plays are also very visual. A playwright doesn't just write dialogue—images must also be written.

I believe that a writer has to step into the threshold of the soul and the heart to reveal the darkest dimensions of the spirit and confess the deepest sentiments, to describe the passions and ideas of hers/his characters, to open the door of absolute truth. To me art yearns for the ideal, and my work aspires to arrest the beautiful—and as an artist I humbly submit to that ultimate yearning.

Production History

Night Train to Bolina received its world premiere at San Francisco's Magic Theatre on December 18, 1994 (Larry Eilenberg, Artistic Director). Mary Coleman was the director, sets were designed by Jeff Rowlings, José Lopez was lighting designer, Derek Sullivan was costume designer and J. A. Deane was sound designer. The cast was as follows:

CLARA	Greta Sánchez Ramírez
MATEO	Sean San José Blackman
TALITA	Minerva García
SISTER NORA	Tessa Koning-Martínez
DOCTOR MARTIN	Luís Saguar

Characters

CLARA, a young girl of eleven.

MATEO, a young boy of ten.

TALITA, a young girl of fourteen.

SISTER NORA, a woman in her late thirties, early forties.

DOCTOR MARTIN, a man in his late forties.

The roles of Clara and Mateo are to be played by actors from ages fifteen to twenty-four.

The roles of the Passengers on the train are to be played by the actors who perform the roles of Talita, Doctor Martin, Sister Nora and the stage manager.

Time and Place

Latin America. The present.

Set

There is a large scrim at the back of the stage in which colors are projected, representing the mood of the scenes. The scrim is also used to project slides, old photographs for the cemetery scenes. To the left of the stage there is a stack of old wooden chairs, a basket of linen and a few hand-loomed rugs. In the second act squares of light and objects define the given locales.

ACT 1

Scene One
Caring for His Bruises

Sound of wind.

In a field. Mateo sits on the ground. He is mending his paper kite. Clara runs to him. She holds a small paper bag.

CLARA: I brought you alcohol for your bruises.
> You got new bruises?

MATEO: Yes.

CLARA: I thought you would. Let me see.

MATEO: Not now, I'm fixing this. Later.

CLARA: They hurt?

MATEO: Yes.

CLARA: They hurt less when you don't pay them any mind.
> They hurt less if you don't scratch them.
> Did they form into scabs?

MATEO: Yeah.

CLARA: Ha! You probably have an infection.

MATEO: What do you know?!

CLARA: The scabs! That's the door . . . That's the door to infection. It lives there.

MATEO: You don't know anything about it.

CLARA: I'm leaving.

MATEO: No stay. Help me to finish fixing it. It almost got lost yesterday. It was twirling in whirlwind. It was already going real high up there. My papa says that when kites get lost, they go to Bolina. It's where kites come undone and disappear. Where they fly loose and die. That's where they go to die.

CLARA: Like the cemetery.

MOTHER *(Voice heard offstage)*: Mateo . . . Mateo . . .

MATEO: She's calling me. Every time she calls for me, I freeze. I start to think she's coming after me to hit me. That's all she does—hit me. Yesterday, she threw a bucket of water at me. And all because I brought flowers into the house.

I can never make her happy. At first she smiled, 'cause she hadn't seen flowers since the drought. Then she threw the bucket of water at me . . . Like that . . . Bushhhhhh . . . And all because I told her that I jumped on the train and I went to the cemetery . . . And I got the flowers from there. Then she started crying 'cause that was the last bucket of water we had. So, I went to my hiding place and started crying too.

Mama is so worried about the drought. I told her it's going to rain. You watch and see. All we need is one cloud over the house. Just one cloud, and we can fill all the buckets with water. And we can go on the rooftop and take a shower.

Shshshsh . . . Mama says that if we continue going to the sea to take a bath, we're going to turn into fish.

CLARA: Did I tell you I got a new hiding place?

MATEO: Where?

CLARA: In my grandma's armoire.

MATEO: They'll hit you more if they find you there.

CLARA: Grandma doesn't use it. She always wears the same old dress.

MATEO: I used to hide in my grandma's armoire. But it was always too stinky there, 'cause Grandma don't wash her clothes. She pees in her bloomers every time she laughs.

CLARA: She can't hold it in?

MATEO: No. She sticks socks inside her panties to soak up the pee-pee. She was stealing all my socks until I caught her. But I told her I wouldn't tell Mama because she'll give her a beating too.

CLARA: Your grandma?

MATEO: My mother hits everybody. She'll hit you too, if you lived in my house. *(Lifts his shirt)* See this mark here. That's from the last beating I got. She hit me with my papi's belt. She said I was stealing my father's socks to give it to my dog Pricila. Every time Pricila goes crazy, she bleeds all around the house and breaks things . . . And Mama gives her my father's old socks and underwear . . . But I didn't take his good socks. I told Mama it was Grandma who took his socks . . . She takes everybody's socks.

So you see this one here . . . *(He lifts his shirt)* Not the one on top. The one on top is from telling Papa that it was Grandma who took his socks . . . He hit me and started saying, "You respect your grandma . . . Respect her." *(Pause)* That's what I get for being honest. For telling the truth.

Let me see your bruises. You got any new one's?

CLARA: No. They don't hit me no more. They just make me kneel down in front of the Virgin. They make me repent for what I've done wrong. Sometimes they leave me there for hours, and my knees start to hurt. Ever since that witch came to my house, she gave Mama new ideas. *(Mockingly)* She said, "You have to educate this child." Every time she sees me, she puts me to read.

MATEO: Who's that?

CLARA: My grandma's sister. I heard her tell my grandma, "That's what I do to the girls in school." So my grandma told Mama. I bet you mama will tell your ma.

MATEO: Don't say that.

CLARA: I bet you it's going to be big here, when everybody hears about it. In every house they're going to start doing that . . . And they're not going to let you wear long pants, even when you're thirteen, so you can feel the floor real hard on your knees.

MATEO *(Slaps her)*: That's mean. Don't say that. Don't ever say that again.

CLARA: Why did you hit me?

MATEO: 'Cause you said mean things.

CLARA: How can you hit me? I never hit you. I thought we made a promise never to hit each other. How can you break that promise? I'm not going to talk to you any more. I'm leaving.

MATEO: I'm sorry.

CLARA: "I'm sorry," is not enough.

MATEO: I'm sorry! I'm sorry! I'm sorry! *(Pause)*

Are you still my friend?

CLARA *(There are tears in her eyes)*: I brought you alcohol and everything. I brought you iodine and cotton for your bruises . . . And . . . And . . . Look at what you do to me. You hit me. I could get yelled at for stealing the alcohol. They'll put me on my knees again, if they catch me. *(Pause)*

Grandma thinks this stuff is like gold. She treats it like holy water. She says we have to start thinking that everything we have is the last of its kind, so we can treat it with respect, so we don't waste things. All she knows how to say is, "We have to

ration our food. We have to ration this. We have to ration that."
Ration! Ration! Ration! But what does ration mean?

MATEO: I don't know. It's probably a new word, something that looks like that, like ration. Like a machine . . . Like a . . . Like a radio . . . *(Pause)* Are you still mad at me?

CLARA: No. Lift up your shirt.

MATEO *(Lifts up his shirt)*: I'm hungry.

CLARA: I brought you a piece of bread.

MATEO: How come your family has bread and mine doesn't?

CLARA: 'Cause my family prepared themselves for the drought. Papa filled the house with bread.

(Clara swabs the wounds.)

MATEO: Aaaahhh! That hurts.

CLARA: I'm sorry.

MATEO: Your family wants to see us starve.

CLARA: I don't want to see you starve.

MATEO: I don't mean you. I mean your father, and the rest of the people around here. Ever since my aunt Julia set her house on fire and ran out naked, they think the rest of us are like Aunt Julia.

CLARA: Why did she do that?

MATEO: Her husband left her and moved to the city. Poor Aunt Julia. They keep her in the crazy house now.

CLARA: I'll set my house on fire if you leave.
Promise me you'll never leave.

MATEO: I promise. And if I leave, I'll fly my kite real high, so you'll always know where I am.

CLARA: But don't leave.

MATEO *(Lies back on the ground)*: Lie on top of me. Pretend I'm your bed.

CLARA: No.

MATEO: Just to hold each other.

(Clara positions herself slowly on top of him and Mateo embraces her.
Lights fade to black.)

Scene Two
Feeding an Animal

Clara places a few hand-loomed rugs on the ground and beats them with a stick. Mateo enters.

CLARA: Go away! Go away! And keep away! I'm being punished.
They put me to beat the rugs because of you.
They put me to do this, for stealing the alcohol.
They put me to sweep the floor and dust the furniture.
I can't talk to you. It's because of you, they have me doing this. Go away! They'll make me beat the rugs again. They'll put me on my knees, if they see me talking to you. You bring me nothing but trouble.

(Mateo starts to walk away. He runs back to the rugs and stomps on them.)

Stop it . . . Stop it . . . Stop it . . .

(Clara struggles with him, trying to pull him away from the rugs. He falls to the ground.)

You stay away . . . I'm punished . . . And what do you want anyway? I haven't seen you in two days.
MATEO: I was hiding. I'm hungry.
CLARA: I can't get you any bread. I'm being punished. See, they have me doing this.
MATEO: Come play with me.
CLARA: I can't.
MATEO: I didn't come to see you 'cause I was hiding.
CLARA: And what did you do this time?
MATEO: Nothing.
CLARA: What did you do?
MATEO: I said nothing.
CLARA: I kept looking for your kite.
MATEO: I buried it.
CLARA: Why?
MATEO: 'Cause I got mad.
CLARA: Well, I'm mad at you.
MATEO: Why?

CLARA: 'Cause . . . 'Cause I'm mad. You disappeared!

MATEO: I'll pee on your rugs, if you don't stop being mad. *(Starts to unfasten his fly)*

CLARA: Mama . . . Mama . . .

MATEO *(Covers her mouth)*: Are you going to stop? I'll leave if you don't want to play.

CLARA: No. Stay. Are you going to get your kite back?

MATEO: I told you I buried it. I took it to the cemetery and buried it.

I don't want Ma to find me. She went around the room with her finger pointed like this . . . She was pointing at everyone in the house. She was asking us, "What are you going to give the pig to eat? What are you going to give the poor animal, huh?" She says he's going to die if we don't give him something. He's got nothing to eat and we need to make him fat. It's all dry out there. We don't even have food for ourselves. But she stood right there, telling us we have to give him something.

Like the time we didn't have food for the goats . . . She went around the room asking the whole family for something to make a stew for those stupid animals. Grandma gave her pillow away . . . Grandpa gave a pair of shoes . . . I gave those goats my favorite toy. My blue car. I closed my eyes and I threw it right in the pot. Mama stirred the stew and I never saw it again. That was it. It was gone. And you know something? . . . I always knew I was going to get it back, 'cause later Mama killed all the goats and we ate them.

Except I don't know if I ate the goat that chewed up my car . . . But sometimes, when I get real hungry, like now, my stomach makes noises, like my car used to make. So I know I ate the right goat . . . And my car is in there, somewhere riding in one of my veins. Like in a tunnel. You want to hear it?

CLARA: You better go to the hospital and have them pull out that car.

MATEO: Uh-uh. If nothing happened to the goats, nothing's going to happen to me. Grandma says she's going to give her fan for the pig's stew. That's all she's got left, since the hurricane took her house and wiped out all her things.

CLARA: But pigs don't eat fans.

MATEO: I know. That's why Mama turned green yelling at Grandma. Mami knows that Grandma can't think straight . . . And . . . And she still yelled and screamed at her. Poor Grandma . . . Just to shut Mama up, she said she would give the pig her yellow canary. But she don't know my sister Flora ate it already. I bet that with all the hunger, Grandma sees visions, and still thinks the canary is inside the cage.

CLARA: What's your grandpa going to give for the stew?

MATEO: He's got nothing to give. Mama said she would throw him out of the house, if he didn't give something. He's got nothing but his tired old body.

Thank God Pricila ran away from home or he would've thrown her in the stew. Then I would've killed Grandpa.

CLARA: Don't say that. You can't kill your grandpa.

MATEO: I didn't mean it. I'm so hungry my mind is leaving me.

CLARA: Shshshsh . . . I'll bring you some bread.

MATEO: Grandpa said he's got nothing to give for the stew. He said he's just going to cut his arm and throw it in the stew.

CLARA: His arm?

MATEO: Uhn-hu. That's what he said. He's got to give something.

And Aunt Ursula, she's got nothing to give so she's going to give her hips away for the stew . . .

CLARA: You're lying. You're imagining things.

MATEO: No, I'm not. No . . . No . . . Aunt Ursula doesn't want them she said. She says that men come to her side all the time because of her hips . . . And she doesn't want no more men. She's tired of them.

My brother Nelson said he was going to give away his left ear. And . . . And Mama crossed her arms, until he said his right one too. That's good, 'cause he don't have to hear Mama scream no more. Then when Mama pointed at me, I started trembling. I said I was going to give my eyelashes, and Mama hit me. Then I said, my eyelashes and my eyebrows, and she hit me again. Then I said my hair, and she started hitting me like a machine gun. And . . . And I didn't know what to say . . . I didn't know what to do. I thought of my finger . . . And Mama kept on saying, "Come on, I'm waiting. Come on."

When I raised my finger 'cause I couldn't talk, my sister pulled out her tongue at me, and called me a copycat. So . . . So, I didn't say anything . . . And I thought of my foot. But how can I walk with just one foot? I thought of my eyes, my nails . . . And I can't give a stupid animal a piece of myself . . . I can't . . .

Then I called Mama to the side 'cause I couldn't decide on anything. And . . . And just before Mama could hit me, Grandpa winked at me and pointed to down there . . . And all of a sudden

I said, my pee-pee. Everybody in the room started laughing at me. So I ran out . . . I ran as fast as I could, so no one could catch me.

Would you kill the pig with me? Would you come with me?

CLARA: We're not strong enough. It takes a big person to kill a pig. Someone who has an ax or a gun.

MATEO: If we don't kill it, they'll turn me into a girl. They'll put me in a dress, and I'll be a girl just like you.

Would you love me if I become a girl?

CLARA: Of course I will. I'll love you even more, 'cause we'll always be together. And you'll let your hair grow. And when it gets long, I'll comb it and braid it.

(The sound of a train is heard in the distance.)

And we'll clean the dishes and wash clothes together. And we'll iron together. And we'll play with my dolls, and dance together.

Come on, let's go wave to the train. *(Clara pulls him by the arm)* Let's go . . . The train is coming . . . Come on . . .

MATEO: I don't want to go.

CLARA: Let's go . . . We'll miss it . . . Let's see who gets there first . . . Let's go.

(They both run to see the train.
Lights fade to black.)

Scene Three
Dressing Like a Girl

Mateo tries on a white dress. He faces upstage. Clara has her eyes covered.

CLARA: One . . . Two . . . Three . . . Four . . . Five . . . What's taking you so long?

MATEO: I'm not finished. Look around you. Is there anybody coming? I don't want anybody to see me.

CLARA: No, I don't see anybody.

(Clara goes to get a mirror.)

MATEO: What was that sound?

CLARA: Nothing. Just me walking. There's no one here.

MATEO: All right, I'm ready. Are you sure there's no one out there?

CLARA: Come out and let me see you.

MATEO: I'm embarrassed.

CLARA: You look beautiful. Turn around. You'll make a beautiful girl. I won't let you look in the mirror yet. First you have to learn how to walk. Like this . . . *(Positions a basket of linen on top of her head)*

MATEO: What's that supposed to be a hat?

CLARA: No. My sister taught me this. It's to keep your balance. *(Demonstrates the walk)* Women have to let their hips move ahead of them, when they walk. Let the hips lead the walk, like if the hips know where they're going. See, they know where they want to go. The hips go, pim, pom, pim, pom, pim, pom . . . The arms go, bim, baum, bim, baum . . . The shoulders go terracata, terracata, terracata . . . Pim, pom, bim, baum, terracata, terra-cata . . . Pim, pom, bim, baum, terracata, terracata . . . Then comes your behind. The behind goes, boom, boom, boom, boom . . . That's the most important part of the walk. You got to move your behind. Look at the cows how they move their tails.

(Clara goes to put the basket on top of his head.)

MATEO: I can't do that.

CLARA: Why not?

MATEO: You don't walk like that.

CLARA: I forget. But that's the way you got to walk.

MATEO: I can't. Let me look in the mirror. Just let me look in the mirror.

(He looks at himself. He throws the mirror against the ground. He takes off the dress and starts to rip it to shreds.)

I'll kill the pig . . . I'll kill him . . . I'll cut its head . . .

(Clara tries to hold him.)

MATEO:	CLARA:
I'll kill him . . .	You can't, he's stronger . . .
I'll cut its head . . .	You can't, he'll bit you . . .
I'll kill him . . .	He's stronger than you . . .

CLARA: Mama . . . Come help me . . . Mama . . .

(Mateo starts to run away. Clara tries to hold him. He gets away. Clara picks up her dress. There are tears in her eyes.)

My dress . . .

(Clara starts to gather the carpets.
Lights fade to black.)

Scene Four
A Prayer

Clara and Mateo are kneeling in squares of light. Mateo's hand is bandaged.

CLARA: Through all my mother's prayers, my father's, my sister's, my grandmother's and my grandfather's prayers, I remain untamed. They say I'm a sheep who's gone astray. Should I stay here awake all night and pray for my sins?

MATEO: I know God. I know. I've been told. They were only evil thoughts. I didn't kill. *(Raises his hand)* And this is what I got for my evil thoughts. That pig bit me because of my evil thoughts. Please forgive me. I promise to be good.

CLARA: I try to hear your voice, but I can't hear your words. Should I burn my knees with the candles of the Virgin? Talk to me. Tell me I'm not bad.

MATEO: I will erase all evil thoughts within me.

Like what Grandma said, "Evil thoughts are like weeds that grow in the garden of the heart and soul. They're like the insects that come in the summertime and eat our fruits."

She says evil thoughts are like the winds of the hurricane that took her house away. I know, Grandma told me. I know.

CLARA: I'll mend my dress. It's torn but I'll mend it. I'll take care of my clothes. Mateo and I were only playing. Please help me to be obedient, so my family won't be ashamed of me. Guide my steps. Send me an angel to guide my footsteps and send one for Mateo . . .

MATEO: Evil thoughts are like dirt. The dirt that sticks to my skin. The dirt in my fingernails. The rocks that break the soles of my shoes.

It's what Mama calls grime, unwashed, unclean . . . What Aunt Ursula calls vile and foul . . . Impure, rotten . . . What my brother Nelson calls garbage, and my sister Flora calls ca-ca . . . I want to call it something too, Lord, so when an evil thought comes to my mind, I can call it by its name and make it go away.

(Mateo gives her a small piece of paper and a pencil.)

Here . . . Start writing. Write down that we want to escape. That we want to escape from here.

CLARA: I don't know how to write "escape."

MATEO: Write something else.

CLARA: What?

MATEO: Write: "Dear God, we want to leave this place."
Write that we want to leave soon.

CLARA: I don't know how to write that word either.

MATEO: Then write that we want to run away.

CLARA: Another word.

MATEO: You don't know how to write.

CLARA: I do. I can write house, light, father, mother.

MATEO: It's not going to work.

CLARA: I can draw a picture. He'll understand. A picture of you and I.

MATEO: He doesn't want to look at a picture. God knows how to read.

CLARA (Draws rapidly): The tombs in the cemetery have pictures of the dead people. They have pictures with their names, so God will know who they are. I can draw a picture. And . . . And . . . I can put our names. Look, like this. And I can draw wings on our backs, like if we want to fly away from here. Fly away from this place.

MATEO: Let me look at it. (Takes the paper from her) This doesn't look like us.

CLARA: Yes, he's skinny like you, and this is me. We go to the cemetery, we get your kite and tie the message to the string, then we let it fly to the clouds. We just have to make sure we send the message on the right day. My mother says that Mondays and Tuesdays are good days to pray because after resting on the weekend, God has a clear mind. That Wednesdays and Thursdays are good days for cleaning your ears, because God speaks from above.

MATEO: What's today?

CLARA: The day for cutting your hair.

MATEO: I don't mean that. Forget it. It's not going to work. (Tears the paper)

CLARA: Let me have it.

(Mateo gives her the torn paper. Clara moves away from him and looks up.)

I know that God will understand. He'll understand what we're trying to tell him.

(Change of light.)

Scene Five
Boxes and the Night Train

Soft Music. In the cemetery. On the scrim a photograph of a cemetery is projected. Mateo flies his kite. The kite is suspended in midair. Clara stands close to him with two large boxes.

MATEO: Look at it fly . . . That's how we're going to be, free . . . Free . . . We're going to be free when we escape. *(Waves to the kite)*
CLARA: Let him go . . . Break the string.
MATEO: No, let him fly higher.
CLARA: Just let him go.

(Mateo cuts the string with his teeth. The kite disappears. They wave to the kite in silence.)

MATEO: Now he can fly and take the message, then he can go to die where he belongs.
CLARA: I want to go to my house.
MATEO: You can't go back, and neither can I. I can't go back. I told you my sister Flora heard me talk in my sleep last night. She heard me talk about our escape. That's why Mama tied my leg to the kitchen table, 'cause Flora told Mama I was talking in my sleep about going to the city. I cut the rope with my teeth. Ha! They thought I couldn't get away. Let's go play with the dead people. This is going to be the last time we play with them, then they'll never see us again. Come on! Let's play pretend. I'll be the man who died in October. You be the woman who died in July. You remember the photograph on her tomb? Let's go look for her.
CLARA: No.
MATEO: You don't like her? You can be another dead woman, if you want. How about the woman who died in 1949? You remember the picture on her tomb? What was her name?
CLARA: Rrrita.
MATEO: Come on . . . You pretend to be Rita. I'll pretend to be the man who died in October. *(Reaches for her hand)* Come on let's go look for their tombs.
CLARA: I'm not going to the city, Mateo.
MATEO: I thought we had it all planned.

Look at me, we jump on the train, I get in this box, you get inside the other box. No one will see us. *(Gets inside the box)*

CLARA: I'm afraid. In the city there are soldiers. They'll take us away.

MATEO: Nothing's going to happen. When the night train comes, we jump on it. I know which wagon to get on. The one with the luggage. We hide in the boxes . . . Come on . . .

In the city we can sell cigarettes. Like my brother, Luis. Five cents each. I know how to do it. We'll make money. And I will buy you a little rug with the money I make. And you can sell fruits and beans on the sidewalk. When I make more money, we can get a table. Like the one's in the market. And we can put all the merchandise on top of the table, like real vendors.

CLARA: And where are we going to live?

MATEO: We could live on the church steps. I've seen people living there.

CLARA: I can't go. I made a promise to be good.

MATEO: If you don't come with me I'll die.

CLARA: Don't say that.

MATEO: All of me will break into little pieces. And I'll be dead. Dead! Watch . . . I'll stop breathing. (Covers his mouth)

CLARA: Don't do that! Stop it! . . .

(Mateo continues to hold his breath. He runs away from her.)

(Clara runs after him) Stop it . . . You're scaring me . . . Stop it Mateo.

MATEO: If you don't come with me, I'll die . . . If you don't come with me, I'll die . . .

(Mateo runs faster.)

CLARA: Stop it! You're going to get sick . . .

(Mateo falls to the ground. He pretends to be dead.)

Mateo . . . Mateo . . . Wake up . . . Don't play dead . . . I know you're not dead.

(Mateo doesn't respond.)

Mateo . . . Oh God! Wake up, Mateo! Mateo . . . Please wake up . . . Wake up!!!! Wake up . . . I'll go with you . . . I promise to go with you . . . Please wake up . . . I promise.

(Mateo opens his eyes.)

You scared me.

MATEO: You promise to go with me?

CLARA: Yes . . . Yes . . . I'll go with you.

MATEO: Tonight.

CLARA: Yes.

MATEO: Good . . . So let's play with the dead people one last time. Come on . . . Let's play . . . I'm the dead man who died in October. My name is Faro. My tomb is right there.

CLARA: I'm the dead woman who died in July.

MATEO: Hello!

CLARA: Hello!

MATEO: What's your name?

CLARA: Rita. My tomb is back there. My tomb has an angel with a horn. He plays music for me.

MATEO: My tomb has a cross and a wreath of laurel leaves. I was a soldier.

CLARA: Soldiers are mean. They kill and steal children.

MATEO: Not me. I was a good soldier.

CLARA: All soldiers are bad. I don't talk to soldiers.

(Runs around looking for another tomb.)

MATEO: All right, then I'll be this man, right here.

CLARA: What's your name?

MATEO: I can't read his name. But they call me Pipiolo like my uncle. What's your name?

CLARA: I'm still Rita. I'm beautiful like her. I was a singer.

MATEO: I was a barber.

CLARA: Would you comb my hair?

MATEO: I lost my comb.

CLARA: Well, find your comb and your scissors. I'm going to sing tonight and I want my hair combed. See that tomb right there, that's my stage.

MATEO: I'll charge you twenty-five cents.

CLARA: I don't have any money. I can give you the flowers on my tomb.

MATEO: I want twenty-five cents.

CLARA: I don't have any money. The soldiers stole my money.

MATEO: The soldiers took my comb. Hide. They'll kill you if they find you.

(Both children run around the stage.)

Ay! Ay! My hand hurts. It hurts a lot.

CLARA: Let me look at it. *(Clara unbinds the bandage)*

MATEO: Ay!

CLARA: Your hand is purple. It's swollen.

MATEO: No, it's not.

CLARA: It's infected.

MATEO: It's not infected.

CLARA: We have to put something on it. Alcohol.

MATEO: No. Leave it like that. There's nothing wrong with it. Leave it like that.

CLARA: Let me wrap it again.

MATEO: In the city you can learn to be a nurse. You could work in a hospital and wear a white uniform.

CLARA: Me?

MATEO: Yes. And you can learn to give injections. And you can be my nurse when I get sick.

(Clara kisses him on the forehead.
Fade to black.)

Scene Six
A Bridge to the City
A Bridge to Each Other

Soft music plays: Satie's Gymnopédies. *Clara and Mateo wear paper hats. They appear on stage with four chairs. They walk on the chairs lifting them up every time they take a step. They place each chair in a line. The chairs face the left of the stage.*

Clara and Mateo establish a game by walking on top of the chairs, as if it was a bridge. They each take turns to walk on top of the chairs.

Clara invents another game. She runs to the basket and gets a sheet. She spreads it on the ground. She gets a dress from the basket and holds it front of her body. She looks at Mateo. She walks holding the dress, as if she was wearing it. She looks at Mateo as she walks around the sheet. There's seduction in all of Clara's movements. She takes the dress and places it on top of the sheet. The dress represents her lying down. Mateo takes notice of her game. He runs to the basket and takes a pair of pants. He looks at her. He follows her game of

*seduction and places the pair of pants by the dress. The pants repre-
sent him lying close to her. Clara walks around the sheet with her eyes
fixed on Mateo. He follows her. Suddenly, she pulls the sheet and
makes a it into a bundle. She runs away with it. Mateo runs after her.*

*The music fades. The steaming sound of a train fills the stage.
The sound of a conductor's whistle is heard. Several passengers
appear on the stage with luggage and sit in the given chairs. A train
whistle is heard. Clara and Mateo appear on the stage hiding inside
the boxes. The two boxes are seen walking slowly across the stage.
The steaming sound of the train fills the stage. There is smoke.*

Lights fade to black.

ACT 2

Scene One
A New Friend at the Mission

At the hospice. There are two beds on the stage. Clara stands stage right. Talita lies in bed to the left of the stage.

TALITA: When the little stick points to seven and the big stick points to twelve, that's the time the bell rings. That's seven o'clock. That's the time we have to wake up. Sister Nora taught us how to tell time. Have you ever seen a cuckoo clock. It goes cuckoo . . . cuckoo . . . And a little bird comes out of the clock. Sister Nora has one in her classroom. Right around this time the bell rings. When the bell rings it's time to go to sleep.

(The bells ring and lights dim.)

CLARA *(Frightened)*: What happened to the lights?

TALITA: It's time to go to sleep. The cuckoo clock must be going cuckoo . . . cuckoo . . . Are you afraid?

Nothing's going to happen to you.

I used to be afraid like you. Natalia, the girl who used to sleep in your bed was afraid, too. She was always afraid the roof would cave in at night and soldiers would come in here.

CLARA: I want to leave this place. I want to get out.

TALITA: You can't. They won't let you.

CLARA: Why not?

TALITA: Because this is where you belong.

Who brought you here? Was it your father?

CLARA: No.

TALITA: Who did?

CLARA: A man from the city. He was cleaning the church steps, and I told him my friend was sick. He took us into a little room inside the church. He gave my friend medicine.

Then he took us to the hospital in a car. But they didn't want us in the hospital, because there were no beds. So he brought us here, me and my friend.

You know where the infirmary is?

TALITA: Yes.

CLARA: That's where they took him. He's sick.

TALITA: Was he dying? Did a soldier shoot him?

CLARA: No. His hand is infected.

TALITA: I clean the floor of the infirmary. I see people die everyday.

When I used to live at the Santa Rosa mission I was sick in the infirmary and I saw a boy die next to my bed.

CLARA: He's not going to die! Don't say he's going to die!

TALITA: Shshhhhhh . . . They'll hear you outside. We're suppose to be sleeping. —See, I hear someone coming. Someone's coming this way, pretend that you're sleeping.

(Sister Nora enters the room. She goes over to Talita's bed and covers her. Then proceeds to Clara's bed and does the same. When Sister Nora exits, both girls open their eyes.)

(Whispering) Run to the door and see if she's gone.

CLARA: You do it.

(Talita runs to the door and sees if the nun has left.)

TALITA: She'll be back later. She's Sister Nora. She's nice. When I can't sleep, because I have bad dreams she tells me bedtime stories. Except she always falls asleep, instead of me. Then she starts snoring.

One time she took us to the zoo and I saw a monkey called Nunu. He was sitting like this *(Sits on Clara's bed and crosses her legs)* like a little man with his legs crossed. He wasn't a boy. He was a woman. Not a woman. A monkey mother. Her little monkey was sleeping and she came to me and looked into my eyes like this. *(Moves her head from side to side)* Then she went like this with her lips. *(Makes monkey sounds. Does monkey movements and spins around)*

CLARA *(Laughs)*: Do it again.

TALITA: Good. I made you laugh.

(Clara becomes serious again. Talita repeats motions.)

The little monkey would put her hand to her nose, like if she was going to sneeze. Like if she had a cold. Like this. *(Places hand on*

*her nose, breathes in and out through her mouth and spins.
Laughs)* She looked like she wanted to be my mother.

(Pause. Faces forward.)

I don't have a mother. I used to have two mothers. I used to. Not
anymore. One lives in America and one disappeared from home.
My papi says she was kidnapped by soldiers. Do you know what
kidnap means?

(Clara shakes her head.)

It means that they steal you. The soldiers that come to our village, they come and do bad things. They put people in bags of
rice and take them away. Then they throw them into a pit.
 Were you at the Santa Rosa Mission?

(Clara shakes her head.)

That's where my father took me, so my American mother can
come for me. I'm going to be her daughter.
 If I show you a secret, promise not to tell anybody.

(Clara nods.)

Stand there and close your eyes. I don't want anybody to know
where I hide my secret. Come on, close your eyes and stand
there. Go on over there.

*(Clara closes her eyes and walks away from Talita. Talita pulls
out a bundle from under her bed cushion.)*

Open your eyes. And don't tell anybody I showed these to you.

(Talita takes out a pair of shoes from inside a pillowcase.)

My mother in America sent them to me in a letter. In a little box.
They didn't fit me when I got them. So my mother gave them to
my sister, because she had bigger feet. Now they are small on
me, because my feet got big. Try them on. They'll fit you. You
have small feet.

(Clara tries them on.)

Aren't they beautiful. But you see my sister scratched them. She
never took care of them. She was going to break them and get
them dirty, so I took them away from her. She was sleeping one

night and I took them from under the bed. I put them inside a sack, I dug a hole and buried them inside the ground, so she wouldn't wear them again.

Wait. Let me see if someone's coming. *(Runs to the door and takes a peek. She runs back to Clara)*

The next day everybody in my house was looking for the shoes. And I didn't tell. I didn't say anything. I used to go out at night and dig them out of the ground and wear them for a little while. Even if they were big on me. Then I would polish them with my nightshirt and dab a bit of saliva to make them shine. They would shine so much you could see the bright moon reflected on them.

Go see if someone's coming.

(Clara goes to the door.)

CLARA: No one's out there.

TALITA: She'll make her round again. Then she'll sit by the door and fall asleep. Let me wear the shoes.

CLARA: But they don't fit you.

TALITA: It doesn't matter.

(Places shoes on top of her head) One day I will melt them into a hat. My grandma had her gold tooth melted into a wedding band. I could do the same with my shoes. And I'll have a hat. Maybe a purse. *(Holds them by the strap, as if they were a purse)* Maybe a pair of gloves, like the one's rich ladies wear to church.

CLARA: Keep them how they are.

TALITA: When I look at them, I remember the smell of back home. Walking on the moist grass. The moon shining on my shoes. My grandma's face.

CLARA: You miss your grandma.

TALITA: Sometimes.

CLARA: I miss Mateo. When will I see him again?

TALITA: Pretend you're sick. They'll take you to the infirmary to see a doctor, then you can see him.

(Blackout.)

Scene Two
A Broken Hand a Broken Lie

This scene takes place simultaneously in both an X-ray room and a doctor's office. Lights are used to distinguish where action is taking place. Mateo sits in a chair stage left. Clara stands stage right.

MATEO: What are you going to do to me?

DOCTOR MARTIN: I'm going to take an X-ray of your hand. Do you know what that is? It's a picture of your bones. It's not going to hurt. It's just like standing in front of a camera.

(Positions Mateo for the X-ray. Lifts his right hand.)

The photographer tells you, "Look at the pretty bird." And . . . voilà he takes a picture of you. —Again with the pretty bird . . . And . . . voilà.

MATEO: What does "voilà" mean?

DOCTOR MARTIN: What does it mean? It means "there it is."

There you go. *(Stands away from Mateo)* "Pretty bird one more time." . . . And . . . voilà . . .

(Freeze.)

SISTER NORA *(Writes and reads rapidly on a chart)*: Clara Maria Prago, eleven years old, complains of abdominal pain and nausea. The child defines the pain or discomfort, as an ill-defined mass in the epigastrium.

(Stops reading from the chart.)

Do you feel pain now?

CLARA: Yes . . . yes . . . Right here by my ribs. The pain doesn't let me breathe sometimes. It goes all the way to my chest and my throat. Like if something was hitting me there with a hammer. More like a knife.

SISTER NORA: Like a sharp pain?

CLARA: Yes.

SISTER NORA: Does the pain extend to your back?

CLARA: Sometimes.

SISTER NORA: Where on your back?

CLARA: It goes all over. It's like a car inside my body. But more like an airplane.

SISTER NORA: Why an airplane?

CLARA: Because the pain goes up and down. It's like a balloon. It's flying inside me. It wants to get out and it gets trapped inside my ribs.

(Freeze.)

DOCTOR MARTIN: I want you to open and close your hand.

MATEO: It hurts when I do that.

DOCTOR MARTIN: I want you to try and do it.

MATEO: I tell you it hurts.

DOCTOR MARTIN: It's going to hurt, but you got to do it. I'll give you a pill and the pain will go away.

MATEO: No. I can't do it. It hurts.

DOCTOR MARTIN: Try.

(Mateo lifts his arm and closes his eyes. He is in pain. He opens and closes his hand.)

Good. Very good. Now I'm going to pull back your fingers, just a little.

MATEO: Aaaaahhhhhhh . . . Aaaaayyyyyyyyyhhhhh . . .

(Freeze.)

CLARA: That sounds like Mateo's voice. Is he next door? I want to see him.

SISTER NORA: There are many children here. I don't think that's your friend.

CLARA: But it sounds like him. I know his voice.

SISTER NORA: You must miss your friend very much.

CLARA: Yes, I want to see him.

SISTER NORA: He's sick. You know he's sick. When he's better you can see him.

Come on, let's listen to your heart. I want you to take a deep breath. *(Places the stethoscope on Clara's stomach)*

CLARA: Aaaaaaaaaaaaaahhhhhhhhhhhh . . .

(Freeze.)

DOCTOR MARTIN: I want you to try one more time. Open and close your hand. *(Pulls back his hand)*

MATEO: Aaaaahhhhh . . . Aaayyyyyhhhh . . . Ahhhh! Ah! Aaaaahh!!!!!!!

CLARA: That's Mateo. I know that's him. *(Stands up on the chair and calls in a loud voice)* Mateo . . . Mateo . . .

SISTER NORA: Sit down . . . Sit down . . . Pay attention.

CLARA: Mateo . . .

SISTER NORA: Clara!

CLARA: I want to see you, Mateo . . .

MATEO: Come see me.

(Mateo stands on the chair.)

DOCTOR MARTIN: Sit down.

SISTER NORA: Sit down, Clara.

CLARA: I can't come see you. They don't let me.
(To Sister Nora) Please let me see him. I feel better. I feel better.

SISTER NORA: Get down from that chair. (Tries to pull her down)

CLARA: What are they doing to you?

MATEO: Nothing. I'm fine.

DOCTOR MARTIN: Stop yelling across the room.

SISTER NORA: Now Clara listen to me, you can see your friend when he's better. And stop yelling across the room.

CLARA: Please let me see him. I feel much better.

SISTER NORA: Get down from that chair. I said get down. You'll see him some other time.

MATEO: Clara . . . Clara . . .

(There is a pause. Clara lowers her head.
    Lights fade.)

Scene Three
Chores for the Day

Daytime. Clara sits on a chair center stage. Sister Nora stands behind her braiding her hair. Clara is braiding Talita's hair, who is kneeling in front of her.

SISTER NORA: There used to be a time when the needs of this place were fulfilled, and children like you spent the whole day in class-rooms, learning how to read and write. Now there's not enough of us and this place is falling apart. Everything smells of mold. As when things become moldy and moth eaten.

There used to be a time when this building was airy and sani-tary, because we had time to scrub our walls and floors. We had time to maintain our gardens, to cut down the branches from our trees and let in the fresh air. And in the summertime we used to throw buckets of water on the floor, flooding the mission up to our ankles, so the tiles could retain the cool moisture and soothe the heat. Our walls were painted and there were no leeks on our roofs.

Then things changed. No missionaries wanted to come here to work. And others left frightened of danger. Afraid of getting killed or lost in our jungles, to end up mangled or mutilated by guerillas or soldiers.

So now if the alms box needs to be painted, we take a brush and paint it. All you children have to help us. If there's no one to mend the altar cloths, we take a needle and thread and mend them. Do you know how to sew, Clara?

CLARA: No.

SISTER NORA: I'll teach you. You know how to sweep and dust?

CLARA: Yes.

SISTER NORA: Good. You can sweep and dust the parish. Take a broom and duster from the room next to the vestry. Talita, you take her there and show her where they're kept. Show her how to sweep under the prayer stools. To get underneath the stools with the broom. Dirt accumulates down there. And show her how to polish the pulpit and the altar rails.

The altar cloths are washed on Mondays. The candles are also changed on that day. I like to change them on Mondays, because Mondays are dull and somber. New candles brighten up the church and bring clarity. When you clean the saints use soap and water. Not too much soap or you'll get too much foam. Then it will take you forever to rinse them. Make sure you dry them well with the cloth I set aside for them. Talita will show you. You know, that's one thing I always liked doing, washing the saints and angels. I like to bathe them as if they were my children. Clean their ears and elbows real good, as I would do a baby. And talk to them. They like it when you talk to them. They like to listen.

(Blackout.)

Scene Four
Take Me to Her

Mateo sits to the left of the stage. He plays with shoes, bottles and cans he has taken out of a box. He lines the objects as if they were a battalion of soldiers. Doctor Martin has fallen asleep by his bed.

MATEO: If you can't bring her to me, take me to her. You can march through the hallways until you get to the girls dormitory. That's were she's at.

I described her to you. Her name is Clara.

First you can take my eyes and put them by her pillow.

Take my eyebrows and lie them by her night table.

Then you can take my hands, and hang them on a nail until I get there.

Then you can take my knees and put them behind the door.

Take my arms and fly them to the ceiling.

Take my whole face and hide it in her pitcher of water. Leave the rest of my body in a corner of the room. I'll take my feet and walk there.

(A bottle from the battalion falls to the side. The Doctor wakes up from the sound.)

DOCTOR MARTIN: What are you doing? What are you doing up from bed?

MATEO: I want to go home.

DOCTOR MARTIN: You're not going anywhere. Get back in bed.

MATEO: Where's my friend Clara?

DOCTOR MARTIN: What's all this stuff? What's this mess? Get back into bed. Come on . . .

(The Doctor tries to get him up. Mateo moves away. Pause.)

Listen, we're not here to hurt you. Now, do as I say.

(Mateo goes back to bed.)

I'll get you your pills. It's time for your medicine.

(Mateo gets up and hides the objects under the bed. A bell rings. Lights change.)

Scene Five
The Confession

An armoire is placed to the center of the stage. Clara and Talita stand to the left of the armoire. A square of light defines the room.

TALITA: Here's a broom and a duster. Let's go to the parish.

CLARA: Why can't I work in the infirmary like you do?

TALITA: Because in order for you to work in the infirmary you have to be prepared. You wouldn't like it there. I make the beds with Sister Nora. Me on one side of the bed and Sister Nora on the other side. How would you like to see bloody sheets, bullet holes on people's skin. Burnt skin. You know why I prefer to work here? I'll show you.

(She opens the armoire which is full of white communion garments.)

Communion dresses. See the veils. Just like wedding veils.

CLARA: Can I try one on?

TALITA: No.

CLARA: Why not?

TALITA: Because you're not ready for communion.

(Tries on the veil.)

See, I look like a bride.

CLARA: Let me wear it?

TALITA: No, I'm going to be the bride. You're not old enough to be a bride. I have breasts. Look at my breasts.

(Opens her blouse and shows Clara her breasts.)

Your breasts have to grow like mine. They have to get bigger.

CLARA: I'll give you my slice of sweet bread at snack time.

TALITA: You can't wear one until you do confession. You have to confess your sins.

CLARA: How do I do that?

TALITA: You have to kneel down and tell me your sins. Come here.

(Talita takes Clara and positions her on the other side of the open door of the armoire. Talita positions herself opposite to Clara, as if the door was a confessional.)

Go down on your knees. Tell me a secret.

CLARA: I don't have secrets.

TALITA: Everybody has secrets. You know what a secret is?

CLARA: Of course.

TALITA: Sister Nora says that secrets are sins. What we're doing is a secret, a sin. My breasts are a secret. A sin. They are dirty.

CLARA: You don't wash them?

(Sister Nora enters from the right of the stage and notices the girls. She remains quiet to listen to their conversation.)

TALITA: They are dirty because they were touched by a man. A soldier. A soldier touched them and bit them, like if they were food. Like if he was going to eat them. He made them dirty. My mouth is dirty because he kissed me, my neck, my shoulders.

Are you dirty too? Did a soldier touch you?

CLARA: No.

TALITA: Then you're not dirty.

CLARA: I'm not dirty. But someone touched my body.

TALITA: Who?

CLARA: Not a soldier.

TALITA: That still makes you dirty. Who was it?

CLARA: His hands weren't dirty. His hands were clean.

TALITA: I know who it is.

CLARA: You don't.

TALITA: Then I won't let you wear the veil. You have to tell me. That's what confession is for.

SISTER NORA: What are you girls doing? What are you doing?

TALITA: We're playing. We are just playing.

SISTER NORA: What is it you don't want to tell her? What is it?

TALITA: It's just a game Sister Nora.

SISTER NORA: Who were you talking about, Clara?

TALITA: She was probably talking about a soldier. But she doesn't want to tell.

SISTER NORA: Leave us alone, Talita.

(Talita exits.)

Why don't you tell me Clara? Why don't you talk to me? It's not good to keep things inside.

CLARA: I'm not dirty, Sister Nora. I'm not dirty. I'm clean! I'm clean!

(Clara runs out of the room.
Lights fade.)

Scene Six
Soldiers and Hearts with Tongues

A cart full of boxes is rolled to center stage. Sister Nora and Doctor Martin stand to the left of the cart. Sister Nora holds a writing pad and a pencil. A square of light defines the room.

DOCTOR MARTIN: Four boxes of evaporated milk, two boxes of canned goods, two bags of rice. A box of soap. I don't know what's in here. *(Opens the box)* Another box of used clothes. Do you want to go through this box?

SISTER NORA: We might as well.

DOCTOR MARTIN: One pair of pants.

SISTER NORA: Those will fit Alfonso.

DOCTOR MARTIN: A blue sweater.

SISTER NORA: Keep that for Luz Maria, she needs a sweater.

DOCTOR MARTIN: A white shirt.

SISTER NORA: That will fit Tato. Let me look at it.

DOCTOR MARTIN: It's kind of small. *(Hands her the shirt)*

SISTER NORA: It will fit him.

DOCTOR MARTIN: Another pair of pants.

SISTER NORA: Those will fit Otilio.

DOCTOR MARTIN: A dress.

SISTER NORA: That's pretty. We'll give it to Leandra. She could use a new dress.

DOCTOR MARTIN: A pair of shoes.

SISTER NORA: What size?

DOCTOR MARTIN: Size five.

SISTER NORA: Those will fit Marita.

DOCTOR MARTIN *(Takes out a pair pants)*: The military stopped us on the way here, just as we were entering the village. They were exhibiting the clothes of the guerillas who had died.

SISTER NORA *(Annoyed. Tries to avoid subject)*: Give me those. They'll fit Francisco.

DOCTOR MARTIN *(Takes out a blouse)*: The militiamen made us get out of the bus. They were doing demonstrations.

SISTER NORA: That will fit Victoria. *(Takes the blouse from him)*

DOCTOR MARTIN: They started to take prisoners out of a truck. Some prisoners could hardly walk, they were so badly beaten. The soldiers forced them to stand in line and face us. They had cut off parts of their skin. Others had their ears missing.

SISTER NORA *(With contained anger)*: They're a bunch of wild dogs! I've never killed. But sometimes I want to take a rifle and shoot the first armed man I see in front of me, whether he's a guerrilla fighter or from the military. Sometimes I wish . . . I feel this thing in my chest. They'll come here and demonstrate. I know they will. As if we need to see another demonstration. There's no need to see soldiers mangling and torturing people.

DOCTOR MARTIN *(Takes out a pair of shoes)*: Will these fit Angelo?

SISTER NORA: What size are they?

DOCTOR MARTIN: Four and half.

SISTER NORA: Those will fit Mateo. I made him a little ball so he could exercise his hand. I made it out of yarn. He's healing quite well. Clara is the one who worries me. She seems anxious. She doesn't want to eat. She draws these little hearts. Little hearts everywhere. I had to take the pencil from her. She was drawing on the altar cloths, the windowsill of her room, on her pillowcase and sheets.

You want to see what they look like? I tell you, all these little hearts everywhere. *(Takes out a piece of paper from her pocket and gives it to him)* See, some of them have crying eyes. Other drawings show bleeding hearts. Look at this one with the tongues. Look at the shape of the tongues. The sexual form of the hearts. You know these hearts lead me to believe that this child was sexually active with her friend. We have to be careful with them. We should keep them apart.

(Doctor Martin looks at her. He turns back to the paper to examine the hearts.

Lights fade to black.)

Scene Seven
Dirt on the Body

Clara stands stage right speaking to her doll. She then sits on a bed. Mateo sits on the floor stage left.

CLARA: Your body is clean, mine is dirty.

I wish I didn't have a body, like the dead people in the cemetery.

If only I could take a bucket of water and wash away all that is bad, then Sister Nora will see me clean.

She's mad at me, because I'm dirty.

They put us in this room because they don't like us here. If we were back home, we would all be together, Mateo you and I. You would like it there.

If we were back home, we could be playing in the cemetery with the dead people. They're so alone inside the ground. Those dead people liked it when we played with them.

(Incantation:)

Mateo, can you hear me! Mateo . . . Come play in the cemetery
. . . Mateo . . .

MATEO *(As if hearing her voice)*: Clara . . .

CLARA: Come play with me . . .

MATEO: Clara . . .

CLARA *(Feeling his presence)*: Mateo . . .

MATEO: I can see you . . .

*(Old photographs of a man and a woman are projected on the
scrim.*

*Clara runs to meet Mateo center stage. They both walk
symmetrically around imaginary tombs.)*

CLARA: Mateo when I die you take a picture of me. I'm going to die
first, so you take a picture of me.

MATEO: Look at her. What do you think her name was?

CLARA: A . . . ma . . . li . . . a. Amalia.

MATEO: That's a pretty name. If I had a canary, I would name it
Amalia.

CLARA: She's looking at us. See how she looks at us.

*(They walk in different directions, as if to hide from the photo-
graphs.)*

MATEO: She wants to be here with us.

CLARA: But she can't. She's dead. She doesn't live anymore.

MATEO: Why don't you let her live in your body? You can pretend to
be her, I'll pretend to be this man. What's his name? Can you
read his name?

CLARA: I think it's Agustin.

MATEO: All right, I'll be Agustin. You be Amalia.

CLARA: Hello.

MATEO: Hello.

CLARA: Where do you come from?

MATEO: From the sky. Where do you come from?

CLARA: I was living in a star.

MATEO: What star?

CLARA: A blue star.

MATEO: What's the name of the star?

CLARA: Pilar.

MATEO: Would you invite me to your star? Would you invite me to dinner?

CLARA: Yes. What do you want me to cook for you?

MATEO: What dead people eat. Flowers.

CLARA: You want carnations?

MATEO: No.

CLARA: You want jasmine?

MATEO: No.

CLARA: I can cook you a bowl of chrysanthemum . . . A dish of petunias with morning glory. How about tulips?

MATEO: I had tulips last night.

CLARA: How about lilies, gardenias, orchids? That's all I have in my kitchen.

MATEO: I want to eat violets.

CLARA: I don't have violets. How about dahlias, geraniums, water lilies, hibiscus. How about hibiscus, Mateo . . . Hibiscus . . . You like hibiscus? Mateo?

(Clara freezes in a pool of light.
    Lights fade.)

Scene Eight
Talita with Fireflies and Plans to Escape

Mateo sits in a chair. He throws the little ball made out of yarn up and down. Sister Nora and Talita are making his bed.

TALITA: You think I'll have a big bed in America?

SISTER NORA: I'm sure you will. And even if you get a small bed, you should be grateful. What matters is that you'll have a bed where you can rest, and a house where you'll be safe.

TALITA: I used to sleep in a little bed like this one. The same size. My father made it out of palm leaves and corn husks. Sister Nora, what does it mean when a firefly comes into a room?

SISTER NORA: I don't know. Why do you ask?

TALITA: My mother used to say that when a big fly gets inside the house, it means we're going to have visitors. And when a dragonfly gets inside, it means the devil is going to visit the house.

SISTER NORA: That's superstition Talita.

TALITA: Last night I let a firefly get inside my mosquito net. You know what I thought when I saw it flying my way? That someone is coming for me.

SISTER NORA: Maybe. You'll find out in a couple of days.

TALITA: Are you trying to tell me something? Is someone really coming to visit me?

SISTER NORA: We'll see in a couple of days.

TALITA: Is my mother coming?

SISTER NORA: Well, I didn't want to tell you until she got here.

TALITA: Oh! Sister Nora, you make me happy. Will she arrive during the day or at nighttime?

SISTER NORA: I don't know.

TALITA: Sister Nora, can I go into the patio at night?

SISTER NORA: What for?

TALITA: To look for fireflies and catch them. I could catch them with my hands and tie them to a thread, and make myself a necklace. That way when my mother comes, I can look beautiful, bright and shining.

SISTER NORA (*Kisses her forehead*): Sure. But I have a better idea. We'll make you a flower necklace instead. We don't want to kill the fireflies.

TALITA: I won't kill them. I'll let them fly free, once my mother sees me.

SISTER NORA: Finish sweeping the floor. I'll get more linen for the other beds.

(*Sister Nora exits.*)

TALITA: Did you hear what she said? My mother is coming for me. When are they coming for you?

MATEO: I don't know.

TALITA: I know who you are. I know how you got that on your hand. A pig bit you. Your friend told me. She told me how you both escaped on the train.

MATEO: Clara.

TALITA: She sleeps next to me.

MATEO: Where?

TALITA: She doesn't anymore. You want to see her?

MATEO: I'm not allowed to see her.

TALITA: You can go see her at night, when the bell rings.

MATEO: How?

(Doctor Martin enters and proceeds to undo Mateo's bandage.
Talita continues sweeping.
Lights fade.)

Scene Nine
Playing with Death

Clara stands stage right playing with her doll. Mateo sits on the floor
stage left.

CLARA: I wish I were dead.
They don't let us do anything here. They took away my pencil so I can't draw anymore hearts. Well, they can all go away
and leave me alone. They can take away my pencil.
(Shrugs her shoulders) I can draw a heart with something
else. I can pull this little scab on my elbow and bleed. And with
my blood I can paint my hearts.

(With her right elbow she draws the shape of a heart in midair.)

With my saliva and the dust from the floor I can draw hearts.

(She dabs saliva on her fingers and draws another heart. She
spins around several times, stomping her feet out of anger.)

My hearts pull out their tongues at them!
If only I could be a soul. A spirit.
The people in the cemetery live without a body, invisible.
If I were dead right now, Mateo could come for me and dig
me out of the earth with his bare hands. He would have to be
dead too. But not gone away. Just dead. *(Lies on the floor)* Just
dead to be with each other. Mateo . . . Mateo . . .

Scene Ten
Escaping with Soldiers

Mateo stands stage left. He continues to play with the objects he has
lined up. He gives orders to his battalion. By the end of the speech
he proceeds to find Clara.

MATEO: The girl said to cross the patio and make a left. To go
through the hallway. You follow me. I'll be watching out for

you. I'll open the doors and see if the coast is clear. When I get to the laundry room, I'll signal you. You can hide behind the old furniture. The helicopters can hide behind the lamps and the light bulbs. I'll find a place for myself. When I tell you to march on, you follow me. When we find the staircase, we'll climb up to the second floor. The third room, that's where she's at. I'll run to the door. You stay outside and keep guard. If anybody comes you shoot. Did you hear me? Shoot. (*Holds an imaginary rifle and shoots*) Poooooommmmmmmm . . .

Scene Eleven
You Can Find Me

Clara lies on the floor. Sister Nora walks toward her and puts her to bed. She exits. The bells rings and the lights dim.
Clara sits up in her bed, making a wish. Incantation:

CLARA: Mateo . . . Find me in the cemetery. I'm this dead woman right here. You can find me if you look for me.
MATEO: Clara . . . Clara . . . I can feel you.
CLARA: Mateo . . . I can almost see you . . . I'm this dead woman right here. I'm turning into a spirit. I'm flying like your kite. You can find me outside this room on the rooftop.
MATEO: Clara I can hear you. I can sense you.
CLARA: You can find me through the hallways. You can find me in the zoo with the monkeys.
MATEO: You can find me in the zoo with the zebras.
CLARA: You can find me in the zoo with the giraffes.
MATEO: You can find me if you look for my kite.
CLARA: You can find me in the clouds.
MATEO: You can find me where kites go to die. Clara, where are you? I can't find you. Clara? Clara . . . I'll find you.

(*Clara closes her eyes as if trying to make herself into a spirit.*)

CLARA: I'm this dead woman right here.

(*Mateo walks around looking for Clara's room.*)

MATEO: I'm this dead man right here.
CLARA: I'm this dead woman right here.

MATEO: I'm this dead man right here.

CLARA: I'm this dead woman right here. Mateo . . .

MATEO: Clara . . .

CLARA: Mateo . . . You're getting closer . . . I'm the woman who died in July.

MATEO: I'm the man who died in October.

CLARA: I'm the woman with the pretty smile.

MATEO: I'm the man with a mustache.

CLARA: I was a singer.

MATEO: I was a baker.

CLARA: I was a seamstress.

MATEO: My name is Manolo.

CLARA: My name is Paquita.

MATEO: I'm Antonio.

CLARA: I'm going to turn into a man.

MATEO: Then I'll be this woman.

CLARA: Then I'll be the man who died in March.

MATEO: January . . .

CLARA: September . . .

MATEO: I had a pretty hat.

CLARA: I had a necklace . . .

MATEO: Pst . . . Pst . . . Clara.

(Stands to the right of Clara's bed.)

CLARA: Mateo . . . *(Turns to him)*

MATEO: Shshshhhhhh . . . I think someone's coming.

(Mateo hides under her bed. Clara covers herself with a sheet and pretends to be sleeping. Sister Nora enters the room and makes sure Clara is well covered. Sister Nora exits.

Clara peeks under her bed. Mateo looks up at her. They both giggle.)

I'm going to live under your bed.

(Clara runs to center stage. Mateo runs at her side. She closes her eyes. Mateo does the same. They express their joy and excitement.)

CLARA: I'm this dead woman, right here.

MATEO: I'm this dead man, right here.

CLARA: I'm this dead woman, right here.

(The voices become faint. The sound of wind.)

MATEO: I'm this dead man, right here. I'm invisible like air.

CLARA: I'm invisible like smoke.

MATEO: I'm invisible like a spirit.

(The voices become whispers. The sound of wind fills the stage. Lights fade.)

END OF PLAY

NILO CRUZ has written several plays, including *Graffiti, A Bicycle Country, Of Storks and Angels, A Park in Our House, Dancing on Her Knees, Drinking the Sea,* and the radio play *Two Sisters and a Piano.*

Cruz has had his work developed and performed in several theatres throughout the country. His play *Night Train to Bolina* received an Alton Jones Award and was produced at the Magic Theatre in San Francisco. *A Park in Our House* received an AT&T award, the Joseph Kesselring Award, and was commissioned and produced by the McCarter Theatre, with subsequent productions at the Magic Theatre and New York Theatre Workshop. *Dancing on Her Knees* was also developed at the Magic, as part of the Bay Area Playwrights Festival, and was produced at The Joseph Papp Public Theater/New York Shakespeare Festival.

Cruz holds an M.F.A. from Brown University. He has taught playwriting at Brown, Hofstra University and University of Iowa. He is a member of New Dramatists and The Dramatists Guild.

SKIN
An Adaptation of
Büchner's *Woyzeck*

Naomi Iizuka

THE WRITER SPEAKS
Naomi Iizuka

I find that I'm often uncomfortable speaking about my work. I have this sense that if you try to speak about your writing in the context of preexisting categories and definitions that are out there in the world, you risk misrepresenting the work, and robbing it, in different ways, of its power. Also, I'm suspicious of the tendency to pin down a writer's demographic or aesthetic identity. I dislike the way a piece of writing can get classified, the labels that are used to say that this person is "this kind of writer," and they're writing "this kind of play" which will speak to "this kind of audience." I think the expectation is that you will depict yourself and your writing in recognizable, and essentially stable ways. It's an expectation I resist. It's an expectation that is, I think, at odds with reality. My experience as both a writer and an individual in the world suggests to me that the way identity is configured is more complicated (and more interesting) than the demographic and aesthetic labels afforded us.

The word "political" is a word that means both too little and too much. I think at times writing has been defined as "political" by virtue of its subject matter or by virtue of its author's demographic affiliation or stated ideology. For me, political writing is political on the level of form and structure. How you're saying what you're saying has to be as significant as the content of what you're saying. I think writing that gets us out of familiar rhetorical grooves, that gives voice to that which is left out of daily discourse, and that gives shape to thoughts and desires that are otherwise unspoken is, by definition, political writing. In its form and structure, in its poetry and profanity, political writing needs to pose an alternative to the vision of the world articulated by more mainstream or conventional sources. It should unsettle. It should startle.

I started writing for theatre because I found that it let me explore in very vivid and multivalent ways basic questions of what it means to be in the world, how we engage with one another, how we come to terms with our public and private selves, how we sort through our respective histories. For me, theatre is about creating a piece of writing with elements from a known world in order to generate within the context of theatrical performance an experience that adumbrates the unknown. It's about working with language in order to get at that which is unspoken, inchoate. At its core, I think writing for theatre is (and should be) unparaphraseable. It should evoke the more elusive, inexplicable realms of human experience, at the same time making possible a renewed attentiveness to the concrete realties of the world.

Production History

In 1995, *Skin* received its first full production at the Forum Theatre, University of California–San Diego. Robert Woodruff was the director. Later that year the play received a production at SoHo Repertory Theatre, New York City. John McGrath was the director. The play received a production also that year at Dallas Theater Center. Matthew Wilder was the director. In 1998, *Skin* received a production at Printer's Devil, Seattle. Kip Fagan was the director.

Scene 1

in the dark. Mary is all voice. her words travel up through the earth and into the air where the sound is like a swarm of tiny insects being born.

MARY: and then later, this is way later, after it got dark, we'd go down to this place out by morely field, it was like a meadow, all flat and long and grass and empty

and it'd be me and this guy sean I used to know, I forget his last name, and he and I, I was like maybe 14 and I was all wearing my hair all ratted out back then, and this crazy black stuff all around my eyes like a real live punk even though there was no such thing anymore cause that happened like a thousand years ago, before I was born, before I even remember

and I was running all around the city and hanging out up by mission bay, ditching and getting high, and everybody was all, do this, do that, and I was all fuck that, I didn't even want to hear any of that shit so then sean and me

so then sean and me, we'd go, we'd go down to this place out by morley field, out by where the airport was, and we'd smoke some thai stick, and we'd get real high, and that was fine, and we'd lie on our backs for a long time, we'd lie there and watch the planes take off and land right above us, so close, that we could see right into the bellies of these huge planes, right into the engines, and it was the most amazing thing, and the sound was so loud, it was everywhere and inside, like something splitting apart inside me

and it was it was like nothing else, and the later sean would roll on top of me and we'd make out a little, and I'd get gravel and dirt in my panties and little cuts from pressing against all the rocks and glass and shit on the ground, and it was ok, and I'd think about the planes taking off and landing above me, and above the planes, the clouds and the sky, and above that, all the stars and planets and galaxies millions of miles away, and on and on like that until all there was was black—

Scene 2

a man named Jones in the city in the night. inside his brain is talk and static and classic rock and jamming z 90 and sweet sweet music from baja california, mexico.

and then the Police slide out of the dark. Jones doesn't hear them. Jones doesn't see them. the Police are sly and invisible in their black and white machine. they have plastic faces the color of flesh. and they are america's finest and they say:

POLICE 1: hey shit head
hey punk
hey motherfucker
hold it—hold it right there—
POLICE 2: he said hold it punk—
POLICE 1: don't move—
POLICE 2: what are you—
POLICE 1: don't you fucking move—
POLICE 2: what are you—deaf—
POLICE 1: understand—do you understand—
POLICE 2: what is with this guy—you want to get smart—you want to be a smartass—boy—I'll fuck you up—
POLICE 1: watch it—punk—
POLICE 2: I will fuck you up—
POLICE 1: you need to listen up now—you need to settle down—
POLICE 2: settle the fuck down asshole—
POLICE 1: do you hear me—do you hear what it is I'm saying to you—
POLICE 2: you want to—you want to—I'll fuck you up—I will fuck you up—
POLICE 1: let's see some ID—we need to see some form of identification—
JONES: my name—you want to know—wait—you want to know my name—my name—hold on—I'm going to tell you—wait—my name—may name is superman—fucking superman—

(and here the dance begins.)

POLICE 1: superman—
POLICE 2: jones.

POLICE 1: this here is superman—

POLICE 2: jones. sean jones. 332-47-7106. 6/25/67.

POLICE 1: what's the matter with you, superman?

JONES: nothing.

POLICE 1: you sure about that?

JONES: yes sir.

POLICE 1: are you high, jones?

POLICE 2: he's asking you a question, shithead, what the fuck's the matter with you?

POLICE 1: are you high?

JONES: no, sir.

POLICE 1: I think you're high.

JONES: no, sir.

POLICE 1: I think you're flying, boy.

JONES: no, sir.

POLICE 2: let me see your eyes, superman—

POLICE 1: settle down—

POLICE 2: let me see your fucking eyes—

JONES: wait—

POLICE 1: I said settle down—

POLICE 2: LET ME SEE YOUR FUCKING EYES, SUPERMAN—

JONES: I CAN'T SEE—

(the dance ends. there is no other sound than the body than the valves and arteries of the body. Jones bleeds. and his blood turns the whole world slowly gorgeous stinking red.)

POLICE 2: you're fucked up, you know that? you're a fucked up individual—

JONES: yes, sir.

POLICE 2: what were you doing back there?

JONES: nothing.

POLICE 2: I'm going to ask you again. what were you doing?

JONES: nothing.

POLICE 2: see, now, jones, that is an untruth. right now, see, I know you're lying to me.

JONES: no sir.

POLICE 2: I'm going to tell you what, jones, I see guys like you every night—I know you. I know what you are. I know every thought that goes through your head. I know every dream. I know what your story is. do you understand me?

JONES: yes, sir.

POLICE 2: don't you ever lie to me—because if you lie, I will know. I will know because I know everything that happens here. you're bleeding, jones.

JONES: yes, sir.

POLICE 2: you're bleeding all over everything.

JONES: I'm bleeding.

POLICE 2: get out of here, jones. you're wasting my time. get lost. I said get out of here. disappear—

Scene 3

a building in the city. Angel is turning the channels of the tv which is all technicolor moving pictures and shiny talking and laughs and everything is pretty and nothing bad happens ever not for real.

JONES: and then so
  they built this whole underground complex out past el centro off the 8 on the way to yuma
  on the way to yuma when yuma was just a couple of shacks in the middle of the desert, nothing nothing nothing for miles this being like in the fifties, this being
desert
from
the
ocean
to phoenix
and
nothing for miles
blank space wide sky
and all these poor shits living in these trailers by the side of the freeway, praying for their shipments of water and propane, waiting for a sign
fuck—
and underground where you can't see, something is happening, some high tech top secret thing, and the only living souls who know shit, they're sitting in some room in washington, dc, and they could give a fuck, and all you know is sounds blasting, inside the earth where you can't see—fuck—and all above, the

ground shaking and dust rising and the sky turning weird yellow into the night.

fuck—

later when they went home, they got sick. their skin turned rotten with all kinds of strange cancer, coughed up their insides in little pieces. they didn't put it together for a long time.

turn the tv off.

ANGEL: what?

JONES: turn the goddamn tv off.

ANGEL: what the fuck's your problem?

JONES: turn it off. listen. listen to that. the air is moving, everywhere it's moving, shifting, ringing, somewhere, so high like a ringing, like some thing shimmering—

ANGEL: I don't hear anything. man, you need to relax—

JONES: listen.

ANGEL: I don't—

JONES: ssh. there.

ANGEL: it's a plane is all it is.

JONES: when I close my eyes, I see all the sky full of plane, in the dark, and I see the way the light cuts through, everywhere I can see, slicing through, I can see right into the belly of it like somebody went and cut it open with a knife, and it was bleeding metal and light—

where have you ever been to, angel? where have you ever been that's not here?

ANGEL: I don't know.

nowhere.

JONES: sometimes I fly. I have no body, no bones, and I am flying in the air, all eye, all light, invisible, electrified, vaporized—wait. listen. listen to that.

ANGEL: alright, man, come on—

JONES: it's so close.

ANGEL: come on, knock it off.

JONES: it's so loud, it's right there. can't you hear it?

ANGEL: I said, knock it off. fuck.

(and then Angel switches on the tv. and everything is happy and noisy like a whole party erupting right before your eyes.)

Scene 4

the boardwalk. the sun is a big white hole. the air is hot and still. the sounds of the radios and the cars cruising by all get lost in the folds of a dress. the ocean is a slit of bluest blue so narrow you forget it's even there. men pass by with their shirts off and their eyes hidden behind dark glasses. Mary and Lisa watch them. Mary's Girl plays by herself. she is a very little girl.

MARY: I'm dreaming of men—

LISA: mary says to me, she says—

MARY: I'm dreaming of men beautiful men—

LISA: we're out in mission bay just hanging out, this was a long time ago, and it's hot and the sun is so bright everything looks warped and wavy like it's melting, and I can't even move, and mary tells me she tells me this crazy ass dream, she says she says to me—

MARY: I'm dreaming—

LISA: mary—

MARY: this was a long time ago—

LISA: mary—

MARY: I'm dreaming of men. they fall out of the sky. they fall and they crash into buildings and some of them get caught in the trees. some of them hit the ground and break into a lot of little pieces and I pick up all the pieces I see and I take them home with me and I sew the pieces all together anyway into this thing.

LISA: that's crazy.

MARY: and I think it's going to be this amazing thing, but it's ugly and fucked up and all I want to do is throw it away.

LISA: still.

MARY: and all I want to do, all I want to do.

LISA: the sound of water.

MARY: I'm dreaming of men.

LISA: the sound of water. this is a long time ago.

MARY: I listen to the men. they talk and laugh. I try to hear the words they say.

LISA: once upon a time, a long time ago.

MARY: it's so hot. I want to sleep.

LISA: last night I'm at work and this guy asks me if he can put his hand on my thigh for five bucks, and I tell him, you have got to be kidding, so then he says, ok I'll buy you a drink, and I'm like, ok whatever, so the hostess comes over and he pays, and then he says he'll give me ten bucks if he can put his hand on my thigh, and I say sure why not, and after a while I'm like, ok that's ten bucks worth, and he was cool, and then later, I saw he had a scar on his hand, and the skin was all smooth and see through kind of, and I asked him how he got it, but he told me some bullshit story—

MARY: still.

LISA: and I thought, what an asshole you are, I'm asking you a fucking question, I'm looking for a fucking answer, asshole. what's it to you to tell me the truth.

MARY: I have a scar on my belly from when my baby was born. it didn't close up for a long time. now it's so white. when I touch it, it's all glossy, the skin, and shiny. sometimes I wake up and I think it hurts, but the doctor says it's all in my head. what time is it?

LISA: I don't know. late.

MARY: I'm hot.

LISA: I am so hot.

MARY: hey, look. look at that.

(a Navy Man appears. his head is shaved. his eyes are invisible behind dark green glass. there is a whole entire world in that dark glass, twisted and glowing.)

LISA: he's so fine.

MARY: mmhm.

LISA: I like that.

MARY: he is hot.

LISA: I like that. I do like that.

MARY: I swear I'd like a piece of that all for myself.

LISA: ssh.

MARY: what?

LISA: he heard you.

MARY: so?

LISA: he's looking at you. girl, he's looking you up and down. you see that?

MARY: I see.

(Navy Man goes away.)

LISA: you better watch yourself.

MARY: I'm just playing.

LISA: I saw how you were looking at him. I know what you're thinking.

MARY: oh?

LISA: just stick your eyes back into your head. do yourself a favor.

MARY: excuse me.

LISA: you know what I'm saying, don't act like you don't.

MARY: why don't you explain it all to me.

LISA: you know what it is.

MARY: I really don't.

LISA: please.

MARY: you want to fight?

LISA: I ain't the one fighting.

MARY: I think you're jealous. bitch.

LISA: please, you ain't all that.

MARY: I get what I want.

LISA: yeah, you get knocked up is what you get.

MARY: fuck you. hag.

LISA: slut.

MARY: you better get out of my face before I kick your ass, bitch.

LISA: fuck you.

(Lisa goes away.)

MARY: fuck you. fuck her.

(a song from a car radio gets real loud, and the bass is like something underground, and the music almost feels like it's coming from inside your head, and then the car drives away, and it's quiet again. Jones appears.)

JONES: mary?

MARY: you scared me. what's wrong. you look all fucked up and strange. where were you last night anyway?

JONES: I don't know. all over.

MARY: what happened to you? were you in a fight or something?

JONES: yeah I've been fighting, I've been fighting with the demons.

MARY: oh yeah?

JONES: big red demons with horns and blood coming out of their mouths. they tore me up, chewed me up good. they kicked my ass, but then I ran away and I was fast and they couldn't catch me.

MARY: you're so full of shit.

JONES: I started thinking about things, mary, and I could not stop—

MARY: baby—

JONES: —I was thinking about all the things that need to happen for it to be perfect. I was thinking about perfection, mary. I was thinking about being perfect, I was thinking how there's something that takes all that is perfect and beautiful and makes it into shit, everything you do, everything you say becomes shit, I was trying to get it all straight in my head last night, but I can't, it's too much—

MARY: stop it.

you think too much, baby. it'll fuck you up.

JONES: I need to get out of here, mary, I need to be someplace else—

MARY: it's so hot. I want to go inside. my skin feels like it's burning off me. the sun is so bright. it's so bright. are we going to have some fun tonight? I want to have some fun. tell me. tell me something, quick.

JONES: tell you what? what do you want me to say?

MARY: I don't know. something stupid. something really stupid. I don't care what.

JONES: I don't know what to say.

MARY: it doesn't matter what. just say something.

JONES: I don't know.

MARY: say something to me say something—

JONES: mary—I got to go. I'll see you later. I'll see you tonight.

(Jones goes away.
Mary closes her eyes, and the world goes black.)

Scene 5

later Mary's Girl is talking and her words are super 8 moving pictures in her head. a man and a woman at the beach. they are so young. this happened a long time ago. there is no sound.

MARY'S GIRL:

my mom's hands are big and white.

my mom's hands are big and strong.

she has long white fingers. they smell of cigarettes and lotion.

my mom paints her nails. she paints them pink. they are so pink like the inside of a seashell.

when my mom picks me up her hands spread out wide. and they
are so big. they block out all the sound and all the light and
everything there is. and when she holds me they wrap around
me and become the whole world all there is all there ever was.
in my head I have a picture of my mom.
she's at the beach. this was a hundred years ago.
and all around her are strangers. behind her is the ocean. above
her is the sky. and she's looking out at me. and her eyes are
half-closed like she's looking at the sun.

Scene 6

*night. outside a club. a parking lot. lights. a crowd of people. they
gleam in the dark with sweat. when they talk, their teeth are so
white. there is laughing and laughing a woman laughing. Jones and
Mary appear out of the dark.*

MARY: sometimes she says these things, and she don't even know
where they come from. it's like she wants to swallow them back
up until there's nothing left.

JONES: mary—

MARY: baby, I'm just talking. don't look at me like that. you got a
smoke?

JONES: yeah. here.

MARY: it's your last one.

JONES: take it.

MARY: sure?

JONES: yeah, here, take it.

MARY: oh, wait, listen. oh man, I love this song. it makes me think of
like junior high, you know, and being out in the parking lot after
some dance and everybody going home, and all the lights and
cars, and I'm so stoned I can't even move, and some guy's got his
hands all up and down me—
        what? what is it? just say it.

JONES: I don't know. nothing.

MARY: I like this song. I like it a lot.

JONES: you want my jacket?

MARY: I'm fine.
        tonight I feel like playing. do you feel like playing?

JONES: yeah.

MARY: yeah? you do? you feel like playing? you crack me up.

JONES: you look beautiful tonight, mary.

MARY: it's too dark right this second, but if you look at me close, you can see, I got lines here and here, all around my eyes, little tiny ones. they didn't used to be there. you can hardly see unless you really look.

JONES: I think you're beautiful.

MARY: yeah, beautiful beautiful.

JONES: you are, mary. I look at you, and I see something beautiful.

MARY: what a stupid word. I fucking hate that word.

JONES: what are you saying, mary? what are you saying to me?

MARY: nothing. I didn't mean nothing. baby, I'm just talking. I'm just—I don't know

(Jones and Mary go in. the Navy Men appear.)

NAVY MAN 1: wait up, did you see that?

NAVY MAN 2: what?

NAVY MAN 1: over there, man. check it out.

NAVY MAN 2: sweet. man, that bitch has a set.

NAVY MAN 1: check out those legs.

NAVY MAN 2: nice.

NAVY MAN 1: I could get lost between those legs.

NAVY MAN 2: "I think I'm in love."

NAVY MAN 1: get off.

NAVY MAN 2: "1 think I love you, baby, I think I want to spend the rest of my life with you."

NAVY MAN 1: quit it.

NAVY MAN 2: "you're so handsome. you're so fine. what's your name, baby? can I touch you all over?"

NAVY MAN 1: get off me, man.

NAVY MAN 2: "kiss me, baby. kiss me quick or I will die."

NAVY MAN 1: shut up.

NAVY MAN 2: "don't you want to kiss me, baby?"

NAVY MAN 1: fucking get off me, man. what the fuck's the matter with you?

NAVY MAN 2: lighten up, man. just relax. come on.

(the Navy Men go inside.)

Scene 7

inside. a crowd of bodies pressed together. a band plays a song. the music is so loud it makes your skull hurt.

and then everything stops. and all is darkness. and all is stillness. and there is nothing in the world except for Mary who is all light like an angel or something.

MARY: and then I'll unzip your pants and pull them off, and I'll hold your dick in my hand, and I'll rub my thumb up and down the bottom of your dick from the base to the tip, where the vein is, I will rub, and I will take the tip between my fingers, and I'll move my fingers back and forth until it's hard and growing, and then I'll lick it until it's wet and shining, and I will make circles with my tongue, I will do this, all around the tip and where it curves in and then out again, my tongue will find that place, and I will trace the vein the length that it goes, and then I'll take it, all of it, in my mouth, and pull it back and in and gently, I will do this, gently press it against my teeth so that it catches a little, that is what I will do

JONES: mary—

MARY: what are you looking at? why are you looking at me like that? if you look at me like that, I swear I'll turn you into stone.

JONES: I can see all the way inside of you.

MARY: yeah?

JONES: it's like you have no skin.

MARY: what do you see? tell me. what do you see?

JONES: naked bone. so white so perfect—

MARY: what are you thinking about?

JONES: nothing.

MARY: tell me.

JONES: white. bone. white. nothing.

MARY: tell me.

JONES: there's nothing there.

MARY: is your head empty? is that how it is with you?

JONES: yeah, I guess.

MARY: what's wrong with you? why don't you say something? sometimes you make me want to laugh. I don't even know why.

JONES: you want a beer, mary?

MARY: I don't believe you. yeah. sure. go get me a beer. go do that.

(Jones disappears into the dark. Mary dances by herself. she spins and spins. the Navy Man emerges from the crowd. the music stops and Mary is still.)

NAVY MAN 1: what's your name? you have a name? I've been watching you.

MARY: oh yeah?

NAVY MAN 1: yeah, I've been over there, like gazing at you from afar. I think maybe I know you. I think maybe I've seen you before.

MARY: I don't think so.

NAVY MAN 1: I've been taking you all in. I think you have bewitched me, see.

MARY: yeah?

NAVY MAN 1: yeah.

MARY: and what is that supposed to mean?

NAVY MAN 1: bewitch—you know—witchy stuff. I look at you and I can't take my eyes off of you. it's like magic.
    what? what's funny? I asked you, what's funny?

MARY: it's like magic. fuck. are you for real?

NAVY MAN 1: yeah I'm for real.

MARY: it's just funny, that's all.

NAVY MAN 1: yeah, you think I'm funny?

MARY: yeah, I think you're funny. I think you're a fucking funny man. you walk up to some girl you don't know talking some witchy bullshit you make up and like that, and so I'm thinking who is this clown, he's got a line, he must have some kind of line. maybe something like you buy me a beer

NAVY MAN 1: yeah.

MARY: and you tell me how nice I look tonight. and you tell me how pretty my eyes are. you tell me how you like the way I wear my hair.

NAVY MAN 1: those ain't the things I like about you, bitch.

MARY: fuck you.

NAVY MAN 1: you want me to back off, you say the word, I'll go.

MARY: do what you want.

NAVY MAN 1: I like this place. I like how you're all packed in tight and it's loud and everybody's sweating. I like that. I like how hot it gets like you can't even breathe. you know what I'm saying. it makes me feel, I don't know, kind of fucked up. I like getting fucked up. I like that a lot. what's your name? I asked you your name.

MARY: mary.

NAVY MAN 1: you got a boyfriend, mary? or maybe he's not here right now or something. you're beautiful, you know that. you are so beautiful. I bet guys tell you all kinds of things. don't they?

so what do you say, mary? do you like to get fucked up? you look like maybe you like getting fucked up. you look like you know what that is.

MARY: I don't know.

NAVY MAN 1: yeah you do. what do you say, mary? what do you say?

(Mary and Navy Man 1 disappear into the crowd.)

JONES: mary?

NAVY MAN 2: hey, fuckhead.

JONES: mary?

NAVY MAN 2: watch where you're going, dumbshit.

JONES: where did she go? mary?

NAVY MAN 2: you better fucking watch your step. hey, I'm talking to you, punk—

(Jones leaves.)

hey. hey—

Scene 8

the music is very loud. and then nothing. a parking lot. cold air and cars driving away and the smell of pot.

a man and a woman are fucking in a room. they are like flesh-colored pieces. you can't see their faces.

JONES: and once you're underneath, see, you can't tell top from bottom, you can't hear anything because all the sound is messed up, and things that are right above you sound like they're coming from miles away, doesn't sound like anything you know, vibration, and sunlight is a memory, is something not real, and all around you is black so black you cannot see, and all you can hear is your heart and your blood pumping, and it is so loud, it fills your head, the inside of your head, and you would lose your mind listening to the sound inside yourself, how can there be so much inside a single body, how can that be.

when I was a boy, my father threw
me into the ocean
when I was a boy, my father threw
me into the ocean
when I was a boy, my father threw
me into the ocean
when I was a boy, my father threw
me into the ocean
and I sank into the dark, and I saw a forest of trees like I have
never seen, tall, strange shapes, beautiful, a forest of shadows,
and I knew
this is where the dead go.

(Mary's Girl is alone.)

MARY'S GIRL:
one plus one is two.
two plus two is four.
three plus three is six.
four plus four is eight.
five plus five is ten.

(a Navy Man appears from out of the dark.)

NAVY MAN: one two three four five six seven, all good children go to
heaven.
    what's your name?
MARY'S GIRL: I can't tell.
NAVY MAN: you can tell me. I won't tell anybody.
MARY'S GIRL: my mom says not to talk to strangers.
NAVY MAN: I'm not a stranger. your mom and me are good friends.
    do you like magic? you want to see a trick?
        watch. I can make things disappear. now you see it.

(and then the Navy Man makes everything disappear.)

    now you don't.
MARY'S GIRL: where's my mom? where is she?
NAVY MAN: she'll be back.
MARY'S GIRL: where did she go? I want to see her. mom?

*(and then Mary's Girl sees a woman who looks like her mom, and
she goes toward her, but when she gets close, she sees it's not her.)*

Scene 9

Mary's apartment. late at night. Mary and Mary's Girl.
Mary's Girl is sleeping, dreaming.

MARY: ssh. ssh. time to sleep. close your eyes, sweet one. sleep. nothing bad. there's nothing bad. everything is ok. ssh.
     who's there?

(jones appears.)

you scared me. it's late.
JONES: I called before.
MARY: yeah, I was out.
JONES: what's the matter with you, mary?
MARY: rent's due. rent's due and I just got a shut off notice from the
     fucking gas company. what do they expect me to do? fuck.
JONES: I was thinking of you, mary. I was thinking all day long of
     you. I was thinking about things—
MARY: don't. I said, don't. I'm tired, OK? I don't want to hear any of it.
     what? what are you looking at?
JONES: what's that?
MARY: nothing. it's nothing.
JONES: is it real?
MARY: how should I know?
JONES: it looks real. somebody give that to you, mary?
MARY: what do you care?
JONES: it's nice. it's pretty, mary.
MARY: I know what you're thinking, and you're wrong. I lifted it,
     alright? I walked right into that place in the mall, and I snatched
     it. they had a whole bunch of stuff out, and I just walked right
     up and slipped it in my bag, and I walked right out of the place,
     I just walked right out, and nobody saw, nobody stopped me,
     nobody said anything, and I know maybe you're thinking it's
     wrong, but I don't care. it's pretty. I like pretty things. why
     shouldn't I have some? just because I'm not some rich cow with
     all the money in the world.
     it's the truth, and I don't care what you think.
JONES: she's sleeping. how can she sleep all twisted up like that?
     she's pretty. she's pretty, mary, just like you.

MARY: she's a good girl. she never gives me any problems.

JONES: her fingers are so little. she's like a little doll.

MARY: I'm a good mother. I love her more than anything.

JONES: I know that, mary.

MARY: she's going to have good things. she's going to have so many good things.

JONES: it's hard, mary. I don't know how people make it. I don't know the secret.

here. it's not much of anything.

MARY: I don't want it.

JONES: just take it. I'd blow it on something stupid anyway.

MARY: wait.

you can stay, you know you can. it's ok. I'm just tired is all.

JONES: no, I got to go. maybe I'll come by tomorrow night or something.

(Jones goes away.)

MARY: fuck.

Scene 10

work. Jones feeds the machine. the Manager supervises.

MANAGER: watch it, watch it, watch what you're doing, you're going to jam the machine, slowly, you need to slow down, slow it down, slow and easy, one step at a time. watch. WATCH IT. YOU'RE GOING TO JAM THE MACHINE. you don't watch what you're doing, you don't think. you need to think. take the time, do it right. common sense. basic. time is tight, every minute every day every cent counts, it's how we do things here. figure it out. what's the matter with you? are you sick?

JONES: I'm fine.

MANAGER: you don't look it. you need to eat better. take a pill. exercise. what's wrong with you, jones? you look sick.

JONES: I'm freezing.

MANAGER: speak up.

JONES: it's freezing in here.

MANAGER: it's hot today. it's hot every day. we live in a desert. figure it out.

JONES: it's hot today, but I'm freezing.

MANAGER: in my apartment, I have a top of the line frigidaire. it makes ice. crushed or cubed. I make a lot of ice. at night, I tuck myself in with bags and bags of ice. that's the only way I can sleep. in the morning, the ice is melted and I have to be careful the bags don't leak or else the water gets everywhere and it's a big, disgusting mess. tell me, jones, tell me your thoughts on life.

JONES: I don't know.

MANAGER: tell me about the future? what are your plans?

JONES: I don't know.

MANAGER: that's a lot you don't know, jones. do you have kids?

JONES: yeah. a girl, a little girl.

MANAGER: is that right? and how do you expect to provide for your little girl?

JONES: I work.

MANAGER: it's not enough. what about your wife?

JONES: I don't have a wife. she's not my wife. I mean we're not married.

MANAGER: and that's ok with you?

JONES: I don't know.

MANAGER: if you don't mind, if you don't mind me saying—that's the thing with you people, you think you can screw around, make babies, keep making babies, and you think, you seem to think taxpayers like myself are going to bail you out and support you and yours forever—THAT JUST BURNS ME UP. do what you want. fuck who you want. get sick. die. I don't care. it's a free country. just don't you expect me to pay for it. WATCH THAT, WATCH IT. one at a time. what did I say?

JONES: I have to take a piss.

MANAGER: what was that?

JONES: I have to take a piss.

MANAGER: there's other ways of saying that. I need to take a break. I need to use the restroom. what's the matter with you? learn to speak the fucking language like a civilized individual. you don't get paid to relieve yourself. when you finish, take your break.

(the sound of a vast machine in motion.)

Scene 11

Jones goes outside and takes a giant piss. and the world turns bright yellow. the sun turns bright yellow. the sun is a yellow flower. it is the color of golden piss sprayed against the blank white sky. and it is ecstasy. whereupon Jones beholds a beautiful cholo standing on the street outside gaslamp liquor. and the cholo is naked from the waist up. and the skin on his back is brown like something you want to eat. chocolate. meat. he is a handsome young god, and the crowd moves up close to him, wet-eyed and hungry for something they do not know. they shove and push to get a better look, and see that on his beautiful brown back is the virgin mary

> *the virgin of guadaloupe*
> *the virgin of san juan de los lagos*
> *la milagrosa*
> *mother of god.*

she's carved into his nut brown flesh, her face frozen in a divine smile, her eyes half closed, her mouth forever shut, her hands fused together flesh fused in a stance of eternal rapture. she stands atop a mountain of flowers. the cholo turns and shifts his weight. the muscles of his back ripple beneath the skin. and as he does this, the flowers open up and shiver with divine delight. god's coming.

> *"oh dulce corazon de maria sed mi salvacion."*

Scene 12

Mary's apartment. Navy Man 1 and Mary.

MARY: I'm dreaming about men—
NAVY MAN 1: tell me—
MARY: I'm dreaming about men—
NAVY MAN 1: yeah and—
MARY: I'm dreaming about your arms and your chest and your back and your neck the back of your neck. I'm dreaming the way your muscles go and how they get all hard under the skin—
NAVY MAN 1: you like that—
MARY: yeah I like that—
NAVY MAN 1: you dream about it—
MARY: yeah I do.

NAVY MAN 1: tell me—

MARY: I'm dreaming of the way your fingers and the skin and the smell of your skin the way the skin is wet and how it tastes like metal and ocean water—

NAVY MAN 1: I see women all the time.

MARY: yeah.

NAVY MAN 1: and what they need.

MARY: yeah.

NAVY MAN 1: I know what it is they need.

MARY: is that so?

NAVY MAN 1: truly. it's like I'm psychic.

MARY: are you—

NAVY MAN 1: what?

MARY: are you my—

NAVY MAN 1: what?

MARY: are you my psychic friend?

NAVY MAN 1: what's so funny?

MARY: you. you are.

NAVY MAN 1: shut up. shut the fuck up.

MARY: I'm tired. it's late.

NAVY MAN 1: you're fine. you got a nice body. you know that, though, don't you?

you got guys coming up to you all the time telling you how hot you are, don't you? oh mary, don't you look at me like that. it doesn't work with me. I know what you are.

don't play with me.

MARY: let go—

NAVY MAN 1: I want to know—

MARY: let go of me—

NAVY MAN 1: I want to know what you want. I want you to say it to me.

MARY: nothing.

navy man 1: bullshit.

say it. say it out loud.

MARY: I don't want a fucking thing from you.

NAVY MAN 1: I think you want to. I think you want to disappear. I think you want somebody to make you. I think you want somebody to fuck you up. I think you want to be fucked up. I think that's how you get off. I think that's how you feel it.

MARY: I used to—I used to want—fuck it. it's stupid. it's the stupidest thing in the world.

Scene 13

Jones follows the freeway back home. a white sun. the cars are so loud they make the ground shake. the sound of a vast machine in motion.

JONES: it goes it goes it keeps going it goes to places I can't see I don't dream I don't sleep. space is cold space is black space is where I can get some sleep. the smell of gasoline gets in my hair on my hands on my face through my skin. it burns. inside my head, I hear the cars go by. they make the sound of giant ocean they make the air moving in my head they make it moving always moving. inside, the million eyes stare out at me, so tiny so fucking tiny in the sockets of their skulls. fuck. so much sky. the sky is white. cut open the sky, there is space. inside the sky is space. inside the sky is black. peel it open. see it bleed.

Scene 14

Mary's apartment. Mary's Girl and Jones.

JONES: where's your mom?

MARY'S GIRL: I don't know.

JONES: where did she go?

MARY'S GIRL: away.

JONES: where did she go?

MARY'S GIRL: my mom says it's time to sleep and then I close my eyes. what do you see when you close your eyes?

JONES: nothing. black.

MARY'S GIRL: when I close my eyes, I see red and purple and orange and yellow and blue. I see so many colors moving and sparkly like lights at night. it's pretty.

JONES: do you remember me? do you remember who I am?

MARY'S GIRL: are you going to tell me a story?

JONES: I don't know any stories, mary.

MARY'S GIRL: that's not my name. I can't tell you my name. I'm not supposed to. my mom says not to. it's a secret. what are you looking at?

JONES: nothing.

I have to go now.

MARY'S GIRL: don't go.
JONES: ssh. go back to sleep.
MARY'S GIRL: aren't you going to tell me a story?
JONES: what kind of story?
MARY'S GIRL: a bedtime story. a happy story.
JONES: I don't know a happy story. I don't know any.

(Jones goes.)

Scene 15

a bar. Lisa and Man. Jones watches.

MAN: can I, can I—
LISA: what?
MAN: I want to touch you.
LISA: oh yeah?
MAN: I want to put my hand on your thigh. I'll give you five bucks.
LISA: you must be kidding me. who the fuck do you think you are?
MAN: come on now, don't be, don't get mad. how about I buy you a drink? will you let me buy you a drink?
LISA: I'm not thirsty.
MAN: you're so pretty. you're a very pretty girl and I would like to buy you a drink. I would like to put my hand on your thigh. I'll give you ten bucks.
JONES: hey.
LISA: what? what are you doing here? what do you want?
JONES: was she in here?
LISA: who?
JONES: did you see her just now? did you see if it was her?
LISA: what the fuck are you talking about?
MAN: she's so pretty.
JONES: did you see her? did you see her face? I'm asking you a question.
MAN: she's a pretty pretty girl.
JONES: listen to me. I'm going to kill you. I'm going to rip your fucking head off. now I'm asking you a question. did you see her? answer me, you piece of shit.
MAN: yeah. yeah, I saw her. I saw her and I'll tell you what. she looked like she was having a good time. she looked like she was having a blast.

(Jones goes into the night. he hears the Man laugh until the laughing dies away.)

Scene 16

Mary's Girl plays house in the dark. her voice is like a broken machine. it goes so fast.

MARY'S GIRL: beautiful beautiful. you are so beautiful. mommy is beautiful. mommy is beautiful and pretty and good. and daddy is big and strong. they say, I love you. I love you. I love you, too. and we all live in a house. daddy and mommy and little baby. she's just a little tiny baby. and they are so happy in their house. this is the upstairs and this is the downstairs and this is the door where you go outside. and she goes to sleep after a while, and it's so quiet, and they're outside, where it's dark and you can't see anything, and she hears them say, good night, little baby. good night. sleep tight.

Scene 17

Mary's apartment. early morning. Jones and Mary.

JONES: mary—
MARY: don't.
JONES: can you feel my eyes?
MARY: no.
JONES: you can't feel them on your skin? on your back like the sun. you don't feel them burning? I'm superman. I can see through skin. I have x-ray eyes. I can see, I can see through everything. it's like I cut a little hole and put my eye right up to it and I was looking straight inside of you.
MARY: don't.
JONES: do you love me, mary?
MARY: yeah. yeah, I do.
JONES: I don't believe you.
MARY: I do love you. what do you want me to say?
JONES: how much?
MARY: I don't know.
JONES: how much do you love me, mary?

MARY: stop it.

JONES: I think you lie to me. I think you're always lying to me. I think you say things.

MARY: what do I say?

JONES: sometimes I'm looking at you, and it's like you were sick, it's like your body was rotting from the inside out, and I go to touch you, but your skin comes off in my hands, and I go to kiss you, but I see your lips are covered with sores.

MARY: I don't know what you want from me.

JONES: I know he was here.

MARY: he was here and he was there and you were there and you were here and I was here and there and there and here.

JONES: don't make fun of me.

MARY: people come and go. I don't keep track. I could give a fuck.

JONES: I saw him, mary.

MARY: oh yeah? what did you see, superman? I bet you see lots of things with your x-ray eyes. I bet you see all kinds of things. I'll tell you, though, it don't take x-ray eyes to see most things.

JONES: fuck you.

MARY: don't you hit me. don't you even try. if you touch me, I'll fucking kill you, I swear I will.

JONES: bitch.

MARY: call me a bitch. you don't even know me.

JONES: mary.

MARY: you don't even know me.

JONES: I'm sorry. mary.

MARY: you don't know what I have inside me. I don't give you that. I don't give anybody that.

JONES: mary—

MARY: get out of my place. fucking get out.

JONES: I didn't mean anything. I don't know what I'm saying. I don't know what I mean. I don't know anything anymore.

(Jones goes.)

Scene 18

Jones dances with the Virgin Mary. she is all long hair and through her hair all through her hair there are so many flowers, they fall over

everything they cover everything they bloom so many you can't count
them all. the Virgin is electric. her lips are electric. her hands burn.
Lisa tells the little girl the story.

LISA:
> once upon a time she
> into the ocean she
> she goes very far she keeps going she
> floats on her belly she floats far out so
> far she can't see the shore anymore
> she can't touch the bottom. she
> forgets. no sound.
> she opens her eyes and she sees blue
> water
> and she sees
> sting rays and blue fish
> and she sees
> tiger sharks and giant squid and huge
> man o war
> she sees coral red coral she sees
> a hundred million tiny fish like silver
> stars
> so many a whole entire world
> they shimmer and glow in the dark.
> she sees them. they swim through the
> pupils of her eyes.

(Jones falls. he is electrified. the Virgin Mary disappears.)

Scene 19

night. Jones hears all the sounds of night. they are so loud, they
crack his skull.
and then the Police slide out of the dark like they have been for-
ever there, invisible, waiting for a sign.

JONES:
> when I was
> when I was
> when I was
> when I was

POLICE 2: hold it—hold it right there

JONES: every thing, in my head

POLICE 1: don't

JONES: in my skull

POLICE 1: don't move—

JONES: I hear it

POLICE 1: don't you fucking move—

JONES: a whole world. I hear it and it's so loud, it's so loud it hurts.

POLICE 2: what is it with this guy—you want to get smart—you want to be a smartass—boy—I'll fuck you up

JONES:

when I was

when I was

when I was

POLICE 2: I will fuck you up

JONES: every thing every thing

POLICE 1: what's the matter with you

JONES: in my head. fuck.

POLICE 1: do you hear me—do you hear me talking to you—what the fuck's the matter with you—answer me

JONES: wait. stop.

Scene 20

a bar. music. Man and Woman sit drinking. Jones enters bleeding.
Woman sings a song.

MAN: shut up.

WOMAN: I want one dollar. give me a dollar.

MAN: go to hell.

WOMAN: oh now—why do you—why do you talk like that? shit. you shouldn't talk to me like that—

MAN: shut up.

WOMAN: a dollar is nothing. it's shit. come on. a fucking dollar. what's it to you—

MAN: I'm not going to say it again. you shut up or I'll fuck you up. do you understand me? shit. look at this. you're bothering this guy over here. see. he's looking at you like you're some kind of freak. you got to excuse her. you got to excuse her language.

she's drunk, you see. you're drunk. you stupid bitch. you're a goddamn drunk—you know that?

(Mary and the Navy Man enter the bar. they are all laughter and touching. Jones watches them. Mary and the Navy Man dance.)

JONES: mary. I can hear you breathing. I can hear your heart beating inside your body. I can hear the inside of you. it sounds like an ocean in my head, it sounds like a fucking ocean. I'm drowing, mary. my heart is exploding.

(Jones falls to the cold ground.)

MAN: jesus, look at this guy. this guy is drunk. he's had too much to drink. he can't control himself. he can't even stand up on his own two feet. what is he? what is he? what is a man? he eats. he drinks. he fucks. he shits. he dies. man is what he is and then he dies. god made it so. if I was a junkie, I would shoot up. if I was a pimp, I would pimp. if I was a killer, I would kill. if I was a drunk, I would drink. man is what he is and then he rots in the ground. this is how it is for us. the world is a shithole. all is folly. therefore, thus, in closing—friends—drink. drink up. and be happy, be happy in your hearts.

(Jones goes our into the night.)

Scene 21

in the darkness. outside the city. planes fly overhead.

JONES: I want to cut my hair. I want to cut it off.

I want to feel my head inside.

I want to pass through rooms and sky, and feel my head inside.

I want the bone, I want the shape of the bone and the feel of the air.

last night, I had a dream, I let my hair grow long. I let it grow so long, I could wrap it around my girl's ankles in a knot. that was a long time ago. I didn't feel a thing. I cut my hair myself. I used a mirror and a razor blade. I watched my hair fall down, I watched it fall down to the ground in soft, broken piles.

Scene 22

Mary's apartment. Mary's Girl is sleeping
Jones appears. she wakes up.

where's your mom?
MARY'S GIRL: I don't know.
JONES: where did she go? do you remember? did she say when she'd
be back? did she say anything? did she?
MARY'S GIRL: I had a dream just now.
JONES: what am I saying.
MARY'S GIRL: I had a dream. but I forget.
JONES: on and on and on and on—
MARY'S GIRL: on and on and on and on—
JONES: ssh. go back to sleep. it's late.
MARY'S GIRL: when I close my eyes, I see all colors. it's all kinds of
colors like the fourth of july.
JONES: ssh. time to sleep. time to go to sleep.

(Jones goes.)

Scene 23

through the air
through the voices of men and women
through the glass and laughing shouting
through the cars speeding by on infinite concrete freeways
through the helicopters overheard,
through empty lots and alleyways,
through canyons of brush and vine and wildflower,
through the shower of bright white light, raining over a thousand
    dogs. invisible, barking in the dark—
the sweet sweet sound of mexican music, metallic and crackling
it fills the crevices of night, it fills the passage of her ears, the folds
    and caverns of her brain, flowering in the blackness
this is what she hears before she falls asleep.

Scene 24

Mary's apartment. Mary and Navy Man. Navy Man holds a child's toy.

NAVY MAN: hey.

MARY: hey.

NAVY MAN: I called before. I guess you were out or something.
    what are you doing?

MARY: nothing.
    what do you want?

NAVY MAN: I don't know. I was thinking we could get together this
    weekend sometime. do something.

MARY: do what?

NAVY MAN: I don't know. see a movie or something.

MARY: whatever. yeah. yeah, that'd be OK.

NAVY MAN: here. I got this. I thought maybe your little girl, she'd get
    a kick out of it. it's just a little thing. I mean, it's nothing.

MARY: look, that's really nice of you, but she doesn't need anymore
    toys. she's already got plenty.

NAVY MAN: it's just a little thing.

MARY: no.

NAVY MAN: just take it.

MARY: I said, no. I don't want it.

NAVY MAN: it's nothing. it's just this stupid thing.

MARY: look, I'm sorry.

NAVY MAN: what are you sorry for? why are you sorry? fuck.

(Navy Man goes.)

Scene 25

*the boardwalk. music and voices. men and women appear and dis-
appear. the ocean is so blue it doesn't seem real. the sky stretches into
oblivion. stillness. the Navy Man and Jones.*

NAVY MAN: hey. hey you. what are you looking at? I'm talking to
    you, asshole.
    what the fuck are you looking at?

JONES: nothing.

NAVY MAN: what did you say?

JONES: fuck you.

NAVY MAN: what did you say? what did you say to me?

JONES: go fuck yourself.

NAVY MAN: what are you saying to me?

(Jones and the Navy Man fight. Jones falls.)

what are you saying to me, what are you saying to me, what are you trying to say to me, you little piece of shit.

JONES: nothing.

NAVY MAN: nothing. shit. nothing. you're funny, you know that? you're a fucking gas.

(the sound of music and voices. Jones goes away.)

Scene 26

the gun mart. Jones and the Gun Mart Employee.

EMPLOYEE: can I help you?

JONES: how much?

EMPLOYEE: which?

JONES: this one.

EMPLOYEE: that is a very nice piece. automatic. u.s. made. superior craftsmanship. feel. see. light. like a feather.

JONES: it's too much.

EMPLOYEE: can't beat that price, not anywhere, I promise you. trust me.

JONES: I don't have that kind of money to spend.

EMPLOYEE: fine.

JONES: how about that knife?

EMPLOYEE: which?

JONES: in back. there.

EMPLOYEE: this?

JONES: yeah.

EMPLOYEE: this knife, this is a beautiful knife. made in germany. stainless steel. eighteen inches. superior craftsmanship. cuts through anything. clean. feel. careful. comes with a lifetime guarantee. if you're not completely satisfied with your purchase, your money back. no questions asked.

JONES: how much?

EMPLOYEE: for you—cheap. a steal.

JONES: how much?
EMPLOYEE: $39.99 plus tax.
JONES: alright.

(Jones pays and goes.)

Scene 27

Mary's apartment. Mary reads to her Girl, but her Girl is half asleep, and doesn't hear the words.

MARY: "But I say, Walk by the Spirit, and do not fulfill the lust of the flesh. For the desires of the flesh are against the Spirit, and the desires of the Spirit are against the flesh; for these are opposed to each other, so that you cannot do the things that you would. But if you are led by the Spirit, you are not under the law. Now the works of the flesh are plain: fornication, impurity, anger, strife— and I warn you, as I warned you before, that they which do such things shall not inherit the kingdom of God. But the fruit of the Spirit is love, joy, peace, patience, kindness, goodness, gentleness, faith: against such there is no law. And those who belong to Christ have crucified the flesh with its affections and desires."

Scene 28

the sound of a plane tearing through the sky. Angel and Jones on the roof of a building. in the city.

JONES: look at that.
ANGEL: fuck. it's so close, you can smell it
    they spill gasoline right before they land. it's like a mist.
JONES: there was a plane that crashed over the city. this was a long time ago. it was all fire and pieces of metal. I saw pictures on the tv. I saw people's shoes scattered all over the sidewalk and the street. I'm tired. I don't sleep I can't sleep.
ANGEL: that's fucked up. you got to close your eyes and just relax. you got to let yourself fall asleep.
JONES: I can't stop moving everything is always moving. I think I'm dying.
ANGEL: you're not dying.

JONES: we all die.

ANGEL: man, you think too much. that'll fuck you up.

JONES: I can see the future, angel. I can see straight into the future.

ANGEL: oh yeah? so what's my future?

JONES: you're going to get old and then you're going to die.

ANGEL: fuck you.

JONES: I see the world burning. I see it going up in flames. it's like a star you see in the sky and then it's gone and all there is is space. when she died, she was skinny like a doll. she didn't look real. she looked like a white, plastic doll. I touched her skin. I put my face against her ribs. I listened for her heart. I thought, I am never going to be like that. I am never going to be that thing.

ANGEL: what the fuck are you talking about?

JONES: nothing. are you happy, angel?

ANGEL: yeah. yeah, I'm happy.

JONES: that's bullshit.

ANGEL: man, shut up. you don't know me. you got some fucked up ideas about things. like you know me. you don't see me every day. you don't know how I live my life so just shut the fuck up.

JONES: if I died

I have some tapes. and my clothes. that's all. I'd leave them to you. you could sell the tapes. trade them in.

ANGEL: they wouldn't be worth shit.

JONES: maybe you could keep them.

ANGEL: for what?

JONES: I don't know for what. fuck—

ANGEL: look, I'd keep them. if that's what you wanted. I'd keep them with my stuff. I'd take care of it if that's what you wanted.

JONES: fuck—

ANGEL: what? what is it?

JONES: it's so loud. all I want to do is make it stop.

(the sound of another plane overhead, and then all is blank sky.)

Scene 29

the beach. Mary and Lisa. music. Mary's Girl plays in the sand.

LISA: I hate that song.

MARY: it's sad.

LISA: that's not why.

MARY: I'm sick of sad songs.

LISA: you could sing.

MARY: no, I can't.

LISA: yeah, you could. you got a nice voice. I've heard you. you sing really good. somebody could discover you or something, and then you'd be rich and famous, and you'd live happily ever after.

MARY: that's not how it goes.

LISA: why not?

MARY: I don't know. because.

LISA: because why?

MARY: I don't know.

(Jones enters.)

you scared me. what's the matter? you look all fucked up and strange. what's going on? where've you been all this time?

JONES: I don't know. all over.

MARY: are you ok?

JONES: yeah.

MARY: you look like you've been in a fight. what's wrong? say something. say something. quick.

JONES: what do you want me to say?

MARY: it doesn't matter. it doesn't matter what.

JONES: there's nothing to say.

MARY: it could be anything. it could be the stupidest thing in the world.

JONES: I want to go now, mary.

MARY: go where?

JONES: I want to see the planes take off. I want to see them up close.

(Jones and Mary go.)

Scene 30

a field by the airport. the ocean is a slit. the sky is vast. the moon is rising. Mary and Jones.

MARY: look. you can see mexico from here. the mountains and all the lights. it's so beautiful. a thousand sparkling lights.

JONES: mary—

MARY: it's late.

JONES: wait—

MARY: it's late. I got to get back.

JONES: it's too far.

MARY: what?

JONES: it's too far already.

MARY: what are you talking about?

JONES: it's too far to go back now.

MARY: what's the matter with you?

JONES: how long has it been since you and me started all of this? how long have we been?

MARY: I don't know.

JONES: how long does it last? how long does love last? does it last till the end of all time, till the end of time, till everything goes away?

MARY: I don't know.

JONES: where are you going, mary?

MARY: I want to go now. I want to go home.

JONES: are you cold?

MARY: yes.

JONES: all of a sudden.

MARY: yes.

JONES: but how can that be—you're so hot, you're burning up, your lips are burning, your skin is burning, your face—

MARY: wait—

JONES: when I look at you, don't you see—

MARY: wait—

JONES: when I look at you, mary, I see how it is, I see all the world, I see it all light up and then the night, I see it become so cold like the desert in the night—

MARY: look at the sky. look at the moon. how red it is.

JONES: it's bleeding, mary. it's like it's bleeding.

MARY: I used to watch the planes take off, I used to try to imagine all that sky, all the stars and planets, all the galaxies I couldn't see—

JONES: the sky is dark, it is so dark—

MARY: I used to close my eyes—

JONES: mary—

MARY: I used to imagine these things—
     no. wait. stop.

(Jones stabs Mary again and again, and then he runs away.)

Scene 31

a bar. music. Lisa and a Man drinking.

MAN: it's nothing.

LISA: fuck you.

MAN: I'm telling you, it's no big thing.

LISA: fuck you.

MAN: ssh.

LISA: man, you are such an asshole.

MAN: I'm just teasing.

LISA: are you deaf? I asked you a fucking question. I'm looking for a
    fucking answer, asshole. what is it to you to tell me the truth?

MAN: lighten up. oh come on—

LISA: get the fuck away from me—

(enter Jones.)

    hey. where have you been?

JONES: hey.

LISA where were you just now?

JONES: I don't know. around.

LISA: it's hot. there's a wind in from the desert. you're shaking. are
    you sick or something?

JONES: I feel like I'm burning up. buy me a beer?

LISA: maybe.

JONES: look at you.

LISA: what?

JONES: your skin is burning. your face. your lips. feel.

LISA: fuck. what are you doing? what's wrong with you?

JONES: nothing.

LISA: what is that on your hands? it's all over your hands.

MAN: jesus, just go get the man his beer.

LISA: look at me—

JONES: it's nothing.

LISA: it's all over you.

MAN: will you leave the man alone. jesus—

LISA: shut up—what is it—what is that—

JONES: don't—

LISA: jesus. it's blood, what's going on? what happened to you?

JONES: nothing. nothing happened. what are you looking at? don't. don't look at me. who are you to look at me? don't look at me like that. fuck—

(Jones goes.)

Scene 32

Jones at the edge of the desert. night.

JONES: and once you're underneath, you can't tell top from bottom, you can't hear anything, and things that are above sound like they're coming from miles away, do not sound like anything you know, vibration, and sunlight is a memory, is something not real, and all around you is black so black you cannot see, and all you can hear is your heart and your blood pumping, and it is so loud, it fills your head, it is so loud in the inside the inside of you, and you would lose your mind listening to the sound inside you, how can there be so much inside a single body, how can that be.

　　so still. so quiet.
mary—
when I was a boy, when I was—
mary—
I sank into the dark, and I saw a forest of trees like I have never seen, tall, strange shapes, a forest of shadows, and I knew this is where the dead go—
mary—
I wanted to
I wanted to peel off my skin.
I wanted to peel off my skin, and fold it up, and put it in a box.
I wanted to disappear

(Jones goes into the night.)

Scene 33

Mary's Girl is talking afterward. and she is so far away, you can't see her. and her words break apart as everything breaks apart.

MARY'S GIRL:
    my mom's hands are big and white.
    my mom's hands are big and strong.
    and when she picks me up
    all the sound all the light
    my mom
    this was a hundred years ago
    and all around her are strangers. the ocean. the sky. all there is
    all there ever was. and she's looking out at me. and her eyes are
    half-closed like she's looking at the sun.

    END OF PLAY

NAOMI IIZUKA's plays include *Aloha Say the Pretty Girls*, *Polaroid Stories*, *Scheherazade* and *Tattoo Girl*. Iizuka's work has been produced at the Actors Theatre of Louisville, Frontera (Austin), Dallas Theater Center, Undermain (Dallas), Seattle's Annex, Printer's Devil (Seattle), Magic Theatre (San Francisco), Campo Santo/ Intersection for the Arts in San Francisco, SoHo Repertory Theatre (New York City), the Theatre at St. Clements (New York City) and San Diego's Sledgehammer Theatre. Her plays have been workshopped at Princeton's McCarter Theatre Center, Seattle's A Contemporary Theatre, the Bay Area Playwrights Festival, New York's En Garde Arts, Bottom's Dream in Los Angeles, Midwest PlayLabs, A.S.K. Theater Projects, New York Theatre Workshop and The Joseph Papp Public Theater/ New York Shakespeare Festival.

Her published work includes *Aloha Say the Pretty Girls* (Smith and Kraus), *Polaroid Stories* (Dramatic Publishing) and *Tattoo Girl* (included in *From the Other Side of the Century*, an anthology of twentieth-century playwriting, Sun and Moon Press).

Iizuka has received the Whiting Award, the PEN Center USA West Award for Drama, an NEA/TCG Theatre Residency Program for Playwrights grant, Princeton's Hodder Fellowship, a McKnight Advancement Grant and a Jerome Playwriting Fellowship.

She received her B.A. from Yale University and her M.F.A. from the University of California-San Diego.

RAGGED TIME

Oliver Mayer

THE WRITER SPEAKS
Oliver Mayer

I find myself shifting as a Latino artist. I based my initial artistic aspirations on Luis Valdez and *Zoot Suit*, which I saw as a teenager and which is still emblazoned in my brain. Chicano sensibility and history in this country seemed such a great subject, still nearly untouched by other writers and full of amazing stories. I made it a point to fill my plays with Latinos to examine past and contemporary U.S. history from a decidedly Chicano—if *pocho*—vista. Now as I approach my mid-career, I intend to keep writing for and about Latinos. But after having spent some quality time recently in Mexico City, my vision of "Latinidad" has undergone dramatic change. My sense of identity as a Chicano feels so different away from home, in a place where Latino is not the *other*, where Latino is not a hybrid culture, and if it is, then it's a deeply ingrained hybrid. Post-Mexico, I feel less need to prove my Latino bent. It's just there, to be seen or ignored. So now I think my ongoing theme may exist similarly, not punched up, but very much there if you want to look.

I feel hybrid. I call myself mixed-blood or half-breed, Mexican-American with the stress on the hyphen. I'm fascinated by the border, the wall itself. The way you think it can be permeated, the way it cannot. The false borders. I think border culture belongs to me in all its insanity and illicitness and noise. I feel privileged to live in Southern California now with this world changing all around me and the rest of us. I think this is the future. The border creeping northward and eastward. And I think it's about time.

I think my generation of writers is intensely political, and that the best of us try to be responsible in our portrayals of the truth as we see it. I don't mean political correctitude or uplifting storylines or characters. I mean clarity of vision. I mean our response to the country we're living in, the myriad inequities we're surviving. More and more, I try to be directly political in both dialogue and in what's being said or stated *underneath*. Of course I try to do this with a sense of humor—ideologue I am not. What's more I think my generation doesn't get sufficient credit for its political writing in plays. The British are supposed to be more developed politically, but I'm not so sure. I think we're ahead of our time. Theatre producers and newspaper critics are simply going to have to catch up with us. And by then we'll be writing something even newer.

Beauty for me is music first. Literally music. The way it hits your heart. What it says as much as how it sounds. I don't think there's near enough music in the contemporary theatre. On another level, beauty for me is surviving. Whether elegantly or not, I think those who struggle against the impossible—against slavery or homophobia or simply lack of self-esteem, those who fight and survive the big struggles—are in their way beautiful. In their way they become gods. And my art is to try to correctly deify them. Human gods are more beautiful.

Production History

In 1994, *Ragged Time* received a production at Royal Court Theatre in London, and also at Mark Taper Forum's New Work Festival. This printed version of *Ragged Time* was read at The Actors Studio West on January 26, 1999, in a production directed by the author. The cast was as follows:

IGNACIO	Vanessa Marquez
BLIND GARY	John Friedland, Jr.
BLIND ROSS	Abdul Salaam El Razzac
ABE	John Diehl
FREDA	Sabrina LeBeauf
THE YELLOW KID	Natsuko Ohama
THE SANCTIMONIOUS KID	Cynthia Mace
WHITE SHADOW	Howard Hesseman

Characters

IGNACIO, a Mexican boy, played by a woman.

BLIND GARY, a black street singer.

BLIND ROSS, a black street singer, his mentor.

ABE THE NEWSBOY, a Jewish pugilist.

FREDA, a mixed-blood lady of the evening.

THE YELLOW KID, a cartoon comic, played by a woman.

THE SANCTIMONIOUS KID, a cartoon comic, played by a woman.

WHITE SHADOW, a white gentleman with a Winchester rifle.

The parts of Ignacio, The Yellow Kid and The Sanctimonious Kid are "pants roles" to be played by women.

Time

1898.

Place

A Deep South of the Mind.

for William Saroyan and Luis Valdez,
spiritual godfathers

So here I am, so here I am
fake mammy to God's mistakes.
And that's the beauty part,
I mean, ain't that the beauty part.

—ROBERT HAYDEN
"Aunt Jemima of the Ocean Waves"

ACT 1

A crunched view of Charleston. Harbor in the distance, waves splashing against the Battery, antebellum villas just out of reach. Aromas of Catfish Row and the syncopations of the redlight district.

On a rickety porch, White Shadow sits in a rocker, rocking the time away. A Winchester rifle resting on his lap. A happy, smiling, twinkly faced, white man, yet with an air of blackness about him.

Blind Ross plays guitar.

WHITE SHADOW: Play me a song. In the old style.

ROSS:
Some folks call abolition
Try to mend the nigger condition
I say leave us babies alone.

WHITE SHADOW: Niggers will always have a home. *(Laughs)*

(Lights up as Ignacio plays ragtime on an upright piano. Freda frowns at him, standing in her red-lit doorway. Her face is heavily powdered. When she questions him, Ignacio does not respond with words. Rather, he plays on, and the music serves as a kind of surrogate voice.)

FREDA: This ain't gonna work. You can't stay here! I can't feature no kid. Why'dya have to come here? Why didn't your damn parents stay in Mexico 'stead of coming here? What'dya think, the streets was paved with gold? And why'dya have to end up at my door?

(Ignacio turns his soulful eyes upon her—the ragtime grows more languorous.)

Well you ain't mine! Just 'cause your parents gone and half killed each other and left you here alone don't make me responsible! What the hell good are ya? Lovechild of a couple dirty Messicans!

They're the ones cursed you with them damn Creole tunes. Play that stuff, people think I'm some kinda ragtime girl, some kinda two-bit boogie fuckstress! Can't ya play no white music?

(He plays on.)

Dontcha see? You're bad for business!
    (To herself) If this ain't whore luck I don't know what is.

(A spot on Abe out front. On the street, by the bay:)

ABE: Papers! Get yer papers!!! *(To us)* Buy a paper! Educate yer mind!

(No takers.)

Live a little. Knock yerself out. How you gonna know nothing if you don't read the papers?!! I love papers. Got yer front page! Got yer funny pages in the back. And in color on Sundays, thanks to Mister William Randolph Hearst. And in between— well ya got yer adverts there! A triple-decker sandwich for the mind! Even if you can't read, especially if you can't. 'Cause they're fulla pictures!!! What a product! It's a can't-miss!!!

(Scratching himself.)

So what's wrong with these Southern jigs? Up North they sell like hotcakes. Down here I can't sell a stack to save my life. Maybe I shouldn'ta got off the boat. Maybe I shoulda stood in bed.
    (To himself) Buck up, kid. If you die the day you was born, you die a fool. And if you live a hundred years you die a fool. So what's the difference?
    (To us) Buy a paper!!

FREDA *(To Ignacio)*: And *quit that nigger music*!!!

(Ignacio stops.)

Kids give me the uglies.

(From offstage, we hear guitar blues. Piedmont-style, with a heavy African rhythm. Blind Gary enters, singing.)

GARY:
    It was a time when I went blind
    It was a time when I went blind
    Was the darkest day I ever seen
    It was the time when I went blind.

(Sniffs the air.) Smell a town. Sure you right. Funky town. Try to pretty it up with sugar and spice, but it's funk all right. Down 'neath the petticoats.

(Strides) This is my town.

(He steps in a ditch and falls hard on his ass.)

ABE *(As Gary falls)*: Criminy. *(Helps him up)* Buy a paper, Jim.

GARY: What town is this?

ABE: I hate a daytime drunk. What you s'posed to do at night if you're drunk by day? Drink?

GARY: I wish I was drunk.

ABE: You punch-drunk?

GARY: I'm blind!

ABE: Blind? Ha! That's a good one.

GARY: Can't see a damn thing.

ABE: Where's yer boy?

GARY: Don't got one.

ABE: Whoever heard of a blind man without a boy?! You need a boy to lead ya!

GARY: To hell with boys. I'm a man.

ABE: A blind man.

GARY: It's a free country.

ABE: You said it. But even I know a blind man without a lead boy is up shit's creek without a paddle.

GARY *(Sniffs)*: It's Charleston, ain't it. Charleston sho nuff. Smell the funk.

(Abe sniffs cluelessly.)

Done reached Slavetown.

ABE: You say something, Winkie?

GARY: Glad to be home.

ABE: This is home? My condolences. We got real towns where I come from. I'm a Yank.

GARY *(Meaning the opposite)*: I'da never guessed.

ABE: Pride of New London, Connecticut. Home of the World's Greatest Newsboy.

GARY: "... boy"—

ABE: Sure.

(Gary snorts.)

What of it?

GARY: Jew?

ABE: Yeah.

GARY: What the hell's a Jew doing down here?

ABE: I'm trying to sell papers!

GARY: Some newsboy.

ABE: Some blind man. Kinda surly for a darkie.

GARY: Kinda stupid for a Hebe.

ABE: What'd you call me?

GARY: "Stupid"?

ABE: Why I oughta—

GARY: You wouldn't hit a blind man.

ABE: You wouldn't see it if I did.

(Backing away from Abe, Gary trips and falls hard.)

Ha! Walk just like an Irishman! Ain't ya got no cane or nothing?

GARY *(Spits)*: Kids took it.

ABE: Kids are like that. Boy, when I was a kid I did lots of fun stuff—

GARY: I hate kids.

ABE: Guess that's why you ain't got no lead boy. Up where I come from we got dogs to lead the purblind.

GARY: To hell with dogs.

ABE: Sure you don't wanna buy a paper? Just a joke.

(Gary pulls out a coin, takes a paper and stuffs it into his vest.)

I'm not sure if that's what Mister Hearst had in mind.

GARY: Cold coming on.

ABE: Where you sleep, side of the road?

GARY: I been known to sleep in a featherbed on scented pillows. But a ditch'll do me just fine long as it don't rain.

ABE: My boat put me off at the docks. I found me a good dosshouse down East Bay Street.

GARY: Say what?

ABE: Doss . . . Hotel de Gink—bit of a stinkeroo at first. I had to knock sense into the clerk 'cause he called me Yid. Ishkabibble, to be exact. But after I got through with him he gave me my own room and for free too. Better than a ditch any day. Wanna kip with me?

GARY: To hell with that. I'll be fine. Just show me which way the whores is.

ABE: The whores? Oh so that's how it is.

GARY: Point me in the general direction, I'll be fine once I catch the scent. *(Sniffs the air)*

ABE: I thought you blind street singers was s'posed to have the gospel in ya.

GARY: Who says I don't? Whores got souls. Whores and orphans and blind mens and all the folk what can't afford to hide who they really be. God loves 'em. He loves 'em to death. I'm just following God's will.

ABE: And looking for a scented pillow.

GARY: Ditch or featherbed, I'll get to Zion some way.

ABE: Zion? I think you mighta taken the wrong turn somewhere.

(Gary stumbles.)

You need eyes, a cane, something.

GARY: Believe you me, I'll get something.

You got any idea where the blackfolk hang out?

ABE: See that tree limb . . . ?

GARY: Aw, to hell with you.

ABE: You ever in New London, I'll show ya the sights.

GARY: You know about as much as a pig knows about napkins.

(Ignacio resumes the ragtime on the piano. The music wafts on the wind. Gary listens, smiles.)

FREDA *(Grumbling to Ignacio)*: You're getting on my last nerve . . .

GARY *(Suddenly walking confidently)*: I'm fine. Fine as wine.

ABE: Sure you can't see?

GARY: This is my town.

(Gary walks toward the music. Abe watches him go.)

ABE: I don't like the cut of his jib.

(Smells the air) Can't smell a durn thing. *(Closes his eyes)* Just think, kid. If you had to see through yer nose. But what if you had to sneeze?

(Opens eyes) Papers! Get yer papers from the World's Famous Newsboy!

(Abe walks off. Gary approaches Freda's red light, he listens to the music.)

GARY: Hands are small. Li'l gal? Nah. See how he's always rushing ahead of the tune? That's a boy sho nuff. And not just any little bastid. That kid was born to ply.

FREDA *(To Ignacio)*: I'm no mom, kid. Neither are any of the women 'round here. Especially the ones with kids. See, we're working women. Get me? Comprende?

IGNACIO *(Slight Mexican accent)*: I get you.

FREDA: Good! Now what do they call you? Ig-something?

IGNACIO: Ignacio.

FREDA: Yeah, Ignatz. Look. Kids is bad for business. So when I'm entertaining, it's out the door with you. There's a ditch out back. Okeydokey? Friends, right? Then let's shake on it.

(Ignacio stops playing to shake hands.)

GARY: Don't stop now!

FREDA: This'll work out fine.

(Ignacio starts to play again. Gary smiles.)

(Glowering) If I don't kill you first.

(Gary approaches, then bumps into something close by. Freda hears it.)

Damn! I got a date, kid. Shoo!

(Ignacio is slow to react. She grabs him by the scruff of the neck and shoves him out the door.)

Skiddoo!

(Ignacio bumps into Gary. Beat. The boy runs off. Freda applies powder to her face; calls out:)

Come hither!—

(She sees his blackness.)

Hmmph! You're a bold one.

GARY: Lovely perfume may I say.

FREDA: You may not.

GARY: Deelightful piana you ply.

FREDA: I don't play.

GARY: Then your son—

FREDA: Son? Ha!

GARY: My apologies. Your brother.

FREDA: That boy ain't none of mine.

GARY: You don't say?

FREDA: God no. Just some little bastid Messican boy.

GARY: Messicans is some fine musicianeers. Some deelightful practitioners of song. A taste sensation for the ears—

FREDA: A lotta words about a buncha nigger music.

    (Uncomfortable) Why you stare at me like that?

GARY: It's just you look good enough to eat.

FREDA: You wanna get your head broke?

GARY: Long as I can lay it on your pillow.

FREDA: You are a sexy old buck.

    (Looks around, no one watching) There's laws, you know. But it's been a slow day. Got money?

GARY: Right here in my pocket.

FREDA: Well come on in then . . . And hurry up.

(Gary stumbles on the threshold.)

    What's wrong with—Ugh!—You're blind!

GARY *(Grabbing her)*: Yeah, but that never stopped me none.

FREDA *(Pushing him out)*: I got my standards! Black and blind? What would people think?

GARY: Believe me, I'm quite developed in my other senses—

FREDA: Get off me, ya damn coon!

GARY: You sure are one uppity geechee tarbaby!

FREDA: Oh!!!

GARY: You better be fine and yellow 'cause that mouth of yours is mighty bad for business!

FREDA *(Checking her makeup)*: Sir. You are under a misconception!

GARY: Don't give me that, girl. I smelt you a quarter mile off. Don't be bashful, honey. It's a respectable trade for a brownskin gal—

FREDA: Am NOT!!

GARY: You mean—? You mean you ain't a whore?

FREDA: OH!!!!

GARY: Or you ain't bla— *(He stops)* Uh-oh. Done put my foot in it this time.

FREDA: How DARE you.

GARY *(Checking his nose)*: Never been wrong before.

FREDA *(Applying more powder)*: I've never been so insulted!

GARY: You oughta get out more.

FREDA: You could get strung up for less.

GARY: Well I am blind! . . .

FREDA: Guess you couldn't help yourself.

GARY: A thousand apologies, all lined up with Valentines.

FREDA: Well all right then, but watch it now.

(Ignacio sneaks back in to the piano.)

GARY: But seriously, just between us folks—Ain't ya got at least a smidgeon of the good stuff—?

FREDA: The what?

GARY: The brown betty? Hot fudge and raisins—?

(Freda growls.)

Okay, okay, I gotcha!—

FREDA: Not black!! You hear me?!!

(Ignacio begins to play.)

IGNATZ!! QUIT THAT JIG PIANO!!

(Ignacio stops.)

GARY: That boy is music to my ears.

FREDA: You're the only one. Nobody wants him. It's fallen on me to take care of him. I guess I don't got no choice.

GARY: You got all the choice in the world.

(Gary reaches for something inside his sock.)

FREDA: What do you think you're doing?

GARY: You're free, babe. This is America. You don't gotta do nothing you don't wanna do . . .

(He pulls out his surprisingly large billfold.)

FREDA: I said I won't take your business.

GARY: Not you. The boy.

FREDA: What do you want the boy for?

(She crosses herself.)

Don't tell me.

GARY: It will be my pleasure to take him off your hands.

FREDA: Pervert! Get away from here!

GARY: Boy got talent. I can give him life experience. Show him what music is all about. Can you do that?

FREDA: I don't even like music.

GARY: Then give him over.

FREDA: You one of them kind.

GARY: I could show what kinda man I am. But if'n you won't let me, then let's us do some business.

FREDA: I'm a Christian woman.

GARY: Sure you right! *(Pounding out the gospel:)*

Gimme that old time religion
Gimme that old time religion—

(Conspiratorial) Kid'll be solid gone. Outta your hair. Hard cash, babe.

FREDA *(Eyeing the billfold)*: How much?

GARY *(Counting them off)*: Squoze the nickel till the buffalo roared, and the eagle cried mercy.

FREDA: Someone like to roll you, blind man, carrying all that cash alone—

GARY: Not alone. Not no more.

(He places the roll of bills in her hand. She weighs the options.)

FREDA: Oh, Ignatz—?

(Ignacio comes forward. Freda pushes him Gary's way.)

Go on now. Go on with the nice man.

(Gary feels Ignacio like a piece of bread.)

GARY: I do believe I have been hoodwinked.

FREDA *(Counting cash)*: Now what are you going on about?

GARY: This boy ain't worth a tinker's damn! Never worked a day in his life! Shoulders like a bird! What kinda Messican is he?

IGNACIO *(To Freda)*: Mama!!—

GARY: Shut yer damn mouth! *(Finishes frisking him)* This kid ain't nothing!

FREDA: What about his musical gift?

GARY: To hell with that, I need a kid can lift a rucksack ten miles a day plus Sunday. Ain't ya got no other kids? Ain't there no other little tykes running around here? I'll trade ya, get 'em outta your hair right quick. You can have this one back.

FREDA: We made a deal.

GARY: This is bad business. What if I wanted my money back?

FREDA: I'd scream rape and the men of Charleston would string you up and set fire to your raggedy ass.

GARY *(Clears throat)*: Well, in that case, I'll take the boy.

(Gary throws his sack at Ignacio—it is heavy.)

(To Ignacio) Steady now! You drop that, your ass is grass!

FREDA: What if the mom comes back looking for him?

GARY: Tell her finders keepers.

(Gary pushes Ignacio ahead, then stops.)

One thing. This here boy—he's dark, ain't he?

FREDA: Excuse me?

GARY: Dark. Of skin. 'Cause Messicans is dark peoples, that's the way I remember anyways. And if he's gonna be my lead boy, well then he's gotta be dark. 'Cause we don't want no trouble.

(Freda knows what he means. Ignacio is light of skin, but Freda says nothing.)

FREDA: No trouble.

GARY: Then it's all right?

FREDA: It's made in the shade.

GARY: Then there's no trouble.

       (Cuffs Ignacio) Snap to it, you little so-an-so!

FREDA: It's Ignatz.

GARY: What kinda fool name is that? Ignatz ain't gonna win no favors.

FREDA: Look how much he's won already.

GARY *(To Ignacio)*: You so much as think of running and I'll skin you alive and roast the rest for Sunday dinner.

IGNACIO *(To Freda)*: MAMA!!—

GARY: I'm yer mama now.

(They exit together. Freda pockets the cash.)

FREDA: See how far you get beating on a white boy. Dirty mangy dog!

(Beat.)

Ah well. Kids ain't your style, gal. Hell, if you got a kid, then a husband can't be far behind . . .

(Abe reappears in the distance, hawking fruitlessly.)

ABE: Get yer papers! Don't nobody read the papers in this town?

(Shift to the rocking chair. The sound of guitar picking: Piedmont-style and syncopated. Ross plays masterfully.)

WHITE SHADOW *(Twinkly)*: Just like the old days.

(Blows the dust off his rifle barrel.)

ROSS: Just like 'em.

WHITE SHADOW: This new generation ain't worth shucks. They don't know their history. They just don't know where they come from. And they sure as heckfire don't know where they're headed!

(Darkness comes. Blindness. Gary's voice is on the wind—the voice of a mean god.)

GARY: Lemme tell ya about blind mens. Don't never try sneaking out on one. 'Cause we'll find ya. We' like bloodhounds, we'll sniff you out sho nuff. And don't never try to fight a blind man. We may not got eyes, but we gots some unnatural big hands, and when we gets to fighting, we let it all hang out. We ain't got so much to lose—I mean, hey, if you put an eye out, what's the diff? So if you value your life, say yassuh and do exactly as I say.

(Pause.)

And one thing. Don't ever . . . ever . . . even try to steal one of my songs.

(Lights rise on Ignacio and Gary. Gary has a hold of the boy's shoulder. They are out of sync. Gary cuffs him.)

Too fast!

(Beat, then cuffs him.)

Too slow! Move yer damn feet! Look where you going, you little wetshoes!

(Gary is about to cuff him again, but Ignacio anticipates the blow. Entangled, both fall to the ground.)

IGNACIO: Mama!

GARY: I'll mama you! I'll mom and pop you!!!

(Ignacio wriggles free and flees. He hides behind a tree.)

Think you can run back home? Where's that? Nobody wants you there. Miss Lady sold you for a song. You can't go back, boy. So what you gonna do? Go to the white man? Try talking Messican to the white man. See how far you get.

(Beat.)

I put my money down, boy. Done good business. I got my rights. I paid legal tender. I put my money down.

(Stalemate. Then Gary has an idea. He removes the newspaper from his vest and sets it down on the ground. He lies back.)

You'll come back. I got all the time in the world! Catch me some beauty sleep, forty winks do sound good!

(Gary sleeps, or seems to. Soon he's snoring loudly.
The wind rustles the paper. We see a flash of bright color— the funny pages. Sounds of manual typewriters, printing presses, freight train whistles. The tune "Yankee Doodle" plays fast. All this is coming a long way on the wind.
Ignacio approaches stealthily. Disembodied Voices egg the boy on.)

VOICES *(Cartoony)*: Have a look! Go on!

(Ignacio looks around but there's no one, nothing, just the paper. Ignacio hesitates. Then grabs the funny pages.
Immediate spot up on The Yellow Kid and The Sanctimo- nious Kid in primary colors as if from a cartoon. Their style is broad vaudeville.)

YELLOW: If it ain't The Sanctimonious Kid!
SANCTIMONIOUS: The Yellow Kid. Fancy meeting you!
IGNACIO: Who are you?
YELLOW: We just told ya! Can't ya read? We're what's funny in the funny pages!
SANCTIMONIOUS: Haven't you ever heard of yellow journalism? We got a special way of burrowing into young minds.
YELLOW: We was drawn that way.
SANCTIMONIOUS: But that's another story.
YELLOW: We'll take a shine to ya. Seeing as you're so bug ugly and pitiful.
SANCTIMONIOUS: Real Mama's boy.
YELLOW: Except he don't got a mom!
        (To Sanctimonious) So whatdya say?
SANCTIMONIOUS: I say we get started.

(He stares at Ignacio.)

So get started!

(Ignacio reads the funny pages as they act it out.)

YELLOW: How about a little burley-Q—?
SANCTIMONIOUS: A bit of Ethiopian minstrelsy—?
YELLOW: Coonshows?
SANCTIMONIOUS: "Yankee Doodle" played fast. We're out for fun and must have it. Let's get to work!
YELLOW: 'Cause when I woiks, I woiks haaaard!

(They fall into a series of pratfalls and somersaults, like a pair of old pros. They are just about to get into their gag when Gary grabs Ignacio's wrist.)

IGNACIO: Ow!
GARY: Kids and cartoons. Just like flypaper.

(Wrestles Ignacio down, sits on him.)

Don't even try running out on old Gary. Ain't no kid gonna get the better of him. Never again.

(Gary stuffs the newspaper back in his vest. He puts a kind of dog chain and collar on Ignacio. Yellow and Sanctimonious watch.)

SANCTIMONIOUS: I thought Lincoln freed the slaves.

(Lights out on them.
Ross spit-shines White Shadow's shoes.)

WHITE SHADOW: Lincoln got the credit, but what'd he really do? What's freedom anyways? Negro's in as bad a way as he ever was. And look what they done to our business! Pulled the heart right outta the South. You know and I know. Civil War got nothing to do with slavery. Who in their right mind would fight a damn war over a buncha black folk? North just wanna keep us down. *(Twinkly grin)* But we ain't dead yet. Is we?
ROSS: No, suh!

(Spot up on Abe. He is reading the funnies. The Yellow Kid and The Sanctimonious Kid reappear.)

ABE: Heh-heh. Funny.
SANCTIMONIOUS *(To Yellow, at Abe)*: What a rube.

(Freda appears at her doorway. Abe sees her. He drops the funny pages, arranges his hat and clothes the best he can. Yellow and Sanctimonious stare at his stack of newspapers.)

Golly!

YELLOW: Look it all dis paper!

SANCTIMONIOUS: We're in every one of them. We've made our mark up North. Now we're taking it on the road, thanks to gentlemen such as this 'un.

YELLOW: Whosipuss?

SANCTIMONIOUS: Whatchamaface.

YELLOW: You mean the boob? He don't look too reliable.

SANCTIMONIOUS: You'd be surprised. These immigrant types, they throw themselves into the selling of our wares.

(Abe sniffs the air in imitation of Gary. Freda appears at the doorway once again.)

ABE: Wow!

YELLOW: Cheese-it!

SANCTIMONIOUS: This is rich.

YELLOW *(Whistles at Freda)*: Whistlebait!

SANCTIMONIOUS: The newsie is a mamaphiliac.

YELLOW: Gee, his ma must be pretty old by now.

SANCTIMONIOUS: Pshaw, my foolish friend! A tit man!

YELLOW: Well she's sure got a pair!

ABE: *(To Freda)* Hiya Kid.

(Yellow and Sanctimonious watch as Abe tips his hat. Freda double-takes at his appearance. The Kids crack up.)

YELLOW: Duh!

SANCTIMONIOUS: The mater's rendered speechless.

YELLOW: He got a face that cud stop a clock.

FREDA *(To Abe)*: Are you all right?

ABE: Sure. This is how I look all the time. I been called the homeliest man in three states, but I can kid with the best of them. The name is Abe the Newsboy.

FREDA: Did somebody hit you?

ABE *(A bell rings, an idea comes)*: Somebody?!! I had a thousand fights. How many you had? You're looking at the Middleweight Champ of New England, known in betting circles as the Connecticut Tiger. Gee, I like to fight. Fighting is like wine to me. They are wrong who think a Jew won't fight. I'm what you Southerners call a "Fighting Po' Fool." —I get carried away with patriotism. I feel romantic towards women, I can see the old stars and stripes waving in fronta my eyes when I'm in ring center and the old fists are going sock, sock, sock—so yeah, I been hit a few times.

(Sniffs the air) May I compliment you on your lovely perfume.

FREDA: What is it about my perfume today?

ABE: You must draw men like flies.

FREDA: I guess that's a compliment.

ABE: Say, if I didn't know better I'd say you was a Jew too.

FREDA: This is not my day.

ABE: Jews are beautiful people. Lucky no. But beautiful. People say Jews is lucky, but if every Jew was lucky there wouldn't be poverty with the Jews. And no Russian pogroms—

FREDA: Russian what?

ABE: Dontcha read the papers? Here. (He gives her one. Yellow and Sanctimonious cackle) On the house. Don't say I never gave you nothing.

FREDA: A paper?

ABE: Greatest invention since outdoor turlets.

FREDA: Usually where I read 'em.

(They accidentally, on purpose, touch hands.)

YELLOW: Wouldn't it be funny if they—?

SANCTIMONIOUS: You mean, kisses at twilight?—

YELLOW: Moons in June and all that guff—

SANCTIMONIOUS: And nine months later—

YELLOW: Puke and screams!!

SANCTIMONIOUS: Pee-filled diapers!!

YELLOW: Poop in the bathtub!!

SANCTIMONIOUS: And no nooky to be had. Not with a kid around.

YELLOW: Wouldn't it be a laugh?

SANCTIMONIOUS: Would the kid look like him or her?

YELLOW: Would she sell it?

SANCTIMONIOUS: She did last time.

YELLOW: Selling kids is good business.

SANCTIMONIOUS: Especially if you're selling yourself and no one's buying!

YELLOW: Say, maybe I oughter sell you.

SANCTIMONIOUS: Long as it's paper money.

(They crack themselves up. Abe continues, he's on a roll.)

ABE: Some say a goat is lucky. Every U.S. navy ship's got one for a mascot. Once I put fifty bucks worth of papers on a navy ship, and when I went to get 'em a certain Mister William Goat had chewed 'em all up. Now the Jew boy and the goat couldn't both have been lucky on that job. Abie may have been good for the goat, but the goat wasn't so hot for Abe the Newsie. Not this boy.

FREDA: Why do you let them call ya "boy"?

ABE: What's wrong with boys?

FREDA: I prefer men. I steer clear of kids—you end up a slave to them.

ABE: Don't talk to me about slaves! I left that stuff behind in Russia. Hey, every time a Russian has a problem, he socks a Jew for luck. But here, no matter who you are you're free. You're in Americker! This place beats all!

SANCTIMONIOUS: This fellow's got more gags than we do.

FREDA: Took too many punches, Yank.

ABE: 'Cause I love my country? Go on. You smokes oughta learn—

FREDA *(Overlapping)*: Hey!—

ABE *(Overlapping)*: Something from us Jews. You darkies oughta—

FREDA: HEY!!—

ABE: be wiser than a buncha Bohunks and Russkies. Heck, you was born here, in good old Dixieland, under The Flag That Makes You Free!!

(Yellow and Sanctimonious melt in fits of laughter. Freda laughs bitterly.)

Go on and laugh.

YELLOW: Ikey!

SANCTIMONIOUS: Ikey Finkelstein!!

ABE: Go on. Show yer ignorance.

FREDA: "The Flag That Makes You Free"?

ABE: Go on. Give it the deep six.

FREDA: You're in the South, little man. You're in Charleston for chrissakes. The home of the whipping post, the auction block, the very mouth of the dark trade. See the fine buildings? The pretty harbor? Where do you think the money came from? You never heard of the cargo of Charleston Bay?

ABE: You never heard of the Cossacks?

FREDA: You're about thirty cents away from having a quarter, boy.

ABE: Guess I just don't understand you shines—

FREDA: And don't *never* say them words to me!

ABE: Which?

FREDA *(Applying powder)*: I am a lady, if you haven't noticed.

ABE: I noticed.

(Beat. They look each other over.)

FREDA: I've a good mind to go back inside.

ABE: No! Please, miss. I forget how to talk to a lady. Guess I got my bell rung one too many times at that.

FREDA: Is your face always like that?

ABE: They say when I'm asleep I look just like an angel.

(Yellow and Sanctimonious watch them disgustedly.)

YELLOW: Mushy stuff.

SANCTIMONIOUS: Let's get outta here!

(They see the papers. They wink at each other, and each takes an armful. Both grin.)

YELLOW: Sometimes you just gotta sell yerself!

(They disappear.)

FREDA: Jews. I know all about Jews. Worked a whorehouse next door to a synagogue. "Psst. Kumt Arien." Chains of whores. If you wanted one, the fancy dan would say sure, dollar for a colored, dollar fifty for a white girl. But a Jewess was a bargain, only a dollar twenty-five. *(Beat)* I knew a Jewess once, with a big belly. Fella would come, she'd ask, "You wanna marry? I marry you. I make money." The dan would come in and slug her in the mouth. "When he comes to fuck you, you fuck him. Don't tell no stories about marrying, you sonofabitch, you lousy whore, you." But she never stopped asking.

ABE: Guess she wasn't too lucky neither.

FREDA: Guess it's tough all over.

(She holds his hand) Didn't mean to bring ya down, Yankee-Doodle. Yankee-Doodle doo.

(They are about to kiss.)

ABE: Hey, you wanna paper?

(She shows him the one he already gave her. Then Abe notices that his stack has been pilfered.)

Well I'll be rogered!

FREDA *(Takes his hand)*: Kumt Arien, tiger.

(She takes him inside. Lights up on White Shadow and Blind Ross.)

ROSS:
Nigger's hair am very short
White folks hair am longer
White folks dey smell very strong
Niggers dey smell stronger.

WHITE SHADOW: Now dance.

(White Shadow sits back and sips his mint julep.
Blind Ross does a shuck an' jive—part softshoe, part minstrel show, complete with waving arms and shit-eating grin. At the finale, Ross sticks out his hand for a coin. White Shadow, chuckling, drops a dime into his palm.)

Now that's entertainment. I like the way you do business. Don't change a thing now. *(Pats his head)* You my boy.

(Winchester over his shoulder, White Shadow ambles off. All that's heard is the empty rocking chair, rocking in the wind.)

ROSS *(Flips him off)*: Dumbass whitetrash piece of cow doo-doo. You sure the fuck ain't my boy.

(Ross bites on the dime.)

Gots one song for the white folk to see, but the real song belongs to me.

(As he slings his guitar over his shoulder and makes his own blind way off into the shadows, the lights come up on Gary and dog-collared Ignacio.)

GARY: Try to give Gary the bum steer. But this fella don't flummox easy. *(Pulls the chain)* Let's go to work.

(They walk into town.)

We need provender. Thanks to you I'm clean broke. Time to earn your keep.

(It starts to rain.)

Well ain't this a blivit. Five pounds of shit in a three pound bag. Damn, I hate the rain.

IGNACIO: It's just the sky is crying.

GARY: What are you, a poet too? Up shits creek with a little Messican oarsman.

IGNACIO: Whoresman?

GARY: Naw, that's me.

(They reach a busy street corner. Gary pulls the chain. They stand together. Gary gives Ignacio a tin cup.)

Now look pitiful.

(Ignacio holds the cup out while Gary plays pitifully.)

Mother and father both gone
Mother and father both gone
Ain't nobody's darling
Nobody don't care for me . . .

(Hissing) I said pitiful!!! *(Resumes:)*

What am I gonna do?

(Clink: a single coin jangles in the cup.)

IGNACIO: Gracias.

(Gary kicks him.)

GARY: Much obliged.

IGNACIO: Moch obliged.

GARY *(Retrieving the coin)*: One penny. We'll go hungry for sure. *(To the boy)* Ain't there nothing you can do? Little shuck and jive? Little harmony? *(Snorts)* 'Course not! Now hold that damn cup out there and look pitiful!

(Ignacio tries.)

That ain't it!
    (Gary grabs Ignacio's face and makes a mask out of it)
There. Don't move.

(Gary starts to play. A lot more lively) We gotta make something happen here. *(Sings:)*

Oh my soul is a witness for my lord
My soul is a witness for my lord
What's that rumbling unner the ground
Must be the devil turning around
What's that rumbling in the sky
Must be Jehovah passing by
Down came the chariot with the wheels of fire,
Took ole Elijah higher and higher
Now Elijah was a witness . . .

(Ignacio starts to sing. It just pours out.)

IGNACIO:
    For my Lord.
GARY *(Stunned)*:
    Elijah was a witness
IGNACIO:
    For my Lord.
GARY:
    Elijah was a witness
IGNACIO:
    For my Lord.
GARY:
    Yes Elijah was a witness
IGNACIO:
    For my Lord.

*(Ignacio begins to dance, a rather delightful innocent shuck and
jive.)*

GARY:
    Now Daniel was a Hebrew child
    Went to pray with God for a while
    King at once saw Daniel descend
    Cast him into the lion's den.
IGNACIO *(Stopping on a dime)*:
    The lord sent an angel
    The lion for to keep
    And Daniel lay down and went to sleep.

(Long pause.)

GARY:

Daniel was a witness

IGNACIO:

For my Lord.

GARY:

Yes Daniel was a witness

IGNACIO:

For my Lord.

GARY:

Now Daniel was a witness

IGNACIO:

For my Lord.

GARY:

Yes Daniel was a witness

IGNACIO:

For my Lord.

GARY:

Now who'll be a witness

IGNACIO:

For my Lord.

GARY:

Who'll be a witness

IGNACIO:

For my Lord.

GARY:

who'll be a witness

IGNACIO:

For my Lord.

GARY *(Climaxing)*:

Who will be a witness

IGNACIO *(Outclimaxing him)*:

For my Lord.

(Coins pour in. The sound of a shower of silver.)

Much obliged! Much obliged!

GARY: Hoo baby! The eagle shits today! Where the hell did that come from? Don't answer, sing another quick. We got 'em on the run! Coupla more like that, we'll be on scented pillows in no time flat. Where'd you learn your stuff? Sedalia? New Orleans? New York City? You grow up with a minstrel show? Rufus, Rastus, Juba, Uncle Jasper, Oyster Man? —One of them coons musta taught you how to shuck and jive, buck and wing—you got the touch, boy!

(The more Gary talks, the sadder Ignacio grows.)

I got new eyes for ya, kid. We might just have us a road act. Catch us a train, we'll be in Pittsboigh-Zinnzinati. They go for kid acts up there! Somebody musta taught you how to pull the heartstrings but good!!!

(Ignacio has tears in his eyes.)

You know "Rock of Ages"?

(No response.)

"Get on Board Li'l Chillun"?

(No response.)

"Ezekiel Saw de Wheel"? "Joshua Fit de Battle"? Boyo, you blowing our chances here . . . *(Plays:)*

Joshua fit de battle ob Jericho
oh yeah, oh . . .

(Gary waits for Ignacio to chime in. Nothing.)

That's just fine! Hold out on me. Think you some kind of artiste? Too good for the shuck and jive?
  (Grabs him) Well listen. T'aint art. It's business. You give the bucra what they want. You know these songs. Anybody darker than a suntan knows these songs. So don't be holding out on me! *(Takes the cup back)* You ain't gonna get my goat. I done fine without you. I don't need you.

(Ignacio cries.)

And quit sniveling!!

*(They sit in the rain, looking pitiful.
   On the wind, Ignacio hears his ragtime. He stands.)*

IGNACIO: I miss . . .

GARY: Who? Your mama?

IGNACIO *(Plays the air)*: I miss . . . The piano.

GARY: That's what's wrong with pianos. Can't cart them out in the rain. That's why God made these babies. *(Strokes his guitar)*

IGNACIO: But I don't play guitar.

GARY: Well maybe you gotta learn to play piano on the guitar.

(Ignacio stops crying. The music wafts away. We hear only the sound of rain.)

Goddamn this rain! Damn newspaper sticks to ya!

(Gary violently pulls the newspaper from his vest, throws it onto the street. He falls into a silent funk.

Ignacio stares at the funny pages. Waiting for them to come to life. Finally he picks them up. As he reads:)

YELLOW: Hook, line and sinker!

SANCTIMONIOUS: Let's break the kid in easy.

YELLOW: Or just break him.

("Yankee Doodle" plays fast. A cartoon backdrop appears, a fence with a hole in it and a sign that says: BEWARE OF EVERY-THING, ESPECIALLY THE DOG. *Like two old vaudevillians, Yellow and Sanctimonious bow.)*

(Taking center stage) THE YELLOW KID LOSES SOME OF HIS YEL-LOW!

(Runs to fence) Here comes that other kid. I'll just hide. *(Stands at the hole)* Boy, he'll be surprised to see me standing here.

(The Sanctimonious Kid approaches. Then something pulls Yellow from behind. His face contorts. Sanctimonious laughs.)

(Responding to the tug) Somebody has took unfair adwantage of me! *(Another tug)* I'm behind in my rent or vice versa!

(Sanctimonious helps pull him away from the fence. A dog—Tige, who looks suspiciously like Abe—has the backside of Yellow's smock in his jaws.)

TIGE: Yow!

YELLOW: Hully gee.

SANCTIMONIOUS: Good dog, Tige.

TIGE: Arf!

(Yellow turns his back, exposing his torn backside to us. "Yankee Doodle" and a laugh track are heard as Yellow and Sanctimonious bow.
But Ignacio does not laugh.)

SANCTIMONIOUS: Hmmph!
YELLOW: How come he don't like the funnies?
SANCTIMONIOUS: How should I know?!!

(Yellow and Sanctimonious frown down at Ignacio.)

YELLOW: No respect for art. Whatdya want? The Mona Lisa?
SANCTIMONIOUS: Maybe it's you.
YELLOW: ME?!!
SANCTIMONIOUS: Maybe his tastes are a little more . . . how shall I say . . . sophisticated?
YELLOW *(Turning up his nose)*: You mean soup-an-fishticated?
SANCTIMONIOUS: Swellegant!
YELLOW: So the spic is a swell! Rat bastid.

(Ignacio keeps reading. More "Yankee Doodle" and vaudeville.)

SANCTIMONIOUS: I'm on!
YELLOW: Break a leg! for starters . . .
SANCTIMONIOUS: THE SANCTIMONIOUS KID JUST PRACTICES ON HIS VIOLIN!

(Sanctimonious produces a violin and saws upon it. Cats shriek and smoke emits from the prop. Meanwhile, Yellow hangs up a sign which says: MUSIC TAUGHT BY THE FOOT, YARD OR MILE. Then Tige appears.)

TIGE: Yow-Yow.
SANCTIMONIOUS: Tige, I've an idea to get rich quick, but you must help me.
TIGE: I'm with you, buster.

(Sanctimonious and Tige put on dark glasses. Sanctimonious resumes playing while Tige holds out a sign which says: WE ARE BLIND. They ape Gary and Ignacio. Coins pour in.)

SANCTIMONIOUS AND TIGE: Much obliged! Much obliged!

(Then a cop whistle.)

YELLOW: Cheese it, the cops!

(Mad scatter.)

SANCTIMONIOUS *(Pointing at Tige)*: Run! This dog is mad!!

(Tige froths at the mouth. Backdrop flies off. Tige and Sancti-monious come together to count the change.)

Resolved! That there is money in music and with money one can be kind and generous and good! Here, boy! *(Gives Tige his cut)*
TIGE: Thanks, kid.
SANCTIMONIOUS: Blindness pays in aces!
YELLOW: Aw feed it to the fish!

(Again "Yankee Doodle" along with laugh track and bows. Ignacio is stone faced.)

SANCTIMONIOUS: Gee. Nary a titter.
YELLOW: Tough nut to crack. *(Inspects Ignacio)* Kid thinks he's some pumpkins.

(Ignacio is not even looking at them. He stares at Blind Gary, who stares directly into the face of nothingness.
Darkness. Abe and Freda in bed together.)

ABE *(Awakens from a dream)*: Mommychen hilf mier!
FREDA: Nummdich zusammen.
ABE: Where the heck am I?
FREDA: How soon they forget.
ABE *(Flexes muscles)*: I'm a new man.
FREDA: I'm the same woman.
ABE: I dreamt I was in my mama's arms. We was on a boat, kinda like the one brought us to Ellis Island. But youse a lot darker than Mom. Prettier too—sorry Ma!—mit hips. That old boat nearly sank, right there off Manhattan. There we were, come halfway 'cross the world with the Cossacks giving chase, and now at the very mouth of Lady Liberty, the freight goes and sinks on us! *(Puts his hand on his heart)* God Bless the U.S. navy. Brought us into port. Otherwise we'da been goners for sure. That's when I figured out, this is a pretty swell country.
FREDA: I see the navy a little different.
ABE *(Oblivious)*: That's why I'm heading down to Cuba.
FREDA: You going to war?

ABE: Sure, seeing as it's all about liberty and freedom and such. We're gonna liberate them Cubans from the shackles of Spanish slavery. *(Abe rises. He's wearing a red union suit)* We gotta set an example for our kids! Show 'em what's right and what's wrong. So if the papers say go, then I'm going! The papers gave me my education. My kid's gonna learn the same way.

FREDA: Your kid?

ABE: When I get one. I love kids.

FREDA: They don't give you the uglies?

ABE: No more than usual. Kids are swell! *(Off her reaction)* Whatsa matta, babe?

FREDA: Just wondering why you're talking about *kids*! Kinda funny if you ask me.

ABE: It is kinda funny at that. You'd think we was getting married or something! *(Laughs uneasily)* You'd think.

FREDA: That's a laugh.

ABE: Yeah, a real hoot.

(*Watches her dress*) When I woke up and saw ya, I swear, I thought I was in heaven. You was Faith, Hope and Charity all rolled up in one hot little package!

FREDA: You got the charity part right.

ABE: Checked my wallet, did ya? You don't know where I keep my secret riches—

FREDA *(Holds his cash)*: You mean this?

(He snatches it back.)

You got about enough to buy a cup of coffee.

ABE: Times is tough.

FREDA: I thought you Yanks was supposed to be rich. Now I feel like offering you a loan. But how about I let you have a free one instead.

ABE: I don't accept charity.

FREDA: Me neither.

(Now Abe is ticked off. Freda plays with his ear.)

I prefer handsome men, but with you I'll make an exception. If you play your cards right.

ABE: I don't like cards. I like fighting.

FREDA: I swear I don't know what I see in ya.

ABE: It's the muscles. Gals go for 'em.

FREDA *(Plays with his ears)*: Nope. It's the ears.

ABE: But they're two cauliflowers!

FREDA: They do look like flowers, kinda.

(They make out a little. Then he looks her in the eyes.)

ABE: Look, I been around the block, but I'm confused here. Help me out. You took to me like a Jewess, but you looks like a Negress. What does that make you, some kinda Mulatress?

FREDA: Babe, down these parts there's a lotta mud in the water. But you oughtn't to say them things. That kinda talk can hurt business.

ABE: Whose business?

FREDA: MY business! Don't you understand nothing? We got a song down here. *(Sings:)*

I went to Charleston
Never been there before
White folk sleep on feather bed
Nigger on the floor . . .

(Shrugs) I prefer beds. I'm the kinda gal who wants to go top dollar. So I put my best foot forward.

ABE: What foot?

FREDA: Being black gets awful inconvenient. So I accentuate the positive, get me?

ABE: Ta hell with color. I say give it up. One woman's the same as another.

FREDA: But—

ABE: You know one, you know 'em all. Give it up.

FREDA *(Angering fast)*: Who do you think you're talking to?

ABE: I'm telling you something. I meet all kinds in my business.

FREDA: So do I.

ABE: What you get all outta joint about? I never saw you before and you never saw me before.

FREDA: I never saw you before and I never want to see you again!

(She storms out. He likes her spunk.)

ABE *(Shouting after her)*: I don't give a hoot what color you are!
(To himself) What a woman.

(Abe gets up, throws on his clothes.)

I'll look for ya later!

FREDA *(From offstage)*: Fat chance!!

ABE *(Out the door)*: I'm in love!

(*Abe walks onto the street, still tucking in his shirt. He sees Gary slumped over like a dead man.*)

Hey Winkie!

GARY: What you looking at, Bucra?

ABE: Guess you didn't find your scented pillows, after all.

GARY *(Sniffs the air)*: Guess you did.

ABE: I got lucky, I sure did.

(*Abe sees Ignacio. Winks at him. Tucks him under the chin.*)

Guess you did too! Pretty little gal you got there . . . Yessirree . . . Hey, wait a—this is—it's a boy!!! I thought you was a regular guy, not one of them Greek types!

GARY: Don't worry, News dummy. He's my new lead boy.
   (Cuffs Ignacio for show) Mind yerself.

ABE *(To Ignacio)*: Ow! You don't gotta take that!

GARY: Yes he do.

ABE: What are you? Some kinda cossack? One of them black Russians?

GARY: I'm always rushing one way or the other. But simmer down.
   Kid's legal. I don't play no bad business. This here's my son.

ABE: Your son?!! *(Breaks out laughing)*

GARY: What?!!

ABE: Don't you know? This child is *white*! He is a member of the
   white race, once you dust him off a little.

GARY: But the kid's a Messican!!—

ABE: A Greaser? He's toasted awful light if you know what I mean.

GARY: But Messicans is dark! And I bought me a Messican!

ABE: You been sold a bill of goods.

GARY *(Faltering)*: Bad business. How white is he?

(*Abe rubs Ignacio's cheek, smudges it pink.*)

ABE: Not near dark enough for you.

(*Gary sinks back, stunned. Abe pokes Ignacio playfully.*)

Lemme see yer hands, kid. Good knuckles. Real good knuckles.
Here, make a fist. Not bad. Hey Smokey. This kid has a future.
You ever think of fighting, kid?

GARY: She said Messican . . .

ABE: Don't take it so hard. Just looks kinda funny. White kid leading a smoke.

GARY: Backwoods Bucra would skin me alive, once they finished laughing.

(Gary approaches Ignacio, without malice) Well kid, Ignatz, whatever the hell. I guess this is it. See, I thought we was the unbleached Americans. I thought deep down we was the same. So that, bad as I was, you'd see I was still better than the white man. But now I see. You can do better. Than me. So I guess it's me that owes you now. *(Gary shakes Ignacio's hand)* Can't figure it out. You got the music like I do. You got the touch, like I did. That rag of yours, white folk just don't ply it quite the same, quite so sad. Just don't smell the same, you know? *(Sniffs the air)* Damned if you still don't fool me.

ABE: You smell color?

GARY: We all stink.

(To Ignacio) I gotta give you up, kid. Coulda taught you things, not the shuck an' jive, but the stuff from the other side, from our people over there. *(Gestures beyond the bay)* Our father's fathers. But I gotta let you go.

(Ignacio kneels down in the mud.)

What you doing? What you up to?

(Ignacio puts mud on his face.)

ABE: Hey! Whatdya know? The kid he's browning himself right up!!

GARY: What?

ABE: He's putting on the blackface for ya! Well if that don't beat it!

GARY: Jesus, kid. You know what you're doing?

(Ignacio stands, nods.)

IGNACIO: I'm playing the piano . . . on the guitar.

(Gary embraces him.)

ABE: Why you wanna go with him? Hell, if you go with him, why not go with me?

(Beat. The possibility of the thought hits them all.)

Yeah! Why not? I can teach ya all kinds of stuff! How to box! And fold papers! I'll take ya to Cuba with me!

GARY: Hey wait a—
ABE: Go with him, go with me! Shake hands with Abe the Newsboy!
Hero of a Thousand Fights! Whatdya say?—
GARY: Now looka here—

(Abe shoves him aside.)

ABE: I'm no boob and I'm not about to bamboozle you neither. The
papers, they could be your future—

(Gary shoves his way back to Ignacio.)

GARY: Let's get outta here, boy.
ABE: And boxing! I can teach ya how to swat, how to come to
scratch! How to hit and not get hit!—
GARY: Hit? You been mashiated!
ABE: Why you say that?
GARY: The wheeze of your busted nose, rattle of your Adam's apple.
ABE: I hadda thousand fights, how many you had? I fought bears, I
fought a kangaroo. Hell, I even fought a Porta Rican!

(Gary grabs Ignacio by the arm.)

GARY: Let's go!

(Abe grabs Ignacio by the other arm.)

ABE: Offer stands, kid.

*(It seems they might tear the boy in half. Ignacio, saves himself
by slipping out of his coat. Gary and Abe lose their balance and
fall on their asses.*
*Ignacio looks from one to the other. Then he picks Gary up.
They exit fast, nearly running into White Shadow, Winchester
under his arm. Gary, smelling him, sensing the rifle, backs off fast.)*

GARY: Excuse me, Mister White Man, suh!

*(Gary pulls Ignacio off by the leash. White Shadow watches
them go, unsmiling. Then Ignacio runs back, dragging the leash
behind him, and picks up the funny pages. He exits even faster.
Abe scratches himself. He watches Ignacio go.)*

ABE: Aw what the hey. What's a kid if you ain't got a wife? Sheez.

(White Shadow takes a paper from the stack.)

WHITE SHADOW *(Not very twinkly)*: WAR WITH CUBA? Niggers down
there getting outta line.

(White Shadow gives Abe a coin.)

Niggers getting outta line here too. Since this *freedom business,*
some folks don't know their place no more. Piece of free advice:
watch who you go consorting with. *(Winks)* The war ain't in
Cuba, my friend. The real war is right here. Down home.

(White Shadow tips his hat, walks on.)

ABE: Huh? *(Examines the coin)* You just sold yer first paper in
Charleston, kid! First piece in silver in two days.

(Beat.)

How come it feels so cold?

*(He shivers. As he pockets the coin, the lights shift—out of
town, a country road. Train tracks, the sea close by. Hunter's
moon on the rise. Gary and Ignacio walk. Ignacio holds the
papers in his hand.)*

GARY: Whatchyu doing? Reading them funny papers? How come
you ain't laughing?
IGNACIO: 'Cause they're not funny.
GARY: That kinda stuff never made me laugh neither.

(Beat.)

Can you read? What the front page say?
IGNACIO *(Reads headlines)*: WAR WITH CUBA.
GARY: Hrmph. What else it say?
IGNACIO: AMERICA DEFENDS HONOR OF RAVISHED CUBAN WOMAN-
HOOD.
GARY: That's a laugh.
IGNACIO: NAVY STOPS IN CHARLESTON HARBOR—NEXT STOP HAVANA.
GARY: Hope they take the Newsbozo with 'em. Ain't ya got no other
news?
IGNACIO: SEA SERPENT SWALLOWS BATHER IN EAST RIVER.
GARY: Now that's more like it!
IGNACIO: SPARSELY CLAD BEAUTIES FROM POLYNESIA.
GARY: Read on.

IGNACIO: "They have silks and a theatre and are worldly and sump-
tuous with the wicked walking on every side."
GARY: Sounds like Charleston.

(Takes the paper away from Ignacio. Tucks it in his vest.)

Lemme tell ya something, boy. This is a damn rag. And I don't
mean no ragtime. Oh it's fun. But it don't sing and it don't ply.
(He starts to play and sing) Ain't no paper can do dat.
IGNACIO: Can I? *(Offers to take Gary's guitar. Gary slaps his hand
away)*
GARY: Think I'm stupid? Try to steal my songs. Try to rob me blind.
IGNACIO: You blind for real?
GARY : Unfortunately, yeah. Brick to the side of the head. Thought it
was the worst thing they could do. Thought to break me, take
my independence, my roving eye. But it take more than pain to
stop this dark horse. Hell with them!
IGNACIO: Who?
GARY *(Spits)*: Kids! Since then I see everybody the way they looked as
kids.
(Suddenly lashes out) Go on! Leave me be!

(Ignacio gives Gary distance.
He hears the sound of distant waves, looks up at the moon,
hums his ragtime.
Then Gary sniffs the air.)

Well I'll be goddamned . . .

(Enter Blind Ross, sniffing. Gary and Ross face off like two big
mangy dogs.)

ROSS: Blind Gary.
GARY: Blind Ross.

(Each spits.)

Nice to see ya.
ROSS: Nice to be seen. Long time.
GARY: Not near long enough.

(Then Ross sniffs the air. In the direction of Ignacio.)

ROSS *(To Ignacio)*: Son?
GARY *(A hiss)*: Watch yerself!

(Ross offers the boy his guitar.)

ROSS: Hold this fer me, will ya?

(Ignacio takes his guitar. It is the first time he's ever held one—he holds it like a lifeline.)

I'm an old man, son. When I catch my breath, we'll share some songs. What's mine is yours. 'Course, knowing Gary, you prob'ly know all my songs by now, seeing as he done pilfered alla mine.
  (He sits down like he's home) Gonna be a cold night. What say we make us a fire? Just like old times, Gary. Like when you was my lead boy.

(Gary glowers. Ignacio strums, like a miracle he picks out the opening notes to his ragtime on the guitar.)

Well looka here! This boy's got the touch! So whatcha gonna ply?

ACT 2

In darkness.

GARY: See? Dark, ain't it. Maybe after a while you might start to see things, or think you do. A flash here. Streak of blood there. Maybe. Now try moving. Kinda clumsy, huh? Gets a little better over time, but you still bound to end up bassackwards and obsocky and basically on your ass.

(Beat.)

Just think. Always this. Always wondering about the next step. Unless. Unless you find a way to see. Second sight. Third eye. Or maybe you use yer nose. Maybe you find yerself a lead boy. Something. And once you got that thing, you ain't wanna lose it.

(Beat.)

Hell, if we ain't losing something, we're trying to hide it. Like it was never there. So what you missing? And what you gonna do to keep it?

(Lights up slowly. Campfire near the train tracks. Moon shining overhead, water lapping in the distance. Ross plays and sings. Ignacio, like a sponge, soaks it in. Gary sits apart, deathly still.)

ROSS *(Singing and playing)*:
   I don't know where I will be,
   Since my good child will be leading me,
   I will pay my last visit in this land somewhere . . .
GARY: Like hell.
ROSS: You know this song. Sing it with me, Gary boy.
GARY: Ross, you kill me.
ROSS: Gary and me, we come to Charleston onct, many years ago.
GARY: Leave off, old man—

ROSS: He don't like to talk about it. But me, I don't hold no grudges, I don't hold nothing in. I let it out. That's why I come back to Charleston.

GARY: You was a slave in Charleston.

ROSS: That was long time ago. Gotta let that slave stuff go. *(To Ignacio)* I went down to the Old Slave Mart this morning. Strange to walk there free as I please. Not have nobody lay a hand on me. Don't nobody spit no more when you brush shoulders on the street. Can you believe I even got a coin or two? And the smell . . . *(Sniffs the air)* Not that old slave smell. No African funk nowheres. Not like in our time, eh Gary? Now they got them a bakery right there in the middle of the Old Slave Mart, right there on the auction block. Right there where they used to . . . to sell our mamas and our papas in the noonday sun . . . *(Plays, sings:)*

Smell of baked bread instead.

GARY: Funk's there. It's just gussied up. But it don't fool me.

(Ross tosses the rucksack to Ignacio.)

ROSS: Here, boy.

(Ignacio pulls out a loaf of bread.)

IGNACIO: Hungry!

ROSS: Keep looking.

(Ignacio pulls out a can of beans.)

Make yerself a beans sandwich.

(Ross opens the tin. Gary is suddenly animated, grabs the loaf from Ignacio and tears into it. Ross grabs the loaf from Gary. Next, Gary goes for the beans. The two blind men enact a ritual of hobo dining: lots of grunts and elbows and full mouths. Ignacio gets nothing. Between mouthfuls Ross takes notice.)

Like this. *(Shows Ignacio how)* Pull the insides out the bread, throw the beans in, you got yerself a beans sandwich.
    (Examining Ignacio's hands) Guitar hands.

GARY: Piana!

ROSS: Guitar!

GARY: Aw you blind!!

ROSS: Wish I had me a boy.

GARY: You had many a boy.

ROSS: For to pass things down. Just like I taught you. *(To Ignacio)* If you was mine, I'd teach you that and more.

(Gary growls.)

Lucky man, Gary. To have warmth and companionship in your dotage.

GARY: My dotage? Then what does that make you?

ROSS: No secret. I'm older than water.

(Ross grins at Ignacio. He may be blind, but he's got his sights on the boy. He sets aside his food.)

Come here, boy. Lemme show you how.

(Ross gives his guitar over to Ignacio, who begins to strum and then pick out his ragtime. Ross laughs like the Buddha. Gary emits a bearlike growl, turns away.
White Shadow in a spot.)

WHITE SHADOW: Slave days? Y'all shoulda been there. Sure we worked hard, but we played too. We had us some times, especially on Sunday. Great day on plantation. Everybody got biscuits on Sunday. Where they gonna get biscuits now? See, I love 'em. I love 'em just like my own children. Just like puppies. Just like little floppy-eared puppies.

(Light shift. The Charleston Battery. Moon overhead illuminating Abe, trying to hawk papers to no success whatsoever.)

ABE *(To Audience)*: Come on! Be a man! Buy a paper!

(No response.)

Come on! Don't be shy. We're Americans, we ain't a shy people! We see injustice, we set it right! Don't we? Dontcha see? This ain't just paper! This is history! This is our country here! This is how people are gonna remember us!!

(He is met with utter disregard.)

Holy smokes! What kinda Americans are we anyway?

(Freda promenades in, dressed to the nines.)

Wow.

FREDA: If it ain't the news butch. Long time no see.

ABE: T'ought you didn't want to see me.

FREDA: That was hours ago. So how's tricks?

ABE *(Scratching himself)*: Business is up.

FREDA *(Adjusts a stocking)*: Up all over.

ABE *(Scratching)*: Nothing like a war.

FREDA: I walk down Broad Street, I lost count how many men of Charleston come looking to plant their little American flags in me. Like I'm Cuba! And all I wanted was a cup of sugar. I'm baking a cake. Wanna piece?

ABE: Cakes are for kids.

FREDA: Well you call yerself a boy.

(He keeps scratching.)

Got fleas? Take a bath in sand and a rubdown in alcohol. Fleas'll get drunk and kill each other throwing rocks.

ABE: No fleas.

FREDA: Good, 'cause then I'd have 'em.

ABE: I gotta sell these.

FREDA: Sell 'em at my place. Set you up right in fronta the turlet—

ABE: It ain't turlet paper!

FREDA: Why are we talking about paper? when you can have your cake and eat it too? Angel food. My special recipe . . .

ABE: Devil's food was good enough last time.

FREDA: Why do you insult me to my face? Have the decency to do it behind my back like everybody else in this godforsaken town. And let's face it . . . I mean—I don't look . . . *(Can't say the word)* I mean my features aren't Afri—And my pigment, I've worked very hard on my pigment! I've put good money down for the best Parisian face wash—

ABE: They got stuff for jigs?

FREDA: On second thought, no cake.

ABE *(Scratching himself)*: Look, sometimes I don't say what I mean. I like you. And heck! with them voluptuous features of yours, you could be anything!

FREDA: Anything but American.

ABE: American as me!

FREDA: Ain't saying much, Abe Hollandersky.

ABE: I'm pretty voluptuous myself. We're equals!

FREDA: Equally lousy.

ABE: Not lousy! I told ya, no lice! I been doused!

(Abe stops scratching and shows Freda his scalp. In response, Freda takes the paper out of his hands.)

FREDA: You don't think this is lousy? *(Reads from it)* CUBAN MON-KEYS—Are Cubans really monkeys?

ABE: Monkey chasers, maybe.

FREDA *(Reading more)*: DARK-SKINNED DEVILS . . .

ABE: Okay, I know, jigs are people too! I don't write 'em, I just sell 'em!

FREDA *(Stamps her foot)*: That's not good enough! Kids read this!

ABE: Kids? Whatcha talking about kids for?

FREDA: Feed 'em the same damn mistakes!—

ABE: Mistakes? What mistakes!

FREDA: Mistaking me for a darkie!!!

ABE: What do the papers gotta do with that?

FREDA: Everything!! It's all in black and white! Everything's black and white!!

ABE: Well there's color supplements on Sundays—

FREDA *(Grabbing him)*: I'm saying you miss what's in between!

ABE: I didn't miss you.

(Pause.)

FREDA: No, you got what you wanted.

ABE: Well, I guess, but . . .

(She starts crying.)

Well if this don't take the rag off the bush! How come you're cry—?

FREDA: You don't care!

ABE: I do too care.

FREDA: You talk nice now, but you want to plant your flag in me same as the next guy!

ABE: Well, yeah, but—NO!!

FREDA: You judge me.

ABE: Babe, take a hard look. Who am I to judge? I'm a Jew pug been hit more than the Liberty Bell. And the papers? You saw my finances. I can't even give 'em away. The South is killing me! The only reason I haven't shipped out of here is . . . well, I hoped we might see each other—and not like that! I mean for a walk, arm-and-arm like and the whole shabang. My steamer left a couple hours ago. I watched it go, southbound to Jacksonville, then Cuba. And now you're here.

FREDA: Am I your Cuba?

ABE: You're my All-American gal.

(They embrace.)

FREDA: Liar.

ABE: See, that's the thing about this country. It's a rainbow of color. A dream of beauty. A wild bust of laughter. And regular hot stuff!

FREDA: You tryna sell me one of your papers?

ABE: Don't blame the papers. Life seems pretty black and white to me. But maybe that's why you stand out.

FREDA: Like a sore thumb.

ABE: Like a lady. But you oughta settle down someplace and make a life. You got a mighty fine head on your shoulders, and I don't much care what color it is.

(They kiss. As they move off slowly together, Sanctimonious and Yellow pop up from behind the papers.)

YELLOW: I hate this gooey stuff.

SANCTIMONIOUS: Funny how a person can go and sell a child, then turn around and kiss and hug like nothing happened.

YELLOW: People is funny.

SANCTIMONIOUS: Hylarious!

YELLOW: We could give him a hot-foot. Tie his shoes together?—

SANCTIMONIOUS: Too easy. But we can't go empty handed, now can we?

YELLOW: Let's swipe his precious newswipe!

SANCTIMONIOUS: We already did once.

YELLOW: But you can never have enough toilet paper!!!

(Giggling, because they do. Horsing around, they make paper airplanes and other projectiles.

By now Abe and Freda have retired to her bedroom, and are in the midst of undressing. Both are shy, tentative.)

FREDA: You married?

ABE: Nah. You?

FREDA: You kidding?

ABE: So what's all this about kids?

FREDA: You're the one always talking about—
ABE: So you want one or what?
FREDA: Do you?
ABE: Sure t'ing!
FREDA: Oh.
ABE: You mean you don't?
FREDA: Does mess with the figure. Not so young as I used to be.

(Beat.)

I'm not one for kids. My dad, he had a bit of the Irish. Thought every time you drop your pants you make a baby. I got sixteen brothers and sisters. Ma never knew what hit her.
ABE: Couldn't he listen to reason?
FREDA: Dad? He had a great capacity for reason. He reasoned with me by lifting up my shirt. Liked his horse sugar, coupl'a lids he loved to reason. So the thought of birthing a kid doesn't seem so romantic as it oughta be.
ABE: What if ya didn't start from scratch? What if there happened to be one ready-made?
FREDA: What are you t—?
ABE: I saw this kid who just about fits the bill.
FREDA: What bill?
ABE: Aw he's a great kid.
FREDA: Was he . . . ? Was he . . . with somebody?
ABE: He was leading some blind spook—I . . . I mean spade—I . . . I mean—
FREDA: Black bastid!!
ABE: That's the ticket! Kid's a pip! I almost decided to take him along with me, give him a life, you know? Maybe I should . . .

(She vigorously shakes her head no.)

Whatsa matta? Look a little green about the gills. (Snaps fingers) Oh, I get you. He a local kid? Can't be that bad. Lemme guess. Is he yours?
FREDA: No!!! I mean— (Struggling) He was given me . . . I mean he was—I was . . . It was just business!!!
ABE: Kids are great for business! What? He clean up for ya?
FREDA: Abe, it wasn't like that.
ABE: You don't gotta apologize, I'm looking for free help myself—
FREDA: The blind fella took! . . . He took!— The boy!—

ABE: You mean he—? *(Puritan pause)* A prevert and a pedicure to boot.

(The Yellow Kid and The Sanctimonious Kid appear.)

YELLOW: A pedicure?

SANCTIMONIOUS: This is getting pediculous!

(They disappear.)

FREDA: Well not quite.

ABE: He took the kid, didn't he? I wasn't born yesterday, I can see the writing on the wall! You got tooken! And so did the kid!!

FREDA: Well I guess.

ABE: Say no more! He made inquiries not befitting a gentleman—

FREDA: Well, he certainly did that.

ABE: He snake-charmed you with his sultry ways and voodoo mumbo-jumbo. You're innocent. He's the one to blame! Why, if I were from these parts I'd lynch him—but I'm not. There was bad business here, and I've an idea to set it right.

FREDA: How?

ABE: Well, they got a headstart. But then again, we got eyes. *(Throws on clothes)* We're gonna free the kid!!

FREDA: But what if the old bastid don't want him freed?

ABE: He'll listen to reason.

FREDA *(Fingering her billfold)*: But what if we have to pay?

ABE: You mean money? Who'd sell a kid for cash? Even he couldn't be that much of an animal!

(Freda squirms.)

Get your clothes on.

FREDA: Why dontcha just give him one good shot behind the ear?

ABE: We're gonna play this fair and square. Hell, even if we do gotta pay him a coupla bucks so he don't go away mad.

FREDA: You don't got a coupla bucks.

ABE: I know.

FREDA: All right, all right . . . *(Pulls out her wad of bills)* It's not as much as it looks. Most of it's spoken for. Rent, groceries and the cops . . . *(He reacts quizically)* You got to pay, one way or the other.

ABE: Naw. You ain't doing that no more.

FREDA: It's my business.

ABE: Not no more. You and me are going into business together. We're gonna make a go of it. We got it all lined up.

FREDA: What kinda business?

ABE: The Family Business! *(Hugs her)* We better shake a leg! We'll find the blind fella. We'll reason with him. And if he don't wanna give the kid up, then we'll reason some more. And if he still don't say uncle, well . . . *(Makes a fist)* He won't know what hit him.

(As he swats the air, scene shift to the campfire. Ross sings and plays, Ignacio in his lap. Gary staggers off, still growling.)

ROSS:

> I don't know and I cannot tell where
> I may be somewhere sailing in the air
> I will do my last singing in this land somewhere . . .

Easy as pie, Longboy.

IGNACIO: Longboy?

ROSS: You oughta have a name to look up to.

IGNACIO: Longboy . . .

ROSS: You'll get used to it. You can get used to anything.

IGNACIO: Did you get used to being blind?

ROSS: You learn to see other ways. Me, I was born blind. Big, strong, happy and blind. This was back on plantation. Wasn't much work I could do. Boy, did it burn the foreman to see a big black baby sitting in the shade, blind or no. One day he throwed a guitar at me. Said keep a rhythm going, ply a song to keep 'em working. So I did. Then alla sudden, we was free. At least that's what they said up North. I could go wherever I pleased. So I hit the road. Trouble is, I was going hungry fast. I was fat and sassy on plantation, but ain't no three square a day on the road. Didn't much take to this *freedom business*. All that time I went hungry I never onct remembered. I didn't have to suffer. All I had to do was ply. *(Plays the guitar)* When you' blind, it's a wild bust of color. The way it looks, the way it busts and dances and jumps and fools around, almost like a buncha crazy kids in your head. *(Ross holds him tighter)* Yep. Just like a buncha kids. When you're blind, you can see it better. But it's there. Right there for the taking, Longboy.

IGNACIO: Do I have to go blind?

ROSS: You don't gotta do nothing you don't wanna do. I know you' Gary's boy, but you know there's him, and then there's me. Now

Uncle Ross he's a little different from Uncle Gary. Ross got faith in the little things in life. Ross, he's easy. And affectionate. The road's a lonely place, and Gary he don't know nothing but womens. But Ross, Ross been on the road a long time. Ross been many a boy's companion on a cold dark night when the wind is blowing hard and ain't nobody else give a damn if you lives or dies. But Ross gives. He gives with all his heart. So you can come with me . . .

(Ignacio tries to squirm away, but can't.)

Ross needs ya more than Gary . . .

GARY *(Sniffing)*: Boy!

(Ignacio tries to rise, but Ross holds him down.)

ROSS *(Whispering fast)*: You and me, we cut out toward Lady Island, Distant Island, Gary don't know that place, I got people there, feed ya good—

GARY: Boy!!

ROSS: Nice soft bed, lots of kids—

GARY *(Approaching)*: BOY!!!

ROSS: And I don't hit! Never hit a soul in my life. Come on!

GARY *(Finds them)*: Shoulda known.

ROSS: Easy now Gary boy—

GARY: I ain't yer boy no more!

ROSS *(To Ignacio)*: He was onct. And I didn't have to buy him or steal him. Gary come of his own accord.

GARY: You know what this fella's all about, don't ya boy?—

ROSS: I got nothing to hide.

GARY: Tryna turn his head!

ROSS: Turned your head. *(To Ignacio)* Back then Gary had eyes. For stealing chickens and fine womens and finding trouble.

(Ross stands, suddenly hulking and dangerous.)

But mostly he had eyes for my songs. Damned if that son-of-a-seacook didn't go and steal my damn songs!! Always looking at my hands. I could feel it. You robbed me blind, Gary boy. I could rip that lying tongue out yer throat!!

GARY: BULLPIZZLE!!!

ROSS: FOOL!!!

(Suddenly they are swinging at each other, missing wildly. Part melee, part ballet, both men tough as all hell.)

Don't study me, I din't put yer eyes out!

GARY: Them bucra kids took my eyes 'cause I plyed too good!

ROSS: Them bucra took yer eyes 'cause you was showing off to they women folk! You couldn't see the danger you was in.

GARY: I seen my own blood. So don't preach on me. You can't see a damn thing, Ross.

ROSS: I could see you wasn't taking care of business, fool!

GARY *(So angry he's crying)*: Business! That's all you ever cared about! Sure I stole yer songs. You never gave me nothing! Beat me like a redheaded stepchild! I caught a whupping for any damn thing! Just for the fun of it! Just for the show! *(Weeps)* I shoulda run off a thousand times!!!

ROSS: I didn't make ya blind, Gary. All I did was teach you how to ply.

GARY: I was just a kid! And the whole time, when that damn brick came flying and hit me upside the head . . . To when them hellions, the Devil's own, come down on me laughing and carrying on and pulling on my ears and leaving me lying there and my eyes bleeding . . . And the whole time this here piece of business kept on "plying" his guitar just like nothing happened. Just kept on singing and crying.

(Beat.)

That was the time that I went blind.

ROSS: Gary. You got to let things go.

(Ignacio goes to him. Gary pushes him away.)

Let the man alone, Longboy. Let him go. That's the way he wants it.

(Ignacio stands midway between the two blind men, torn.)

What you gonna do, Longboy? Who you gonna turn to?

(The sounds of feet tramping. Abe and Freda enter.)

ABE: Hi Folks!
(To Freda) Looks like we hit paydirt!
(To Gary) Hi, neighbor.
(To Freda) That's him, ain't it? I got lousy night vision.

(Abe offers his hand for Ross to shake, not realizing the man is blind. Ignacio freezes as he sees Freda.)

FREDA: Hello there . . . son.
GARY: When it rains it pours.
ABE: Hey, kid.
FREDA: We come to bring you home.

(Abe clamps a hand on Ignacio's shoulder. Gary rises, protective, yet knowing he's helpless. Ross sits Buddha-like—que será, será.
Ignacio looks from one person to the other. Abe's hand feels like a shackle around his neck. Then he bolts. Abe ends up with nothing but the boy's coat. Ignacio runs full speed into The Yellow Kid and The Sanctimonious Kid.)

YELLOW: Say!
SANCTIMONIOUS: Going somewhere?
YELLOW: You're already gone!
SANCTIMONIOUS: Said we'd keep you under our wing.
IGNACIO: Let go!!

(They take Ignacio up into an as-yet-undisclosed treehouse full of swiped papers, projectiles, toys, grafitti. A turn-of-the-century kid's paradise. Ignacio is like a kid in a candy store. Yellow and Sanctimonious watch smugly.)

ABE: Where'd he go?
ROSS: I din't see nothing.
ABE: Is blindness catching?

(Ignacio plays with a slingshot.)

SANCTIMONIOUS: Careful there, you'll put out an eye.
IGNACIO: What happened?
SANCTIMONIOUS: You climbed a tree.
IGNACIO: I did?
YELLOW: Well you're up one now.
SANCTIMONIOUS: Let the kid have a look at what he left behind.

(They all look down.)

FREDA: You said you'd get him!
ABE: I will, babe.
FREDA *(Glancing uneasily at Gary)*: Do it quick.

SANCTIMONIOUS: Go back down if you want to.

IGNACIO: I don't want to.

SANCTIMONIOUS: Suit yourself.

YELLOW: Nah, let's us suit him!

(Yellow puts a cartoony sombrero on Ignacio.)

IGNACIO: What's that for?

SANCTIMONIOUS: Come up here, you gotta be like us. That's the deal.

YELLOW: It's us or them.

SANCTIMONIOUS: That's why you gotta be like us!

YELLOW: We don't like the way you been treated. This is Americker! People can't tell you what to do! Be like us! People can't do that to us!

SANCTIMONIOUS: Except for Mister Hearst.

YELLOW: Except for Hearstie.

SANCTIMONIOUS: And we don't like the way these so-called adults keep playing ya like a poker chip! You're a kid by gosh by gum, and you're not gonna take it anymore! No one can push us around!

YELLOW: Except the Hearstmonster.

SANCTIMONIOUS: But I don't see anyone remotely like Bill Hearst around here? Do you?

YELLOW: Just a coupla mashiated blind guys and an overgrown newsbaby.

SANCTIMONIOUS: Not to mention the lady. The lovely lady who sold you in the first place.

YELLOW: Without even offering you a percentage!

SANCTIMONIOUS: The nerve!

YELLOW: You been taken unfair adwantage of! But we're here for ya!

SANCTIMONIOUS: Regular Rough Riders at your service!

YELLOW *(Very Teddy Roosevelt)*: Bully!

SANCTIMONIOUS: It's a little like this Cuban War. There wouldn't be a war if it weren't for our beloved Boss Hearst.

YELLOW: We started a war. Just think, kid. The power of paper!

SANCTIMONIOUS *(Reading from the paper)*: AN AMERICAN NEWSPAPER ACCOMPLISHES IN A SINGLE STROKE WHAT THE BEST EFFORTS OF DIPLOMACY HAVE FAILED UTTERLY TO ACHIEVE!

YELLOW *(Reading from another)*: HOW DO YOU LIKE THE JOURNAL'S WAR?!!

SANCTIMONIOUS: Just think! A pound of toilet paper with a raving lunatic's ink smears; and out comes the U.S. navy no less to do

Boss Hearst's bidding and crush the aforementioned enemy, whoever they may be! So we figured, what the hey! If a newspaper can start a world war, then why can't a pair of fine upstanding Kid Celebrities—

YELLOW: That means us!

SANCTIMONIOUS: Why can't we come to the aid of a poor little Messican bastid orphaned in the jungle camps of the Deep South? Why can't we take a moment out of our busy schedules to take History by the scruff of the neck and give her a good swift kick in the slats, for a friend in need?

YELLOW: So here we is!

SANCTIMONIOUS: Cheer up, sad boy, and let us show ya the power of paper. You need us, and by gosh by gum we need you too.

IGNACIO: For what?

YELLOW: For *Business*!!

SANCTIMONIOUS: We're on a promotional tour. Hearst wrote us a carte blanche!

(The Yellow Kid and The Sanctimonious Kid produce an oversized check.)

YELLOW: Don't it make your mouth water?

SANCTIMONIOUS: Leave it go, you'll smudge it!

(They gesture toward the piles of kid stuff.)

We got all this merchandise!

YELLOW: Try this on for size!

SANCTIMONIOUS: No charge!

YELLOW: Hold him down!

(They overpower Ignacio and force him to dress up as a cartoon character—specifically a cartoon Mexican. They have all the paraphernalia—poncho, cigar, fake mustache, ukelele. Ignacio ends up a cartoon kid—part Keaton, part Cantinflas, with a Pierrot-like melancholia.)

SANCTIMONIOUS *(Introducing)*: Ladies and Gentlemen: The Lost Boy!

YELLOW: I dunno . . . Still bug-ugly. Who's gonna laugh at him?

SANCTIMONIOUS: He may lack our particular genius for comedy, but there's something innately ridiculous about his very being that tends to make the common man chuckle.

YELLOW: You mean 'cause he's a spic?

SANCTIMONIOUS: The unwashed phenomenon. *(Laughs)* It's fun to condescend.

    (To Ignacio) So Ignatz! Longboy! Whatever the heck! Enjoy the world of two dimensions! The land where cause has no effect, or the other way around. Be a kid cartoon, go on!

YELLOW: The world is your erster!

SANCTIMONIOUS: Oyster.

YELLOW: Aw feed it to the fish!

("Yankee Doodle" plays fast. The Kids look to Ignacio.)

SANCTIMONIOUS *(Stage whisper)*: That's your cue.

YELLOW: Do something!

(Ignacio picks up the uke, and plays the tune to his ragtime. Yellow sticks his fingers in his ears.)

Whodya t'ink you are? Paganinny?

SANCTIMONIOUS: Put some pep in it! Where's your get-up-and-go?

YELLOW: Guess it got up and went.

(Ignacio begins to really play the rag. Even on the uke, it is beautiful.)

SANCTIMONIOUS: Argggh! Don't ya see? That's what's holding you down!

YELLOW: That kinda music's too real! You'll never get free!

SANCTIMONIOUS: Don't ya see? We're your Abe Lincoln! We freed ya from those shackles!

(Ignacio loses himself in the ragtime, the hint of tears in his eyes.)

Feeling? Feeling's just a great big leg iron. And music? Music is a whipping post! We freed ya from all that! And what do you do? You sit there and stare at us with the shackle in your hand!

YELLOW: It's enough to gimme the blues.

SANCTIMONIOUS: And what do you do? You ply the uke!

YELLOW: Really gimme the blues.

SANCTIMONIOUS: Americans are happy! They like to laugh! They like a joke! Even if it happens to be on them! They don't want blues! They want action! Thrills!

(Ignacio starts to cry.)

What is it with you people?!!

YELLOW: Yeah, what gives?

(Ignacio plays with feeling and soul not heard before on a ukelele. The Kids can't helping being affected, no matter how much they may fight the feeling.)

Real laff riot.

SANCTIMONIOUS *(Huffy)*: Oh great. Make us feel two-dimensional. You think we have no hearts? Well we don't! Cartoons aren't supposed to feel. It gums up the burleyque.

   (Almost pleading) We're offering you an out from the infinite sadness of your life, and you insist on staying human! I thought you said you didn't want to go back!

IGNACIO: I don't.

YELLOW: Then what the heck are ya doing?

SANCTIMONIOUS: Yeah! What are ya trying to be?

(Ignacio stops playing, wipes his eyes, smiles.)

IGNACIO: Free, I guess.

(Scene shift: Ross plays, Gary sniffs around near Freda. Abe and Freda are searching fruitlessly.)

ABE: Kiddio!

FREDA: C'mere pumpkin! *(Under her breath)* Little bastid.

GARY *(Sniffs the air)*: If it ain't the funkytown gal!

FREDA: Shhh!

ABE: Say something?

FREDA: Nothing snookums. Try over there . . .

(Abe ruts around out of earshot.)

(To Gary) Keep it down.

GARY: We done bad business. You sold me the boy under false pretenses. You knew if I went backwoods with a white boy they would lynch me good and proper. You knew—

FREDA: Hoped, maybe.

GARY: Well I want my money back.

ABE: You say something?

FREDA: Nothing, snookie!

   (To Gary) For godsakes, quiet.

GARY: Well?

FREDA: Put out your hand.

(She puts her wad of bills in his hand.)

GARY: What's this?

FREDA: Now I don't wanna hear no squawking, you ol' rangtang. This is payment in full— *(This pains her)* with interest. Now gimme the kid.

GARY: Now you want the kid?

FREDA: I got a chance at something. And I don't wanna mess it up.

GARY *(Sniggering)*: You want the kid!

ABE: Wha—?

FREDA: Nothing, puddin'!

    (To Gary) You got your money. So shush.

GARY: The Yank don't know you sold the kid?

FREDA: Please. Don't say nothing.

GARY: Why shouldn't I?

FREDA: 'Cause I'm asking. I'm asking ya nice.

(He keeps sniggering.)

    Don't refuse a lady.

GARY: You refused me.

FREDA: That was business!

GARY: And now it's more than business, in't it, puddin'?

FREDA *(Despairing)*: What do I got to give ya? *(Gary grins)* All right, all right.

(Freda maneuvers him professionally behind a tree.)

    Just try not to make any noise.

GARY: Little ol' me?

    (Then to Abe) Hey Newsbaby!!

FREDA: Bastid!!

(Abe approaches. Freda jumps away, applies makeup as fast as she can.)

GARY: Whatcha up to, boy?

ABE: Well I'm looking for a kid about yea high.

GARY: Why in hell wouldya want to do that?

ABE: 'Cause I'm gonna be his pop. And she's gonna be his mom!

(Gary sniggers.)

    Don't snigger at the lady, there's a good scout, eh Jim?

GARY: Well, Deacon, you'd snigger too if you saw what I'm seeing.

ABE: I got this lousy night vision.

FREDA: Dirty mangy dog.

GARY: Smell the air, Ross.

ROSS: I'm smelling it.

GARY: You know what it smell like.

ROSS: Sho nuff.

GARY *(Sniggers)*: Smell like sex.

ROSS: And cabbage.

GARY: Say what?!!

ROSS: Cabbage, sho nuff.

GARY: Ross getting a little long in the tooth.

ABE *(Taking charge)*: What say we quit the pleasantries. We're here on business.

FREDA: Abe—

ABE: I'll take care of this, babe. Now we want the kid, and we're ready to offer you—

FREDA: Abe!—

ABE: Not now, babe! We're doing business.

GARY: Some business!

ABE: We're prepared to pay!

GARY: Kid's value done skyrocketed! None of us can afford him!

ROSS: Much less find him.

ABE: He'll turn up.

GARY: If he does, then he ain't for sale.

ABE: It's been my experience that most men can be bought.

(Gary tosses Freda's money on the ground.)

GARY: Not this time.

(Freda snatches it up violently.)

ABE: Is that yours?

FREDA: Just take the damn kid!

GARY: Over my dead body.

FREDA: That can be arranged.

ABE: No need threatening—just yet.

(Abe looks at Freda.)

FREDA: Abe, I swear! I'll tell you all about it, soon as we get home. *(Seductively)* I promise. I'll make it all right.

GARY *(Sniggers)*: So you're gonna mom-and-pop-it. Know what you're getting into, newsboy?

ABE: Listen, Jim. You're a good fella. But I've seen ya play dad and you really stink up the joint. Now the lady and me, we plan to make a go of it. With us, the kid's got a future. Not some dead end playing tunes for pennies by the side of the road—but a real trade! See, it all comes down to who you are and what you put your faith in. Now the future missus and me, we got faith in God and Country and the Almighty Dollar, and we plan to pass that faith onto the boy. The papers made me what I am today. you watch what they do for the kid.

GARY: You think the papers, let alone *god* and *country*, give a god-damn about you?

ABE: I do!

(Gary removes the funny pages from his vest.)

GARY: This? Ain't nothing but a rag! And here you wanting to take the boy and feed him all that guff! All the guff been crammed down your gullet all these years, and now you want the boy to choke on it too! Stick that rag clear down to his soul and gag it for good! Raggedy ass—

FREDA: I wouldn't talk.

GARY: No, you oughtn't to. We all know what kinda business the lady runs.

FREDA: Watch it!

GARY: The Passing Business! Putting on a face, but it don't fool a dog like me. Go on, gal. Lessen the lips, lower the ass. But you can't lose the funk. I can almost taste the blackness—

FREDA: Bastid!!

(Freda runs at him. Abe has to hold her back.)

ABE: You really wanna call a spade a spade? You beat the boy. I seen ya.

GARY: What the hell do any of us know, but beating? Beat every damn day of our godforsaken lives!

(He slaps at Abe, mock playfully.)

Eh, tigerman? What the hell else do we know but beating? What else we got but shame? Eh, slabberchops?—

(Gary suddenly swings at Freda, a near miss. Freda screams, then attacks. Abe can barely hold her back.)

FREDA: What I got to be ashamed about? I can't help it if I was born lucky!

ABE: Shouldn'ta taken a poke at a lady. You're lucky you're blind—

GARY: You think a blind man can't fight?

FREDA: Cream him!!!

ABE: Come on, now. Let's not be rash.

GARY: I'll raise a rash on yer ugly puss. You assified auntie-man! You lapdog! You Navy Boy! I'll knock ya piss-to-windward. I'll mash ya front to back!!

ABE: Talks a good show, don't he?

FREDA: All bark and no bite.

(Gary punches Abe, hard.)

ABE: Ow! Well whatdya know? He jooked me in the eye! If that don't beat it!

(Gary punches again. This time Abe the professional eludes the blow, then wraps Gary in a half nelson.)

FREDA: MURDER HIM!!!

GARY: OW!!!!

ABE: This doesn't have to be like this, friend. Now. Apologize to the lady.

GARY: Never!

(Abe applies his trade.)

OW!!! I'm sorry, damnit!

ABE: There's a good scout. *(Looks at Freda)* Now. You gonna sell us back the kid?

FREDA: Abe!

ABE: Well that's what you did. You sold the boy. Right?

GARY *(Still struggling)*: Not as stooopid as you look!

ABE *(Applying more pressure)*: I asked you a question.

GARY: To hell with— *(Abe squeezes)* ARGGH!!

ABE: Think about it. Take your time. We got all the time in the world . . .

GARY: Damn! I hate pain!

FREDA: Just kill the bastid and we'll keep the money.

(Abe lets Gary go.)

ROSS: No wonder the boy done gone.

FREDA: Shut your trap unless you want some of the same.

ABE: Quit volunteering me to fight old blind guys, okay? I'm a professional!

GARY: Professionals I'll say! Professional liars and sluts and punching bags!!!

(Freda hits Gary in the eye. Drives him to his knees. Gary grabs his eyes, he shakes head to foot as if doused in cold water. Then he stands, looks out at the water and the moon. He seems to be undergoing a change, some kind of revelatory moment. He has a weird gleam in his eye.)

I see.

FREDA: You're blind!

GARY: All this time I heard my way through the world. Used my ears to see. It was all I had, there was no going back, and anyway I had the music. But I never saw. I never had that freedom. It got took from me, see? Long before anybody ever throwed a brick my way. See, I had to find a way to live. And knowing no different, I lived like a slave. And I put that in the music. And I gave that music to the boy. I made him my slave. And you all would do the same, if you could.

FREDA: Us? Wake up! Slave days over!

ROSS: Young lady, my folks was slaves. Your folks was slaves. All our folks was slaves. That's something we got in common. Then, by god, how's it come to pass that we become the slavers now?

ABE: Slavers?

FREDA: I ain't no slaver!

GARY: You just sell the meat.

FREDA: You bought it.

GARY: Indeed I did.

ABE *(Chastened)*: Guess I did too.

FREDA: Abe! Abie! Don't listen to these raggedy fools!

GARY: Ragged is the word. All our faith, a buncha rags. All our songs, all our shuck an' jive. All the crap we put our faith in. Like a kerchief over my eyes. Couldn't see a thing, least of all myself.

(Approaches Ross) Ross, the very mention of your name makes me spit. But you done hit the nail on the head this time. Here we be, slaving with the best of 'em.

ROSS: I'da done it too. Tried to turn the boy's head, but not for him. For me.

GARY: Most dreadful day I ever did see. 'Cept it's a bit of laugh too.

ROSS: 'Cept it ain't really.

GARY: No it ain't.

    (Shouts at the sea) Sail away, boy!! Sail the hell away from us!! BE FREE!!!!

FREDA: To starve. He'll never get free. But we'll find him. Right Abe?

ABE: Naw, babe. It's late and I'm bone tired.

FREDA: You giving up on me?

ABE: No one should ever call Abe Hollandersky a slaver. My mom and pop would be sore ashamed.

FREDA: Abe!

ABE: Maybe it's all been a big mistake.

FREDA: I swear I'll never sell a kid again! I'll never sell a living soul!!

ABE: What about yerself?

FREDA: I'll give it up! I will. Starting right now I'm turning over a new leaf.

(Abe sighs heavily.)

What.

ABE: Watch the ones who turn over new leafs. You tend to find the old one underneath. Sorry, babe.

FREDA: Oh. So it's like that.

ABE: We musta been crazy. I got papers to sell. And you, you got yerself a thriving business. I'm keeping ya from yer business, and yer keeping me from mine. I took a real bath since I dropped anchor—

FREDA: So to speak.

ABE: Hey. No hard feelings. Friends? *(He offers his hand to shake. She bats it away)*

FREDA: I don't got any friends. See ya down Charleston Bay. And don't you say a word unless you got your money ready.

ROSS: Talk about rags. That's all we brought with us. Our people. Just rags and faith and songs to ply. Everything else got tooken. But it's an old story. My mother sung it to me, my mother's mother sung it, my grandmother's mother's grandmother sung it back in Bible days. And wouldn't you know, here we go again.

GARY: Just like the Children of Zion.

(Scene shift to the treehouse.)

YELLOW: Ain'tcha glad you ain't down there?

IGNACIO: They're sad.

SANCTIMONIOUS: People get sad. That's their problem. Spend enough time with a person, they'll get sad.

YELLOW: Chances are you will too!

SANCTIMONIOUS: My pitiful friend . . . Some people are born sad, some achieve sadness and some have sadness thrust upon them. In other words, who knows—

YELLOW: And who cares!!

IGNACIO: I do.

YELLOW: There's yer problem!!

SANCTIMONIOUS: In a nutshell! Why care for them when they don't give a cowslip about you?

YELLOW: Why be a slave?

SANCTIMONIOUS: Give up yer shackles, kid. They only weigh you down.

YELLOW: Laugh 'n' play. And do what we tell ya!

IGNACIO: My mama—

SANCTIMONIOUS: The one who left you high and dry?

IGNACIO: My papa—

YELLOW: The one who beat yer ma?—

IGNACIO: They came across, from Mexico—

SANCTIMONIOUS: Swam?

IGNACIO: They came—

YELLOW: For a quick buck?

IGNACIO: For me. They came for me. They tried—

SANCTIMONIOUS: To kill each other!

IGNACIO: They tried to give me—

SANCTIMONIOUS: Shitty pomes and nigger music—

IGNACIO: They tried to give me—

YELLOW: They gave you nothing!

IGNACIO: This one chance.

(Ignacio plays the uke sadly. Then a string breaks. The Kids take it back from him. Ignacio seems very sad.)

SANCTIMONIOUS: These feelings? They'll pass. Like the measles and the mumps and poison ivy.

YELLOW: Like scabies! Hey, it's just one life, and a pretty lousy one at that!

SANCTIMONIOUS: See, kid—it's just you. Now envision this scenario. No parents, no history. No history, no memory. No memory, clean slate. Think of that—a clean slate! That's what boss Hearst sent us out to look for! You! You and the million other yous coming into Ellis Island and wading across the Rio Grande and getting born into the lovely tenements of the Lower East Side! Kid, you're the New American. You're gonna build our pyramids! You're gonna be the company boy! You're gonna save your pennies, you're gonna make a buck or two here or there, and you're gonna spend 'em on the funnies, or whatever technological equivalent thought up by the mind of Hearst, and all the other Hearsts to come. You, kid, may be the Lost Boy, but believe it—You Have Been Found.

(Ignacio removes his cartoon finery.)

YELLOW: Hey. What the hey?
SANCTIMONIOUS: Be careful, that's a store model—
IGNACIO: Let me be free.
YELLOW: No way! You can't escape us!
SANCTIMONIOUS: Freedom? Ha! You belong to us!

(Sanctimonious puts a hand on Ignacio. Surprisingly, Ignacio pushes Sanctimonious, and he falls in a big way.)

YELLOW: Hully gee.

(Yellow does the same. He gets pushed and falls just as big.)

SANCTIMONIOUS: What . . . whatdya know?
YELLOW: Kid's got potential!
IGNACIO: I have a mother! A father! I have a history! People! Even if they're not here. Even if they never come back. I have them. I have them here. *(Pounds his heart)*
YELLOW *(Pointing down to the adults)*: You have them?
IGNACIO: Them too.
SANCTIMONIOUS: They're your history? Gee, our condolences.

(Ignacio begins to climb down.)

Wait! If you go back, what do you go back to? One guy beats ya for fun. One puts his arms around and kisses ya kinda funny. One would make ya take up boxing and hawk papers in places like Cuba. And the lady, well she'd turn ya inta some kinda bordello boy—
YELLOW: Which would be a laugh.

SANCTIMONIOUS: But not a gag. That's what's down there for ya.
YELLOW: It ain't safe!

(Ignacio shrugs. He takes the uke.)

IGNACIO: I'll keep this.
YELLOW: Nuh-uh!
SANCTIMONIOUS: It's an original.
YELLOW: It ain't in stock.
SANCTIMONIOUS: Don't got all the kinks out yet.
YELLOW *(Sad)*: And besides . . . It ain't real.
SANCTIMONIOUS *(Sadder)*: The real one's down there.

(Ignacio smiles, gives it back. Then he climbs down.)

YELLOW: Think we shoulda stopped him?
SANCTIMONIOUS: What are ya gonna do? People.

(Ignacio joins the others, but stays out of sight. Abe and Freda stand apart, neither willing to exit first.)

FREDA: Why ain'tcha pushed off yet?
ABE: Maybe I ain't so swift as you. Maybe I gotta think about my next step.
FREDA: Put one foot in fronta the other. Usually does the trick.
ABE *(To the blind men)*: I feel like the Children of Zion too, ya know. I happen to be one!
FREDA: Aw, go sell a paper!
ABE: I don't care about papers. I'm talking about history.
FREDA: I thought papers was history.
ABE: This is history. You, me. Even if nobody gives a damn. This is real. See, I hadda thousand fights. Coupla them was pretty tough. But none so tough as what my old man had to go through back in Russia. The way they treated him, the way he suffered. He came here in rags, babe. Bottom of the barrel. They even said he was retarded 'cause he couldn't spick de Inklish. But he didn't let it get him down. He saw the chance. In this country, hell you make your own history. 'Cause we all start with a clean slate. *(A fighting pose)* I was the slate. And look at me now! Abe the Newsboy!
FREDA: Real step up.
ABE: I think so. And my kid is gonna do better than me. And his kid. And all the way, till we can finally rest. Till we get to Zion. That's what it's all about, see. Rub the slate clean. Make a clean

go of it. That's what a kid can be to folks like us. *(Tenderly)* You done a bad t'ing. I done bad t'ings too. But it's got to stop. It's got to stop! This is a free country!

FREDA: Nothing free. You pay with your blood. We both know that.

ABE: But one day it'll stop. *(She shakes her head no)* Don'tcha wanna stop fighting?

FREDA: Naw. I'll be fighting past my grave.

(Abe shivers.)

What you shivering for?

ABE: I dunno, babe. Guess someone stepped over my grave, that's all.

GARY: Let's quit fighting each other.

FREDA: I got no more fight with you. Let's consider ourselves older and wiser.

GARY: Each day closer to the grave.

(Abe offers Freda his arm.)

ABE: Lemme walk you back to town.

FREDA: All right, but you know you're not coming home with me!—

ABE: Heck no! I'm going to Cuba!

(They start to go. Abe stumbles blindly.)

FREDA: What's wrong?

ABE: It's awful black out there!

ROSS: Hey, white man! You blind?

ABE: Right now I am!

ROSS *(Claps him on the shoulder)*: Well then god bless ya brother.

GARY *(Claps him on the shoulder)*: Never thought I'd call ya brother, brother!

FREDA: This dark, I'm pretty blind myself—

GARY: Oh yeah? Well then god bless you, puddin'.

(Gary moves to cop a feel. Ross pushes him aside.)

ROSS: Godspeed. And keep each other warm.

(Freda leads Abe like a lead boy with a blind man.)

FREDA: Come on, kid.

ABE: You jigs—I mean dar—I . . . I mean—Criminy! You fellas are okay by me!!

(To Freda) Come on, pussil.

FREDA: That sounds dirty . . .

(They start to exit into the night. Before they can go, White Shadow appears, pointing the Winchester at them.)

WHITE SHADOW: Hold on now.

(Everyone freezes.)

Ain't nobody going nowhere.

(White Shadow walks among them, pointing the rifle from one frozen body to the other.)

What kinda business you all up to?

(Silence.)

Where's the kid?

(He looks them over. They all look down.)

What's really going on here? Blind men, whores, jews, niggers? Talk about a motley crew! Must be looking to make a fast buck. So what's the deal? What kinda evil thing y'all up to? And where's the boy fit in? *(Beat)* White slavery?

(Gary looks up, looks him in the eye.)

That's it, ain't it.

GARY: Slave days over.

WHITE SHADOW: You think so? *(Laughs)* You really think so?

ABE: No slaves in this country, friend.

(White Shadow slings the rifle over his shoulder. He grins at Abe.)

WHITE SHADOW: Don't believe what the papers say. Slavery won't die. Take a lot more than a little war to kill off an idea that good. Look at yourselves. Even you mudbabies figured out how good it can be. Maybe you call it something different now. But a rose by any other name smells just as much to high heaven.
(He winks at Freda. Sniffs the air) Nice perfume you got on. Too bad you had to go and sweat all over it.

FREDA *(Desperate)*: The kid's gone! *(Beat)* I wouldn't lie to you.

WHITE SHADOW: What would you do to me?

(Ross shuffles over, flashes his shit-eating smile.)

ROSS: Sorry, boss. We's jus' tryin' to make a few dimes. We don't mean no harm, we knows our place, we jus' plyin' the ragged time. We don't want no trouble.

WHITE SHADOW (*Looks them over*): Your life is trouble. Just know. I'm watching you. You're my children, and I'll beat you like I'm your father. Don't forget. You're in America. So you can all rest easy. 'Cause Daddy's home. I make the decisions now.

(*Beat.*)

The kid'll turn up. And when he does I'll be here waiting. He'll make me a nice houseboy. Ply me a good nigger song and keep the bed warm on a cold night . . .

(*Something breaks inside of Abe. He hits White Shadow on the jaw. White Shadow aims the rifle, but Abe knocks it aside. He hits White Shadow once more, with purpose. He hits him, but it's as if the punch is for everyone. Then he stands above the prone body of White Shadow.*)

FREDA: Oh, Abie. You gone and done it now.

GARY: He dead?

ABE: He'll come to, eventually.

(*Freda embraces Abe.*)

FREDA: I may just have to get outta town. Better safe than sorry.

ABE: You can come with me. There's a steamer tomorrow morning.

FREDA: Ain't there a war down in Cuba?

ABE: Something tells me things is a lot safer there.
    (*To the blind men*) You fellas gonna be all right?

GARY: Don't you worry about us.

(*Gary goes to the body of White Shadow, picks up the rifle. Everyone ducks.*)

This'll make a mighty fine cane.

ABE: Don't shoot!

GARY: I don't shoot my people.

FREDA (*To Gary*): Y'all be careful out there.

GARY: Death ain't far. But I plan to live.

(*Abe and Freda exit. Gary and Ross are alone. Only the sound of the water lapping on shore.*)

GARY: Just me and you.

ROSS: And the boy.

GARY: Boy's long gone.

ROSS: Maybe.

(Ross begins to pack up.)

GARY: Where you headed?

ROSS: How the hell should I know?

GARY: Them Gullah Islands? I heard you talk to the boy. You was gonna—

ROSS: But I didn't.

GARY: Always wondered what I'd do, running into you after all these years. Blamed you for my troubles. Dreamed I'd split you down the middle with a broken bottle. Do you like you done me. Oh I had my dreams. But here we sit. Like nothing ever happened.

ROSS: Everything happened.

GARY: Thing is, Ross. I missed ya. Feeling ya around, near. Feeling . . .

ROSS: Feeling.

(Awkwardly, the two men touch hands. Not unlike the Sistine Chapel image. Then Gary clears his throat and starts to pack up his things.)

GARY: Well if you find him somewheres, don't spoil him too much. I know you can't keep your hands off, but go easy. And let him watch ya good when you ply. Let him learn yer damn secrets, so's he don't gotta go waste time stealing 'em from ya. Let him have a leg up. Let him have it better than I did.

ROSS: And you . . . If you happen to run into . . . somebody . . . Treat that somebody with a little warmth now, ya hear? Warmth. That's what a body's good for.

GARY: I can do that in any old cathouse.

ROSS: Not that.

GARY: You talking about the nasty?

ROSS: Quite the opposite, quite the opposite. But you'll be nicer. Next time you'll be nicer.

(Ross starts off.)

GARY: Ross.

ROSS: Gary.

GARY: See ya around.

ROSS: In a manner of speaking.

(Ross is gone. Gary is alone. He checks the body of White Shadow, dead to the world. Then he lifts the rucksack.)

GARY: I could never be a mom or pop. Me, of all people. You're lucky to be free of me, boy. Guess it's all for the best.

(Then he sets the rucksack down, breathes in deep.)

Songs belong to everybody. (Then he plays Ross's song. He sings:)

I will do my last singing in this land somewhere
I will do my last singing in this land somewhere.

(Ignacio approaches the body of White Shadow.)

I don't know and I cannot tell where
I may be somewhere sailing in the air
I will do my last singing in this land somewhere . . .

(Ignacio covers White Shadow with the funny pages, like a blanket, like a shroud.)

I will take my last journey in this land somewhere
I will take my last journey in this land somewhere . . .

(Ignacio begins to sing:)

IGNACIO:
    I don't know where I will be
    I may be out on the ocean,
    Way out on the sea . . .
GARY AND IGNACIO:
    I will take my last journey in this land somewhere
    I will do my last traveling in this land somewhere
    I will do my last traveling in this land somewhere
    I don't know where I will be
    I may be somewhere way over the sea
    I will do my last traveling in this land, child, somewhere.

(Song ends.)

GARY: You was up that tree. (Laughs) Smelt ya all along.

(Ignacio takes the rucksack and the guitar.)

Ain't gonna be easy.

(Ignacio plays the guitar like a man. Like a musicianeer.)

Whoa baby! Who taught you that?
IGNACIO: My people.

(Yellow and Sanctimonious watch from above.)

SANCTIMONIOUS: Gee.
YELLOW: Another sucker bites the dust.

(As they go off together . . .)

END OF PLAY

OLIVER MAYER is the author of numerous plays, including *Blade to the Heat*: premiered at The Joseph Papp Public Theater/New York Shakespeare Festival; was revised at Mark Taper Forum in Los Angeles; is being adapted for film (Madonna and Showtime, producers). His newest play, *Conjunto*, is being developed in conjunction with Mark Taper Forum's Latino Theatre Initiative after being workshopped at the 1999 Taper New Work Festival. *Joy of the Desolate* will receive its world premiere at the Apple Tree Theatre in Chicago in 2000. *The Road to Los Angeles*, a play in homage to David Alfaro Siqueiros, was recently produced by Campo Santo at Chabot College in Hayward, California, following a production at SPARC in Venice, California, and development at San Jose Repertory. *Joe Louis Blues*, which premiered at LATC in 1992, and is being revived at Thick Description in San Francisco.

His screenplays and teleplays include *Boxing Illustrated*, *Manifest Destiny* (co-written with Robert Glaudini); *Slow Blind Curve* (co-written with Robert Glaudini); *Sins of the City: The Hurt Business* (episode three, USA Cable); *The Wetback Academy* (co-written with Alfonso Arau); *Caliente* (a Latino rock musical; Alfonso Arau, Ben Myron, producers) and *Joy of the Desolate* (Gerraint Wyn-Davies producer).

Mr. Mayer is the recipient of numerous awards, including an OBIE Award, two Drama Critics Circle awards, eight Dramalogue awards and three Jeff awards, including Best Production for *Blade*.

He was literary associate at Mark Taper Forum from 1989 to 1997. He has been a lecturer/panelist at Columbia, UCLA, UCONN, San Diego State, University of California–San Diego, Stanford, University of California–Riverside and California Youth Authority. He was voted "100 coolest" by *Buzz* magazine in 1996. He is the author of *Circus Flora's* "Homage to Alexander Calder." (His literary archive is available at the Stanford University Libraries.)

My. Mayer attended Worcester College, Oxford. He received a B.A. in English, magna cum laude, from Cornell University and an M.F.A. in Theatre from Columbia University.

TRASH
A Monologue

Pedro R. Monge-Rafuls

THE WRITER SPEAKS
Pedro R. Monge-Rafuls

I write of my experience, and the world I know, the world that
surrounds me. This is a world of immigrants. Many "Latinos" have
similar experiences being Puertorican, Nuyorican or Chicano, and in
that sense I have similarities with them. But, at the same time I feel my
experience as an exile is far from theirs. My work delves into the
Cuban, the Anglo and the African-American idiosyncrasies, and is
very concerned with including the possibilities of modern media in
staging my plays. This is not necessarily true of other Latino/a writers.

I see my work as Cuban. This is a concept that can be controversial.
I belong to the "Latino" culture, a term created by the mainstream
which I do not fully accept, as I identify myself with my Cuban roots. I
can see how we "Latinos" are starting to be recognized more and more
as part of the literature of our home countries by the writers there, but
at the same time we belong to the American theatre as we are an important part of this country. It is a sense of dual identification which is difficult to define, especially if you are not part of this bicultural reality.

In some cases, the "Latino" and the American realities get together as an important part of my plays' action. This is the case in *Noche de Ronda* and *Solidarios (United)*. At other times the Cuban reality faces the American one in plays such as *Trash*. Another possibility includes the presence of a Cuban or a "Latino" reality with some depiction of the American way of life. This is the case in *Nadie se Va del Todo* and *Easy Money*. Lastly, other plays deal with oppression devoid of a specific ethnic culture. Here what matters is how man is governed by outside political, moral and social pressures.

My interest is to write about oppression. Not only of "political" oppression, but mainly all oppression that imprisons us as Latin American immigrants in the United States. As a Cuban exile.

I don't describe myself as a political writer, but my work is a result of political situations. My preoccupation is to present how man suffers through political circumstances and how he is obligated to react. These reactions are not always the most desirable, but it is how we live through these situations that concerns me.

Beauty is a very relative concept. The beauty of my writing is to express things, create characters and/or situations that through their images create thought. If this is achieved then the image created is beautiful, even though it is rough or cruel.

I didn't select theatre. Theatre selected me as a medium of creative expression. I think it is a very difficult means of expression that many times is not valued in our "Latino" society, nor in Latin America, as it is recognized in Europe or the United States.

I live in a society where to be "Latino" and write in Spanish, as I usually do, is not an advantage in regards to being produced. I am in the middle of two societies: the American, which does not care at all for so-called minority playwrights, especially if he/she writes in Spanish. On the other hand, there is not yet a recognition in the Latin American countries and Spain of our work, especially in my country, Cuba, where I am considered *persona non grata* for my political attitudes. It is also difficult to be produced in U.S. "Latino" communities, which do not care for Cuban theatre written outside the Island. So this hinders the production of my plays, which are written structurally and aesthetically different from the traditional theatre expected of "Latinos." The themes of my theatre, my perspective on life, is erotic and unflinching.

Production History

Trash had a staged reading at Hunter College, M.S.A. Studios on February 9, 1995, in a production directed by the author.

JOSÉ   Tom Starace

Trash was first produced by Do-Gooder Productions at Theatre on Three on November 8, 1995, under the direction of Mark Robert Gordon.

JOSÉ   Sam Valle

For those Cubans who escaped
during the Mariel Exodus in 1980.
Especially all those I met in New York.

1988. Daytime. No scenery. Through mime the actor should indicate the presence of any object. He is in direct contact with the audience unless otherwise indicated.

José, Latin mulatto, masculine, muscular. He has a "St. Barbara" tattoo which is visible to the audience. Barefoot, shirtless.

He is boxing, punching the air. Then he stops and faces the audience. He speaks English with a Spanish accent and with his particular grammatical constructions.

JOSÉ: Hi! I am José . . . a lot of people call me Joe. I am not Joe, I am José. *(Talks while making boxing motions)* If your name is William and you go to Puerto Rico you wouldn't like people calling you Guillermo. I don't like to be called Joe. *(Stops boxing. Serious)* My real name is Jesús *(Pronounced "Ha-sus")*. I know some foreigners who wanted to sound American and changed their names to English names. I changed mine because people laugh at me when I tell them my real name . . . I am Jesus. Yes, that's it . . . and any time I say, "I am Jesus," people laugh. No American is named Jesus. Why? That's a very common name in Latin American countries. *(Pause)* I have another problem with my name. Some people call me Fidel when they find out that I am from Cuba. Isn't that ridiculous? Will you like to be called Bush? *(Or use the current president's name)* Those people think that calling me Fidel is a great joke.

(Goes to a pair of sneakers and a shirt. He takes the sneakers, sits in front of the audience and starts putting the sneakers on while he talks.)

I'm a *Marielito*. You know, a boat people. Everybody in this country is afraid of Cuban boat people. They say that we kill everybody and rape all the women. You heard a lot of stories about us. Remember the Fourth of July when that crazy man killed those people in the ferry that goes to the Statue of Liberty?

And the other one who ran nude through St. Patrick's Cathedral and stabbed an old man? Not all boat people are bad.

Castro put a lot of criminals and crazy people in the *flotillas*. They went to jails and mental hospitals and pulled prisioners out and sent them here in the boats, but most of us wanted to be free when we decided to come to this country. I couldn't live in Cuba anymore. Cuba is like a big hell! It's not even easy to go to your girlfriend's house. *(Remembers)* I had a nice girl back there. Nedy; she is beautiful, man. I keep thinking about her after all these years.

(Starts boxing again. Talks while making violent boxing motions, as if in the climax of a match. Wants to forget about his girlfriend.)

I went to visit Nedy every day. I ran from work to her house. *(Feels he must explain)* You see, I worked in a store for foreigners—those who were invited to visit Cuba. Those stores have everything Cubans can dream of. They trusted me. I had dreams over there. Nedy and I dreamed together. *(Stops boxing. Remembers)* I wanted to go to finish school and marry Nedy. We will have a house near the beach and twelve children: a dozen. Don't laugh. It's true. *(Wakes up)* Then, something happened that everyone was wishing to happen—the chance to get out of the country and be a free human being. No one was ready when it finally happened (the takeover of the Peruvian Embassy) and there I was. That's how I got to came to this country. People don't understand Castro's ways. They think that he behaves like the Americans, and that's a big mistake. But do you think that one of the White House experts cares for what I have to say? Noo! Anyway, I'm not going to talk about American foreign policy. It's not my business, man! I'm proud of being a Cuban. *(Pause)* I am also proud of being a *Marielito*. You can see how boat people are doing in Miami and New Jersey. They're doing good. Like my buddy Roberto; you see, we came together to this country. He stayed in Miami and started to work in a mirror factory—he learned the trade and he opened his own business. He's doing good, and now he even has four guys working for him.

(He sits.)

D'you know why I speak English well? Because the first thing I did when I came to this country was to go to school. I had good teachers. My grammar teacher was Desi Arnaz and my American literature teacher was Charo. Do you know them? That's a joke! Let's be serious. Do you know how the Cubans call Fidel? *El caballo.* The horse. We call *caballo* to someone who is the most powerful, the best in everything. *Eh, tú, tú eres un caballo.* It means, "Hey, you are a horse." A foreign language is not an easy thing to learn. It hasn't been easy for me. *(Pause)* I came here and didn't understand a thing. If you asked me what my name was, I smiled and said yes and moved my head up and down with a smile on my face. If you asked me where did I live, I smiled and said yes. It was my "yes period" of time.

(Thinks) Some people said they didn't believe Castro, but they believed we were all criminals as he had said. I was no criminal in Cuba. I haven't been a criminal anywhere. Some people tried to take advantage from us. Not all of course. I remember the first job I got. I had to fix roofs with that sticking tar for two dollars and twenty five cents per hour. I had to spend almost every penny I made on transportation and didn't have any left to buy food. Smart people, they are! They paid us less money than they were supposed to, by law, and abused us any way they could. You know it's hard to come here from a Communist country. A Communist society is very different from the American way of life. Over there, you don't have anything. When we came here, the American government put us in camps—you know army camps. Once you got there, you were interrogated to find out whether you were a criminal or not. You had to find a sponsor. Only a sponsor can take us out of the camp. We were desperately looking for sponsors so we could take the last step to freedom. My Aunt Felicia, my mother's aunt, sponsored me and took me to her home. She was nice but she died soon. Her son didn't help me, and there I was out in the street with no trade—nothing. It wasn't easy . . . We were solicited for sex at the camp. Outside people used to come to see what they could get. You know that we Caribbean people are known to offer big *(Discreetly touching his penis)* pleasure. You know what I mean? Women were sponsoring us, helping us out. *(Imitating)* "I help you to make a good life in the U.S. You'll see, we'll be good friends."

Well, to tell you the truth, some of us did anything in order to survive. D'you know how we call homosexuals in Cuba and Puerto Rico? We call them *patos.* Ducks. *(Realizes)* I think we love to identify people with animals. In the Dominican Republic they call "tigers" those who you call hustlers. Well, I won't mention any other animal 'cause I'll end up mentioning the whole zoo. Do you think a psychiatrist will be interested in doing a research on this subject?

(Transition. Angry at himself) Humans are animals, man; we're animals but not beasts. There's a difference. Animals don't do what beasts do: horrible things.

(Pause. Starts throwing punches.)

The truth is, I wanted to start a new life in this country. I came here very young. I wanted to learn English and go to college. That's why I stayed in New York, because I was told that was easier here, but no way. Every door was closed for me. I tried to study but didn't have any income. Then I tried to work but didn't have any experience and didn't speak any English either. Welfare could've solved my life but welfare is not good. It doesn't let you advance in life. It kills your drive to do positive things. I was forced to live in slums, surrounded by alcohol, drugs and prostitution. Kids stayed up late at night sipping beer and snorting coke. But I kept my distance. Honest. That's the truth.

(Stops punching. Goes back in time.)

That day I went to Nedy's house. We were talking in the front yard, trying to make out when nobody was looking. I loved that woman. Then Roberto came running. *(He speaks as if he is Roberto and himself)* "Jesús, *(Pronounced "Ha-sus")* they went nuts; they're letting everybody go—leave Cuba."

"What are you talking about?"

"Swear to God; some guys barged in the Embassy of Peru and asked for political asylum."

"So what?"

"Well, Fidel made one of his big-shot speeches and said that everyone who wanted to leave is free to go. He said Cubans are happy with his government, so he said he knows no one is leaving."

"And then what happened?"

(Back to the present.)

There were more than eight thousand people inside the embassy in less than three hours. I ran out with Roberto. Nedy was so nervous because she was afraid and she didn't want to come. "Don't go," she says, but no way. I had to go because that was the only chance I had to get out of Cuba. It was hard inside the embassy—women, children, everybody was there and we couldn't move. Thank God they let us go! It isn't easy to leave the country where you were born. I had to leave my mother—and Nedy. If you're against something you try to earn your rights. Being alone out here doesn't excuse you for being bad. Here, I went to school. *(Very frustrated)* But for one year only. Race relations and life for a minority person have gone from bad to worse in the last years. It's not easy. That's when I pray. Yeeaah. I pray. I was born to a good family. My family taught me to respect God and religion. I get so confused when I find out bad people in the church. *(Pointing to his tattoo of St. Barbara)* She's my mother in Heaven. I have faith. I ask her for help, for guidance. I ask her what to do when I don't know what else to do. She has given me good advices.

Suddenly I started to realize that I had to go to Miami and talk to my buddy Roberto. That he would give me a job and help me to put my life together; I thought that maybe I can get a visa for Nedy through the American Red Cross and bring her here and marry her.

(From now on, he forgets the audience. He talks to himself and acts accordingly, sometimes, as if in a trance.)

I went to Brooklyn to see my friend Carlos. I wanted to say good-bye to him. We had a couple of beers, we talked about friends, girls. You know. We had a good time. I told him that I was leaving. It was late and it's not good to be out in the street. I don't want problems, that's not what I'm looking for. I had a gun I had bought for my own protection, but only because you need one in a city like New York. If it's OK for drug dealers, it must be OK for me. So I was waiting for the bus that takes me to the subway station. The bus stop is on a deserted dark street. A van passed by me but I didn't pay any attention until it passed by a second time. A man was looking straight at me. I immediately knew what he was looking for. To have a good time with a young, black guy. It wasn't the first time. He was white, in his late forties and fat. It didn't bother me but I wasn't interested. He went around the corner and came back again. He stopped the van in front of me and asked me, "Is this Brooklyn?" What a stupid way to start a conversation. "Yes," I said, "but I don't know anything else about the neighborhood." He insisted. God, why did he think he had the right to insist? Didn't he see I wasn't interested? He got out of the van and came to me. And here he is, standing next to me. He smiled at me and I smiled right back but moved away from him. He was wearing this white shirt with no collar and black pants. He said, "I like you." "Thank you very much, but I am waiting for the bus." "Oh, I can give you a ride anywhere you like. To my apartment for a drink. It's not that late. I have porno movies." Who told him I liked porno movies? But I understood and I was nice. "Thank you but I'm going home." "Are you Puerto Rican?" "No." "You're not? Where are you from then?" "Cuba." "Oh, Cubans are good people. Very handsome men," and then he started talking to me, and he keeps talking and talking. He didn't leave me alone. He offered me fifty bucks if I let him give me a blow job. I didn't want to do it. It's true that I had done that for money when I first was alone after my aunt died, but not anymore. I am afraid of AIDS. Besides I quit after I did it for a while because that's not my preference. *(As if in a trance)* And the man kept insisting and the bus didn't come and he offered me sixty dollars. I remembered I didn't have enough money to get by the first days in Miami. *(He has given up his internal struggle)* So I went inside the van as he wanted me to. *(Pause. Like it happened a hundred years ago)* He insisted I had to be completely naked. *(Instinctively he goes for his T-shirt and puts it on)* I didn't want to at first but I remember how he insisted when he got me in the van. And first I only had one idea on my mind—I wanted to get done with it and leave. I was naked now and he started to touch me all over. I could feel all the big pleasure he was having while touching my balls. He started blowing. He knew how to give head, let me tell you. I felt guilty at the beginning because I had promised myself I was never going to do this again, and there I was feeling a lot of pleasure. And I came! He enjoyed that. He rubbed my dick around his face, still licking it. He really loved to feel the sperm on his face. I said, "It's over. Take me to the train station. Pay me." And I pushed him away. Gently. That's when he asked me for more. "Come on, man. I'm not a machine." He insisted for more and I said to myself, This man is too much. Too vicious. He said, "I am going to pay you sixty dollars. I have the right to ask you. Latinos are so proud. I'm paying you." "Look man," I said, "that wasn't the deal. Pay me and go." "Why should I pay you so much for something you also enjoyed?" Of course I liked it, how else was I going to get a hard-on. That's not the point. And I started pulling my pants up. I already had my T-shirt on, and he struggled trying to take my pants off. He tore my T-shirt up. I pushed him away but he insisted again. That's when he felt my gun. He started screaming. I pulled it out of my pocket because I thought it was a good idea to scare him, get my money and keep him away from me. But he kept screaming trying to take the gun from me. We struggled and I shot him. *(Lights go down abruptly)* A second shot hit him on the leg. He held his hands to his face, blinking his ice blue eyes as if a helmet strap had frozen his expression. Frightened and humbled. He didn't want to die. But he knew he would. He cried. Sure, we both cried. He wanted to say something, but no words came. *(Desperately)* I don't want to talk about that right now . . . It's too painful. I can't do it . . . I can't begin to understand . . . *(Pause)* I am not willing to make any explanation of why he . . . me? fired.

(Thick bars come from nowhere to surround him. He is in jail.)

This is something you read on the papers, but you never think it can happen to you. It was on the paper the next day. He was a priest. *(Amazed)* He didn't pray when he knew those were his last minutes in life. He didn't even mention God. How can he die like that? How can a priest look for sex? I'm sure God weeps when he sees what happened to me. Who will believe a *Marielito?* He ruined my dreams. My lawyer told me to stop lying for my own good. He said that he can't make a good defense because I gave the police a false name. He said I was probably lying about my name because I didn't want them to find out about my crimes in the past. Who will believe that was something missing to fulfill his nights? The papers said he had a twenty-year career as a good priest. That his parishioners loved him because of his exemplary life. At the funeral mass the bishop said, "This attack is something you would only expect from beasts, not from humans." That's a horrible thing to say. Am I a beast? How can I ask Nedy to understand? We think we can control our destiny . . . and then something like this happens, death comes, pain and suffering come. And then we know in a flash . . . that we can't control our lives. *(His eyes swell with tears)* I am very far from my country. I got nervous, I pulled the gun, and he started to push me around. I told him I had a gun and he grabbed my hand and the gun went off. Boom. Boom. What am I going to do now?

END OF PLAY

PEDRO R. MONGE-RAFULS was born in Central Zaza, Placetas, Cuba, in 1943. He left Cuba by boat in 1962, and after living in Honduras and Columbia he moved to the United States. In Illinois he co-founded the Círculo Teatral de Chicago (Chicago Theater Circle), the first Spanish-language theatre group in the Midwest. In 1977 he founded Ollantay Center for the Arts and in 1993 *Ollantay Theater Magazine*. In 1991, he became the first person to receive the Very Special Arts Award as a New York artist for his comedy *Noche de ronda* (1991). He has written *Cristóbal Colón y otros locos* (1986); *En este apartamento hay fuego todos los días* (1987), produced in IATI's first festival of Hispanic theatre, later published in *Linden Lane Magazine*'s special 1990 issue dedicated to exile literature, later published in *Ollantay* (Vol. III, No. 1, 1995); *De la muerte y otras cositas* (1988); *El instante fugitivo* (1989), produced by Duo Theater; *Easy Money* and *Solidarios* (1990), presented in the FestiArte '90; *Noche de ronda*, produced three times in one year by the Gay Men's Health Crisis (GMHC); and *Momentos* (1993). Mr. Monge-Rafuls is a member of the National Endowment for the Arts' theatre panel for the expansion of the arts.

THE HUNGRY WOMAN
A Mexican Medea

Cherríe Moraga

THE WRITER SPEAKS
Cherríe Moraga

I see my work in the trajectory of Chicano theatre, the theatre that emerged in the sixties and seventies—of flatbed trucks in lettuce fields on strike, of East Los Angeles school walkouts, of protest against imperialist wars, pesticide-poisoned grapes, and illegal landlords. My plays have learned to pray with the "mitos" of El Teatro Campesino and to rage with the domestic- and docudramas of El Teatro de la Esperanza. The bilingualism of my works pays tribute to its origins in a U.S. Mexican Teatro for a Spanish and Spanglish-speaking people. My writings reflect an evolving critique of Chicano Nationalism (*The Hungry Woman* is a case in point), while remaining loyal to our native land and the rights and responsibilities that that knowledge requires. In this sense, I see my work in concert with Native American theatre—our first teachers, our storytellers. I may write down the play, but it returns to its oral antecedents—its original spoken voice and the necessary listener—with each darkening of the house lights.

As a Chicana playwright, my first consciously theatrical writings came forth in dialogue with the Fathers, since in the mid-eighties Chicano theatre remained overwhelmingly male in character and subject matter. Whereas I began as a disobedient daughter, I soon grew veterana enough for unacknowledged sisterhood, until age and war wounds changed the shape of my writings to (not-always-benevolent) mother. Now I work on the young ones to change.

I admit I am one of those writers shamelessly committed to change. This is fundamental to my writing. I am not ashamed to affirm that I write to right a wrong, a distorted picture of our mexicana/americana selves. Each of my plays begins with the Native and Mestiza female body, the body of the woman worker, the daughter, the mother, the lover. She is the lens through which I continue to see and write.

I have also always written as a self-acknowledged Chicana lesbian. With little to lose in the way of privilege in the theatre world (both Euro-American and Chicano) I believe this has helped me get to the heart of the matter in my work. I feel less afraid of breaking taboo, so my characters may be less afraid to tell me what's really on their mind. Sex is often on their minds, their longing for it, their failure at it, their deformed view of it, including the pleasure it brings them. Since homosexuality is always a possibility in my characters, hetero-sexuality can be viewed more honestly, I think, and I hope that the work can provide some insights about the role desire plays in our lives beyond social convention.

To say as I do at the start of these comentarios, that I am in dialogue with Chicano theatre, I mean that this is where my heart resides—in that continuing conversation with my own kind, in spite of the piti-fully shrinking resources to house that conversation. I am still naive enough to believe in a teatro that can show us back to ourselves so that we are improved by the reflection. In short, I am not cynical.

One way or another, I insist on writing plays because the voices of my characters make me feel less lonely, less loca. They make me feel that for a moment, we can speak our minds. As if this América were still, at least in part, truly ours.

Production History

The Hungry Woman: A Mexican Medea was originally commissioned by Berkeley Repertory Theatre, where it received a staged reading on April 10, 1995. It was directed by Tony Kelly.

On December 2, 1995, the play was presented in a staged reading as part of Mark Taper Forum's New Works Festival in Los Angeles. It was directed by Lisa Wolpe.

As part of Theatre Communications Group's National Theatre Artist Residency Program, funded by The Pew Charitable Trusts, *The Hungry Woman* was further developed at The Brava Theater Center of San Francisco and it received a staged reading on June 10, 1997, directed by the playwright.

On May 21, 1999, the play was presented in a staged reading as part of A Contemporary Theater/Hedgebrook Writers' Retreat Women's Playwright Festival in Seattle. It was directed by Richard E. T. White.

Characters

MEDEA, a midwife and curandera in her mid-forties.

LUNA, Medea's lover of seven years;
stone mason and clay sculptor, late thirties.

CHAC-MOOL, Medea's thirteen-year-old son.

MAMA SAL, Medea's aging grandmother, late seventies.

CIHUATATEO (El Coro), chorus of four warrior women who,
according to Aztec myth, have died in childbirth. Here they are
identified by the four directions and four primary pre-Columbian
colors: East (Red), North (Black), West (White) and South (Blue).
The figures wear the faces of the dead in the form of skulls.
Their hands are shaped into claws. Their breasts appear bare
and their skirts are tied with the cord of a snake.
They are barefoot, their ankles wrapped in shell rattles.
The chorus performs in the traditional style of Aztec danzantes.

SAVANNAH, Luna's girlfriend, African-American,
played by Cihuatateo West, wears white.

NURSE, Medea's aging caretaker in the psychiatric hospital,
played by the Cihuatateo East, wears red.

JASÓN, Medea's husband and Chac-Mool's father;
played by Cihuatateo South, wears blue.

THE BORDER GUARD, also plays the Prison Guard and the Tattoo
Artist, played by Cihuatateo North, wears black.

NOTE: All characters are to be played by women,
with the exception of Chac-mool, who should be played by a boy.

Setting

The play takes place in the near future of a fictional past—one only dreamed in the Chicana imagination. An ethnic civil war has "balkanized" the United States. Medea, her lover Luna and Medea's child Chac-Mool have been exiled to what remains of Phoenix, Arizona. Located in the border region between Gringolandia (white Amerika) and Aztlán (Chicano country), Phoenix is now a city-in-ruin, the dumping site of every kind of poison and person unwanted by its neighbors. Scenes shift from the "present," where Medea is an inmate in a prison psychiatric ward, to events in the past leading up to Medea's incarceration. Psychiatric ward scenes are represented by a deadening silence and the glare of hospital lights. Phoenix is represented by the ceaseless racket of a city-out-of-control (constant traffic, low-flying jet planes, hawkers squawking their wares, muy "*Blade Runner*-esque.") The lighting is urban neon. Most people look lousy in it.

Where can I go? Is it possible to imagine a world,
a time, where I would have a place?
There's no one I could ask. That's the answer.

CHRISTA WOLF
Medea: A Modern Retelling

For Marsha Gómez,
sculptor

1951–1998

ACT 1

Prelude

Pre-Columbian Meso-American music. The lights slowly rise on the altar to Coatlicue, the Aztec Goddess of Creation and Destruction, an awesome statuesque decapitated figure. She wears a serpent skirt. Her breast shield is splayed with dismembered hands and hearts. The Cihuatateo flank her.

CIHUATATEO EAST:
This is how all stories begin and end
the innocence of an eagle feather
stuffed inside a mother's apron.

The birdboy growing there
taking shape.
The warrior son waiting in the wings
taking flight.

So, too begins and ends this story.
The birth of a male child
from the dark sea of Medea

at the dawning of an age.

(Pause. Cihuatateo North crosses to Cihuatateo East and hands her a red nurse's cap. As she puts it on, North covers her face in a black ski mask.)

NURSE: This is how all days begin and end.

Scene One

Prison Guard stands upstage in ski mask, hands behind her back. A huge ring of jailer keys (very exaggerated) hangs from her military belt. *There is a domino game set up nearby. Medea is downstage, looking directly into the one-way mirror through which all activities in the psychiatric ward can be observed. Medea senses she is being watched. Upstage is an unmade hospital bed with a vase of wilting white flowers next to it.*

PRISON GUARD *(To audience)*: A prison psychiatric hospital in the borderlands. The near future of a fictional Chicana past.

(Nurse enters, crosses to Medea, studies her chart.)

MEDEA: Cover the mirrors, Nurse. I don't want my son to see me like this, red-eyed, crow's-feet drooping. I am a motherless sight. Nurse, are you listening? Bring out the purple cloths. We'll pretend it is Lent and we await the resurrection of my son, my holy son. I'll sleep until then, until he returns to me. *(Pressing her face against the mirror)* The mirror is cold, impenetrable. You can never get inside it, unless you are a child or un muerto. I am neither, no longer, not yet. *(She spits at the mirrored wall. Nurse perfunctorily wipes it clean. She grabs Nurse's arm)* Tiny ghosts live inside me. The ghost of my own pathetic girlhood. When I met Luna I imagined every touch was a gesture toward that girl-child.

NURSE: Tell your girlfriend, not me. She comes on Saturdays, three o'clock. Today is Friday. That's tomorrow. She's the one in the man's suit jacket who always comes with flowers. She's the face behind the flowers. You can't miss her.

MEDEA: But I do. I do miss my Luna.

NURSE: Why don't you tell her that when you see her. You never talk to her.

MEDEA: No. I only want to be an Indian, a Woman, an Animal in the Divine Ecosystem. The jaguar, the bear, the eagle.

(The Prison Guard and Nurse begin to play dominoes. Medea remains, examining herself in the mirror. Lights rise in Luna's bedroom in Phoenix, early morning. Luna sits up in bed, raises the shade. City sounds. The woman lying next to her under the covers, stirs.)

LUNA: To have somebody read your face in the light of day.

(Luna dresses.)

MEDEA: My chin is dropping, just like all the women in my family. My face is falling into my throat. Next thing I know I won't have a chin at all, just those thick necklaces of flesh strangling me. My eyelids are falling. One morning I'll open my eyes and the shades will be drawn permanently.

LUNA: Medea hid from the light. She always slept in the shadows, the windowless side of the bed, the shades drawn day or night. She slept with earplugs, blindfolds.

MEDEA: I think it's the alcohol that sucks out all your juices, leaves you dry and black-eyed. The obsidian mirror and pulque. Vanity and drunkenness. The gods' downfall and my own. I'm getting old. Old means the circles stay even after the cucumber peels.

NURSE *(Mildly interested)*: Cucumber peels?

MEDEA: You didn't know?

NURSE: What's to know?

MEDEA: During the day when Jasón was at work. I would lay my head down on the pillow and put the slices over my eyelids. They were so cool, one on each eye. I could hear Chac-Mool outside talking to the stonemason. It was paradise.

NURSE: The stonemason?

MEDEA: Yes. The woman, the migrant worker, my husband, Jasón, hired to put in the garden patio.

(Luna and Chac-Mool appear in Medea's memory. Chac-Mool is sitting on a slab of stone. Luna holds a trowel.)

LUNA: You should plant corn.

CHAC-MOOL: My mom didn't say nothing about no corn.

LUNA: What's a garden without corn?

CHAC-MOOL: She's gonna plant medicine.

LUNA: Your mom makes medicine?

CHAC-MOOL: Yeah, she learned from my Bisabuela.

LUNA: Plant corn. A single corn plant can produce enough grain to feed a person for a day.

MEDEA: And the stonemason's voice entered me like medicine. Medicine for my brokenness.

(Luna crosses back to bedroom, puts on a man's suit jacket.)

LUNA: I always liked that tiny fold hanging over Medea's eyes. It was like a delicate little awning, shading her from the world. I liked how that little mistake made her face less perfect. There's something to read in that. Nothing's printed in perfection. Only language I know are worry lines, a brow that looks like the valley floor in planting season. I'd trace my finger like a dumb plow along those furrows, but I could only guess at what Medea was thinking.

(Luna bends down, kisses woman who stirs in bed.)

I'll be back tomorrow night. *(Beat)* I am tired of mourning Medea. I dream of other women to bring moisture to places made dust by her departure.

(Luna exits.)

Scene Two

Prison Guard and Nurse push Medea's hospital bed to a cramped government-funded urban apartment. Outside the neon quality of the lighting and sudden rush of city sounds are distinct from the glaring bright lights and soundlessness of the psychiatric prison hospital. The Guard dumps a load of trash around the floor: old magazines, used tissues, newspapers, junk mail, a few empty pints of booze.

PRISON GUARD *(To the audience)*: One year earlier. The land of the exiled. Phoenix, Arizona. What never rose up from the ashes of destruction.

(She hands a letter to Medea and exits. Medea paces back and forth with the letter in one hand and a bottle of tequila in the other. Luna is on her knees with a wastebasket, picking up the trash.)

MEDEA: He writes me in fucking lawyerese. I hate that! Fucking lawyer, fucking poet-lawyer! There ought to be a law against fucking with language that way. Mira esta mierda. *(She thrusts the letter at Luna)*
LUNA: I've seen the letter, Medea.

(Cross-stage Cihuatateo South appears as Jasón. He wears perfectly pressed military blue.)

MEDEA/JASÓN: "She reminds me of you, Medea. Your once-innocence. Your wide-eyed eagerness. She is the Medea you were before the war, before 'politics' changed you . . . changed us."
MEDEA: ¡Pendejo! She's a virgin, sabes? Bueno . . . *was* a virgin.
LUNA: The bride-to-be? I thought they didn't make virgins no more.
MEDEA: She's nineteen years old.

LUNA: Oh. How does he know for sure?

MEDEA: That she's nineteen?

LUNA: That she's a virgin.

MEDEA: She bled for him.

LUNA: He wrote you that.

MEDEA: Uh-huh.

LUNA: Grosero.

JASÓN: "She bled for me, just as you did once."

MEDEA: Ay, Jasoncito, that was a wound you found too many years ago, a bleeding ulcer between my legs.

(Medea crumples up the letter and tosses it on the ground. Luna picks it up, puts it in the trash. Jasón exits.)

Politics. Men think women have no love of country, that the desire for nation is a male prerogative. So like gods, they pick and choose who is to be born and live and die in a land I bled for equal to any man. Aztlán, how you betrayed me! Y aquí me encuentro in this wasteland where yerbas grow bitter for lack of water, my face pressed to the glass of my own revolution like some húerfana abandonada.

LUNA: You aren't an orphan, Medea.

MEDEA: I have no mother . . . land. *(Beat)* Can you stop doing that? *(The cleaning)*

LUNA: It bothers you?

MEDEA: Yes.

LUNA: It bothers me, too.

(Medea sloshes tequila onto the floor. With intention:)

MEDEA: I need to talk to you.

(Luna stops.)

LUNA: Are you jealous?

MEDEA: No, not jealous.

LUNA: . . . Medea.

MEDEA: I'm a rabid dog.

LUNA *(Beat)*: You've never divorced Jasón . . . why?

MEDEA: You believe in that piece of paper?

LUNA: Yes, when it means you could be taken away from me.

MEDEA: I'm not your custody case. Don't treat me like one.

LUNA: No, Chac-Mool is. Our son is the custody case.

MEDEA: My son.

LUNA: Why don't you get dressed and go to work?

MEDEA: Work! I suck off the seven-pound creations of other women! That's all. I catch their babies and throw them back at them.

LUNA: Just get dressed. *(Starts to exit)*

MEDEA: Jasón doesn't need Chac-Mool now. He'll get his progeny. The teenager waifa will see to that.

LUNA: She's Indian.

MEDEA: Indian enough. And young enough. She'll have a litter of breed babies for him.

LUNA: He's getting old, Medea. He wants Chac-Mool.

MEDEA: He hasn't asked for him.

LUNA: The boy's turning thirteen, he has the right to decide for himself.

MEDEA: No.

LUNA: Medea.

MEDEA: There's time yet.

LUNA: For what?

MEDEA: I don't know. Something.

LUNA *(After a pause)*: I always thought that if Jasón had felt even the smallest part of what I've come to feel for Chac-Mool, that he never would've let him go. He would have held him kicking and screaming to his chest. He would've forced you to choose.

MEDEA: Lucky for you he didn't.

LUNA: That's what I thought. Get dressed, Medea.

MEDEA: Didn't you hear? Jasón wants a divorce. I'm yours forever. Happy?

(Luna exits as Mama Sal enters, laden with a heavy leather satchel.)

(To herself) And our hands are left empty . . . you and I, childless women que chupan each other's barren breasts?

MAMA SAL: You're gonna push her so far away from you, she won't be able to find her way back.

MEDEA: Good. She's a liability.

MAMA SAL: ¿Por qué hablas así?

MEDEA: I can't bring her into this. It'll make things worse.

MAMA SAL: They can't get worse, Medea. We lost it all already. ¿No recuerdas?

MEDEA: Not my son. I didn't lose my son.

MAMA SAL *(Beat)*: You better get dressed. La clínica's got two women in labor.

MEDEA: No puedo. You go for me instead.

MAMA SAL: Ay, Medea. I've burped every border baby from here to Nogales today.

MEDEA: No puedo.

(Medea climbs back into bed.)

MAMA SAL: Medea, you got to get back to work.

MEDEA: I don't trust myself. I feel my hands as liquid as the river.

MAMA SAL: La poet. It's your mind that's liquid from tanta tequila.

(Mama Sal rummages through her satchel pulling out small sacks of yerbas. She hands Medea a few clear capsules of ground herb.)

Ten.

MEDEA: What are they?

MAMA SAL: Tómalos and not with the tequila.

(Medea pops the capsules into her mouth.)

Now, sleep it off.

(Mama Sal closes up her satchel and exits.)

Scene Three

Chac-Mool sits beneath a glaring spotlight. It looks like an interrogation room. Various small rings of silver hang from his eyebrow, ear, lip and nose. The Tattoo Artist, who is the Prison Guard wearing a worker's apron, blindfolds Chac-Mool with a black bandana. Chac-Mool offers his shoulder as Tattoo Artist begins to etch out with a needle the first markings of the tattoo.

TATTOO ARTIST: What's the matter? Why are you covering your eyes?

CHAC-MOOL: To see.

TATTOO ARTIST: To see what?

CHAC-MOOL: The swirls of purple and forest green. If I cover my eyes, I am asleep in a dream. I can dream anything I want. At night, before I dream, I stay up and watch the moon cross the sky. Each night it's a long journey, unless you forget to watch her. Then she can appear in completely different places as if by magic. Have you seen the moon the last four nights? The evening moon?

TATTOO ARTIST: I think so.

CHAC-MOOL: What did you see?

TATTOO ARTIST: A sliver.

CHAC-MOOL: A sliver in the smoggy haze?

TATTOO ARTIST: . . . Yeah.

CHAC-MOOL: A thin brush stroke in the sky. One delicate turn of a silver-haired paintbrush marking the sky with her hue.

TATTOO ARTIST: You talk beautiful for a boy.

CHAC-MOOL: At sunrise, she melts from the sun's glow. Soft, insistent.

TATTOO ARTIST: You watch her all night?

CHAC-MOOL: La luna? Yes, like a lover. *(To himself)* "The Boy Who Fell in Love with the Moon."

TATTOO ARTIST: What do you know about love? You're too young.

CHAC-MOOL: I am a boy who sleeps alone in his pijamas and wakes up in the middle of the night wishing for something.

TATTOO ARTIST: What? Manhood?

CHAC-MOOL: No. Full-grown innocence. Such lightness of flesh that I could rise above my bed and fly to the moon. I believed that once, pumping my swing harder and harder, I believed I could touch la luna. My mom sang me songs of flying to the moon as she pushed my back.

(Singing:)

Up in a balloon, boys. Up in a balloon.
Sailing 'round the little stars and all around the moon.

It seemed possible then.

TATTOO ARTIST: And now?

CHAC-MOOL: Now I know more and my dreams are getting as heavy as my heart.

TATTOO ARTIST: Pity.

CHAC-MOOL: Don't pity me. Pity my mother. She sleeps during the day when la luna has disappeared to the other side of the earth. She can't stand the relentless sun without her, she says. She can't stand the brilliant productiveness of the day.

TATTOO ARTIST *(Cutting deeper into the skin)*: Cover your eyes.

(Chac-Mool puts a hand over his blindfold, wincing as the Tattoo Artist pierces.)

CHAC-MOOL: I don't remember if this is the right way to pray. I was never officially taught. It is not allowed. Everything relies on memory. We no longer have any records, nothing is written down. But I heard. I heard about Aztlán and the piercing of the skin as a prayer.

TATTOO ARTIST: You think that's what you're doing, praying? You think this is holy, driving needles into the paper of your flesh? Hanging metal off your eyebrows, your nostrils, your lips?

(Removing his hand from the blindfold.)

CHAC-MOOL: I pray as you cut. I pray deep and hard and if it pusses, I pray harder for the pain. In the center of pain, there is always a prayer. A prayer where you get up to leave and a whole army of people are there to carry you away. You aren't alone anymore.

TATTOO ARTIST: Is this what they're teaching kids now in this ghetto?

CHAC-MOOL: They don't know what to teach us no more. We only get what's left over.

TATTOO ARTIST *(Pulling the blindfold off of Chac-Mool; to the audience)*: "What's left over."

(Lighting transition. Nurse appears upstage in the corner, spinning a bingo machine.)

NURSE: B-7!

MAMA SAL *(Entering)*: Bingo!

(The Tattoo Artist rolls Chac-Mool over to the "game room" and hands him a bingo card. Mama Sal and Savannah and Cihuatateo South are already busy at the game. The Tattoo Artist joins in.)

NURSE: D-33!

MAMA SAL: By the time I was born Communism had spread all over the world. The Jews and the Italianos had already brought it over in boats to América . . . Are you taking notes, Chaco?

CHAC-MOOL: Yes. Mental ones.

MAMA SAL: But it didn't catch on until it went south . . . a Cuba, El Salvador, a Nicaragua. Then the Cold War thawed and all the small Commie countries began to dissolve también.

NURSE: G-42.

MAMA SAL: In the meltdown, la política changed completely, and the only thing los gringos cared about was the language you used, the Bible you carried, y la lana que tenía en tu pocket.

SAVANNAH: And that you weren't sticking your hand into theirs.

MAMA SAL: You got that?

CHAC-MOOL: Is this the official version?

NURSE: N-16.

MAMA SAL: Of course, it is. I was there.

CHAC-MOOL: I just want the facts, 'buela.

MAMA SAL: Facts. There are no facts. It's all just story.

CHAC-MOOL: Okay, the story.

MAMA SAL: Pues, all this born-again-Christian-charismatic-apoca-lyptic-eucalyptus-que-sé-yo gave fresh blood a la práctica de nazism y la plática de—

SAVANNAH: Wetback go home.

NURSE: S-5.

MAMA SAL: Mientras cancer clustered through every Mechicano farm town and low-income urban neighborhood en Gringolandia. To say nothing of NAFTA—

CHAC-MOOL: NAFTA?

SAVANNAH: North American Free Trade Agreement.

MAMA SAL: Eso.

NURSE: P-9.

MAMA SAL: Which turned México into a Puerto Rico overnight. Maquiladoras and their poisons—

SAVANNAH: Border babies being born without brains.

MAMA SAL: Then came anti-affirmative action, anti-Spanish, anti-Arabe, Ethnic cleansing in the name of Nation and as you can already imagine Fidel began to despair y . . . tengo que decir que . . . me, too.

NURSE: F-14.

MAMA SAL: Until Los Maya en la selva de Chiapas—

CHAC-MOOL: The Zapatistas! I heard of them.

(Mama Sal nods.)

MAMA SAL: They took on the PRI, the Mexican president got shot and bueno . . . the rest is *his*-story. Pan-indigenismo tore América apart and Aztlán was born from the pedacitos. We were con-tentos for a while—

SAVANNAH: Sort of. Until the revolutionaries told the women, "Put down your guns and pick up your babies."

MAMA SAL: Fuera de las calles—

SAVANNAH: And into the kitchen.

MAMA SAL: Just like the Gringo and Gachupín before them.

NURSE: I-27.

SAVANNAH: And then en masse, all the colored countries—

MAMA SAL: Threw out their jotería.

SAVANNAH: Queers of every color and shade and definition.

MAMA SAL: Y los homos became peregrinos . . . como nomads, just like our Aztec ancestors a thousand years ago.

SAVANNAH: And we made a kind of gypsy ghetto for ourselves in what was once a thriving desert.

NURSE: B-33.

MAMA SAL: They call it "Phoenix," pero entrenos, we name it, "Tamoanchan," which means—

SAVANNAH: "We seek our home."

MAMA SAL: And the seeking itself became home.

CHAC-MOOL: God, Bisabuela. You've lived a long life.

MAMA SAL (*Like the "wolf"*): The better to teach you with, malcriado!

NURSE: T-29.

CHAC-MOOL: Luna told me they just finished building a strip of casinos along Cuahtemoc Boulevard.

MAMA SAL: Casinos? . . . In Aztlán?

CHAC-MOOL: With neon, glitter and the works.

SAVANNAH: I guess they figure the Indians are making a killing on gambling throughout the Confederacy, why not the Chicanos, too? No one's gonna leave them in the dust of socialism.

NURSE: P-27.

MAMA SAL: Pues, maybe it's not such a bad thing. Our people is already crazy for the bingo.

CHAC-MOOL: Bingo!

MAMA SAL: No!

SAVANNAH: Ah, man! And I was almost there! Damn!

(*Blackout.*)

Scene Four

Chac-Mool, shirtless in overalls, and Luna can be seen working in a small urban garden (a barely redeemable abandoned lot bordering their building.) City noises persist.

LUNA: After the first rains the planting begins. You burn incense at the four corners of the field. Smoke the seed to be planted with copal and candles. You fast.

CHAC-MOOL: For how long?

LUNA: Seven days is good. I would do seven days.

CHAC-MOOL: Seven days.

LUNA: The first three are the hardest, after that you're high. You don't miss eating, really. Then you place candles at the four points, the four corners.

CHAC-MOOL: I feel like everybody's gonna know stuff I don't know.

LUNA: You know enough. *(Beat)* When you harvest the maize, the ears are broken from the plants in the field. You should bring them back to the house in a basket. The ears are then tied together or braided into clusters. Then they are hung up to dry, separated by color.

CHAC-MOOL: Blue, black, red, white—

LUNA: When you find twin ears, one is kept for seed, the other offered to Tonantzín.

(Medea enters. Chac-Mool spies her.)

CHAC-MOOL: Luna . . .

LUNA: The shelled grain is mixed together again for planting.

MEDEA: Once you're initiated, you have to leave for good. You know that.

CHAC-MOOL: Mom.

MEDEA: Thank you, Luna, for respecting my wishes.

LUNA: I—

CHAC-MOOL: She didn't do nothing, Mom. I asked her to teach me.

MEDEA: And I asked her to wait.

CHAC-MOOL: Mom, I turn thirteen in the spring.

MEDEA: Everybody seems to think that I have forgotten when your birthday is. I know when your birthday is. I was there for the first one, remember?

CHAC-MOOL: Why you getting so pissed off?

MEDEA: This is not a game, Chac. A get-back-to-our-raíces-harvest-moon-ritual.

LUNA: That's not fair, Medea.

MEDEA: Fair? Who's the real warrior here, Luna? You or me? Show me your scars.

(Medea thrusts both arms out at Luna to reveal a trail of scars from shoulder to wrist.)

LUNA: Mine are invisible. You win. *(Handing Chac-Mool the hoe)* Here, Chac. We'll finish later.

CHAC-MOOL: Luna . . .

LUNA: It's okay.

(She exits. There is a pause.)

CHAC-MOOL: Mom.

MEDEA: What?

CHAC-MOOL: I'm gonna go back to Aztlán and make 'em change, Mom. You'll see. Like those Cuban kids who went back to Cuba in the seventies and became Castro sympathizers.

MEDEA: Who told you about that?

CHAC-MOOL: Bisabuela. Except the revolutionaries, I mean the people who call themselves revolutionaries, like my dad . . . They're the traitors to the real revolution. And I'm gonna—

MEDEA: What?

CHAC-MOOL: . . . Make them see that.

MEDEA: . . . Oh.

CHAC-MOOL: You'll see.

MEDEA: Did Luna tell you it was four years? Four years of Sundance until you can even visit us again.

CHAC-MOOL: No.

MEDEA: That's a long time, Chac-Mool.

CHAC-MOOL: I guess I really didn't think about that part.

MEDEA *(After a pause)*: Your father hasn't asked for you to come back, you know.

CHAC-MOOL: But I thought—

MEDEA: He's getting married.

CHAC-MOOL: Oh.

MEDEA: To an Apache. He's thinking of other things right now. He's thinking of her.

CHAC-MOOL: Is she gonna have a baby?

MEDEA: Not yet.

CHAC-MOOL: He's an old man, Mom. I mean, to get married again.

MEDEA: Men are never old, Chac-Mool.

(Medea looks up to the evening sky. Chac-Mool watches her.)

If your father comes to get you, and he could come at any time, you have to know, for sure, what you want. You can't change your mind. He has the right to take you, but only if you agree to go.

CHAC-MOOL: And if I don't go?

MEDEA: You don't get another chance.

CHAC-MOOL: But Mom, I don't know if—
MEDEA: I know you don't. *(Beat)* Vente.

(Chac-Mool goes to Medea. She wraps her arms around him.)

It's okay, hijo. You don't have to know. Not today. It's okay.

(Beat.)

What's this?
CHAC-MOOL: A tattoo. It's Chac-Mool.
MEDEA: Ya lo veo. Why'd you do it?
CHAC-MOOL: I dunno, I thought it'd be cool.
MEDEA: Cool.
CHAC-MOOL: I was preparing myself. A tattoo couldn't hurt no more than getting pierced.
MEDEA: Tattoos last forever.
CHAC-MOOL: So do scars.
MEDEA: Déjame ver. *(She traces the tattoo with her finger)* You know what that bowl is for . . . there on his belly?
CHAC-MOOL: For sacrificed hearts. Chac-Mool carries them to the gods.
MEDEA: He's the messenger. Entre este mundo y el otro lado.
CHAC-MOOL: And he's a warrior, right? Isn't that what you always told me?
MEDEA: Sí . . .
CHAC-MOOL: What, Mom?
MEDEA: He's a fallen warrior, hijo.
CHAC-MOOL: Well, why would you name me like that, for someone who didn't win.
MEDEA: Well, it was better than your other name.
CHAC-MOOL: Yeah, but—
MEDEA: But what?
CHAC-MOOL: You never told me that part before is all.
MEDEA: I didn't think to.

(Mama Sal enters.)

MAMA SAL: Por fin. Somebody's putting a damn hoe in the dirt out here. *(She bends down to finger the earth)* It's more sand than anything else.
CHAC-MOOL: The corn's gonna be blue, Bisabuela.
MAMA SAL: Blue maíz.

CHAC-MOOL: It's an experiment. Everybody says it grows best in Aztlán, but Luna says—

MAMA SAL: Blue corn. Bueno, just don't start putting huevos on top of your enchiladas like they do en Nuevo México.

CHAC-MOOL: Ugh.

MEDEA: That's how they eat 'em in Aztlán.

MAMA SAL: Ni modo. If you can grow corn and you know how to light a fire, you'll never be hungry, Chac-Mool. Never.

(A sudden blast of salsa music from a small radio. The Prison Guard enters, announces:)

PRISON GUARD: The Hungry Woman.

(She grabs Medea's hand to escort her over to the hospital. Medea hesitates, looks to her son. Chac-Mool and Mama Sal reluctantly exit. In the hospital, Medea sits and begins pumping her breasts, one at a time. She puts her index finger below the breast and places her thumb above, her fingers rolling down to meet at the nipple. Medea looks for milk at the tip of her nipple, touches it lightly, brings the faint yellow liquid from her fingertips to her lips.)

MEDEA: It was true what Jasón claimed, that I was unfaithful to him. True, I was in the midst of an insatiable love affair. No, it *did* satiate. Did it begin when my son first put his spoon-sized mouth to my breast? Yes, there our union was consummated, there in the circle of his ruby mouth. A ring of pure animal need taking hold of me. It was a secret Jasón named, stripped to expose us—mother and child—naked and clinging primordial to each other.

(Jasón appears isolated in his own light. He paces nervously.)

JASÓN: I want a wife, Medea. It's not natural!

MEDEA: Each night I could hear Jasón circling outside our bedroom window, over and over again, pissing out the boundaries of what he knew he could never enter. Only protect. Defend. Mark as his domain. *(Suddenly)* Nurse! Nurse! They're spilling again. ¡Ay diosa! ¡Apúrate, vieja!

(Nurse tosses a box of nursing pads onto the bed.)

NURSE: If you'd leave your pezones alone, you wouldn't be needing these.

(Medea opens up the box, stuffs a pad in each cup of her bra.)

MEDEA: I never really weaned my son. One day, he just stopped wanting it. It was peer pressure. He was three years old. I call him over to me. "Mijito," I say, "¿quieres chichi?" He is on his way out to play I remember his playmate, that little Rudy boy at the doorway. And I show Chac-Mool my breast. His eyes pass over me. Lizard eyes. Cold. "Not now, Mom," he says. Like a man. I knew then that he already wanted to be away from me, to grow up to suck on some other woman's milkless tit.

NURSE: Took it personally, did you?

MEDEA: There's nothing more personal than the love between a mother and child. You wouldn't know. You are childless, a dull mule who can't reproduce. I will always be more woman than you.

NURSE: I was sterilized. Puerto Rico. 1965.

MEDEA: I . . .

(Sound of phone ringing, ringing, ringing. Medea rushes to the mirror excitedly, finger-combs her hair, speaks into the mirror as if it is the telephone. Jasón observes her.)

There's no need for name calling, Jasón.

JASÓN: Just old wounds, Medea. *(Beat)* Why did you call?

MEDEA: I was wondering about my status.

JASÓN: Your status? I thought this was about the boy.

MEDEA: You will abandon his mother again?

JASÓN: I didn't—

MEDEA: Technically I still hold the right to return. My land—

JASÓN: Is in my custody.

MEDEA: Yes.

JASÓN: You want to come back then?

MEDEA: I want to know my status.

JASÓN: That's simple. Give up the dyke. Nothing's changed.

MEDEA: Her name is Luna, Jasón.

JASÓN: Yes, Luna. How could I forget?

(Beat.)

MEDEA: And your marriage?

JASÓN: My marriage is another matter.

MEDEA: It matters to me.

JASÓN: It does . . . ?
MEDEA: Yes.

(The phone begins to ring again. Blackout.)

Scene Five

Luna is in the laundry room of their apartment building. She and Savannah fold clothes.

LUNA: I come down here just to get away from Medea sometimes. I sit up on top of the dryer and my thighs stay warm in winter. In the summer, it's cooler here in the darkness.
SAVANNAH: Yeah, a regular paradise down here.
LUNA: I feel like I can breathe better. I got all my sculpting stuff down here, locked up in that cupboard. I'm just waiting to save up for enough clay to put my hands onto something. The rest of the stuff in there is mostly household tools. Sometimes I open it just to see all the glass jars of nails and screws all lined up on the shelves and my hand drill and wrenches all hanging real neat. She never comes in to mess things up. She never knows where a hammer is or a Phillips. She doesn't need to. She lives on beauty alone.
SAVANNAH: Rent still gotta be paid by somebody.
LUNA: Upstairs it's pure chaos. It's like I can't stop moving, working, cleaning. I hear my voice and it's my mother's voice, nagging. I'm nagging like a frustrated housewife. I bitch. I bitch about the laundry that I never stop doing, the dishes that never stop piling, piling, the newspapers . . . news from the rest of the world, always a dozen days old, recycled magazines, fourth-class mailers never opened. All she does is read and discard, read and discard, right where she finished the last line of print. The couch, the toilet, the kitchen table, the bed. Her shoes and stockings and bra come off right there, too. She says she doesn't give a damn if I feel exploited. She says who asked you to be a housewife? "¿Quién te manda? I want a lover, not a vieja." I think what she really wants is a man. I hear her on the phone negotiating with that self-conscious lilt in her voice. I didn't even like it when she used to "lilt" me.
SAVANNAH: Who she talking to?
LUNA: I don't know. Friends. Enemies. She says it's for Chac. That's all she says.

SAVANNAH: Luna, stop waiting on her.

LUNA: I can't. I feel like I can't breathe. Like all the shit in the house—the plates with the stuck-on egg, the chorizo grease in the skillet, the spilled powder milk and crumbs on the floor, the unmade bed, the towels on the floor of every room in the house . . . that all of it is conspiring against me, suckin' up all the air in that apartment.

SAVANNAH: You trippin' bad.

LUNA: Maybe I am. *(Putting a clean T-shirt to her face, breathing in)* No smell sweeter.

SAVANNAH: What's that?

LUNA: Liquid Tide.

SAVANNAH: Imported?

LUNA: Terrible for the environment, but who gives a shit about the environment here.

SAVANNAH: Nobody I know.

LUNA: It's such a clean smell. The cotton. I put my nose inside here and everything is organized. Everything is sweet and well placed.

(Medea enters. Savannah spies her first.)

SAVANNAH: Don't look now, here comes Beauty's Beast.

MEDEA: Sniffing clothes again?

LUNA: Do you want something, Medea?

MEDEA: Oh, am I interrupting?

SAVANNAH: No, I was just leaving.

MEDEA: Not on my account, I hope.

SAVANNAH: See you tonight, Luna.

LUNA: See ya.

(Savannah exits.)

MEDEA: What was that all about?

LUNA: What do you want, Medea?

MEDEA: Why are you hiding from me?

LUNA: I'm not hiding from you.

MEDEA: No? Then what's this?

(Medea stretches out a long strand of hair in front of Luna's face.)

LUNA: What? It's hair.

MEDEA: It's not my hair.

LUNA: Okay . . . so?

MEDEA: It's not yours . . . too coarse. Who's is it? I found it in our bed.

LUNA: I don't know whose hair it is.

(Beat.)

MEDEA: Are you having an affair?

LUNA: That's too easy, Medea! You can't get rid of me that easy?

MEDEA: Answer me.

LUNA: Look, there are forty-five apartments in this project, housing every kind of queen and queer and party animal in Phoenix. I don't know who puts their clothes in the dryer ahead of me and got their pelito stuck onto our sábanas.

MEDEA: Take the whine out of your voice.

LUNA: I'm not whining.

MEDEA: You're weak. You don't love me. You just follow rules. You're afraid of me. Do you think that makes me feel safe?

LUNA *(After a beat)*: No, I imagine it doesn't.

(She gathers up the clothes basket.)

MEDEA *(Grabbing Luna)*: Don't you give up on me. ¿M'oyes?

LUNA *(Breaking her hold)*: I'm getting out of here.

MEDEA: Where to? To see one of your "girlfriends"?

LUNA: Yes, to tell you the truth I miss them a lot right now. Just thought I'd drink a coupla beers with some plain ole unequivocal tortilleras.

MEDEA: Fight for me—for me, cabrona. You're worse than a man.

LUNA: You oughta know.

(Luna exits.)

Scene Six

A mournful animal cry is heard in the darkness, then city noises. Mama Sal sits outside the building, where the corn is steadily growing. She packs a pipe, lights up. Chac-Mool sits with her. The cry is heard again.

MAMA SAL: Gives you chicken skin, doesn't it?

CHAC-MOOL: Sounds like a baby crying.

MAMA SAL: They moan like that when they're lonely for their machos. *(Pause)* I had a cat like that once. She was wanting it so bad, she clawed a hole through the screen door to get out. In no time, I had a small mountain of gatitos in my closet. Están locas when they're in heat.

(The cry continues.)

She got such a lonesome llanto. Es el llanto de la llorona.

CHAC-MOOL: La llorona never scared me like she's supposed to.

MAMA SAL: No? Even when you was a little escuincle?

CHAC-MOOL: No, I felt sorry for her, not scared. *(Pause)* When I was real little back in Aztlán. I used to wake up in the middle of the night just when the wind would kick up and the whole cañon would start crying. I'd go outside and stand out there under the stars and just listen to her. I felt like she was telling me her side of the story. I felt like I was the only one that heard it.

MAMA SAL: Maybe you were.

(Chac-Mool watches the sky. The sounds of the city in the distance: sirens, screeching cars, low-flying police helicopters.)

CHAC-MOOL: They're fighting all the time now, you know, my mom and Luna.

MAMA SAL: Yo sé. Blood is strong, hijo. Don't make a mother choose between blood and love.

Scene Seven

The local bar. "Crazy" plays on the jukebox. Savannah and Tattoo Artist are dancing a slow number.

LUNA: Turn off that white girl shit!

(Savannah crosses to Luna who's been watching the dance floor and nursing a beer.)

SAVANNAH: Let's go now, Luna. It's almost closing.

LUNA: Shit, in Aztlán the night would barely be starting right now. In Tamoachan everything closes up tight as a virgin's thighs.

SAVANNAH: You're drunk.

LUNA: I'm not drunk. I'm bitter.

SAVANNAH: You're talking like a drunk.

LUNA: And you're just an old lesbian prude, like the rest of our generation. All that twelve-stepping and disease in the nineties turned us into a buncha deadbeats. Let's go to la taquería, I need to soak up that tequila.

SAVANNAH: Nothing's open now.

LUNA: The taquería is.

SAVANNAH: Which taquería?

LUNA: The one that leaves all the jalapeños out on the table. St. Josie's or whatever it's name is. You know how they have those sweet little plastic bowls in pink and yellow and turquoise on the table filled with jalapeños floating around with slices of carrots. Shit, the carrots are as hot as the chiles after floating around so long in the same juices.

SAVANNAH: You see you got to be careful who you float around with. You ready?

LUNA: Wait. I have to go to the head. *(She crosses to the bathroom, goes into a stall)* Hold the door will you, baby? The lock's busted. *(Savannah does)* This place is such a dive. You ever known a nice lesbian bar? What did gay liberation ever do for colored dykes? We might as well be back all-closeted-up like Mama Sal's stories of "the life" half a century ago, sharing the dance floor with drag queens and 'ho's, waiting for the cops to come in and bust our butts. This place is a dump.

SAVANNAH: You wanna talk about it, Luna?

LUNA: What? About what a dump this place is? Shit. No toilet paper. Pass me a paper towel, baby.

SAVANNAH: There isn't any.

LUNA: I hate drip-drying. You got anything?

SAVANNAH *(Takes a Kleenex from her bag, passes it to her)*: Girl, here.

LUNA: Thanks. I *am* talking about it, talking about all the things Medea says every time I try to bring her to a joint like this.

(Luna comes out of the stall. Savannah half-blocks the door with her body.)

What? What is it, Savannah?

SAVANNAH: Luna, I'm tired.

LUNA: Well, let's go—

SAVANNAH: I'm tired of seeing someone I love being played. Medea wants out Luna. The writing's on the fuckin' bathroom wall.

LUNA: I know.

(Small pause.)

SAVANNAH: And I want . . . in.
LUNA: Ah, Savannah. Don't tell me that.
SAVANNAH: How long have you known me?
LUNA: I don't know. A long time.
SAVANNAH: Five years.
LUNA: Okay.
SAVANNAH: I'm here when you want it.
LUNA: "It." Like that?
SAVANNAH: Like that.
LUNA: But you're my buddy.
SAVANNAH: Fuck your "buddy."
LUNA: I don't wannu!

(They both bust up. Savannah pins Luna up against the wall.)

Savannah, I—

(Savannah kisses her deeply. Luna responds.)

She's always been jealous of you.
SAVANNAH: I know. She ain't all crazy.
LUNA: C'mon. I gotta get home.

(They wrap their arms around each other's shoulders, and sing "Crazy" as they exit.)

Scene Eight

Medea lies on top of her bed still dressed after a night drinking alone.

MEDEA: You once thought me beautiful, Lunita. My hair the silky darkness of a raven's, the cruelty of Edgar Allan Poe's own, I know. I know you think me cruel. But you must like it, in a way, the cry of the dead seeping through floorboards, all my angry ancestors mad at you for some reason you haven't figured out yet. For your seamless face, for the natural blush on your peach down cheeks, for a mama who loved you, if only too much.

(Luna enters. She quietly removes her shoes when she realizes Medea is still awake.)

LUNA: Medea.
MEDEA: Oh, good. It's you.

LUNA: Medea, why are you still up?

MEDEA: Take my body, baby.

LUNA: Were you waiting up for me?

MEDEA: I don't want to watch it descend into the earth.

LUNA: C'mon, let me get you into the bed.

(Luna stumbles across an empty fifth of tequila.)

Shit.

MEDEA: Gravity, fucking gravity.

LUNA: How much did you drink?

MEDEA: The earth has become my enemy.

LUNA: I'm gonna get you some aspirins.

(Medea stops her.)

MEDEA: I don't even remember being nineteen. *(Beat)* Where you been, amor? You shouldn't leave me alone so much.

LUNA: You never want to come with me.

MEDEA: I don't like being alone. It's not . . . safe. I don't trust myself.

LUNA: Let's get your clothes off.

(Luna starts to undress Medea.)

MEDEA: I used to have spectacular thighs. Remember, Lunita?

LUNA: You still do.

MEDEA: Remember how I'd wrap my thighs around your boy's face. *(Holding her face)* How come I called it a boy's face when you're so female?

LUNA *(Pulling away)*: Just macha, Medea.

MEDEA: A boy's hunger, that's what I saw there in those dark eyes resting between my legs. Luna, why would you look at me that way?

LUNA: What way, amor?

MEDEA: Like you didn't have what I had, like you didn't have nalgas, senos mas firmes que yo, a pussy . . . that perfect triangle of black hair . . .

LUNA: I'm just a jota, baby.

MEDEA: That's a stupid response.

LUNA: Don't be cruel.

MEDEA: I'm not cruel, I'm dying. Dying to make sense of it. How does it start? How does it vanish? How is it you used to drink from me as if you yourself didn't taste the same coppered richness when you brought your own bloody fingers to your mouth. As if when you drew a woman's shape with your sculptor's hands, you didn't find the same diosa curves and valleys when you bathed yourself each day. Eres mujer. But for you, falling in love is to think nothing of yourself, your own body. In the beginning all was me.

LUNA: Yes, in the beginning.

MEDEA: And now . . . ?

LUNA: It's different now. You get used to each other. It's . . . normal.

MEDEA: I loathe normal. At night, I would lay awake and wonder, how is it she could worship me so and not be banished? But then you were already banished. And now, that's the road I walk, too.

LUNA: Medea, that was seven years ago.

MEDEA: I had always imagined we'd return to Aztlán, one day with my son grown. I thought they'd change their mind, say it was all a mistake.

LUNA *(After a beat)*: Medea, did you talk to Jasón tonight?

MEDEA: Yes.

LUNA: What does he want?

MEDEA: Chac-Mool.

LUNA: When?

MEDEA: Now. Tommorrow. Soon. He's sending custody papers. *(Beat)* She's barren.

LUNA: What?

MEDEA: The virgin bride. Está vacía.

LUNA: He's still going to marry her? *(Medea nods)* Damn, he must love her.

MEDEA: She can still fuck, Luna.

LUNA: I'm . . . sorry.

(Medea starts to get up.)

Don't. C'mere.

(Medea stands at the edge of the bed.)

Medea.

MEDEA: He wants my boy . . .

LUNA: I know. Come back to bed. Please.

(Medea goes to her. They embrace. Lighting transition. Cihuatateo East enters.)

CIHUATATEO EAST: Creation Myth. In the place where the spirits live, there was once a woman who cried constantly for food. She had mouths everywhere. In her wrists, elbows, ankles, knees . . . And every mouth was hungry y bien, gritona. Bueno, to comfort la pubre, the spirits flew down and began to make grass and flowers from the dirt brown of her skin. From her greñas, they made forests. From those ojos negros, pools and springs. And from the slopes of her shoulders and senos, they made mountains y valles. At last she will be satisfied, they thought. Pero just like before, her mouths were everywhere, biting and moaning . . . opening and snapping shut. They would never be filled. *(Pause)* Sometimes por la noche, when the wind blows, you can hear her crying for food.*

(Cihuatateo East exits. Luna and Medea are in bed, after sex.)

LUNA: Tell me who you were with him.
MEDEA: It still interests you?
LUNA: Yes.
MEDEA: Why?
LUNA: It gives me something . . . somehow.
MEDEA: What?
LUNA: I don't know. That I have you that way, like he did, but knowing he wasn't—
MEDEA: . . . Enough?
LUNA: Yes.
MEDEA: I . . . I've missed you.

(They kiss.)

LUNA: Some days I think I have been with you forever. Seven years . . . forever. Chac-Mool is our measuring stick, like the pencil scratches on the kitchen wall, marking out our time together. When that last mark passed the height of my own head, I thought . . . Where do we go from here? No growing left to do.

(Pause.)

I can hardly remember being with other women.
MEDEA: I remember. You being with other women.
LUNA: So, do we just go back to where we started? Do we return to zero?

*From The Hungry Woman: Myths and Legends of the Aztecs. John Bierhorst, ed., New York: William Morrow & Co., 1984.

MEDEA: Zero. A good place to be. I wish I had the guts.

(Luna tries to bring Medea into her arms again. Medea stiffens.)

LUNA: Medea.

MEDEA: It doesn't matter now. I am the last one to make this journey. My tragedy will be an example to all women like me. Vain women who only know to be the beloved. Such an example I shall be that no woman will dare to transgress those boundaries again. You, you and your kind, have no choice. You were born to be a lover of women, to grow hands that could transform a woman like those blocks of faceless stone you turn into diosas. I, my kind, is a dying breed of female. I am the last one to make this crossing, the border has closed behind me. There will be no more room for transgressions.

Scene Nine

Medea rises from the bed, slips on a black dress.

MEDEA: Help me.

(Prison Guard enters, announces:)

PRISON GUARD: Phoenix, Arizona. The month of June. It is stifling hot in exile.

(Luna zips Medea's dress.)

LUNA: Where are you going . . . ? To him?

MEDEA: Yes.

(Medea arranges her face in the mirror. Luna observes. Prison Guard hands Luna a small stack of letters.)

LUNA: Why are you courting his illusions, Medea?

MEDEA: What illusions?

LUNA: That you're not a lesbian.

MEDEA: I'm not?

LUNA: Does he? You know lesbianism is a lot like virginity, you can't recycle it. You don't get to say, oops, sorry, I changed my mind, I didn't mean those seven years in her bed.

MEDEA: What do you want me to do, shove it in his face?

LUNA: Yeah. I want you to shove it in his face. I want you to tell him, "Recuerdas, Jasón? The mother of your son is a dyke. She licks pussy and loves it."

MEDEA: So, he can take my son away for good.

LUNA: Oh, he doesn't just want the *Warrior-Son*, he wants it all: *Virgin-Bride, Aztec-Goddess.* Or can't you read between the lines?

(She throws the letters to her.)

MEDEA: Where did you find them?

LUNA: Where you left them.

MEDEA: You rummaged.

LUNA: Not much.

MEDEA: I'll keep my son any way I have to.

LUNA: That's what I'm afraid of.

MEDEA: ¿No ves? You've seen the letters. I still have allies there. People don't forget so easy. I'm building a bridge back. For both of us. I'll send for you.

LUNA: I don't think so, Medea. I'm not the revolutionary they have in mind.

(She starts to exit. Stops.)

I don't know what's going on with you. It's like the thought of losing Chac . . . no kid between us . . . and we got nothing to disguise what we are to each other. Maybe for you, Chac-Mool somehow makes us less lesbian.

MEDEA: Maybe.

LUNA: Well, it's too late, Medea. You can't go back there. I know your secrets. Your secrets have been safe with me. All of them, like sacred relics carefully guarded. I watch them spill out of you in our lovemaking. I tell no one. I don't even tell you what I can testify to in every sheet you drenched with your desire. Let me remind you of the first time. The magic. The disappearing act. My hands vanishing inside you, your grito. "Where are your hands?" you cry. They move inside of you and you thank me with your eyes. For this, I forgive you everything. And we start another day. *(Beat)* You've changed, Medea. You don't know it yet, but you won't ever be able to go back to Aztlán or to any man. You've been ruined by me. My hands have ruined you.

(There is a pause.)

MEDEA: I'm not you, Luna. I wasn't born that way, the way you like to brag. I'm just a woman worried about keeping her son. You act so damn free. You're not free.

LUNA: No, I live in the fuckin' colony of my so-called liberators.

MEDEA: You don't even know your own prison. I'm right in your face every day. We sleep together, eat together, raise my child together, and a man walks into our lives and you give him all your attention. I'm not even in the equation, except as the premio at the end of your contest with each other. You can't beat him, Luna. Isn't this queer ghetto proof of that?

LUNA: Tell yourself that. I don't want to beat him.

MEDEA: No?

LUNA: No.

MEDEA: You're lying. First to yourself, then to me. When you stopped wanting to beat him, you stopped wanting me.

LUNA: That's not true.

MEDEA: Now he's back in our lives and you're on top of me like a teenaged boy.

LUNA: Are you complaining?

MEDEA: Yes. I want to be left alone.

LUNA: . . . With your thoughts?

MEDEA: Yes.

LUNA: They betray me.

MEDEA: They betray my unhappiness.

LUNA: With me.

MEDEA: With all of this. Failure.

LUNA: You hate it here that much.

MEDEA: That much. But I promise you, I hate my countrymen even more.

LUNA: He can hurt us, Medea.

MEDEA: Yo sé.

LUNA: He's already hurting us. You don't flirt with power. You fight it.

(She exits and crosses out the front of the building. Mama Sal sits smoking her pipe!)

MAMA SAL: In a hurry?

LUNA: I . . . No. You got a cigarette?

MAMA SAL *(Feigned innocence)*: Moi?

LUNA: Give me a cigarette, Mama Sal.

(She does. Luna lights up, paces.)

MAMA SAL: When you're a girl, hija, and a Mexican, you learn purty quick that you got only one shot at being a woman and that's being a mother.

LUNA: Tell Medea. She's the mother, not me.

MAMA SAL: I'm telling you, so you know. You go from a daughter to mother, and there's nothing in between. That's the law of our people written como los diez commandments on the metate stone from the beginning of all time.

LUNA: Well, that ain't my story.

MAMA SAL: Exacto. You go and change the law. You leave your mother and go and live on your own.

LUNA: Right.

MAMA SAL: You learn how to tear down walls and put them up again. Hasta tu propia casa, you build with your own hands. But you don't forget your mother. You search for a woman. You find many womans . . .

LUNA: Sal, I—

MAMA SAL: But still you feel your daughter-hands are sleeping. You meet Medea—

LUNA: . . . Yes. Medea.

MAMA SAL: And your whole body wakes up to the empty places inside her. You twist and deform yourself to fill her. You come out crooked. *(Beat)* Leave her, Luna. She's not the woman for you.

LUNA: She's your granddaughter.

MAMA SAL: Leave her, te digo. I say that out of love for you both.

(Luna tosses the cigarette to the ground, puts it out with her foot and exits.)

Scene Ten

Medea in black silk dress before the altar of Coatlicue.

MEDEA:
Madre, Coatlicue.
I want to know your sweet fury.
Teach me your seductive magic,
your beauty and rage.

Make Jasón small and weak.
Make him shiver
within the folds of my serpent skin.

He feared me before.
Help me make him remember why.

(Lighting transition. Jasón appears. He stares out a window. Moonlight bathes his face.)

JASÓN: There was a time when I remembered being no one or as close to no one as possible. As no one as any Mexican man on that midnight train passing through Puebla. A full moon. A lonesomeness so full, so complete.

(Medea crosses to him.)

MEDEA: Does being with me te da tanta nostalgia?
JASÓN: A little, I guess. I'm glad to see you face-to-face. The letters . . . your words are very persuasive.
MEDEA: I was a writer once, too, remember?
JASÓN: Of course.

(Jasón crosses to a table, unwraps the plastic off a glass.)

Drink?
MEDEA: Yes, thank you.
JASÓN: Sorry, the glassware's not too fancy.
MEDEA: Border motels.
JASÓN: Yeah, I'm sorry. I didn't know where else to meet. Somewhere out of the public eye.
MEDEA: I'm a big girl, Jasón. I can take care of myself.
JASÓN: Obviously. Still, you certainly dressed for the occasion.
MEDEA: It bothers you?
JASÓN: No, I wouldn't say "bother." "Torment" is the word I'd use.

(She laughs.)

(Enjoying it) Are you trying to torment me, Medea?
MEDEA: Don't flatter yourself, Jasón. I wore this dress for myself. That's something few of my lovers have ever understood. The clothes are for me. The feel of silk against my thigh, the caress of a satin slip over my breasts, the scent of musk when I bury my own face into the pillow of my arm.

JASÓN: You should live on an island.

MEDEA: No, occasionally I need someone to accuse me of tormenting them with my beauty. *(Pause)* Do you find me beautiful, Jasón?

JASÓN: You know I do.

MEDEA: Still?

JASÓN: Yes . . . Very.

(She looks hard at him for a moment, then:)

MEDEA: You're kind. Nos 'stamos poniendo viejos. ¿No, Jasón?

JASÓN: No tanto. You look fine . . . good for your age.

MEDEA: Yes. My age. My eyelids—

JASÓN: You've got beautiful eyes. I always told you that.

MEDEA: Obsidian jewels you called them.

JASÓN: I did.

MEDEA: It's different for a man. They're young at fifty. Sixty, even. Look at you, marrying a woman a third of your age.

JASÓN: I guess I . . .

(They smile at each other.)

MEDEA: I'm jealous of her, Jasón. Your new young love.

JASÓN: You're jealous?

MEDEA: My vanity is no secret. In an odd way, I grew to kind of rely on your devotion, safely distanced as it was. I derived comfort out of knowing that, even in my exile, you thought of me. You did think of me, didn't you?

JASÓN: At one time . . . daily.

MEDEA: No longer?

JASÓN: One doesn't stop thinking of you, Medea. The thoughts merely grow less . . . insistent.

(Medea smiles. Jasón takes hold of her hand.)

Medea, why the sudden change of heart?

MEDEA: I want what's best for my son. He'll be forgotten here in this ghetto.

JASÓN: I'm . . . sorry.

MEDEA: Are you?

JASÓN: You don't have to stay here either, you know.

MEDEA: I don't know that.

JASÓN: You're not a lesbian, Medea, for chrissake. This is a masquerade.

MEDEA: A seven-year-old one?

JASÓN: I'm not saying that you have no feelings for the relationship, but . . . you're not a Luna.

MEDEA *(Sadly)*: No, I'm not.

JASÓN: I want you to reconsider.

(There is a pause.)

MEDEA: After the war . . . before Chac-Mool, I felt completely naked in the world. No child to clothe me in his thoughtless need, to clothe the invading lack of purpose in my life. I can't go back to that.

JASÓN: You don't have to.

MEDEA: Then I wasn't mistaken?

JASÓN: No.

(He takes her into his arms. They kiss and begin to make love.)

ACT 2

Prelude

Pre-Columbian Meso-American music. In the semi-darkness, the stone image of Coatlicue becomes illuminated. The Cihuatateo stand sentinel beside it.

CIHUATATEO EAST: This is how all nights begin and end.

(Medea emerges as the living Coatlicue. She wears the slip she had on beneath her dress. Her dark hair is disheveled and her eyes are shadowed from lack of sleep. Still, Medea possesses a dark and brooding allure, akin to obsidian: a razor-sharp edge with a deep and lustrous sheen.)

A long time ago, before the Aztec war of the flowers, before war, Coatlicue, la mera madre diosa, was sweeping on top of the mountain, Coatepec, when she encounters two delicate plumitas.

(Medea begins sweeping as Coatlicue.)

She stuffs the feathers into her apron and, without knowing, becomes pregnant. *(Pause)* Now, Coatlicue es una anciana, bien beyond the age of fertility, and when her daughter, Coyol-xauhqui, learns of the boy-to-be-born, traición is what she smells entre los cuatros vientos.

(Luna appears as Coyolxauhqui.)

COYOLXAUHQUI: You betrayed me, Madre.
CIHUATATEO EAST: So, along with her 'manitos, "The Four Hundred Stars," Coyolxauhqui conspires to kill the Mother-God.
CORO:
    The light of the son
    will eclipse your daughter's glow

hold you under fire
in the heat of his embrace . . .

(Chac-Mool as Huitzilopotchli, in full Aztec regalia, emerges from the icon.)

CIHUATATEO EAST: Pero, Huitzilopotchli, that's him, el diosito inside Coatlicue, he ain't gonna punk out on his mami. A humming-bird buzzes by and gives the little Sun-God the 4-1-1 about the planned matricide, and the vatito is quick to respond.

HUITZILOPOTCHLI: Cuenta conmigo, jefa. I got it all under control.

CIHUATATEO EAST: He is born with filero flying and chops off his sister's head.

CORO:
Y sus senos
las manos
las piernas
los dedos . . .

HUITZILOPOTCHLI: I hold my sister's moonface bleeding between my hands . . . Sas! *(He tosses "the head" into the sky)* I exile her into darkness.

(Huitzilopotchli and Cihuatateo East watch the moon rise into the night sky.)

CIHUATATEO EAST: This is how all nights begin and end.

Scene One

The psychiatric ward. The Prison Guard stacks dominoes in the corner. Medea stands at the window. The shadow of the bars from the moon's reflection crosses her face. Nurse observes her.

NURSE: The moon was beautiful out tonight, did you see it?
MEDEA: No Luna. Ya no Luna.
NURSE: Whad ya say, honey?

(Medea does not respond. She cranes her neck to feel more of the moon on her face.)

(To Guard) Bendita. She's been walking around in a funk all day. The girlfriend didn't come.

MEDEA: No Luna. It was a moonless night. Black sky. There had to be stars, but I don't remember any. All four hundred vanished into thin mountain air. And the Brother-God was born back into our family, returned a warrior decorated. I remember the decoration, the medal leaving an imprint in my cheek when he brought me to his chest and squeezed. He taught me how to squeeze, not too hard, just the right amount of pressure, the right curve in my little girl's palm. *(Pause)* At first, when he opened his zipper, it was like, "Let's make a deal!" "What's behind the curtain?" And what was behind the curtain was grown-up and a mystery machine, the way it could inflate and deflate just by thinking he told me, he could think it hard and tried to teach me hard thoughts, too. And Mami told me . . .

(Lighting transition. Nurse becomes Medea's mother. "/" indicates when their lines overlap.)

NURSE: Wait on your brother. Give your brother whatever he wants.

MEDEA: Shoes shined, shirts ironed, money from your torito piggy-bank / for putas and pisto.

NURSE: Give him whatever he / needs.

MEDEA: Cuz he's the only man in the / family.

NURSE: Your father isn't worth two cents, / not mean enough.

MEDEA: Just a lloron who don't know how to cheat a little / to make a little extra.

NURSE: Be good to your brother, give him / whatever he wants.

MEDEA: Cuz God has been good to us bringing him home in one piece / and not crazy.

NURSE: When the rest of the barrio boys are coming home in burlap bags.

MEDEA: And stiff canvas flags folded into triangles.

(Medea lets out a deep wail. Nurse goes to her.)

Saturday is almost over and she didn't come, Nurse.

NURSE: She musta been otherwise occupied.

(Prison Guard stands, announces:)

PRISON GUARD: "Otherwise occupied."

Scene Two

Nurse escorts Medea offstage. Border Guard crosses to Luna, who wears a kind of sack dress. She has bare legs and feet. The Border Guard ties Luna's hands behind her back with the black bandana that Chac-Mool wore earlier.

BORDER GUARD: Luna is arrested at the border.

(The Guard sits Luna down in the interrogation room. A huge spotlight glares in Luna's face.)

Why did you cross the border?
LUNA: I was on my way to her.
BORDER GUARD: To whom?
LUNA: I got distracted.
BORDER GUARD: Whom were you to meet?
LUNA: No one. I was visiting the sick. It was a Saturday.
BORDER GUARD: Today is Monday.
LUNA: There was a song on the bus. It was her song. *(Half singing:)*

Soy como el viento que corre
alrededor d'este mundo . . .
BORDER GUARD: But you hadn't a work permit.
LUNA: I was denied one.
BORDER GUARD: You knew it was illegal.
LUNA: Yes.
BORDER GUARD: Then—
LUNA: I longed for Aztlán.
BORDER GUARD: Why did you break into the museum?
LUNA: I wanted to free them.
BORDER GUARD: Who?
LUNA: Those little female figures. Those tiny breasts and thick thighs, those ombligos y panzas de barro.
BORDER GUARD: Who were they to you, these figurines?
LUNA: Ancient little diosas, the size of children's toys. They were trapped, sir, behind the museum glass. They belonged to us. I remember them from my youth, going to visit them in my Catholic school uniform. I wanted to free my little sisters, trapped by history. I broke the glass.

BORDER GUARD: You stole them?

LUNA: No, ma'am I wanted only to hold them in my hands and feel what they had to teach me about their maker.

BORDER GUARD: And . . . ?

LUNA: We were not as we are now. We were not always fallen from the mountain.

BORDER GUARD *(Announcing)*: "Before the Fall. Mexican Pussy."

(Border Guard unties the handcuffs and hands Luna a mirror.)

Ten, take a look.

(Music. Amalia Mendoza. Luna brings the mirror up between her legs, studies herself. Medea enters, then hides as if in a game.)

MEDEA *(Singing)*:
Háblanme montes y valles
Grítanme piedras del campo . . .

LUNA *(Spying her)*: Hey!

MEDEA: Don't stop.

LUNA: You busted me.

MEDEA *(Very playful)*: Nah, go on with what you were doing.

LUNA: I can't. Not with you watching me.

MEDEA: What were you doing?

LUNA: Seeing.

MEDEA: That's my mirror you're holding.

LUNA: Yo sé. I wanted to see through your reflection.

MEDEA: See what?

LUNA: What I got.

MEDEA: You don't know.

LUNA: No.

MEDEA *(Going to her)*: I can tell you what you got.

LUNA: I want to know for myself.

MEDEA: Well . . .

LUNA: Well, what?

MEDEA: What do you got?

LUNA: Hair. God, lots of hair all over the place. Unruly hair. Undisciplined hair. Pelo de rebeldía. *(Medea smiles, kneels at Luna's feet)* I have a Mexican pussy, did you know that? Definitely a Mexican pussy.

MEDEA: How's that?

LUNA: Mexican women always hide our private parts.

MEDEA: I'm Mexican.
LUNA: Yeah, but you're . . . different. Less hair.
MEDEA: Más India.
LUNA: Prouder, more . . . available.
MEDEA: I don't know about that.
LUNA: I love your pussy.
MEDEA: I love your mouth.

(Medea kisses her.)

LUNA: My private parts are a battleground. I see struggle there
before I see beauty.
MEDEA: I see beauty.
LUNA: You have to dig for it. You have to be committed.
MEDEA: I'm . . . committed.
LUNA: You weren't supposed to see me doing this.

*(Medea takes the mirror out of Luna's hands, kisses her again,
first on the mouth, then grabs Luna by the hips, and goes down
on her. Luna holds medea's hair like a rope between her fingers,
she pulls her deeply into her. The Border Guard enters.)*

BORDER GUARD: So, you confess to being a lesbian.

*(Luna and Medea separate in a panic. The Border Guard stands
between them. They hold each other's eyes from a distance.)*

LUNA: Can I be tried twice for the same crime?
BORDER GUARD: Answer the question. Do you desire—
LUNA: There was no passion there. By the end, it was a mindless
reflex. The desire was gone from us months before or was it
years? We fought about it. We slept as sisters. When she began
to dream and the dream was bad, I just drew her closer to me,
placed her hands one on top of the other, and folded them into
her belly with the unconsciousness of a sonámbula.
MEDEA: I am sleepwalking still. Even the smell of the sea has abandoned us.

*(Sudden police sirens and the spinning of blue and red police
lights. Medea stands amid the circling colored lights. Trance-
like, she cradles her arms as if holding an infant. Luna
approaches her.)*

Do you smell my baby's death?

LUNA: I can't.

MEDEA: Open the holes in your face and breathe. The breeze smells of sulfur. Do you smell it?

LUNA: I . . . don't know.

MEDea: Where were you, Luna, when I needed you?

LUNA: In my cell, always in my nun's cell.

MEDEA: I hardly recognize you, wearing the skirt of a woman.

LUNA: I dressed to visit you. I visit you weekly. But you won't speak to me. Is it . . . *(The infant)* heavy?

MEDEA: A dead child weighs nothing in your arms. He is light as balsam wood, hollow inside. The spirit gives weight to the flesh. His spirit ya se fue.

LUNA: The child I carry is heavy.

MEDEA: Tienes que dar a luz.

(Luna turns and exits, the Cihuatateo enter.)

CIHUATATEO *(Chanting)*:
All, viene La Llorona.
Rivers rising.
Cold-blooded babies at her breast.

(Wind rises, blends with the wailing of children. Then the cry of la Llorona, an ominous and chilling wail, fills the air.)

A-y-y-y-y-y-y! *MIS HIJOS! MIS HI-I-I-I-JOS!*

(The Cihuatateo dance as warrior women. They draw out maguey thorns, the size of hands, from their serpents sashes. They pierce and slash themselves, wailing. They encircle Medea with the ghostly white veil of La Llorona. It is a river in the silver light. Medea and the sound of the children's cries drown beneath it. Blackout.

Luna is back in the interrogation room. Hours have past, she is clearly exhausted. She speaks almost deliriously. Jasón appears in shadow behind the Border Guard.)

BORDER GUARD: Do you confess?

LUNA:
I am
awake
to the sound
of screaming

her voice, too, she is
screaming I
can't remember when they merge
Medea's voice
with my own
only opening my mouth
swallowing
air
the cry coming out
the man
in the doorway, a shadow
a stranger
a lover
a rapist
I
can't know
for sure
I
inside time stop time
what to do
when he
enters
the room
his size immense
filling the doorway
what to do
when he
steps
one
foot
inside
the room
I . . .

BORDER GUARD: Stop it. Speak sensibly. You are talking in circles!

LUNA *(After a pause)*: When Jasón . . . found us—

BORDER GUARD: Yes. Go on.

JASÓN: When I found them in bed together, I remember I just stood
there, staring at them.

BORDER GUARD: And then?

LUNA: Then . . . nothing.

JASÓN *(Simultaneously)*: Nothing.

BORDER GUARD: Nothing?

LUNA: He had a very . . . sad look on his face . . . disappointed, kind of.

JASÓN: I just turned away and walked into my study. I was waiting for her, waiting for an explanation.

LUNA: She got up and left me in the bed. I could hear them down the hall.

JASÓN: We fought.

LUNA: In hushed voices. I slipped out without their noticing. What else was there to do? The next morning, she shows up with the kid on my doorstep. He was five years old. She didn't know where else to go, she told me. I was the reason for it. I was the lesbian.

JASÓN AND (LUNA): I (He) never even came looking for them (us).

BORDER GUARD: That's it?

LUNA: No. She was exiled.

JASÓN: Medea was never to return to Aztlán.

Scene Three

Lights rise on the kitchen back in Phoenix. It is again a year earlier. Chac-Mool enters angrily with an armful of blue corn. He finds a cooking pot, begins to strip the corn furiously, tossing it into the pot. Medea enters.

MEDEA: Why are you doing that? I'm going to make dinner.

CHAC-MOOL: I'm not hungry.

MEDEA: Then what are you cooking for?

CHAC-MOOL: It's Luna's corn.

(Medea goes to the pot, lifts the lid.)

MEDEA: It's blue.

CHAC-MOOL: Where is she? She doesn't even get to see it. She planted it. Why can't she see it? Why did you send her away.

MEDEA: I didn't send her away. She left.

CHAC-MOOL: You did. You made her unhappy. You make me unhappy. Stupid corn. *(Starts to exit)*

MEDEA: Chac-Mool.

CHAC-MOOL: The corn's ready to harvest. Bring her back.

MEDEA: I'm trying to save you, ingrato!

CHAC-MOOL: From what?

MEDEA: From . . . him.

CHAC-MOOL: You made Luna go away. He didn't.

MEDEA: To keep you.

CHAC-MOOL: To keep me for what?

MEDEA: For—

CHAC-MOOL: For yourself.

MEDEA: Yes. Is that such a crime? We can go back together. Start all over again.

CHAC-MOOL: You can't leave her like that, Mom. It's not right. You don't even love him . . . Do you love him?

MEDEA: . . . No. (Beat) Luna's found someone else, hijo.

CHAC-MOOL: I don't believe it!

MEDEA: Believe it.

(After a beat, Chac-Mool crosses to the pot and dumps out its contents.)

CHAC-MOOL: You were a warrior woman, Mom. You were a fucking hero!

MEDEA: I'm almost fifty. I'm tired of fighting. I wanna go home.

(Blackout.)

Scene Four

Jasón sits at the table in Medea's home. There is a briefcase on the table.

MEDEA: I sent the papers back because they were unacceptable. You ignored my conditions.

JASÓN: You aren't in the position to negotiate, Medea.

MEDEA: I'm not?

JASÓN: Frankly, I think I'm being quite generous.

MEDEA: To live as your ward. I could stay here for that.

JASÓN: Semantics.

MEDEA: I know what "ward" means, Jasón.

JASÓN: It means I will take care of you. Your grandmother, too.

MEDEA: I'm not your Juárez whore, Señor. A woman is nothing in Aztlán without a husband.

JASÓN: Then stay here if you want. It's your decison.

MEDEA: Then we both stay. Chac-Mool's not going anywhere without me.

JASÓN: Medea, I . . . don't want you.

MEDEA: And I don't want you, but I'm not going back to my land on my knees. I thought we gave up Catholicism with the revolution.

JASÓN: I'm in love with somebody else.

MEDEA: Love! You love a tight pussy around your dick, that's what you love. Why do you have to marry it? It will not make you younger.

JASÓN: Ah, Jeezus.

MEDEA: You raped me. Now pay up.

JASÓN: Oh, Medea. You orchestrated the whole damn thing.

MEDEA: When the prostitute is not paid as agreed, she is raped.

JASÓN: You said it. I never agreed to stay married to you.

MEDEA: She's a child in bed, you tell me. I want a woman. (Mimicking him) "I miss you. I miss your breasts, tu piel, that smell, how could I have gone so long without that smell."

JASÓN: It was the passion of the moment.

MEDEA: And the moment has passed.

JASÓN: . . . Yes.

MEDEA: Get out!

JASÓN: Not without my son!

MEDEA: ¿Qué crees? That you'll be free of me? I'll decide, not you. You'll never be free of me!

JASÓN: Free! You're the slave, Medea. Not me. You will always be my woman because of our son. Whether you rot in this wasteland of counter-revolutionary degenerates or take up residence in my second bed. You decide. I'm not afraid of you, Medea. I used to be afraid of that anger, but not anymore. I have what I want now. Land and a future in the body of that boy. You can't stop me.

MEDEA: Watch me.

JASÓN: If you really loved your son, you'd remove him from your tit.

MEDEA: So his mouth can suck your dick?

JASÓN: That how your dyke friends talk, Medea? Look at you. You hate men. And boys become men. What good are you for Chac now? He needs a father.

MEDEA: My son needs no taste of that weakness you call manhood. He is still a boy, not a man and you will not make him one in your likeness! The man I wish my son to be does not exist, must be invented. He will invent himself if he must, but he will not grow up to learn betrayal from your example.

JASÓN: You left me.

MEDEA: And you sent away your son and his mother to live in exile.

JASÓN: You would not be separated.

MEDEA: That's one version of the story, Jasón. Would you like to hear the other? Or do you believe in your own mythology? The "Minister of Culture" marrying una niñita. ¡Qué conveniente!

JASÓN: It's hardly convenient, Medea. I've had to defend this relationship—

MEDEA: She'll never call you by your true name, Jasón, so you may fortunately begin to forget it. Forget the U.S. Air Force father, the quarter-breed mestizo-de-mestizo cousins, your mother's coveted Spanish coat of arms. That girl can't know you because your lies were sown long before she made root on this earth. Send me your wife. I will teach her of her own embattled and embittered history. I will teach her, as I have learned, to defend women and children against enemies from within. Against fathers and brothers and sons who grow up to be rapists of women, traídores de una cultura más anciana que your pitiful ego'd life can remember.

JASÓN: That bitterness in you . . . you'll never change.

MEDEA: Oh yes, I've changed. I married you when I was still a girl, not a woman, but a girl with a girl's naïveté who still looked for a father's protection. But that was a long time ago. I am a woman. A Mexican woman and there is no protection and no place for me, not even in the arms of another woman because she too is an exile in her own land. Marry your child-bride. A mi no me importa. No, in that lies no traición. Betrayal occurs when a boy grows into a man and sees his mother as a woman for the first time. A woman. A thing. A creature to be controlled.

JASÓN: If it is so inevitable. Give me the boy. Spare yourself the humiliation.

MEDEA: No, my son is still an innocent. He will love you in spite of me, for his body requires that that animal memory be fulfilled. To that I do not object, nor to the fact that he must one day grow away from me, but he will leave me as a daughter does, with all the necessary wrenching, and his eye will never see me "as woman." I promise you that.

(Jasón opens his briefcase, takes out a document, puts it on the table, rises.)

JASÓN: The courts have already made their decision, Medea.

MEDEA: Which courts? Those patriarchs who stole my country? I returned to my motherland in the embrace of a woman and the mother is taken from me.

JASÓN: You agreed. Age thirteen. You signed the—

MEDEA: My hand was forced.

JASÓN: Bueno, the Sundance starts in a matter of weeks. I'll be back for the . . . *(Spying Chac-Mool entering)* Adolfo . . .

CHAC-MOOL: Chac-Mool. It's written on my arm, so I won't forget.

MEDEA: Hijo . . .

JASÓN: Chac-Mool, yes. You're . . . big.

(Silence.)

MEDEA: Tell him the truth, Jasón. Since my son is standing here in front of you, tell him to his face.

JASÓN: What are you talking about?

MEDEA: That my son makes you legit, just like I did. That's why you've suddenly appeared on our doorstep con tus papeles in hand.

CHAC-MOOL: Mom . . .

MEDEA: He is your native claim. You can't hold onto a handful of dirt in Aztlán without him. You don't have the blood quantum.

JASÓN: I'm a practical man, Medea.

MEDEA: I believe the word is opportunist.

JASÓN: Yes, there is that requirement, but that says nothing about my love for my son.

MEDEA: That's right. It says nothing.

JASÓN: There are the custody papers, Medea. The divorce is already a done deal. There's really nothing more to discuss. *(Beat)* Chac-Mool, regardless of what your mother has said to you, I want to be with you. I admit, it's taken me a long time to . . . to grow up. I never should've let you go, but I'm coming back for you now. Once these papers are . . . taken of, I hope you'll—

CHAC-MOOL: Go willingly?

JASÓN: Yes. *(Beat)* Bueno—

(There is a pause.)

MEDEA: Get out.

(He glances over to Chac-Mool one last time. Chac-Mool does not return the look. Jasón exits.)

Chac-Mool.

CHAC-MOOL: I barely remember him.

MEDEA: I'm sorry you had to see this.

CHAC-MOOL: Him?

MEDEA: Yes.

CHAC-MOOL: He's old. Small.

MEDEA: Yes.

CHAC-MOOL: Why didn't you tell me he was coming?

MEDEA: He brought papers. It was business.

CHAC-MOOL: Did he come for me?

MEDEA: I never would've let you go. Así. Without time to prepare.

CHAC-MOOL: Mom, I've been preparing.

MEDEA: I mean in your heart.

CHAC-MOOL: How do you do that?

MEDEA: . . . I don't know.

CHAC-MOOL: I didn't know he even wanted me.

MEDEA: Didn't you hear him?

CHAC-MOOL: He wants me.

MEDEA: He wants you for a piece of dirt! He didn't deny it!

CHAC-MOOL: You didn't tell me.

MEDEA: He's using you! Just like he used me and when he's done with you, he'll toss you back here like so much basura.

CHAC-MOOL: Why you talking like this? Let's just go.

MEDEA: I can't go.

CHAC-MOOL: Why not?

MEDEA: Nothing's changed, Chac-Mool. They want a public disavowal.

CHAC-MOOL: A what?

MEDEA: I can't deny what I am, hijo. I thought I could, but I can't.

CHAC-MOOL: He doesn't want you, does he? That's why.

MEDEA: Did you just hear what I said?

CHAC-MOOL: I want to be initiated, Mamá.

MEDEA: You want to cut open your chest?

CHAC-MOOL: I—

MEDEA: Is that what this is all about! Toma! *(Grabbing a letter opener from the table)* Then start your initiation right here.

(Mama Sal enters, she drops her satchel on the floor, and rushes to restrain Medea.)

MAMA SAL: Medea!

MEDEA: Cut open your mother's chest first! Dig out her heart with your hands because that's what they'll teach you, to despise a mother's love, a woman's touch—

CHAC-MOOL: I won't do that.

MEDEA *(Breaking Mama Sal's hold)*: You say that because you're still young. Your manhood, the size of acorns. When you feel yourself grown and hard as oak, you'll forget.

CHAC-MOOL: I won't forget. I'll come visit you. I promise.

MEDEA *(Bitterly)*: You'll visit.

CHAC-MOOL: I gotta get outta here, Mom. I can't carry this no more, I'm just a kid. It's not normal!

MEDEA: You want normal? Then go with your father. He's perfectly normal. It's normal to send your five-year-old child and his mother into exile and then seven years later come back to collect the kid like a piece of property. It's normal for a nearly sixty-year-old Mexican man to marry a teenager. It's normal to lie about your race, your class, your origins, create a completely unoriginal fiction about yourself and then name yourself la patria's poet. But that's normal for a country who robs land from its daughters to give to its sons unless of course they turn out to be jotos.

CHAC-MOOL: Stop it, Mom. I don't wanna hear no more.

MEDEA: Well, I've got more to say.

MAMA SAL: Ya, Medea! Basta!

(Blackout.)

Scene Five

Chac-Mool sits beneath a glaring spotlight in the interrogation room. The Border Guard circles around him, holding a clipboard.

BORDER GUARD: What is your name?

CHAC-MOOL: Adolfo.

BORDER GUARD *(Checking the notes on the clipboard)*: What about Chac-Mool?

CHAC-MOOL: If you knew already, why did you ask me?

BORDER GUARD: For the record.

CHAC-MOOL: For the record, my real name is Adolfo.

BORDER GUARD: And Chac-Mool?

CHAC-MOOL: It's my mom's name for me. It's written in my skin. You wanna see?

BORDER GUARD: No, they don't approve of graffitti en Aztlán. They do murals.

CHAC-MOOL: It's not—

BORDER GUARD: Let's get back to Adolfo, shall we? For the record.

CHAC-MOOL: For the record, I hate that name. It's a Nazi name. Every kid named Chuy has to live up to the legacy of being named Jesus. Well, me . . . I got Adolfo to follow me into the grave.

BORDER GUARD: Who named you?

CHAC-MOOL: My father, after some revolutionary, long-dead gun-runner uncle of his. But it's still a Nazi name. Sure there are other Adolfs in history . . . plenty of them, including my revolutionary uncle, but nobody with an impact even close to that of Hitler or Christ. I was born to be a Nazi, to have a Nazi life, to be denied a free life. Is nobody listening to me?

BORDER GUARD: We all are. It's your play.

CHAC-MOOL: Who says?

BORDER GUARD: You're the source of conflict. You're also the youngest one here, which means you're the future, it's gotta be about you. *And*, you're the only real male in the cast.

CHAC-MOOL: And who are you?

BORDER GUARD: Think of me as your revolutionary conscience, the mirror to that elegant yaqui body of yours, inside and out.

CHAC-MOOL: Is this about a confession?

BORDER GUARD: What do you mean?

CHAC-MOOL: Like are you trying to get some kind of confession outta me.

BORDER GUARD: I'm trying to ascertain your readiness to make the return.

CHAC-MOOL: I don't want to be here no more.

BORDER GUARD: Where?

CHAC-MOOL: Tamoachan.

BORDER GUARD: Phoenix?

CHAC-MOOL: Yes.

BORDER GUARD: Where do you want to be?

CHAC-MOOL: Aztlán.

BORDER GUARD: Right answer. Tu patria.

CHAC-MOOL: Sí, mi patria. I am my father's son. I've got a right to be there. He tried to deny me. I was born from the sweat between my mother's thighs. He wanted to forget those campesina thighs.

BORDER GUARD: Who told you that?

CHAC-MOOL: My mother.

BORDER GUARD: And now?

CHAC-MOOL: And now . . . what?

BORDER GUARD: What does he want now?

CHAC-MOOL: Well, now he wants me back. To make a man outta me, to keep the Indian in him.

BORDER GUARD: He's not an Indian?

CHAC-MOOL: Not enough, according to my mother.

BORDER GUARD: And that's a problem?

CHAC-MOOL: In Aztlán it is. God, I thought you knew the place.

BORDER GUARD: Not really. I hardly remember. I only work the border. And what do you want outta the deal?

CHAC-MOOL: The return?

BORDER GUARD: Yes.

CHAC-MOOL: I just don't wanna have to hurt nobody.

BORDER GUARD (Untying the handcuffs): Nazi, let me introduce myself.

CHAC-MOOL: You said it was my play.

BORDER GUARD: You want this play?

CHAC-MOOL: I don't know . . . yet. I don't know if I want you in it. I know I don't want you to be a man. Men scare me.

BORDER GUARD: Your father's a man.

CHAC-MOOL: I've got nowhere else to go.

BORDER GUARD: I'll be a woman.

CHAC-MOOL: Be my mother. I miss my mother. I'm leaving her.

BORDER GUARD: No, not your mother. I am your revolutionary conscience. Today using modern methods I could convince you of anything. That you are no more than your father's son. The son del nuevo patrón revolucionario, a landowner from whom you will inherit property and a legacy of blood under the fingernails. Today using modern methods, I am landless. A woman without a country. I am she whom you already know to hate. I wipe your infant ass in another life, sensitive Nazi-boy.

CHAC-MOOL (Rising): I've had enough of this.

BORDER GUARD (*Pushing him down again, hand on his shoulder*): It's cold out. Where could you possibly go in such weather? It's too hot to move.

CHAC-MOOL: I have a country. I am not despised as you are. There is a piece of dirt a few hundred miles away from here that still holds the impression of my footsteps. I belong somewhere. I am going.

BORDER GUARD: Footsteps, the size of boys' feet?

CHAC-MOOL: I am not ready to be a man.

BORDER GUARD: No?

CHAC-MOOL: I was blessed always blessed to be a boy. My great-grandmother literally traced my forehead with the cross of her thumb and index finger and my brow was tranquil then. I didn't then have these violent thoughts of a man. At four, my father drilled his fingers into my chest, held me at the gunpoint of his glare. You are blessed, he told me. Open your nostrils and flare like a bull. I want you to smell this land. I remember the wings of my nostrils rising up to suck up his breath. It was a birthing of sorts. He penetrated and I was born of him. His land was his mother and mine and I was beholden only to it.

BORDER GUARD: Aztlán.

CHAC-MOOL: Yes, Aztlán. And then my mother stole me away with the stonemason. A sculptor.

BORDER GUARD: Get up now.

CHAC-MOOL (*Standing*): Did I pass? Am I ready?

BORDER GUARD: We caught you just in time.

(*Border Guard pushes Chac-Mool out of the scene, then the Guard crosses to the hospital.*)

Scene Six

PRISON GUARD (*Announces*): Too late. Prison Psychiatric Ward. Back to the future.

(*Medea sits in a stupor in the psychiatric ward. The Prison Guard hands her one of the wilted white flowers from the opening of the play. She caresses it. Nurse enters with tray of food.*)

MEDEA: I have gone without campanitas on my kitchen table, I have gone without a kitchen table, a kitchen, a hearth for . . . how long has it been, Nurse?

NURSE: Many months.

MEDEA: Enough months to become years?

NURSE: Not yet.

MEDEA: Without a kitchen, my meals are brought to me on plastic trays, everything wrapped in plastic—the forks, the napkin, the salt and pepper, like on airplanes. I want to fly away.

(She lifts the lid to the food tray.)

Is this soup?

NURSE: It's breakfast. We don't serve soup for breakfast.

MEDEA *(Stirring it with her spoon)*: It's gray soup.

NURSE: It's mush.

MEDEA: I like avena.

NURSE: Avena.

MEDEA: Oatmeal. It sticks to your ribs, like that commercial. *(Singing a little jingle)* "Sticks to your ribs all day."

NURSE: I remember that. *(Starts to exit)*

MEDEA: You're leaving me?

NURSE: I got more patients than you. Eat your breakfast.

(Nurse exits.)

MEDEA: She's leaving me. Now I will have no one to talk to. I could talk to the man on the Quaker Oats box but she did not leave me the box or the man, just the mush. *(She pushes at it with her spoon)* Avena. That's my baby's word. One of his first words because oatmeal was one of his first foods. *(She wipes the spoon clean with a paper napkin, tries to glimpse her reflection in the bowl of the spoon)* I live inside the prison of my teeth. My voice can't escape. This wall of maize white tiles sealed shut. "Perfect masonry," Luna'd always say . . . about my teeth. I wish I had a mouth of corn, sweet baby corn. A mouth of baby teeth sucking at virgin purple pezones. How do I live now without her breasts? I can't open my mouth to suck her. Luna . . . ?

(Luna enters in memory.)

LUNA: Say it. Say what is hardest to say.

MEDEA: I would've respected you more, had you just left. You don't have the courage to be alone. You'll flop from woman to woman for the rest of your life.

LUNA: That's not it. That wasn't hard. Try again.

MEDEA *(Softening)*: I had a dream.

LUNA: Good.

MEDEA: I dreamed our land returned to us.

LUNA: Go on.

MEDEA: You were there. It was the most natural evolution in the world to move from love of country to love of you.

LUNA: And—

MEDEA: There was a road of yellow dust, sagüaro and maguey. You were laying down the cactus stones one by one to my door.

LUNA: Why did you shut the door, Medea?

MEDEA: My son.

LUNA: No. The truth.

MEDEA: My son.

LUNA: Look. *(She holds out an empty hand to Medea)* The corn is going to seed.

MEDEA: Ya lo sé.

LUNA: I tried to warn you, Medea.

MEDEA: Fucking means nothing!

LUNA: I warned you about me.

MEDEA: . . . And your negra?

LUNA: She's a friend.

MEDEA: A friend!

LUNA: Yes! You're right. I don't want to be alone. Not now.

MEDEA: I sacrificed Aztlán for you!

LUNA: Aztlán was uninhabitable.

(Luna exits. Medea begins shoveling spoonfuls of oatmeal furiously into her mouth, then spits it out.)

MEDEA *(Shouting)*: This tastes like shit. Hey! Nurse, somebody! This takes like shit!

Scene Seven

Mama Sal sits out by the entrance to the projects. She smokes her pipe. Chac-Mool approaches, carrying a small backpack.

MAMA SAL: You should've called me. I would've met you at the bus station.

CHAC-MOOL: That's all right.

MAMA SAL: I love the bus station. Everybody goin' someplace. *(Beat)* Are you going, hijo?

CHAC-MOOL: Yeah. Just came to get my stuff. Say good-bye.

MAMA SAL: Who knows maybe I'll even follow you there in a few years.

CHAC-MOOL: I'd like that.

MAMA SAL: It don't matter no more. Lesbiana ni lesbiana. I have outlived all the lovely womans in my life.

(Chac-Mool smiles.)

You do me one favor, Chaco?

CHAC-MOOL: Dígame.

MAMA SAL: If I don't get back there, you don't let them bury me here, eh?

CHAC-MOOL: I won't Bisabuela.

MAMA SAL: Just fire me up como un cigaro and put me en tu bolsillo—

CHAC-MOOL: I'm not gonna do that!

MAMA SAL: I mean it. And take me out there by those ruinas . . . out there en las montañas de Jemez.

CHAC-MOOL: I don't know where that is.

MAMA SAL: You'll find out. Just spread me around out there with all that red rock. I'm tired of this pinche city.

CHAC-MOOL: I promise.

MAMA SAL: Bueno. *(She gets up, putting her pipe in her pocket)* Oh, mira. Luna came by. She wanted me to give you these.

(She takes out a small bag of corn seeds from her pocket, hands them to Chac-Mool.)

CHAC-MOOL: They're from the garden?

MAMA SAL: Uh-huh. She thought maybe you could throw a few of the seeds over there in Nuevo México. See if they take root.

CHAC-MOOL: She see my mom?

MAMA SAL *(Nods)*: Sí.

CHAC-MOOL: She gone?

MAMA SAL: Sí. Go on in there now, talk to your mamá.

(She kisses him on the cheek and starts to exit.)

CHAC-MOOL: You're not coming?

MAMA SAL: Hell no. Talking about my own damn burial, I'm gointu go find me some beer.

(She exits. Chac-Mool crosses to the garden. He throws the seeds back into the cornfield. The lights fade.)

Scene Eight

Medea dumps the contents of Mama Sal's satchel onto the kitchen table. She is in frenzy, nervously searching through the various bags of herbs. She sniffs one, then tries to pour it into a measuring cup. She spills it, her hands shaking uncontrollably. She crosses to a bottle of tequila. It is half empty. She takes a shot. Chac-Mool enters.

MEDEA: I tried getting her back. But I wouldn't beg. If you expected me to beg, I didn't.

CHAC-MOOL: I didn't expect nothing.

MEDEA: You been to the border?

CHAC-MOOL: Yes.

MEDEA: Then go pack your bags.

CHAC-MOOL: Mom.

MEDEA: You've decided, haven't you? You've been approved.

CHAC-MOOL: Yes.

MEDEA: Then go pack your bags.

CHAC-MOOL: I don't wanna leave you like this.

MEDEA: Now, that's a line I've heard before. But they leave you anyway, don't they? The line-givers.

CHAC-MOOL: It's not a line.

MEDEA: They're all lines, mijito. Rehearsed generations in advance and transmitted into your little male DNA.

CHAC-MOOL: Why you turning on me, Mom?

MEDEA: I think that's the question I have to ask you.

CHAC-MOOL: What am I supposed to do? Who am I supposed to be, Mom. There's nobody to be. No man to be.

MEDEA: So all the tíos I've surrounded you with, aren't men.

CHAC-MOOL: That's not what I mean.

MEDEA: Jotos aren't men.

CHAC-MOOL: They're not my father.

MEDEA: You are not the first boy in the world to grow up without a father.

CHAC-MOOL: And without a country? You made me want it, Mom. More than anything. It was "our blood got spilled. Yaqui

blood." You said that to me, every day. Every day like a prayer.
I can't help it that they took it away from you.

MEDEA: But you'll take it away again, won't you?

CHAC-MOOL: How?

MEDEA *(Grabbing him by the shoulders)*: You're my land, hijo.
Don't you see that? You're my land!

(He pulls away.)

CHAC-MOOL: How is that any different from my father?

MEDEA: I'm an Indian. And a woman.

CHAC-MOOL: That's not my fault!

(She freezes.)

MEDEA: I've held my breath for thirteen years in fear of those words,
to hear you finally absolve yourself of me.

CHAC-MOOL: But what did I do? You chose to leave Aztlán! You
chose for yourself, not for me!

MEDEA: That's right. I chose Luna. Remember Luna?

CHAC-MOOL: I remember. Where is she now?

*(After a beat, Medea crosses back to the table. Takes another
shot of tequila, she keeps her back to him.)*

That's it? You're not gonna talk to me no more?

MEDEA: You win. Vete.

(He doesn't move.)

Go, Chac-Mool.

(He still doesn't move.)

(Turning to him) What? You want my blessing, too? ¡Qué dios
te bendiga! Lo siento mucho, hijo, pero no soy tu mamacita
davidosa. *(Grabbing her breast)* The chichi has run dry.

CHAC-MOOL *(After a beat)*: You're crazy. He's right. He told me you
were crazy. He met me at the border. He told me to come with
him. Right then.

MEDEA: You should have.

CHAC-MOOL: I didn't. I didn't because you taught me loyalty. Because
I wasn't going to sneak away from you like a punk. When I leave
here tomorrow, I'm walking out that door like a man.

MEDEA: A man.

CHAC-MOOL: Yeah, a man. Just the way you taught me. You fucked him, I didn't. You fucked yourself.

(Medea goes to slap Chac-Mool, then stops herself. He stares at her. A stoned silence, then he exits. Mama Sal stands at the doorway, the sack of beer in her hands. Medea slumps onto a chair at the kitchen table. She reaches again for the bag of herbs.)

MAMA SAL: ¿Qué 'stás haciendo?

(She lets the herbs run through her fingers.)

MEDEA: All the babies, they're slipping through my fingers now. I can't stop them. They've turned into the liquid of the river and they are drowning in my hands.

MAMA SAL: Medea . . .

MEDEA: I lost her. I lost my baby. We were splintered, severed in two. I wanted a female to love, that's all, Abuelita. Is that so much to want?

MAMA SAL: No.

MEDEA *(Holding up a bag full of herbs)*: How much?

MAMA SAL: No, Medea. You don't have to do this.

MEDEA: A stranger has inhabited me, taken possession of my body, disguised himself innocently in the sexless skin of my placenta. *(Extending the bag to her)* How much?

MAMA SAL: Half of that. Es suficiente.

(Medea dumps the herbs into a pot as the lights cross-fade to Cihuatateo who enter as women warriors. They perform a stylized enactment of a traditonal midwife birthing. There is chanting in Nahuatl and deep moaning. Nurse stands between Medea's legs awaiting the birth of the infant. As the infant emerges, we see that it is Luna, in the lifeless form of a woman. She is shapeless liquid. The others cannot revive her. They all scatter, leave her abandoned onstage, except for Cihuatateo West, who, as the lights change, takes on the shape of Savannah. She draws a huge white sheet over Luna and herself. When the couple reemerge, they are joined together in the sack of sheet. It is a kind of tableau of the Aztec codex, symbolizing marriage. The Guard enters and announces.)

GUARD: "Blood Wedding."

LUNA: Medea was pregnant within weeks and the matter of names came up again—what to call that he/she clinging fish-gilled and hermaphrodite inside her liquid belly. She loved her belly more than the man but was grateful to Jasón for that first effortless conception. He took her virginal and spineless. Except there was no blood, no stain upon the sheet. The blood was only under her tongue, I found. A small pool behind the bottom row of her teeth, a dam holding back the ruby kiss, the original name of which she once spilled into my mouth. I, who would never give her children. I, who would always make her sweat and bleed every month. Our shared moons, a marriage of the most bitter, sweet-lipped kind.

SAVANNAH: Just keep talkin' that talk, girl, and I'll never leave you.

(Savannah pulls Luna back down under the sheet. Blackout.)

Scene Nine

As in the beginning of the play, the figure of Coatlicue is illuminated. Medea, wearing a long white nightgown, stands before the statute in prayer, holding a cup in her hand, then raising it in offering to the Diosa.

MEDEA:
Coatlicue,
this is my holy sacrifice.

I would have preferred to die a warrior woman,
like the Cihuatateo
women who die in childbirth
offering their own lives
to the birthing of others.

How much simpler things would have been.
But what life do I have to offer to my son now?

He refuses my gifts and turns to my enemies
to make a man of him.
I cannot relinquish my son to them,
to walk ese camino triste
where they will call him
by his manly name
and he goes deaf
to hear it.

But the road I must walk is sadder still.

(Chac-Mool enters. Medea turns to him, a bit offguard.)

CHAC-MOOL: I just came in to say good night. It's a habit, I guess.
MEDEA: You going to bed already?
CHAC-MOOL: Yeah, it's a long trip tomorrow.
MEDEA *(After a beat)*: Forgive me, hijo.
CHAC-MOOL: Mom, I—
MEDEA: I know that's stupid to say after so many words. Harsh words. But, if you let me, could I bless you now, before you go?
CHAC-MOOL: Now?
MEDEA: I got the copal burning.
CHAC-MOOL: Okay.

(He goes to her, opens his hands in front of her. She brings the smoking resin to him, wafts his body with it.)

MEDEA: Our ancestors are watching, hijo. They pity us. They know what is in our hearts.
CHAC-MOOL: I'm . . . sorry.

(She prays over him softly, then returns the burning copal to her altar.)

MEDEA: Can you stay up with your mami for a little while?
CHAC-MOOL: I'm tired, Mom.
MEDEA: I made you some atole. It may not be as good as Luna's pero no quieres probarlo? I made it with the blue corn.
CHAC-MOOL: Sure.
MEDEA: Vete. Go put on your pijamas first. Yo te espero.
CHAC-MOOL: Okay.

(Chac-Mool starts to exit, then suddenly turns and runs over to Medea. He throws his arms around her. Medea starts to pull him away and he clings all the tighter.)

I love you, Mom.
MEDEA: Sí, hijo. Ya lo sé. Now, go get changed, then come outside. You can drink your atole out there. The moon is so clear.
CHAC-MOOL: Okay.

(Chac-Mool exits. Medea takes out a bag of herbs from her gown, sprinkles them into the atole. She addresses Coatlicue.)

MEDEA: Can you smell it, Madre? Mi hijo's manhood. He wears it in his sleep now. In the morning I find it in a heap on the floor, crumpled in his pijamas. Like Luna, I bring the soft flannel to my nose. I inhale. No baby smell. No boy. A man moving inside his body. I felt a small rise against my thigh just now, a small beating heart hardening against that place that was once his home. Where is my baby's sweet softness now?

(Chac-Mool reenters, naked from the waist up and wearing pajama pants. Medea holds the cup of atole.)

CHAC-MOOL: Mom?

MEDEA: Vente, hijo. It's too hot in here. Let's go watch the corn grow.

(She grabs his hand and escorts him outside into the backyard, next to the field of corn. They sit down together. She puts her arms around him.)

El maíz 'stá muy alto.

CHAC-MOOL: Yeah, too tall. I feel kind of bad I didn't harvest it. I forgot somehow.

MEDEA: You were thinking of other things. No te apures. In Aztlán, there's plenty to harvest.

CHAC-MOOL: Yeah.

(There is a pause.)

MEDEA: Toma, hijo. This will help you sleep.

(He drinks. Beat.)

CHAC-MOOL: Mom—

MEDEA: Don't say anything more, hijo. No mas palabras.

(Medea takes Chac-Mool into her arms. She rocks him, singing:)

Duérmete mi niño
Duérmete mi sol
Duérmete pedazo
de mi corazón.

My sleeping little angel. *(He is instantly drowsy. She strokes his hair)* Sleep, mi diosito. Sleep the innocent sleep of the childless.

(He passes out. It is a pietà image, Medea holding him limp within her arms. Then, with much effort, she tries to drag Chac-

Mool's body into the small field of corn. She is unable to. The Cihuatateo enter, dressed in the traditional Aztec. They lift Chac-Mool and take him into the center of the field. Meanwhile, Medea starts pulling up all the overgrown corn stalks in the field, piling them into a mound higher and higher. She becomes frenzied, a frightening image, her white nightgown flowing in the sudden wind. The pile of blue corn stalks have formed a kind of altar. The Cihuatateo heave Chac-Mool's body on top of it.)

¡Hijo! ¡Mensajero!
How much simpler had you been born a daughter
that first female seed inside of me.
You would have comforted me in old age
held vigil at the hour of my death
washed my body with sweet soap
anointing it with oil.

You would have wrapped me in colored cloths
worthy of the meeting of mothers.
My finest feathers and skins would adorn me
as you returned me to the earth.

(Calling out against the wind and to the illuminated figure of Coatlicue.)

What crime do I commit now, Mamá?
To choose the daughter over the son?

You betrayed us, Madre Coatlicue.
You, anciana, you who birthed the God of War.

Huitzilopotchli.
His Aztec name sours upon my lips.
as the name of the son
of the woman who gave me birth.

My mother did not stop my brother's hand
from reaching into my virgin bed.
Nor did you hold back the sword
that severed your daughter's head.

Coyolxauhqui, diosa de la luna.
(Her arms stretch out to the full moon)
Ahora, she is my god.

La luna, la hija rebelde.

Te rechazo, Madre.

¡Ay-y-y-y! ¡Mi hi-i-i-i-jo!

(The Cihuatateo echo her.)

CIHUATATEO: ¡Mis hi-i-i-i-jos!

(Their lament is accompanied by the soft cry of the wind in the background that swells into a deep moaning. It is the cry of La Llorona. The moon moves behind the mountains. The lights fade to black.)

Epilogue

Flauta and tambor. The Cihuatateo North and South appear upstage. They are positioned together in the statuesque pose of the original icons: kneeling, sitting on their heels, their hands pushed forward in a kind of martial arts stance. They begin to dance in slow ritualized movement. Lights rise on Luna who sits before a potter's wheel. She leans into a mass of clay. Mama sal's satchel sits at her feet.

LUNA:
In her absence she is all the disguises she wore. She is
the flood of fever that fills my veins
with a woman's passing perfume. She is
la música flamenca, the gypsy allure,
the lie.

She is the painting of a woman fractured and defiant.
Cueva of clay opening como flor.
Coyolxauhqui's unnamed star sister. She is

renegade rebozo, el tambor's insistence,
a warrior's lament.
Slender hips of silk.
She is silk.

(Moving more deeply into the clay with her hands.)

I could sing of her breasts with my hands.

With my hands, I could sing
she was a woman who never stopped being naked to me.

(Luna rises. The Prison Guard enters, helps Luna put on a suit jacket, hands her a bouquet of fresh white flowers and Mama Sal's satchel. She escorts Luna to the psychiatric ward. The Prison Guard joins the Cihuatateo upstage. Medea waits on the edge of her bed.)

Medea?

MEDEA: You've come back? I thought you'd never come back.

LUNA: I was stopped at the border.

MEDEA *(Turning to her)*: It must be Saturday. Again.

LUNA: Yes, it's Saturday.

MEDEA: Thank you for the flowers. *(She doesn't take them)* How is my grandmother?

LUNA: She's old, Medea. Old and tired.

MEDEA: She should be less tired now. I was a burden to her.

LUNA: Yes. How are you?

MEDEA: I'm old and tired, I think, too. *(She crosses back to the window)*

LUNA: I dreamed of you last night.

MEDEA: I thought so.

LUNA: In the image of a maguey exploding from a vagina.

MEDEA: More flowers?

LUNA: No, desert cactus. There was nothing sweet about it.

MEDEA *(After a pause, turning to her)*: You know what I always loved about you, Luna?

LUNA: No, what?

MEDEA: Your innocence.

LUNA: I'm . . . innocent?

MEDEA: Your hands. *(Medea goes to her, wraps her hands around Luna's)* Your hands have handled dozens of women and somehow they remain virgin hands. You left her, didn't you?

LUNA: Who?

MEDEA: The other woman.

LUNA: . . . Yes.

MEDEA: Not me, I'm not innocent. I am spoiled. What I touch is spoiled and I am spoiled by the touches of others.

LUNA: Did I spoil you, Medea?

MEDEA: You said it yourself, you ruined me.

LUNA: I didn't mean—

MEDEA *(Letting go of her)*: You were right. You made me good for no one. Man, woman or child.
LUNA: I'm sorry.

(There is a pause.)

MEDEA: Luna?
LUNA: . . . Yes?
MEDEA: Was the vagina yours? In the dream?
LUNA: Maybe.
MEDEA: And I was the maguey?
LUNA: Maybe. Maybe it was all you. You giving birth to yourself.

(Medea smiles.)

I brought you something.
MEDEA: No more flowers, Luna. They remind me of death.
LUNA: No.

(She opens Mama Sal's bag and pulls out a small bundle.)

MEDEA: You have Mama's bag.
LUNA: Toma.

(Luna gives Medea the bundle. Medea unwraps it, stares at it, awed.)

It's a Cihuatateo.
MEDEA *(Suddenly urgent, she grabs Luna)*: Is that how I died, Luna? Giving birth to myself?
LUNA: I—
MEDEA: Is that what you came to tell me?
LUNA: I . . . don't know.

(Nurse enters. Medea and Luna's eyes are locked onto each other.)

NURSE: You want me to put those flowers in some water, negrita?
LUNA: What? No. She doesn't want them.
NURSE: But they're so gorgeous.
LUNA: Yes, you take them then. Put them in some water. They've been hours out of water.
NURSE: Chevere.

(Nurse takes the flowers and exits. She joins the Coro of Cihuatateo.)

MEDEA: Thank you.
LUNA: Sure.
MEDEA: Luna, go away now.
LUNA: You—
MEDEA: Please.

(Beat.)

LUNA: Good-bye, Medea.

*(Luna leaves. Medea holds the Cihuatateo figure in her hands.
She looks upstage to the Coro.)*

CIHUATATEO AND MEDEA:
And though banished from Aztlán
Medea and Luna kept the faith,
fasted by the phases of the moon
but did not pierce their flesh
for they bled regularly between their legs
and did not die.

(Chac-Mool suddenly appears in Medea's room.)

MEDEA: Are you a ghost?
CHAC-MOOL: No.
MEDEA: You're mistaken. You are a ghost. You're the son I mourn,
the one I pray to, that his heart may soften when I join him on
the other side.
CHAC-MOOL: It's me.
MEDEA: Daily, I try to join him . . . and my hands are always emptied
of the instruments of death. They steal my fingernail file and
panty hose and yerbas. They give me no yerbas here, just pathetic
pastel pills that numb me, but won't kill me. They're useless.
CHAC-MOOL: Mother.
MEDEA: Mother. I had a mother once, for a moment. Do you have a
mother?
CHAC-MOOL: Yes.
MEDEA: Is she beautiful? I imagine she's beautiful. You are beautiful,
or maybe you are the image of your father.
CHAC-MOOL: She's beautiful.
MEDEA: That's nice how you talk about her. I'd like to meet her. I
love beautiful women, but it's best not to touch them too much.
Touch yourself better, if you're beautiful. Another beautiful

woman is hard to take sometimes for too long. It's confusing. I mean, for a woman. It's not confusing for a man. But you're not quite a man yet, not fully. But it's coming. I can see it in your eyes. If you had been my son, the dark of your eyes would mirror me. And we would blend together sexless.

CHAC-MOOL: Mom, I'm Chac-Mool.

MEDEA: Chac-Mool. No.

CHAC-MOOL: It's true. I—

MEDEA: No, stop. Don't speak anymore. Go away.

CHAC-MOOL: Mom, don't make me go.

MEDEA: If you live, then why am I here? I've committed no crime. If you live, why then am I strapped into the bed at night? Why am I plagued with nightmares of babies melting between my hands? Why do I mourn you and no longer walk the horizon at the hour of sunset as I used to? Why are there locks and I haven't the key? Why?

CHAC-MOOL: You're in a hospital. A prison.

MEDEA: An insane asylum?

CHAC-MOOL: Yes.

MEDEA: Then I am insane.

CHAC-MOOL: I don't know.

MEDEA: Oh. *(Pause)* Why have you come here?

CHAC-MOOL: To take you away.

MEDEA: Away . . . where?

CHAC-MOOL: Home.

MEDEA: Home. *(She stares ahead blankly)*

CHAC-MOOL: Come look out the window, Mom. See the moon.

MEDEA: Yes. Nurse told me it's a nice afternoon. A beautiful woman brought me flowers today. Is today still Saturday?

CHAC-MOOL: Come here, Mom. ¿Ves la luna?

(Chac-Mool grabs his mother's hand, takes her to the small window.)

MEDEA: La Luna. That was her name.

CHAC-MOOL: Mom.

MEDEA: Mom. The sun is too bright.

CHAC-MOOL: No, mira. Do you see the moon? There to the left, just above those hills.

(Medea cranes her neck to see.)

MEDEA: Oh yes. She's droopy-eyed

CHAC-MOOL: No, she's waxing. Watch the moon. By the full moon, you'll be looking at saguaros. You're going home.

MEDEA: How will I get there?

CHAC-MOOL: I'm taking you.

(He leads her by the hand back to the bed. He holds a handful of herbs and puts them into a small paper cup of water.)

MEDEA: Mijo?

CHAC-MOOL: Here, drink this. *(He gathers Medea into his arms—a pietà image)* It'll help you sleep.

(He holds her head while she drinks. The lights gradually fade. Only the shimmering moon remains, and the figure of the four Cihuatateo dancing silently in its light.)

END OF PLAY

CHERRÍE MORAGA is a poet, playwright and essayist, and the co-editor of *This Bridge Called My Back: Writings by Radical Women of Color* (New York: Kitchen Table Women of Color Press, 1983). She is the author of numerous plays, including *Shadow of a Man* and *Watsonville: Some Place Not Here* (both won the Fund for New American Plays Award in 1991 and 1995, repectively) and *Heroes and Saints*, which earned the Pen West Award for Drama in 1992. Her two most recent books include a collection of poems and essays entitled *The Last Generation* (Boston: South End Press, 1993), and a memoir *Waiting in the Wings: Portrait of a Queer Motherhood* (Ithaca, NY: Firebrand Press, 1997). Ms. Moraga is also a recipient of the National Endowment for the Arts' Theatre Playwrights' Fellowship and is the Artist-in-Residence in the departments of Drama and Spanish & Portugese at Stanford University.

GREETINGS FROM A QUEER SEÑORITA

Monica Palacios

THE WRITER SPEAKS
Monica Palacios

When I first started out in this writing/performing business—we're talking 1982—I was doing standup comedy and I felt very different from the other Latino artists. Everybody was talking about nationality but no one was really talking about sexuality like I was. And not to say I was peddling pornography, I was simply talking about my life as a lesbian and as a Chicana—mix the two together and society creates a "controversial comedian." The majority of Latino artists that I knew at this time were doing material—I don't want to judge but—that was not creative. How many times can you hear, "What does a Mexican order at McDonald's? McTaco." And not that I was the most intelligent Latina comic on this planet—please—I'm still trying to figure out how to use a VCR. But my work was "off the wall" and refreshing.

Present day, as a writer/performer, I still feel my work stands out because it continues to be a "little off" but I don't feel like I'm the only one anymore—I don't feel alienated. There are artists whose work I respect, who are doing nontraditional Latino theatre, performance and writing, like Luis Alfaro, Michele Serros, Marisela Norte, Beto Araiza and Marga Gomez.

My work is bicultural because I create it from a Chicana lesbian perspective. I am never one without the other—I can't be or I can't create. When I started doing standup comedy, talking about my life experiences, I would get questioned by various people, wanting to know why I had to talk about being a lesbian. They said, "No one wants to know about *your* personal life." Yet these same people had no problem listening to straight comics talk about their personal lives. They just didn't get it. And I would tell them, "If you want me to stop talking about my personal life, that would be like me asking you to stop breathing. Can't do it."

I am a story writer and a storyteller, so it was destiny for me to end up doing theatre and performance. As a standup comic I was telling stories, but I didn't appreciate that I had to stick in a joke every twenty seconds. And I hated the club scene: dealing with hecklers, drunks, smoke, getting stuck on stage at two in the morning. And if that wasn't bad enough, I had to put up with homophobia, racism, sexism—not an ideal creative environment. Experiencing the harsh comedy scene truly made me realize that I needed to create the space where I could feel safe and be in control of my subject matter.

Theatre has truly allowed me to explore my story writing and storytelling. I believe theatre and performance go hand in hand. I love the fact that present day theatre and performance have no limits. In the last five years, I have seen some wild things on stage which make me feel very hopeful for my theatre future.

Production History

Greetings from a Queer Señorita is a combination of Ms. Palacios's two autobiographical pieces: *Latin Lezbo Comic,* which has been seen Off-Broadway and featured on PBS; and *Confessions . . . A Sexplosion of Tantalizing Tales.*

Greetings was first produced in 1995 by One in Ten Theatre Company (Tucson, AZ). Productions followed at MIT, USC, Brown University, San Diego State and the Women & Theatre Program at the Association for Theatre in Higher Learning Conference. In 1996 the play was produced at UCLA, University of Redlands, International Women's Day (West Hollywood) and Mujeres Activas en Letras y Cambio Social Conference. In 1997 *Greetings* received productions at Mexican Fine Arts Museum Center (Chicago), University of Riverside, Carleton College (Minnesota), New World Theatre, University of Massachusetts and Pomona College at Claremont Colleges. The majority of these productions were produced or cosponsored by gay and lesbian organizations.

A black stage. Then general lights up. A cordless microphone on a mike stand is upstage right. Monica is downstage left in a muscle man pose.

MONICA: In the eighth grade I was this jock! *(Emphasizes present pose, exaggerates two more poses and stops)* I loved getting sweaty with a bunch of girls—but I didn't know why! I felt frightened—yet HORNY!

I was a good basketball player and that year we got a new coach. She was tough but it paid off because we won the championship.

CHEERLEADER: Beat 'em at the jump ball goooooooooooo! Sink it *(Sensuously bends her knees down)* Monica. *(Slowly stands up, thrusting out her pelvis and breasts)* Sink it!

MONICA: I loved that! Anyway, this coach—she was a Chicana, she was a tomboy, she was attractive, she had girlie long hair and she was funny! So of course the cool people got chummy with her and we would hang out. Go to the movies, get a pizza—you know, she had a car.

But then one day, my mom and my sister stepped in and said a woman her age—which was about twentyish, shouldn't be hanging out with kids and maybe she even likes girls. Heaven forbid!

"Mother!" I would say like Samantha in *Bewitched*. "You are so unfair to teenagers!" Then I'd storm upstairs to my room. Forgetting we lived in a one-story house. I agreed she was hanging out with us too much but it never tripped me out to think she could possibly be a—LESBIAN!

I've noticed the word *lesbian* makes some people cringe. And I think this is happening because the word *lesbian* makes people think of some yucky sexual activity that has to do with a *tractor*! *(Mimes driving a tractor, then raises right hand and waves)*

And that's silly! But I used to call myself a "gay woman" because the word *lesbian* was soooo upsetting to me!

YOUNG COLLEGE COED: I mean, like, why do we have to use that word?! It's sooo gross! Why can't there be a different word like—*precious*! If men are gay, *I Want to Be Precious*!

MONICA: I'm so glad I've matured. And as I became more involved in the gay and lesbian community, I started using the word more. And one day I said the word a bunch of times *(Repeats the word lesbian seven times)* and I got over it! Because folks, it's just a word. I was making a big deal out of nothing. It seems to be the American thing to do!

I was pleased to find out that the producers of this show went out of their way to attract a good amount of lesbians to this event. As I want to attract a good amount of lesbians. It's kind of a hobby of mine. OK, it's an obsession. —All right, I'm seeing a counselor for it!

So they put billboards along Interstate Ten: ENTERTAINMENT, COMEDY, LESBIANS—5 MILES. HUNGRY? BURGERS, FRIES, LESBIANS—2 MORE MILES. COLD DRINKS, HOT LESBIANS—1 MORE MILE!

(Mimes driving a tractor, raises right hand, waves.)

(Runs to the front, center stage) Hey, remember when I was little and I was a kid and I stole a pack of gum and my mom found out and she made me go back and steal a roast? I love those Kodak moments.

I hung out with my little brother Greg. An adorable stubborn brat but we got along because we did and I was the boss of him. Our favorite times were pretending to be James Brown, cap and all, and the Beatles.

(The Beatles' song "Girl" starts. After the first line, "Isn't anybody going to listen to my story?" tech fades out and stops.)

I was Paul. He was Ringo. I was cute. He was not. I would play the tennis racket left-handed and Greg would play the drums by using empty coffee cans. Ohhhh, we were poor but—crafty!

Our favorite jam was *(Sings:)*

. . . Well my heart went boom
when I crossed that room
and I held her hand in Hawaii!!!!! . . . *(Stops singing)*

No, it's not Hawaii! It's "held her hand in *mine*!" Not Hawaii. So stupid, but—crafty!

We had this "music thing" because my dad, *Guadalupe—Lupe* to his friends. My mom calls him, Pal, it's short for, *Palacios*. Now everybody calls him Pal. He played several instruments and he sang. And my older brother Art was in a band!

I always thought my dad was this pseudo*mariachi* guy because he had the guitar but he didn't have the outfit. And I would always ask him, "Dad why must every *mariachi* song end the same way?! *Tan, Tan!*

Every now and then, my parents would invite friends, relatives, *compadres,* to the house and these people would bring instruments, voices and beer! And they would jam, creating great Mexican music. Everyone loved when my parents did duets because they thought they were Steve and Eydie.

STEVE AND EYDIE *(Singing):* *Cuando caliente el sol. (Stops singing)* Hey, how ya doin'? Where ya from?

MONICA: But the highlight was, my parents knew these two *comadres,* *Lala* and *Trini,* who sang together professionally—sort of. When they would sing, they would rock the house. My favorite song of theirs was, "Cu cu ru cu cu Paloma"—I'm sure it's a favorite here. They would get to that one point where they would be really close together, looking into each other's eyes *(Mimes their activity)* like only Mexican women can who sing together. Just *comadres?* I don't think so.

Comadre Lala would sing: *Cu cu ru cu cu. Comadre Trini* would sing: *Cu cu ru cu cu. Comadre Lala* would sing: *Cu cu ru cu cu.* And then they would both sing: *Palomaaaaaaaaaaaaaaaaa!* Holding it on that one note: *Aaaaaaaaaaaaaaaaaaaaaaaa!* Because this is what you do with these *rancheras: Aaaaaaaaaaaaaaaaaaaaaa!*

And then dramatically and full of *pasion,* they would sing: "No Llores!" And their lips would be really close together— quivering like this *(Quivers lips).* Full of passion and ruby red lipstick. Filling the air with music, culture, makeup, woman sweat, woman breath and beer!

(Cross-fade to dreamy lights: blues, reds, purples. Music cue: the song "Cu cu ru cu cu Paloma" plays the exact part the comadres did, as Monica overdramatically lip synchs. Song ends. Holds pose. Slow cross-fade to general lights.

Kneels down stage right. She attempts to make the sign of the cross three times but seems to be confused and impatient. Finally, quickly, completes her task and then nervously blurts out:)

Hail, Mary, full . . . of—gravy. Blessed be the—taxpayers. He turned water into wine. They ate baguettes and fondue—thank you, very much. Can I go, sister?

I went to an all-girl Catholic high school. *(Big smirk comes over her face)* This is where I got my training. "Thanks, Mom and Dad." *(Stands)* Actually, I didn't know I was a lesbian at this time. I just knew certain women made my uniform feel tight. *(Wiggles out of tight uniform)*

High School was great. I made women laugh. I made them read my short stories and I was their basketball hero—varsity— four years. Go ahead—touch my hand. *(Makes an audience member in the front row touch her hand)*

You'll like this: once during practice, this woman who we labeled as *dyke*, was being very chummy with me. Chummy, chummy, chummy. At the end of practice, we hung out and shot baskets because . . . we're jocks. I got tired so I sat on the floor. She walked over, squatted on top of me, *(Walks across the stage like John Wayne and gets into a straddle position, then shifts into a squat)* and gave me a very cute smirk. Many thoughts ran through my confused head as I looked up at her sweaty body.

(Slowly stands, thinks out loud, looking at woman) I should tell her to get off of me. I'm not supposed to like this.

(Speaks to the audience) Eeewww—tractor! *(Does a tiptoe escape from the woman across the stage)*

After seconds that seemed like *forever*, I told her, *(Hystyerical)* "Get off of me!"

I should have told her to get off—on me. *(Pause)* Get off— with me. *(Pause)* Get me off, baby!

I regret that moment. It would have saved me many awkward, frustrating dates with men. Because I didn't know. Somebody should have told me. A letter would have been fine. *(Mimes writing a letter)* "To whom it may concern, *you're a lesbian*!!!!! Figure it out!!!!!!!!

Toward the end of high school, a microphone appeared to me. I thought it was the Virgin Mary granting me a miracle, but it was a microphone. I did some "standup" for class assembly and I was hooked. After high school, I knew I had to do two things: come out as a lesbian and come out as a comedian. So I headed for the girl bars and I headed for the stage.

(Walks over to the microphone, cross-fade to a follow spot around the mike area giving a standup comedy club look.)

And, a star was born—OK in my own mind!

(Does around five to eight minutes of standup, ending with the following waitress bit:)

. . . I didn't mind being a waitress, I just hated when men would order for women—

WAITRESS: Good afternoon. My name is Monica, what can I get for you?

MAN: Well, my wife will have—honey, what did you want again?

WIFE: I would tell you but she's looking at me. Help! I can't speak!

MONICA: I felt very sorry for these women but I will say this, things started to change drastically in my section of the restaurant.

WAITRESS: Good afternoon. My name is Monica, what can I get for you?

MAN: Well, the little lady—

WAITRESS: Sir, the little lady has a mind of her own and she will order for herself. Ma'am, what can I get you?

WIFE: Hi . . . um, I'll have . . . I'll have a . . . a . . . a steak!

WAITRESS: OK, a steak. A little hesitant but that was good—keep it coming!

WIFE: And ah, ah, ah baked potato!

WAITRESS: OK, a baked potato. Much more assertive. Let it out. Let it out!

WIFE: And a salad!

WAITRESS: OK, a salad. You were fantastic! *(To man)* Wasn't she great? *(To wife)* Don't you feel much better? Now turn to your husband and demand oral sex!—My tips started to dwindle.

(Monica walks out of the spot. Cross-fade to general lights. She walks stage left.)

MONICA: I eventually moved to L.A. because I, like many of you, wanted to be bothered with my environment. As I was stressing out about surviving in Hollywood, I managed to remain sane by performing and writing comedy. I did shows here and there, performing mostly for homo audiences because I could be myself: "Take my lesbian—please!"

But I figured since I was living in L.A., I should attempt the mainstream clubs because some bigwig could discover me, give me a TV series and enough money to pay off my student loan. So I went to these clubs—and I hated it! I was so uptight. No one was to find out I was a lezbo—dyke—queer—homo—butch—*muff diver*!!

(Music cue: surfer song "Wipe Out" blares as Monica does the Swim. Monica does the backstroke and turns around. Music fades.)

And everybody I met was either homophobic, racist or sexist—usually, all three. But I had to give the biz a good shot because I was a fighter . . . sort of.

I tried my darndest to act like a generic comic: straight, white, male—always on, cruising chicks, talking fast, always networking. Always. But it just wasn't me. And every time I'd tell male comics I was from San Francisco, they would respond with a stupid homophobic comment. I wanted to smack them in their abdomens with an oar! Instead, I walked away angry, confused, my tummy ached. So you can imagine how I felt on stage.

(Heads for microphone as general lights cross-fade to a special spot. She continues monologue.)

I did OK but my confidence was low so my punch was weak. And sometimes I really sucked because I couldn't be myself and I couldn't relate to the audience. You try following some jerk doing material on *beaners, bitches, AIDS*—of course he's grabbing *(Grabs crotch like a man)* himself the whole time. The sad part was, the audience laughed.

I just hated how comedy was and still is a boy's game. Club owners don't like to book women because, quote: "They talk about women things and their periods." End of quote.

Yet guys would get on stage, grab their dicks, talk about shit, talk about farts, and the audience was on the floor! I wanted to make them stick their tongues on ice trays!

Bitter?! I'm not bitter. I'm a waitress!

My true frustration was many of these comics were not funny yet they had gigs. Here I was this comic with an impressive résumé but I couldn't boast about it. Performing for gay and lesbian events didn't count!

(Walks out of spot. Spot is empty for ten seconds, then returns with a happy face.)

But hey, life wasn't that gloomy! Because the commercial world of comedy led me to TV auditions. For Consuelo *the maid*! Maria *the maid*! Anita *the maid*!

Believe me, folks, I did not want to go but I figured, this was how every great Latino actor got their start—a foot in the back door.

On my last and final audition, I waited with a bubbly blond blue-eyed woman who asked:

BUBBLY BLOND BLUE-EYED WOMAN: Are you here for the role of Tracy?

MONICA: I could only shake my head no because I was too embarrassed to tell her I was here once again auditioning for the maid. I . . . was . . . too . . . embarrassed.

(Looks down. Pause. Slowly walks out of spot. Empty spot held until Monica stops downstage left. Then a slow cross-fade to general lights.)

After all these run-ins with a cruel world, I had to sit down and take off my bra. *(Pause)* Thump thump!

I had a chat with my creative guru—you know, my higher self. And after a pack of M&M's and a wheel of brie, I decided: Fuck this shit, man! I have to be what I'm about!

Wow! I am so profound!

I stopped going to these clubs and those stupid auditions! I couldn't put my *Latin Lezbo Comic* self into those Hollywood molds.

I figured it out. I now only did shows and got involved with projects that had to do with me: gays and lesbians, Chicanos, Latinos, women, politics—bikini contests!

And you know what—life went on . . . Because as I was dealing with social-political ethics, racism, homophobia, the restaurant that time forgot and heat rash—I was getting into relationships and I was getting out of them. Finally, I reached a point in my life where I declared: "No more commitments! No more compromises! Couples are stupid! I just want to be a Don Juanita!"

DON JUANITA: Hey, mamasita, let me touch those chi-chi's!

MONICA: And just when I was about to conquer *las mujeres*, the babes, those little gazelles, I met a woman at a party. There were people all around. Breasts everywhere. *(Grabs breasts everywhere)* But when I shook her hand, it felt like *we* were the *only ones* in that room.

(Sings the theme song melody from A Man and a Woman *and says:)*

Hi, my name is Monica Palacios.

(Sings melody.)

I make a decent amount of money.

(Sings melody.)

I'd like to have sex with you—please!

Within a month, we were married. It just happened. No invitations were sent out. No one told us to kiss the bride. I just knew she was the woman I wanted to spend the rest of my life with. And . . . she . . . had a . . . gold card. Not just any gold card. Citibank gold card.

It became time for my wife, the Mrs., the little woman, to meet my family because I love them very much. We're very close—and this way I thought I could do my laundry.

We all decided on a Sunday dinner. But we stumped everybody about what to make for dinner because we are vegetarians. My family was confused.

FAMILY: WHAT? You don't eat chicken, fish or cheese?! Well then, what do you eat? What do you eat?!!!!!

MONICA: Finally, after many phone calls and much, much research, we all decided on—Mexican food. Ooooh, that was tough.

The day arrives and they are all excited to meet her. The nieces and nephews all run up to me.

NIECES AND NEPHEWS: Auntie, Auntie, Monica, we've missed you. You don't eat chicken, fish or cheese? What do you eat?

MONICA: Of course my precocious niece starts in on me.

PRECOCIOUS NIECE *(Smart aleck)*: Auntie, Monica, why don't you have a husband? Why are you a vegetarian? Why are you and *your friend*, wearing the *same rings*!?

MONICA: So I just kind of pushed her out of the way and *kicked her*!

(Mimes kicking field goal, using niece.)

My dad was playing the piano and singing away.

DAD *(Singing)*:
You are my sunshine, my only sunshine.
You don't eat chicken, fish or cheese.

MONICA: My mom was great. She warmly welcomed my wife—very sincere. Then she tried to get the kids to eat before the adults but they were not cooperating, so she had to resort to her Mexican mom sound effects and her chin.

(Does Mom making sound effects and points with her chin.)

Finally, the time was right. I gathered everybody around the room and I said, "My family—*mi familia, this is my wife!*"
Everybody stopped talking. After a moment of thick intense silence, my mom says:

MOM: Come on, everybody, let's eat. Food is getting cold. C'mon, *andale*. C'mon, get the baby. Where's the baby?

MONICA: You see, they know but they don't want to talk about it. What for? Why ruin a good meal?!

(Blackout. In the blackout she says:)

Family thoughts around the dinner table. My mom:

(Special spot around head and shoulders.)

MOM: We know that you are but we don't want to know again! Pass the butter! *(Points with chin)*

(Blackout. In the blackout she says:)

MONICA: My dad—

(Special spot around head and shoulders.)

DAD: She's not married. She brings women to family functions.

(Sings:)

Qué será, será,
whatever will be, will be.

(Blackout. In the blackout she says:)

MONICA: My older sister—

(Special spot around head and shoulders.)

OLDER SISTER: Well, I don't approve of it. But she is my baby sister. Her girlfriend is pretty—thank god!

(Blackout. In the blackout she says:)

MONICA: My older brother—

(Special spot around head and shoulders.)

OLDER BROTHER: I guess she knows what she's doing. We don't talk about it. She better not try to hit on my wife!

(Blackout. In the blackout she says:)

MONICA: My other older sister—

(Special spot around head and shoulders.)

OTHER OLDER SISTER: I'm not sure I understand it. Her girlfriend is nice—I guess that's what she calls her! Her woman? Her lover—person?!

(Blackout. In the blackout she says:)

MONICA: My little brother—

(Special spot around head and shoulders.)

LITTLE BROTHER: Hey, man, she can do what she wants. It's her business. She seems happy. Oh my god! My wife is flirting with her girlfriend!!!

(Blackout. In the blackout she says:)

MONICA: My precocious niece—

(Special spot around head and shoulders.)

PRECOCIOUS NIECE: *LEZBO!!!!!!!!!!!*

(Blackout. General lights come up.)

MONICA: But are you ready for this? My other, other older sister, is also a lesbian! You know my family thinks—

FAMILY: Did you guys eat the same thing? How does this happen?!!!

FILM ANNOUNCER *(Commercial voice)*: Just when the Mexican Catholic family thought they had one lesbian daughter, they actually have two! Experience their confusion in: *Double Dyke Familia!*

MONICA: Every year the *familia* had that same holiday wish: *"Por favor,* let them bring home men to dinner. We don't want to march in that gay parade!"

FILM ANNOUNCER: *Double Dyke Familia!*

MONICA: Having a lesbian sister has made my life peaceful. Believe me. She has always been a strong role model. And about our relationship with our family, of course we could never take them to a movie called: *Rodeo Girls in Bondage and Birkenstocks.* But we remain connected and that's important to me. It's the relatives who make me crazy. You know the ones that never encourage their daughters to say hello to me because they think I'm going to hypnotize them!

(Mimes hypnotizing girls with hand and eyebrow movements. Then quickly pops into lesbian character driving a tractor and waves. Quickly pops back to hypnotizing the girls.)

You are getting sleepy but you will soon want the love of another woman. *(Makes the shape of a woman with hands)* You will also want—a meatless dish!

(Continues to hypnotize as lights fade to black.
At this time, stagehands set a simple sturdy chair without armrests center stage; they strike mike and mike stand. Monica exits stage right, where a bar stool with doctor's coat lying across it, sits. Music and V.O. of Monica reading a poem comes up as Monica changes into black slip and heels. Done dressing, she places herself on chair. V.O. poem stops.
Music cue: the song "Jungle Fever" slowly goes up as rich, red back lights fade-up; then slow fade-up of rich blue over-head special.
Monica sits on chair à la Sophia Loren. Legs are crossed, hands are tied behind back and head hangs down. She slowly struggles in chair to get loose; she maintains this throughout poem. When Monica jerks her head back and up, she gets frontal face light.
"Jungle Fever" fades to background. She looks up into light.)

It was turning into a kinky ritual.
What lured me was the way she used her sexy mouth,
and god—
she loved to CHEW!
Yes, I watched her eat *carne asada tacos* from afar.

It all started weeks ago when I looked up after devouring my
vegetarian *burrito*—
and I saw her.
She was a *Chicana*—
brown woman
dark eyes
dark thick Mexican girl hair
about 5' 2"
athletic built and she was,
hungry!

Didn't just wolf down her two *tacos* and *Corona* with two limes.
She consumed her meal creatively, slowly, tenderly—
Con pasion.
Ab-so-lute-ly loved when she closed her eyes after every bite.
Chewing at least twenty times as if she was becoming one with
the *carne asada.*
OOOOMMME!
Peaceful and beautiful she looked as her full *Chicana* lips produced
kisses
as she
mas-ti-ca-ted!

(Uncrosses legs abruptly.)

Added attraction: at every third or fourth bite, she chased it with a
bite
of a
jalapeño.
Ay, pura Mexicana!
And of course, a few seconds after, she had the sniffles.
Her *jalapeño* gestures reminded me of my
parents.

Tíos
their *comadres*
always in need of *jalapeños* with their food.
Even dessert.
It was
intense!

Taquería la Cumbre, my favorite *taquería* in *San Francisco*

because the cashier looks like my *nina* and when she gives me
my change
she always says,
"Thank you, *mija.*"

Added to this dietary delight
because it was a romantic *taco* haven.
Enabling me to peer at
Miss *Sabrosita.*
Watching the *carne asada* grease
trickle from her mouth
down her chin
down her neck
almost down her cleavage,
her cleavage—
Almost.
Ay!

But a ready napkin comes to the rescue.
And I want to be there clutching that napkin.
But then I would have to introduce myself—
and that can't be.
I have to stay in the shadows,
across the room,
behind the *salsa.*

I need to watch her eat
carne asada tacos
from afar.

*("Jungle Fever" ends. Tech stops. Monica hangs head down as
frontal light and red light fade out; blue light remains. Monica
stays in chair dramatically recuperating, inhaling and exhaling
loudly. She unties herself, slips off shoes and places them to the
right. She slowly rises, stretches. Stagehands strike chair and shoes.*

*Conga player places herself/himself in the wings stage left
and waits for cue. Music cue: ocean sounds fade up—waves
moving in and out.*

*Monica gets mike. As she returns to center, cross-fade to light
special: lights up from downstage left and right, creating two huge
shadows of Monica on back wall. Front lights come up to light face.*

Music cue: ocean sounds go to background.)

The warm cool of her ocean
embraces my soul. I see her out there,
riding those big blue waves.
Water is her lover
but I want to quench her . . . thirst . . .
let me be your liquid, baby.

(Music cue: conga starts. Monica sings:)

Surfer, *chola*
you're so fine
I love your Speedos
On your behind.

Low and slow
is your style,
cruising waves
with that smile.

You're my surfer *chola*
my surfer *chola.*
You're my surfer *chola*
my surfer *chola.*

Your bouffant stays perfect
in the salty air,
hard like a shell
with heavy glare.

Forget the Beach Boys
or muscle men,
I'll be your surf
I'll hang your ten.

You're my surfer *chola*
my surfer *chola.*
You're my surfer *chola*
my surfer *chola.*

Malibu Barbie
and suntanned Sue
don't compare
to your tattoos.

I want to do you
on your board
so Annette and Frankie
can yell, "Dear Lord!"

You're my surfer *chola*
my surfer *chola*.
You're my surfer *chola*
GIDGET LOOK OUT!

You're my surfer *chola*
my surfer *chola*.
You're my surfer *chola*
my surfer *chola*.

(Music cue: sounds stop. Conga stops. Conga player exits. Cross-fade to general lighting. Monica gets rid of mike.)

I couldn't believe I finally lured her to my bed.
It took so many dinners.
So many "No On 187" rallies.
So many discussions on the Virgin Mary—whether she was a consumer or a lesbian. And so many poetry readings where poets lamented about *carnitas*.
But we made it. To the love nest. The sex sack. The coochie cot.
Actually, what did it, was the dinner I made. *Salsa, guacamole,* chips, chicken *enchiladas, arroz, frijolitos* and the best *margaritas* west of the 405.
Throughout the entire meal we exchanged:
Mmmmm
Mmm-Mmm
M-M-M
God I'm a good cook.
Then we casually ooozed into the living room where I cleverly hit the remote and presto Barry White started singing what I had been wanting to tell her:

Can't get enough, girl.
Can't get enough.

I pulled her close but thought I might offend her with my onion/*margarita* breath. But I realized she had the same—and quite a bit more—I pulled her closer.

We slowly did the lezbo lambada—my thigh to her crotch, her crotch to my thigh. And I drove. Driving, driving, driving, driving.

I waltzed her into my room and whea-lah! We landed on my bed. I ever so gingerly RRRIPPED her clothes off and I put my hands to work. O, they were all over her delicious body: massaging, sculpting, pinching, sliding, rubbing, rubbing, rubbing and rubbing! Until she gave me wet fingertips.

I could barely contain myself. I wanted so desperately to dive into her sweet thang
her *pan dulce*—
her *empanada* of love.
But she interrupted by asking,
"Did you wash your hands after you made *salsa?*"
Of course I thought she was concerned about safer sex techniques and I assured her in my soothing sexual healing way, "Baby, baby, my love, I'm the safest woman on this planet."

She was so cute. She kind of . . . grabbed my throat and said: "Oh yeah—then why is my *empanada* on fire!"

(As audience laughs, Monica steps to stage right and puts on doctor coat and shoes. She grabs stool and mike and brings them center stage. Lights cross-fade to nightclub look—blues, reds, purples, follow spot. She sits.)

. . . Did you have a nice break? Welcome back to the Lucky Lady Lounge and Women's Health Clinic—where you can hear show tunes and get a Pap smear *(Pulls out plastic speculum from pocket—and keeps it visible)* at the same time.

I'd like to thank the Clinton Administration for keeping cabaret and women's health facilities alive. Thanks, Hillary. You're a doll. *(Wink's at Hillary)*

If I may, I'd like to turn our attention to the word "Love."

(Music cue: cabaret piano music through the entire bit.)

Love, soft as an easy chair.
Love, fresh as the morning air.

And it comes in many shapes, colors—speculums. Sometimes you think you're never going to find it and sometimes it's staring you right in the face.

(Monica looks out to the audience) What's your name, sweetheart? *Concha*—oh, pretty. *Concha*, can I tell you something? *(Sings "I've Got a Crush on You," stopping midway to say)* Lay back put your feet in the stirrups. *(Continues singing until song ends)*

(Applause) Thank you. Thank you for being with me here tonight, but let's stop this gab-fest and sing more love songs— shall we? *(Sings slowly "That's the Way Uh-huh I Like It." Really gets into it, midway humping the stool. Then she lays straight across stool on stomach and dangles feet. Song ends)* K.C., I love you. Mean it.

Is Frances Johnson in the house tonight? Frances, your tests have come back. You do have a yeast infection. I'm sorry, hun. I know it's really hard. It's very difficult. But it's during these times that I . . . well . . . let me tell you what I'm talking about . . . woman to woman . . . *(Sings "Let It Please Be Her")*

(When the song ends, she cries softly) Thank you. Thank you all so very, very much. No, please don't get up. Don't worry about me because I always rise above. I use Monistat 7. And I think of the good times. And I thank the goddess I'm alive and I remember . . . *(Sings "To All the Girls I've Loved Before")*

(Song ends. Music stops. Cross-fade to general lights.

As Monica gets rid of stool, mike, coat, shoes and speculum, lights come up to a softer general.)

When I was four, five and six, I was extremely shy and I had a pixie hair cut.

Adults would stick their faces in my space and ask:
"Are you a boy or a girl?"
"Girl!"
Shouting up into their adult world.
Wishing they hadn't asked me that.
Wondering if I looked like a freak or something.
I just didn't feel like a little girl.
Sugar and spice and everything nice.
I don't think so.
It was raining really hard but my mom, dad and little brother Greg went to the toy store anyway. It was Sunday and we respected our obligations.

Greg got this totally cool machine gun and I—I don't know what possessed me, perhaps societal pressure—I got this doll.

During our drive home I knew I made the wrong choice. By the time I got inside, I was balling my head off because I wanted a machine gun too. I cried so much, my dad went back to the toy store and returned home with a

brand new machine gun.

I was really happy then.

I was always the Dad, the Soldier or the Sheriff.

The Christmas that I was five was the year I got my cowboy drag. "Getty up, Miss Kitty."

I was just getting over the chicken pox, so my week had been hellish.

But waking up Christmas morning to a cowboy hat, shirt, leather vest with fringe, chaps, Levi's, two-tone boots and a holster with two guns—I was spent.

The land of little boys was Adventure—Danger—Buddies! And really cool toys.

Don't get me wrong, I never wanted to physically be a boy.

Although I did try peeing standing up a couple of times— and I did pretend to shave with dad.

I liked my girl body. I just wanted what they had—Power!

I soon reached the age where I was supposed to like boys and they were supposed to like me back.

They liked me back all right—too much!

They were so annoying and I was just in the fourth grade! This is when I started feeling that

Male Sexual Power!

They didn't hurt me or anything, but they would really tease me.

"Hey, Monica, he says he loves you."

"Monica meet José behind the school yard because he wants to kiss you."

"Hey, Monica, come out of your house because we want to *fuck you*!"

Fuck me?! Jeeez, I'm just in the fourth grade and I'm still begging my mother for an Easy Bake Oven!

Because I, like many of you, wanted to bake a cake with a light-bulb.

This Male Sexual Power thing, when I didn't ask for it—made
me crazy! And it continued through elementary school,
junior high, high school and college.
Who told them it was OK to invade
my space—
my body—
my soul—
on their terms?
Who told them it was OK to grab my tits and laugh as I walk
down the corridor to my science class?
Who told them it was OK to verbally, sexually harass me until
I'm in tears as I wash my car in front of my house?
Who told them it was OK to
fuck me even though I said NO????!!!!!!

In high school, I didn't have many boyfriends which was OK
with me but not in my circle of friends. Because I hung out with
boy-crazy girls and all they could talk about were their
boyfriends.

"Monica, you know my boyfriend who I love very much
and I would stick a fork in my eye to prove my love?"

"Yeah."

"Well, we can't have sex unless he can come twice so we
have sex all the time. I can't wait to see him again and his
sperm."

Oh god and that stuff. There was always so much of it.
Where did it come from? Give me a towel!

I couldn't handle it.

Or their tongues down my throat.

Hands up my shirt.

Dicks inside—get that hose away from me!

There were moments when I thought I was enjoying myself—
but no, not really.

And, folks, please note, I don't hate men. I don't want to read
somewhere: ". . . Funny but hates men."

I have close male friends. I do shows with men.

It's just that Male Sexual Power—I allowed it because I was
taught to accept it.

You're thinking, OK, Monica, you were having fantasies of
women all this time.

No I wasn't because the institutions that were telling me to have sex with men were also telling me not to have sex with women because that is like really, really gross!

And during these confusing stressful heterosexual years, I had men—*MEN*—tell me: "I think you're going to become a lesbian. I'll go put on my clothes now."

I wished they would have told me sooner. I wished someone would have taken me aside—preferably an angel and said:

"The reason you felt like an outsider when you were growing up. The reason you couldn't handle all that Male Sexual Power. The reason you've had these unexplainable weird feelings for women—is because you were born a lesbian and NOBODY TOLD YOU!"

But now I know. Because I have reached
Deep in the Crotch of My Queer *LATINA* Psyche.
And it told me to kiss that woman.
And she tasted like honey.
And I kissed her entire body until I passed out!
When I came to—I realized I was a lesbian!
Lesbian—Lesbian—LESBIAN!
(Pops into miming lesbian on a tractor) And I didn't have horns or fangs or this uncontrollable desire to chase Girl Scouts: "Hey little lady, can I bite your cookies?"
I was ready to embrace myself.
I was ready to embrace other women.
And feel safe.
And feel a sense of equality.
And feel myself gripping her sensual waist.
Massaging her inviting curves.
Kissing her chocolate nipples.
And sliding my face down
Lick . . .

(Gets down on knees, eyes closed.)

Down
Lick
Down
Lick
Wanting all of her inside my mouth
And knowing I was never, ever going back

Because honey is
too sweet
To give up.

(Slowly licks fingertips as lights slowly fade to black. In the black she puts on shoes and gets mike. Lights fade-up to follow spot in the mike area.)

Well I gotta go. My carpool is here. But I'd like to leave you with this special song and I want to dedicate it to my parents for going all the way.

(Sings the "Vagina Medley" a cappella:)

Women gather 'round women
we must laugh, we must laugh.

We must learn to be less uptight,
so we can relax our vaginal muscles.

(Speaks) You know, folks, we haven't heard enough about that great word "vagina."

(Sings to the tune of "Lullaby of Broadway":)

C'mon along and listen to
my Lullaby of *Vagina.*
The hit parade and belly-hoo
my lullaby of *Vagina.*

(Sings the next lines in traditional medley style but replaces the key word with "vagina.")

. . . I left my *vagina* in San Francisco . . . *Vagina* Cathedral . . . The days of wine and *vagina* . . . I wanna hold your *vagina* . . . I'm a little *vagina* short and stout. Here is my handle. Here is my spout . . . The shadow of your *vagina* . . . La *vagina.* La *vagina.* Ya no quiere caminar . . . One less *vagina* to answer. One less *vagina* to fry . . . Put your *vagina* in. Take your *vagina* out. Put your *vagina* in and you shake it all about . . . I'm gonna wash that *vagina* right out of my hair . . .

(Sings next line to the tune of "Lullaby of Broadway":)

So you've listened to my melody of ooolllddd *vaaa-giiii-naaaahh*!

(Sings last line exactly like the last line from the Bobby Darin classic, "Mack the Knife":)

Look out old *vagina* is back!

(Blackout—hold for thunderous applause. Lights up. Bow. Blackout.)

END OF PLAY

Venice Beach resident, **MONICA PALACIOS** is a highly acclaimed Chicana lesbian writer-performer whose one-woman shows have been critically praised throughout the United States. They include *Latin Lezbo Comic, Confessions* and . . . *A Sexplosion of Tantalizing Tales.* She has performed Off-Broadway and has been profiled on PBS. Monica is a playwright-in- residence at L.A.'s Mark Taper Forum's Latino Theatre Initiative, where she is developing her play *Clock.* An anthologized writer, she is featured in *Latina: Women's Voices from the Borderlands, Chicana Lesbians: The Girls Our Mothers Warned Us About* and *A Funny Time to Be Gay.* She is an adjunct professor at UCLA, a columnist for the *Lesbian News* and is on the Board of Directors of VIVA, Lesbian and Gay Latino Artists.

ALCHEMY OF DESIRE/ DEAD-MAN'S BLUES
A Play with Songs

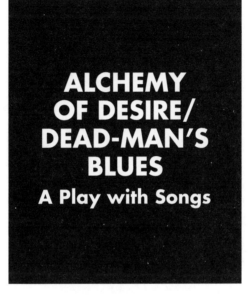

Caridad Svich

THE WRITER SPEAKS
Caridad Svich

Flux is at the core of my writing aesthetic. My work, although an outgrowth of a singular vision, reflects my interest in a variety of structural forms, styles, and tones.

Born in the U.S. of Cuban-Argentine-Spanish-Croatian descent, I am a first generation hybrid, a daughter of a hybrid sensibility, which is neither fully Latina in what may be termed a conventional sense nor fully "American," but rather a sensibility in flux: bilingual, multicultural, female.

My plays are naturally built on the concept of collage, mixing poetry, songs, ritual, traditional Western dramatic scenes, movement and images. They are character based and rooted in a sense of place, be it emotional or geographic terrain, as well as rooted in the notion of giving voice to dispossessed voices. *Alchemy of Desire/Dead-Man's Blues* in particular stems from a desire to re-imagine the United States from within: to take apart familiar structures and reconfigure them in a way that will forge a new theatrical identity, one that is reflective of a multifaceted culture yet rooted in ancient, even primeval impulses and forms. The nature of my work is to always chart anew, building on what has gone before, seeking transcendence and spiritual transformation in a world not yet gone wrong.

The biggest influence on my work, besides my cultural lineage and the influence of growing up bilingual (speaking Spanish in the home and English "outside") would have to be the rather nomadic existence I have lived. Between the ages of five and twenty-seven, I lived in Pennsylvania, New Jersey, North Carolina, Florida, Utah, New York and California, along with twice as many cross-country trips in between.

The process of seeing the country, being constantly uprooted and having to adapt to new circumstances has left a marked imprint in the formation of my work and world view. You can never really escape where you're from, but if you're from nowhere and everywhere, the source of the work is significantly changed. It has meant that I write both consciously and not about location and dislocation, about longing for home and wanting to run away, about feeling like an exile and feeling like a native. The decidedly American obsession with wanderlust is both a topic of exploration and continual de-mythologization.

I have a strong connection to various literary figures: Virginia Woolf, Federico García Lorca, Annie Dillard, Borges, Shakespeare, but also to the work of other artists in dance, art, music and photography, including Velázquez, Ana Mendieta, Helen Leavitt, Charles Ives, to name a few. From Woolf's writings I especially learned about form, the role memory plays, and the necessity for experimentation and the vitality of a woman's voice. From one of my teachers, Maria Irene Fornes, with whom I studied for four years, I learned to not be afraid to speak the truth in my work.

My commitment to theatre even in this technological age is strong and vital. Although I welcome the use of sophisticated technology in theatre, my primary concern is a poet's concern: voice and space, voice in space. My areas of experimentation are never far removed from this basic concern. The language of the theatre with its ability to encompass literary, painterly and musical traditions is the language with which I currently feel most comfortable to address the public and private realms of experience which constitute the focus of my work.

for my parents

Special thanks to Jocelyn A. Beard, Kent Brown, Rebecca Brown,
Annie Castledine, Anne Cattaneo, Maria Delgado, Elyse Dodgson,
Roger Ellis, Michael Garces, Tori Haring-Smith, Mead Hunter,
Dina Ibrahim, Rachel Katz, Wendy Knox, DD Kugler,
Lorenzo Mans, David Moore, Jr., Nadine Pederson,
Jane Peterson, Lisa Peterson, J. D. Steele,
Ed Stern, Sheila Tousey, Ross Willits,
Steve Wise, Jan Woolf

‖‖‖

Production History

Alchemy of Desire/Dead-Man's Blues was originally developed by A.S.K. Theater Projects, Los Angeles, and the Playwrights' Center, Minneapolis.

The play received its world premiere at the Cincinnati Playhouse in the Park as winner of the Lois and Richard Rosenthal New Play Prize (Ed Stern, Producing Artistic Director), in Cincinnati, Ohio, on March 31, 1994. It was directed by Lisa Peterson; the set design was by Neil Patel; the costume design was by Candice Donnelly; the lighting design was by Mimi Jordan Sherin; the sound design was by Dan Moses Schreier and the stage manager was Bruce E. Coyle. The cast was as follows:

SIMONE	Sheila Tousey
TIRASOL	Patricia Mattick
CAROLINE	Camille D'Ambrose
SELAH	Susan Barnes
MIRANDA	Kate Malin
JAMIE	Scott Ripley

Alchemy of Desire/Dead-Man's Blues received further productions in 1994 at the Royal Court Theatre for New American Plays Festival; in 1996: Florida's Bridge Theatre, Seattle's University of Washington; in 1997: Alberta, Canada's Northern Light Theatre International Play Festival, Minneapolis's Frank Theatre; in 1998: New York City's Repertorio Español; in 1999: London's Hackney Empire Studio Theatre, Baltimore's University of Maryland.

Characters

SIMONE, a passionate, restless woman
in her late twenties/early thirties.

TIRASOL, an anxious, determined woman in her early forties.

CAROLINE, a strong, practical, yet slightly melancholic woman
in her forties.

SELAH, a woman in her fifties/early sixties. A seer.

MIRANDA, a curious and spirited woman in her late teens.

JAMIE, Simone's husband, a ghost.

Time

The present.

Setting

An open, fluid space evocative of the swamps
of a burnt-out bayou.

Notes

This play should be performed without an intermission. Selected
scene titles may be used for production purposes. Original songs by
the author featured in the text may be performed a cappella.

Regarding lighting: except where indicated, there are to be no
blackouts in the staging of this play. "Light change" at the end of a
scene indicates a subtle but significant variance in light. "Light shift"
at the end of a scene suggests a fluid shift in light, but that little or no
time has passed. "Lights fade" indicates a breath or rest (as in a piece
of music), and denotes an elongated passage of time.

1.

Dark. Lights reveal Simone seated, surrounded by buckets of Kentucky Fried Chicken. She wears a faded purple dress, and is barefoot.

SIMONE:
Chicken.
Buckets and buckets of fried chicken all over.
Twelve, sixteen, twenty-four piece . . .
Everybody brought one. One kind or another.
Caroline, Selah, Mrs. Hawkins . . .
They all came in with their chicken.
They all came in.
With their mouths open. Gristle stuck between their teeth.
Their faces smeared with grease, and perfume, and liquor.
They all came in.
Came in and flapped their arms. Calling out to God
and Jeremiah and all the powers in the universe.
They all came in with their chicken.
Came in to push their thigh meat in my face.
Push it in my face to make me feel better.

I thought I'd puke.
I thought, One more bucket, I'm gonna get down on my knees
and puke right next to the coffin.

I don't like fried chicken. He sure as hell didn't.
Why'd they bring it, then? Cause that's what you do?
That's what you do when somebody passes on?
Y'know, just because people been doing somethin a long time
don't mean you got to *keep on* doin it.
Ain't nobody said you gotta become a fool to tradition.
Why didn't they bring somethin else?

Sweet potato pie, ice water, hard whiskey . . .
I wouldn't have minded some hard whiskey.
But fried chicken?

It smells up the whole house.
Smells up the house real good.
Why, you can smell the stink of the fat for miles.
. . . Clear up to the river, you can smell it.

Grease all over.
Goes straight through the buckets, stains the wood.
Hell to get grease out once it's stained the wood.
Fingers get oily, sticky. Hands reeking of chicken.
Grease swimming through you til *nothin*
can rid you of its reek.
Gotta get tar soap, wash it off, scrub your hands blood raw
to get rid of it.

And the thing is, who's going to eat it?
Who is going to eat the damn chicken anyway?
I can't eat it. —And he's dead.
What good's it going to do him?

Peel off the skin and fat and throw the chicken bones at him,
that's all I can do.
Bury him with the chicken bones.

Dead. He's just dead.
Some bullet ripped right through him like he was dog meat:
eyes all busted, bones sticking out of the flesh . . .
I didn't even recognize him.
If they didn't say it was Jamie, I wouldn't know who it was,
so little left of him that's really him.

(Sound: slightly distorted shell-fire of battle. Fade-out.)

He was my husband, Jamie was.
Damn war killed him off.
I don't even know where it was.
All I know is: one day, there was a rumor of war
and the next, he was off to some little country somewhere
I couldn't even find on a map.
And then he was dead.

We weren't even married a month.
Made love in some car, got married . . .
And he just *takes off*.

BASTARD.

(Sound: slightly distorted shell-fire. Fade-out.)

I can barely remember him now.
I'll see somebody, he'll look like him,
but he'll turn around and I realize he don't look like Jamie at all.

Not even married a month.
And all I got are buckets of chicken stinkin up the house.
That's all I got.
Fried chicken and a dead body.

(Lights fade.)

2.

Tirasol and Caroline are seated, snapping the last of a batch of beans into a large earthenware bowl. Selah and Miranda are seated to one side. Selah is fanning herself slowly. Miranda is looking out, listening. The bean snapping should serve as a kind of accompaniment to the voices—subtly, discreetly musical.

TIRASOL: You know what they say?
CAROLINE: What they say?
TIRASOL: They say she made a pile of chicken bones in her backyard.
CAROLINE: That what they say?
TIRASOL: That's what they say.

(Beat.)

Know what else they say?
CAROLINE: What they say?
TIRASOL: They say she's going 'round with no clothes on in the dead of night—
CAROLINE: No.
TIRASOL: Calling his name out like he's going to answer.
CAROLINE: They say that?
TIRASOL: I've heard it.

(Beat.)

CAROLINE: You lie.
TIRASOL: I swear on my mother's grave, may the poor woman rest in all-mighty peace.
CAROLINE: They say that?
TIRASOL: Uh-huh.

(Beat.)

CAROLINE: They sure say a lot of things
SELAH: Don't mean it's true.
TIRASOL: Gotta mean somethin.

(Beat.)

SELAH: People talk.
TIRASOL: They talk all right.
SELAH: Talk until their tongues turn blue. Got *nothin* to do.

(Beans falling into bowl. Pause.)

TIRASOL: What's she gonna do?
MIRANDA: Who?
TIRASOL:
Simone. What's she gonna do?
Got to do somethin. Ain't she?
Can't keep grievin forever.
Ain't do a soul no good to *keep on* grievin.
Bring nothin but chaos and misery on a person to do that.
. . . What's she gonna do?

(Beat.)

CAROLINE: Nothin.
TIRASOL: What you say?
CAROLINE: Nothin, I 'xpect.
TIRASOL: Nothin?
CAROLINE: Uh-huh.
TIRASOL: What you mean, "Nothin?" There ain't no such thing.
CAROLINE: Is too.
TIRASOL: What? What you gonna tell me is, "Nothin?" Huh?
SELAH: . . . Goin on. Lettin yourself just *go on.* That's a kind of nothin.
(To Caroline) Eh?

CAROLINE: Uh-huh.

(Beat.)

TIRASOL: Bull. Throwing me bull, that's all you're doin.
  That woman's *got* to do somethin . . . Ain't even married a
  month.
SELAH: Mercy on the child.
CAROLINE: Have mercy.
MIRANDA: What's she gonna do?

(Pause.)

TIRASOL: Heard say she wrote a letter to the guvment.
MIRANDA: Did what?
TIRASOL: Wrote a letter. Cussed them out.
MIRANDA: That true?
TIRASOL: It's true all right. I've heard it.
MIRANDA: A letter?
TIRASOL: Yeh.
SELAH: Bull.
MIRANDA: What'd she say?
TIRASOL: Huh?
MIRANDA: What'd she say in this letter?
TIRASOL: She say all sorts of things. Tell guvment this, that . . . Cussed
  them right out.
MIRANDA: Yeh?
TIRASOL: That's what they say.
MIRANDA: That's somethin.
TIRASOL: It's somethin all right.
MIRANDA: . . . Grand.
TIRASOL: Eh?
MIRANDA: To write somethin like that? To the guvment?
  Grand, I say. Grand and valiant.
TIRASOL: Grand?
MIRANDA: Why, just the notion of it is . . . I couldn't do it.
  It may be a small measure of significance, but writing down
  a letter *is* somethin.
SELAH: . . . Mercy on the child.
CAROLINE: Have mercy.

(Pause.)

TIRASOL: Got a right.
MIRANDA: Course she does.
CAROLINE: What you say?
TIRASOL: To cuss guvment out like that, it's a right.
CAROLINE: Got *no* right.
TIRASOL: What you say now?
CAROLINE: Ain't guvment's fault. People die in wars all the time.
    She ain't the only one.
SELAH: That's right.

(Beat.)

CAROLINE: Your man, he passed on, didn't he?
SELAH: In the second war.
CAROLINE: . . . The second war.
SELAH:
    Sweet boy he was, too. Never bring me no harm.
    Not like the other so-called men in my life.
    No, that boy was as good as can be.
    Hungry, is all. Hungry for war. Couldn't wait to be part of it.
    Wanted the taste of battle more than anythin else, that boy.
    Wanted it more than lovin,
    more than any kind of lovin a woman could give him.
    I'd sit up at night and think, That boy is a fool.
    What's he doin thinkin about war when he's got me
    ready to walk hot coals for him if I had to? What's he thinkin?
    But he didn't know no better. He was young. Young and hungry.
    A thirst for war is simply too much for a young man.
    It's a kind of call: a call to desperate livin.
    Boys listen to it, their ears aflame:
    Oh when the rapture of war comes upon them unbelievable in
        its truth.
    Just didn't know no better.
    . . . Sweet boy. Sweet sweet boy.
CAROLINE: And he died.
SELAH: Yeh, he died. Fell out of a plane and into the sky, body on fire.
    I don't think he ever saw the ground.
CAROLINE: And you ain't wrote the guvment.
SELAH: No sir.
CAROLINE: It was your cross.
SELAH: Mine to bear.

CAROLINE: You just moved on.
SELAH: Had to. Couldn't write.
    Couldn't write, couldn't read. Not at the time.
CAROLINE: You just moved on.
SELAH: Yeah.

(Pause.)

TIRASOL: He was a stupid boy.
CAROLINE: Who?
TIRASOL: Jamie.
MIRANDA: Was not.
TIRASOL: Stupid. Didn't know anythin, that boy: always walkin
    around, not a thought in his brain.
SELAH: She loved him.
CAROLINE: Yeh, she did.
SELAH: He loved her.
MIRANDA: I don't know about that.
CAROLINE: You say he didn't?
TIRASOL: I say he was stupid. I don't think he knew what love was,
    'cept for puttin his thing between a woman's legs.
MIRANDA: . . . He could do that.

(Beat.)

CAROLINE: Oh, child. You just run wild. Got no mind at all.
MIRANDA: Ain't married him. Got some mind to do that.
TIRASOL: Sleepin with the devil, sleepin in the devil's bed.
SELAH: Mercy.
CAROLINE: Mercy on the child.
MIRANDA: It's war. Wartime makes you wild.

(Pause.)

TIRASOL: Say, you know where was that war?
MIRANDA: Which war?
TIRASOL: This war.
MIRANDA: Don't know. Some country, I 'xpect.
TIRASOL: . . . China?
MIRANDA:
    No. China's at the bottom of the ground,
    clear way to the other side of the earth,
    you gotta dig to find it. Not China.

CAROLINE: I used to know where it was.

TIRASOL: Yeh?

CAROLINE: Used to know 'xactly where it was. Can't remember the name.

How come names do that?

MIRANDA: Do what?

CAROLINE: Escape us?

TIRASOL: Too many countries.

SELAH: Too many wars.

(Beat.)

TIRASOL: What's she doin now, I wonder?

CAROLINE: Don't know. Don't know nothin no more . . .

TIRASOL: She could go crazy, with all the talk goin 'round. Could go mad.

CAROLINE: She keep thinkin about him, yeh. She don't . . .

SELAH: I 'xpect she's sleepin. Gotta sleep off your mournin.

TIRASOL: Sleepin. Yeh. She could be doin that.

MIRANDA: I 'xpect she's dreamin.

TIRASOL: Dreamin? What she gonna be dreamin about with her grievin? She got no cause to dream.

MIRANDA: She got cause.

TIRASOL: Yeh?

MIRANDA: She's dreamin.

TIRASOL: What's she dreamin about?

MIRANDA: She's dreamin about his sweet eyes lookin at her . . . his tongue, his mouth . . . dreamin.

CAROLINE: You need some water, child. Gotta cool yourself off.

MIRANDA: It's hot.

CAROLINE: No excuse for talk like that. That's a dead-man you're talkin about.

Gotta respect the dead same as the livin.

MIRANDA: Ain't said nothin.

CAROLINE:

Said plenty, that mouth of yours.

You got no right to talk about that man, especially not about his body.

The man is dead. His body is in the ground.

Ain't no dreamin of any kind about a dead-man's body,

especially not when he's left a widow to remember him by.

MIRANDA: You sayin she ain't dreamin?
CAROLINE:
I'm sayin: you gotta conduct yourself,
no matter how much you ache for him.

(Beat.)

TIRASOL: Hot.
CAROLINE: Yeh.
MIRANDA: And she's dreamin . . .
CAROLINE: Mercy.
SELAH: Mercy on the child.

(Light change.)

3.
Apparition

Sound: slightly distorted helicopter flying overhead. Sound swells.
Jamie appears. His clothes are rumpled, distressed, but he is physi-
cally intact.

JAMIE:
Oh—
I got beat up bad.
Those bullets went right through me.
Got holes all over: arms, chest, thigh . . .
Even my damn breathin's screwed up.
(Breathes audibly) Hear that?
It's like I got no air goin into my throat.
Bullets wiped me clean, clean out of air.
Damn blood and holes and . . .
Can't feel my dick.
Can't feel your dick, you ain't a man, right?

I don't even know where I am. Nothin looks familiar. Spooky.

I was doin good, too. I was beatin up the bad guys left and right,
jumpin on 'em like—
WISH TO HELL I knew where I am.
Feels like I'm all alone on the earth:
alone, and stinkin.

Got somethin. Got some—air—left.
(Indicating ribs) Cracked . . .

I'd get to feel this way—before—yeh—
take out this picture.

(Takes photograph out of pocket.)

Goddamn Blood's right across it.
Gets hard, blood . . . There. Can sorta see it.
Yeh. That's her. That's . . . Simone.

Oh, I got lots of girls, but she's the one I married.
Yeh. I married her.
Nobody believed it when I did it.
"Man, what you doin gettin married for?" they said,
"You got it perfect. Why you go have to ruin it?"
I don't know. Just felt right.
I looked at her one day, and I thought, I'll marry this one.

It was like she was in my skin. Like she'd been in my skin for years,
even though I'd only just met her.
"I'll marry this one."
"'For to desire and to be desired is better than to *burn*.'"

(Sound: distorted helicopter flying overhead.)

Head startin to hurt. That's no good. NO . . .

(Sound fades.)

I married her.

She was so sad when I left.
I was goin out on that bus to here,
and she just kept looking at me. Like I did somethin.

What the hell is she sad about? I thought,
I'm the one who's leavin. I'm the one goin God knows where
to get God knows beat up so bad I can't even breathe.
But she just kept standin there on the side of the road,
the bus drivin off and all I could see was her
standin there on the side of the road with those eyes . . .
and then nothin.

'Cept for this picture.

And she don't even look that good in it:
her mouth's all crooked, eyes kinda cross-eyed—
She don't look good at all.

(He tears the picture. Beat.)

Dear Simone . . .
I am beat up.
I am beat up bad.

(Light change.)

4.

Afternoon. Selah is hunting for stones in the ground. As she finds one to her liking, she picks it up, and stores it in a small pouch she carries. Miranda runs in.

MIRANDA: I've heard say there are ghosts walkin the earth. Is it true?
SELAH: Course it's true. There are spirits 'round us all the time.
MIRANDA: Yeh?
SELAH: Uh-huh.
MIRANDA: Then how come we don't see them?
SELAH: 'Cause we feel them, that's why. Don't you feel them?
MIRANDA: I don't know.
SELAH:
    You got to know.
    Why, don't you sometimes walk 'round,
    and feel like there's someone walkin 'round with you,
    'cept you can't see him?
MIRANDA: Guess so.
SELAH:
    I do. Not all the time, mind you, but sometimes . . .
    Oh, there is a powerful feelin I get
    that there's someone right here beside me. A strong, palpable
        feelin.
MIRANDA: Like a ghost?
SELAH: Yeh. You could call it that: a spirit, presence of some kind—
    walkin the earth with me.
MIRANDA: Must feel scary.
SELAH: No. Feels nice. Like I'm protected.

MIRANDA: Protected?

SELAH:

That I'm not alone, not completely, no matter what I do.
Course, sometimes a bad spirit comes to haunt you,
and that can get scary all right.
Ain't no way that feels nice.
Why, one time a bad spirit got hold of me,
and it took heaven and earth to rid myself of it. Heaven and
      earth . . .
Stubborn spirit, it was. Stubborn and nasty.

MIRANDA: Devil spirit?

SELAH:

Ain't so much the devil, as a meanness that come over me.
It's when it's mean that it's the worse kind of hauntin.
The world's mean enough already—
to have a mean spirit come along and visit you:
well . . . ain't no place for it. No place at all.

MIRANDA: What'd you do?

SELAH: Hmm?

MIRANDA: Mean spirit. What'd you do?

SELAH:

Got myself rid of it. You *got* to with bad spirits,
otherwise they never stop hauntin you.
Ol Lucy Hawkins's cousin, Aster Dean:
she let a bad spirit into her, paid it no mind at all,
figurin it'd let go of her when it done what it had to do;
the woman turned right into a spook before our very eyes:
grown her hair down to the ground white as ash,
speakin in all kinds of tongue,
lettin the meanness rise up out of her like untamed lava.

MIRANDA: Yeh? Bad spirit, huh?

SELAH: Untended.

MIRANDA: . . . Where's she now?

SELAH:

Aster Dean? Don't know.
I stopped speakin to her. We all did.
Woman turns into a spook, can't keep socializin with her.
Figure she must be off somewhere.
In her state, it's better if she be off somewhere . . .

(Beat.)

MIRANDA: And now?

SELAH: Eh, child?

MIRANDA: Right now. Is there a spirit here?

SELAH: . . . Yeh.

MIRANDA: Yeh?

SELAH: Course.

MIRANDA: How do you know?

SELAH: Just a feelin I get. Why are you so worried, child?
You come upon a ghost today?

MIRANDA: I don't know.

SELAH: You know if you come upon one.

MIRANDA: . . . No.

SELAH: Then why the worry? You sick, child?

MIRANDA: No.

SELAH: Then what is it, then?

MIRANDA: Been thinkin about Simone and Jamie, is all.
Thinkin bout her thinkin bout him . . .

SELAH: You feel him?

MIRANDA: Huh?

SELAH: Feel his presence?

MIRANDA: Feel somethin. But it ain't him.

SELAH: How do you know it ain't him?

MIRANDA: 'Cause it ain't. Why would I feel anythin?

SELAH: You slept with the man.

MIRANDA: So? That don't mean *nothin*.
Why, he wadn't even married then.

SELAH: Still slept with the man, shared in his spirit—

MIRANDA: No. Don't mean nothin! Don't mean I gotta believe in ghosts.

SELAH:
Oh, but you do.
If you don't, life just ain't the same. Ain't the same at all.
It'd be like goin 'round seein things one-half, instead of whole.
Don't you know it's up to the livin to recall the dead?
The one obligation we got besides bein born and dyin
is to recall those who have passed on to another life,
to signify their very physical passin.
It is our recallin that keeps spirits alive.
Now, I'm not sayin it's got to be Jamie.

You don't even have to know who it is you're recallin.
Why, there are ghosts who have been walkin this earth
for hundreds of years.
Old, tired ghosts who sit, and watch, and murmur.
Don't you ever feel that? The earth murmurin?
At night. When the world's asleep,
when you're lyin in bed before sleep overcomes you,
and all the sounds of the surroundin world
float in and around where you lay:
cars passin, off, down the road,
their tires squealin and hissin in the darkness;
the cracklin of leaves as they fall off the branch into the air,
their landings broken by hard ground;
split-splat of stones ripplin on water
before the whoosh of the night current takes them under.
Sounds. Floatin in and around,
until the space between you and slumber comes upon silence,
a silence that's so alive, so full of pulse and vibration,
you can hear them murmur: the ghosts of the earth.

'Tis not cause to be a-feared, child.
You got to take comfort in the murmurin,
for spirits wake to rumors of beauty and violence
to shiver our souls and remind us of our mortality.
'Tis not cause to be a-feared.

(Selah pulls out a bone necklace from her pouch, holds it out in front of Miranda.)

Come here. Let's see how this looks on you.

(Miranda turns away.)

It's all right to wander in your mind.
You got to wander before you can come to believe somethin.
That's why they say it like that: "Comin to believe."
It don't just happen. No sir.
You got to find your way to it, whatever it is,
whatever you set down and say you're goin to believe—
you got to find yourself to.

(Selah places necklace on Miranda.)

MIRANDA: I know one thing.
SELAH: Yeh? What would that be?
MIRANDA: I know I ain't loved Jamie. Not like Simone does.
SELAH: That's why he married her, child. That's why he married her.

(Light shift.)

5.

Simone walks in. There are traces of mud on her hands and dress.

SIMONE:
Truth is, I married him.
When you come right down to it,
I'm the one who did the marryin.
Jamie just fell into it.
In fact, I'd say we sort of fell into each other:
he didn't know what he was doin,
and I was still burnin with the memory of havin made love in his
  car.

It's a strange thing: desire.
It makes you do things for no other reason
than a mighty feelin you can't even put your finger on
says you *got* to do it . . . Strange.

Haven't cleaned up the house yet. Haven't even been in the house,
not for more than an hour or two at a time,
not since the wake.
I don't wanna go in there. It still smells like fried chicken.
And what stuff he had is in there, too.
It's too pitiful to sit around, touch it . . . wouldn't know what to
  do . . .

I sleep in the yard.
It's been so hot, the cool nights feel good against my skin.
I like being next to the earth, right up against it,
lettin the moss tickle my belly and my toes,
have it lick at my feet like a strange animal.
Feels good sinkin into the moist earth unencumbered.
Gives a sense of peace to things, kind of peace can't feel nowhere
  else.

Some nights I pretend I'm dead:
that I'm just a body restin on a piece of burial ground somewhere,
waitin for the heavens to take my soul away—
like those bodies you see lyin about sometimes,
people you ain't ever met, never seen even,
forgotten bodies that somehow are at peace on the ground
indebted to the cruelty of nature—
that's what I pretend.
It's gotten to where I can hold my breath for a minute
. . . sometimes two.

I lie on the cool ground, motionless, holdin my breath—
hush—
in hope that no one will find me,
that I will simply be lost forever, gone from this world.

But then a sound or a light in the sky will stir me,
and I am no longer at rest on a burial ground
but lyin all too awake in my yard,
sleepless, stirrin,
eyes that had been dream-less suddenly wide in motion,
searchin for the first signs of light.

I stay there. Eyes open. Starin at nothingness.
Until, sure enough, I see the hard sparkle of the sun
hit the edge of the fence, bounce against Lucy Hawkins window-
    pane,
and cut across my eyelids—close, hot.

I get up. I go into the house. I take off my clothes.
I pour myself a tall, very tall, glass of mint julep ice tea
with much too much ice,
and when I finish the glass,
just as it is beginning to cool itself right through me—
the stench, the wretched stench of the chicken,
and of the candy-sweet perfumes Caroline and Selah wore that
    day,
sends me back outside:
where I throw on an old dress that's been hangin on the line too
    long
over my body,
and take off

down to the water.
Down to the water . . . and go fishin.

(Light shift.)

6.

By the water. Simone is fishing. Miranda walks in.

MIRANDA: Ain't caught anythin yet?
SIMONE: Not yet.
MIRANDA: Gotta be patient. Gotta wait.
SIMONE: Mmm-hmm.
MIRANDA: I used to go fishin, so I know.
SIMONE: Yeh?
MIRANDA: Never actually fished myself, mind you.
SIMONE: Huh?
MIRANDA: My Grammy'd take me. When I was little.
   She's the one who did the actual fishin.
   I'd just watch her. *(Pulls out a cigarette)* Smoke?
SIMONE: No.
MIRANDA: Yeh, she'd take me. I didn't know what was goin on.
   I used to say, "Grammy, what's this? Grammy, what's that?"
"Hush, child," she'd say, "Hush."

(Miranda lights cigarette, smokes.)

SIMONE *(To herself)*: Hush . . .
MIRANDA:
   Swear. I don't know how she put up with me, but she did.
   She'd just smile . . . sit there . . . fish.
   She'd smoke, too.
   Not cigarettes, but a big ol cigar 'bout this thick.
   You should've seen the smoke she'd blow out of that thing.
   Swirls and swirls of it. Like chimney smoke.
   And it smelled too.
   Not sweet like Caroline's perfume. But strong. Like dust and
      ginger.
SIMONE: Yeh?
MIRANDA:
   Used to make them herself, the cigars.
   Grow the tobacco out back,

roll the leaves up in the finest paper,
suck on it til one end'd be completely wet with her saliva and juice,
and then she'd light up, the raw tobacco just envelopin the
    air.
Oh, and she'd smile . . . she'd smile the biggest grin . . .
Teeth turned black, she'd still smile.
I hated it. All of it. The cigars. Everything.
Felt like it was a punishment every time I had to go out with her.
Grammy and her goddamn tobacco.
But after a while, I don't know how it occurred,
the smell of that tobacco became like heaven itself.
"When we goin fishin, Grammy? When we goin?"
"Patience, child. Patience." And she'd smile, gather her gear,
and take me down to the water.
The sun'd be comin up. You could see the rays just peerin.
Flashes of light bouncin off the water blindin you
as you looked into the mornin haze.
And she'd smile, lay out the tobacco, and start rollin them cigars,
her hands movin sharp and quick
like one of those gunfighters on the TV, all eyes and trigger fingers.
Rollin and lightin up. Smokin and castin a line.
It was all of a piece with Grammy.
I'd sit there, wallowin in the smell,
swear all angels had come down to pay us a visit.
Used to try to catch the rings of smoke with my mouth,
like some sort of weird human kind of fish.
I must've caught a hundred rings one time. One hundred.
I swear, it was the best part of goin fishin.
In fact, for the longest time, that's what I thought fishin was:
just somethin you did to go smokin.

SIMONE: Wouldn't she catch anythin?

MIRANDA:
Every once in a while, sure.
Caught a yellow perch once—gutted it, chopped it up, ate it for
    supper.
But I can't say I remember her actually catchin
much of anythin in particular.
Not like you see in those pictures they got all over the walls at
    the diner
of people standin tall next to their big fish and smilin.

> Can't say she ever got took a picture like that.
> . . . Got somethin?

SIMONE: Feels like somethin's on the line.

MIRANDA: Maybe you got somethin.

SIMONE: . . . It's gone.

MIRANDA:

> That happens. Used to happen to Grammy all the time.
> Just when she'd think a fish would bite, it'd go away.
> They're not as stupid as we think—fish.
> I mean, if I were a fish, I wouldn't want to be somebody's supper.
> I'd know better than to jump at the first thing I saw.
> . . . What you thinkin?

SIMONE: Hmm?

MIRANDA: Hmm? What you thinkin?

SIMONE: Nothin.

MIRANDA: Awful quiet. Gotta be thinkin 'bout somethin.

SIMONE: Just thinkin.

MIRANDA: What about?

SIMONE: Thinkin 'bout the world.

MIRANDA: The world? What you thinkin bout the world?

SIMONE:

> Thinkin that it's some place, y'know.
> That it's such a big place, and all these things happen—
> wars, fires, hurricanes, sickness—
> I think, How come the soil don't just *burst*?
> How come it don't just burst from all this excitement?
> I know I would.
> If it were me, I'd *explode* in a thousand little pieces,
> scatter myself in bits all over the earth—
> wars, fires, hurricanes comin up out of me
> in *bile* colored gray, scarlet and indigo.
> Come up and out of me till there'd be *nothin*,
> just open space: a whole other world.
> I don't know how the soil can take it. I really don't.

(Beat.)

MIRANDA:

> Selah says the soil's stronger than all of us,
> on account of that's where we go once we pass on.
> . . . And that's where we get our strength, too, from the soil.

SIMONE: Yeh?

MIRANDA: That's what she says.

SIMONE: How you get strength from somethin that's torn apart, *busted* open?

How you get it then?

MIRANDA: . . . Maybe a different soil come up.

SIMONE: Huh?

MIRANDA: A different soil, a different earth underneath the old one.

Maybe it'd come up and . . . I don't know, it'd do somethin.

SIMONE: . . . Damn.

MIRANDA: Fish ain't jumpin for nothin, huh? They'll come 'round.

Grammy'd sometimes have to wait two, three hours before a fish'd jump.

That's when she really put her time in smokin.

You sure you don't want one? It's good.

SIMONE: I know.

(Beat.)

MIRANDA: So, what you do, you clean the house yet?

SIMONE: No.

MIRANDA: Gotta clean it.

SIMONE: Ain't gotta *do* nothin.

MIRANDA: Selah says you don't clean a house after someone's—

SIMONE: Hell what Selah says! I ain't doin it. I ain't goin in there.

MIRANDA:

Well, she says if you don't clean it, you collect bad spirits.

And then you can't even go into the house. Even if you want to.

Gotta BURN IT DOWN. 'Cause fire's the only thing that'll scare bad spirits off for good.

SIMONE: She say that?

MIRANDA:

Yeh. And she said you don't get rid of bad spirits, they come 'round and turn on you—turn you into a *spook*.

SIMONE: I ain't a spook.

MIRANDA: That's what she said.

SIMONE: Well, I ain't! Hell, who wants to be that?

Nobody talkin to you, nobody lookin at you—nobody wants that.

MIRANDA: . . . So, you gonna clean it? Huh?

SIMONE: Gonna do somethin.

MIRANDA: Yeh? What you gonna do?
SIMONE: Gonna keep myself far away from it. As far from the house
as . . .
    Just stay close to the water. Maybe I can lose myself in it.
    Lose myself . . . That'd be somethin.

(Light change.)

7.

*Evening. Caroline is wringing items of wet clothing into a tin wash-
tub. She sings to herself:*

CAROLINE:
    Take me to the flood, Lilah.
    Take me to the flood.
    I wanna see the moon winkin
    through river of blood,
    through river of blood.

    Take me in a boat, Lilah.
    Take me in a boat.
    And there I'll see the night tumble
    as weary stars float,
    as they float.

    Wash away my trouble.
    Hmm-mmm.
    Send me along.

    Steal away my sorrow.
    Under and gone.

    Take me in a flood, Lilah.
    Take me in a flood.
    And there I'll see the boat sinkin
    through ocean of mud.

(Light shift.)

8.
Visitation

By the water. Night. Ella Fitzgerald's recording of Van Heusen and Burke's song "Moonlight Becomes You" is heard. Simone is listening to a transistor radio, drinking whiskey from the bottle, and swaying to the music. Song plays. Starts to fade in, out, as it is interrupted by static. Simone changes the station. More static. Changes back. Song is heard for a moment, then disappears in static. Simone turns off the radio. Jamie appears.

JAMIE: It's the radio.

(Simone sees him. He does not see her.)

Damn radio's no good. I had me a radio like that once.
Transistor radio? Yeh. Piece of shit.
Only thing it was good for was a bit of rock 'n' roll.
And they only played that at night.
It was hard to listen to 'cause the music was loud,
but the radio had to be kept quiet.
And you know how the volume is on these things—it's either *up*
     or down.
Yeh. It's the radio.

Wasn't the song. No. Song went good. Fit the moon just right.
If it wadn't for the radio, it just might've been perfect.

(Simone circles him slowly.)

Sure don't get those too often. A moment perfect in time?
I don't think I've ever had one.
Maybe the day I was married. And then not even the whole day
     even.
Just that moment when I looked at her. Right before the vows.
Before the words "I do" could even make their way out of my
     throat.
Just that moment. Closest I ever come to perfect.
And it ain't had nothin to do with sex.
Not that I haven't had it good.
Guys in my unit? They're amazed at the number of chicks I've had.

Simply amazed.
But it still ain't got me to perfect.
Hell, you grow up thinkin your whole life sex is the only way
you can get to perfect, but then when your life happens,
somethin else happens.
Ain't nobody tell you about desire. It just come upon you.
Like somethin that ain't even real.
Like it come down from someplace in the ether. Down and
     through you . . .
And it ain't about your dick or . . . It's just a look.
Or the way her hair falls in front of her face, or . . .
Closest I ever come.

(Simone is very close to him now. He moves away.)

Hot, ain't it? Damn near burnin up.
Done nothin but run around all night lookin for my arm.
Got shot off someplace. Thought if I looked for it, I'd find it.
Don't know how many times I come across a part of somebody,
a piece of 'im that's found its way to another part of the land.
Why, I found a whole hand once.
Belonged to some guy named Toomy. Not a bad guy. Just stupid.
I recognized it right away 'cause he had this tattoo on his hand,
somethin like a crossbow and a dragon's tail with flames all
     around it,
I saw it and I said, "Man, this is Toomy. This is Toomy's hand."
And it was clear way 'cross someplace else, miles from the rest
     of 'im.
Just layin there. With no one to claim it.
Course, I picked it up. Only fair thing to do.
Carried it in my pocket for a while.
Then I just threw it away.
I mean, the man was stupid. Got his fuckin hand shot off.
I didn't want Toomy's slow-trigger curse on me, y'know what
     I'm sayin?
Look and look. Ain't seen my arm nowhere.
Thirsty, too. Throat's all . . .

*(She holds out the whiskey bottle. He grabs it. It is as if the bot-
tle has simply appeared before him.)*

Yeh. *(He drinks)* Yeah.

Now, you see? This is good shit. This is real good shit.
This is the kind of shit that's gonna find me my arm.

Puts me in mind of my girl. My girl, she always got the best whiskey.
One night in the car, we went off and parked up by ol man
    Hawkins's mill,
and she pulled out this *absolute goddamn kick-ass* whiskey
that just about set my tongue on fire.

Swear. Everywhere I look now, I see fire.
Nothin but red air splittin itself all around me,
the sky electric with blood and flame.
It's the killin. It puts you in shame.

Poppin bodies, taken 'em down—takes you down with it.
Got no way to cool yourself off. Not deep inside.
You're like tinder: tremble and spark. All the time.
Tremble, and . . .

(She reaches toward him. He walks away.)

Whiskey's startin to hit. Swear, it's got the best kick, whiskey does.

(Looking out) What's that? What the hell is that?
It was like a flare in the sky. Blue-orange.
Off. Behind the stars. See it?
Thought I saw it.

Water sure is still. Storm must be comin.
Water gets still like that, somethin's gonna break.
Gotta keep lookin. Gotta keep movin.
Storm hits, I'll never find anythin. It'll all wash away for sure.

(He walks away. Is almost gone when:)

SIMONE: Jamie?

(He stops.)

JAMIE: Hell of a storm. Hell of a storm come this way.

(He exits.)

SIMONE: Jamie!

(Blackout.)

9.

Night. Tirasol holds a skein of yarn, which Caroline is unwinding and rolling into a ball.

TIRASOL: Must be up to somethin.

CAROLINE: Eh?

TIRASOL: No word? Sure sign a person's up to somethin ain't right.

CAROLINE: Leave her be.

TIRASOL: Can't. It's not in me.

CAROLINE: You know, I think Selah is right: you got *nothin* to do.

TIRASOL: Selah's the one who's got nothin.

CAROLINE: Oh yeh? Then how come you done nothin but spy on that poor woman ever since his body done touch the ground?

TIRASOL: Ain't spyin.

CAROLINE: What you call it, then?

TIRASOL: Don't know.

CAROLINE: Now, that is bull. Clear as can be.

(Beat.)

TIRASOL:

Don't like death. Can't stand to be around it.

So many men died in this town, havin Jamie catch his like that makes me feel rotten.

I go about my business, yeh, but the air's thick with grievin.

Don't have to look close, but you can see the phantoms

sure take shape as the mist comes up on the water:

strange, throttled phantoms jostlin the livin flesh.

Makes me feel hard inside. Like my guts are all twisted.

Don't like bein part of shame. And that's what it is—a land of murder:

bones of the dead suffocatin the earth one war upon the other,

howls of widows ensnared in the wind

crumplin 'gainst the skin of the water

and us, sittin here, goin on.

Well, don't like bein here. And goin on, bein here.

Makes me feel burdened.

To think of her still thinkin of him, and not a word at that . . . can't stand it.

CAROLINE: Don't you miss him, though?
TIRASOL: Jamie?
CAROLINE: Yeh.
TIRASOL: Only as someone who used to be but now isn't.
CAROLINE: I do.
TIRASOL: Yeh?
CAROLINE:
He wadn't no saint,
and I never really took to him like other women did.
But now that I actually think of him,
now that he's in the ground
and his soul is hoverin over the trees and water lookin for mercy,
I think, He had a true expression. A kind of honesty.
I miss that.
TIRASOL *(To herself)*: Yeh.

(Light change.)

10.

Woods. Night. Simone runs in.

SIMONE:
Done run off on me.
You move so fast I can barely catch you.
Where'd you learn to move like that? Huh?
You're like lightin. Just skimmin the surface of the air.

And where is it you run to? Huh?
What the hell are you lookin for?
There's nothin. Nothin here.
Just trees, and water and goddamn branches that got me all cut up.
And all you think about is runnin.
Like the air's gonna take you someplace you've never been.

Well, I can't lose you—can't let myself lose . . .
I heard you. I know I did.
I saw you. I know. —I did.
To have you come back to lose you—
You tell me you're here. You tell me.
You ain't goddamn leavin me again.

I am gonna find the breath.
I'm gonna trespass on the night.
I'm gonna swallow the stars until I find you.

'Cause I am comin to you—yeh—
don't know where I'll find you, but I can feel you in my skin—
oh—like tinder.

(Light shift.)

11.

Woods. Night. Miranda walks in with a jar of fireflies in her hand.

MIRANDA *(As an incantation)*:
A hundred and one fireflies in my jar,
Light my way, near and far.
If I catch them, will you say—
JAMIE *(Appearing)*: What you got there? In that jar?
MIRANDA: . . . Fireflies. Can't see my way round here without them.
Not this time of night.
JAMIE: Dark, huh?
MIRANDA: Don't seem dark to you?
JAMIE: I'm kinda . . . used to it.
MIRANDA:
You mean to tell me you can find you way 'round here
without even so much as a firefly to guide you?
JAMIE: Can—do it.
MIRANDA:
You must be from real far, 'cause I ain't met nobody
who can see in the dark like that.
I bet you're from one of those places with wide water.
JAMIE *(To himself)*: Wide water . . .
MIRANDA: From one of those places where you can roam 'round.
JAMIE: . . . wouldn't mind—that.
MIRANDA: What's it like?
JAMIE: Huh?
MIRANDA: Roamin.
JAMIE:
It's long. Days—long. Nights, too. Can't get no rest.
Just go 'round 'n' 'round on some road ain't got. —Can't stop.

Somethin inside—won't let—
(Indicating fireflies) They're gonna die all bunched up like that.
MIRANDA: Won't.
JAMIE: They're climbin jar like mad. Can't breathe—there.
MIRANDA: They breathe fine.
JAMIE: They'll die.
MIRANDA: What are you worried about? They're just fireflies.
JAMIE: Seen too much death where I've been. Let them go now. Let them go.
MIRANDA: If I do that, I won't be able to see anythin.
JAMIE: What you wanna see this time of night? What you wanna see?
MIRANDA:
I want to see a ghost!
Selah says, "Ghost rise up out of the water, and go in among the trees."
I've been aimin to see one. For some time now. Ain't gonna stop.
Ain't gonna deprive myself of a real-live vision,
just 'cause some stupid fireflies are bunched up in a jar.
JAMIE: Let—them—go.
MIRANDA: You want 'em? Is that it? You want the goddamn fireflies? Here. Take them.

(She exits. Beat. He opens the jar.)

JAMIE: . . . Go.

(Fireflies rise up out of the jar and into the night.)

12.

Morning. Tirasol and Caroline are slicing squash.

TIRASOL: Vanished.
CAROLINE: Hmm?
TIRASOL: Out-right vanished.
CAROLINE: She ain't vanished.
TIRASOL: Ain't been heard from all night. Might as well be.
CAROLINE: Maybe she's wanderin.
TIRASOL: All night and straight to the mornin?
CAROLINE: Could be.

(Beat.)

TIRASOL: What's she doin?

CAROLINE: Huh?

TIRASOL: Can't just wander for the sake of wanderin. Gotta be a purpose to it.

> And if there ain't no purpose, then . . . what's she doin?
>
> What's she doin wanderin about with no shoes on all night, all mornin?
>
> What's she doin?
>
> I think she's vanished. It's simply too long a time without word.

CAROLINE: You worry too much.

TIRASOL: Don't it bother you?

CAROLINE:

> Of course. But I don't go round thinkin about it. I can't live that way. Can you imagine if I went 'round thinkin 'bout every little thing? I wouldn't get out of bed in the mornin. My head'd be heavy. Weighed down with thought. Wouldn't know what to do first. And things gotta get done. No matter what goes 'round. Sure, I worry. I just don't let the worryin occupy me, that's all. Like Selah says, "Got to move on."

TIRASOL: Gotta do somethin.

CAROLINE: Can't you give the woman peace?

TIRASOL: No. Not when her house is sittin there with its smell and his stuff.

> Can't give her *no* peace.
>
> Why, don't nobody want to go near it no more.
>
> Turnin itself into a spook house, it is.

CAROLINE: Just 'cause she's been gone all night don't mean it's come to that.

TIRASOL: How you know? You heard somethin?

CAROLINE: No.

TIRASOL: Then how do you know?

CAROLINE: I just know we got to give it time.

TIRASOL:

> Why? What do we got to wait for?
>
> We wait for ten thousand crows to come down
>
> and start peckin at the house gashin blood from the sky?
>
> That what we wait for? And how long do we wait? Five, ten days? Years?

How long do we wait before we just *do* somethin 'bout it? Huh?
How long?

(Caroline stops slicing squash.)

CAROLINE:
Swear. You've been up too long, y'know that?
You ain't even thinkin what you're sayin.
You wanna *clean house* before you even know what kind of spir-
it's in there?
You wanna mess around when you're not even sure if Simone's out
wanderin, or vanished, or somewhere in the belly of the house
lost in the chicken slime and darkness?
You thinkin 'bout anythin 'cept your own burden?
You thinkin 'bout anythin at all?
Or do you just wanna toy with the spirits?
Play your worryin, see if heaven and earth come down?
You need to sleep a while. Rest your head. Give it time.
Believe me, time come. And when it does—we'll do somethin.

(Light change.)

13.
Specter

Jamie is caught in a flash of unnatural light.

JAMIE:
What I?—
Can't remember
can't remem—you
Simone!

*(Simone appears. She wears a dress of chicken bones and scarlet
ribbons. A handprint of blood across her face.)*

SIMONE:
I am right here. See?
JAMIE:
Brain is
SIMONE:
fragments. Yes.

JAMIE:
  Like fragments
  fallen
SIMONE:
  falling
JAMIE:
  chunks—memory
SIMONE:
  pieces
  falling.
JAMIE:
  Takin me down.
SIMONE:
  Take me.
  Take me.
JAMIE:
  Down
SIMONE:
  Take me.
JAMIE:
  Past light
SIMONE:
  Sky
JAMIE:
  Shadow
SIMONE:
  Stirs me
SIMONE AND JAMIE:
  into somethin
  I don't understand.
JAMIE:
  Not
SIMONE AND JAMIE:
  face
JAMIE:
  name.
SIMONE AND JAMIE:
  Lost.
  Can't remember.

(Beat.)

JAMIE:
Road has unwound.

SIMONE:
Hot
burning.

JAMIE:
I am in
fever,

SIMONE:
Take me.

JAMIE:
Fever.

SIMONE:
Now!
Take me.
Take me.

(Beat.)

JAMIE:
Peckin.

SIMONE:
no.

JAMIE:
Lone bird peckin.

SIMONE:
no peace—no.

JAMIE:
Clawin at

SIMONE AND JAMIE:
skin.

JAMIE:
Rippin

SIMONE AND JAMIE:
vein.

JAMIE:
Tearin past.

SIMONE AND JAMIE:
blood,
bone.

(Jamie and Simone emit a long, silent cry. Beat.)

JAMIE:

Hot.

Sun. Silence.

Hope—wind—

SIMONE:

Jamie?

JAMIE:

comes.

Or I'll burn. I will.

I am burning.

SIMONE:

Can you see me?

JAMIE:

Like one of those Red Demon firecrackers I used to get when I
was a kid.

SIMONE:

Can you see me now?

JAMIE:

True devil . . .

SIMONE:

See.

See.

See.

See.

(She hits herself.)

See?!

(Silence. He looks at her.)

JAMIE:

Yes.

(He reaches out to her.)

Let—me—go.

(Simone lets out a sob. Blackout.)

14.

Lights come up on Selah, Caroline, Tirasol and Miranda, brooms in hand. They speak-sing the following "Spirit Call":

SELAH:
Spirit, you here?
CAROLINE:
Spirit, you here?
TIRASOL:
Get away, spirit.
MIRANDA:
Get away, spirit.

(They repeat lines above. After a beat, they begin to sweep.)

CAROLINE:
Don't wanna take you up to heaven.
Don't wanna take you up, no sir.
Don't wanna send your soul a-temptin.
Don't wanna send your soul nowhere.
TIRASOL:
'Cause I'm gonna sweep you under my feet.
I'm gonna sweep you off this floor.
I'm gonna sweep you straight to the devil.
Ain't gonna sin 'round this house no more.
SELAH:
Oh, Lord.
CAROLINE:
Father, can you hear me?
SELAH:
Oh, Lord.
ALL:
Hey. Uh.
SELAH:
Oh, Lord.
ALL:
Save this house from fallin.
SELAH AND CAROLINE:
Spirit, don't you come 'round this house no more.

CAROLINE:

Don't wanna let you ride to graceland.
Don't wanna let you ride, no sir.
'Cause if I lead you to the graceland,
I'll be in the devil's house for sure.

SELAH:

Oh, Lord.

CAROLINE:

Father, can you help me?

SELAH:

Oh, Lord

Oh, Lord.

ALL:

Keep this house from fallin.

CAROLINE:

Spirit, don't you come 'round this house no more.

TIRASOL:

'Cause I'm gonna sweep you off this floor now.
I'm gonna sweep you out of sight.
I'm gonna sweep you straight to hell now.
I'm gonna sweep you with all my might.

SELAH:

Oh, Lord.

ALL:

Father, can you hear me?

SELAH:

Oh, Lord.

ALL:

Hey. Uh.

SELAH:

Oh, Lord.

ALL:

Save this house from fallin.
Spirit, don't you come 'round this house no more.

TIRASOL:

Spirit, don't you come 'round this house . . .

(Beat.)

MIRANDA:

> Chili pepper
> cornbread
> ice water
> alligator
> Spirit, fly away.

(Beat.)

ALL:

> Chili pepper
> cornbread
> ice water
> alligator
> Spirit, fly away.

SELAH:

> Oh, Lord.

ALL:

> Father, can you hear me?

SELAH:

> Oh, Lord
>
> Oh, Lord.

ALL:

> Save this house from fallin.
> Spirit, don't you come 'round this house . . .

(They stop sweeping. Beat.)

CAROLINE:

> Spirit, fly away.
> Spirit, no more.

TIRASOL:

> Spirit, fly away.
> Spirit, no more.

MIRANDA:

> Spirit, fly away.
> Spirit . . .

SELAH:

> . . . No more.

(Light change.)

15.

In the background, a turquoise sky dotted with black crows. In the foreground is Simone before a garbage can. She is wearing layers of Jamie's clothes.

SIMONE:

You got to burn things. Got to burn 'em so they'll go away.
You don't burn 'em, they just stick around forever.
You burn things, they go away.

(She takes off one item of clothing, draws a lighter from her pocket, holds item out in front of her, burns it, throws it into garbage can. Small fire.)

They disappear down the path of nothinness
where fire and ash and air get all mixed up together
and turn into sky and breathin.
That's what they tell me, anyway.
'Cept the more I burn things, the more they stay in my mind:

The blue shirt
he wore when we were out by the water,
the way he looked at me then, and took his hand
and ran it along inside me,
so a trickle of sweat stayed, restin, on his brow
wonderin where it was gonna go next;
(Throws shirt into fire) You burn things, they go away.

The shape of his torso
permanently outlined
in the small folds and crisp creases
of his grease-stained workshirt
fresh with the smell of gasoline and oil, and . . .
all the other mysteries of the garage;
(Throws shirt into fire) You burn 'em, they go away.

The softness of his skin
in the white jersey
comin up behind me in the kitchen
while I was cookin the chicken fricassee,
and the steam was comin up out of the pot

and he was squeezin me firm, soft, in his white jersey—
jersey he wore with no underpants on,
so that the sweat and smell of his member
became a part of that jersey
as much as its frayed cotton fibers and green number 21;

(She throws the jersey into the fire.)

Things have a way of stayin in the mind.
No burnin can stop your mind from thinkin.
Only by losin yourself completely can you stop yourself from
    thinkin.
Either that, or by dyin.

Nobody knows for sure whether you keep thinkin once you're
    dead,
but I figure once you're gone from this world,
the things of this world can't be the same.
And that's got to be comfortin somehow.
To not think.
(To self) Burn things. Go away.

It's takin my self down that's hard.
Every time I try—
lettin the spark brush against my skin,
holdin my breath
till I feel myself drown in the gulf of fire—
the too-much-ness of this life calls to me
and brings me back from

Ash.
They're all of a piece now: blue, white, sweat, smells—
locked in flame.

Burn things. Don't go away.

*(She takes off the last layer of Jamie's clothing and throws it into
garbage can. She is left wearing a white cotton shift. Light change.)*

16.

*Lights come up on Selah. Caroline, Tirasol and Miranda are lit softly
in the space, surrounding her.*

SELAH:
Lay the flowers out.
Lay them on the hard floor.
The dead-man has come by.

Press the flowers into the cracks in the earth,
flowers with veins of purple and green.
Set them on the ground.
Let the soil swallow them bloom to stem.
Call the blues for the dead-man.

For there's told a story
about a ribbon of petals
that wrapped itself in a garland
'round the circumference of the world
and called out:

ALL *(Sung)*:
Ai-ah!
La-le lai-ah!

Ai-ah!
La le lai!

SELAH *(Spoken)*:
My feet will go on marching.
The dead-man goes by.

(Lights fade.)

17.
Chimera

Sound of a moving train. Jamie and Simone are on the train. Jamie is leaning against her. Train sound underscores the scene.

JAMIE: Simone?
SIMONE: Yes.
JAMIE: Where do you think everybody is?
SIMONE: What do you mean?
JAMIE: People. There's no people anywhere.
SIMONE: They're in their houses. Locked away.
        Protectin themselves from the elements.

(Beat.)

JAMIE: Simone?
SIMONE: Yes.
JAMIE: Where will we end up, you think?
　　　We'll have to jump off. We can't just keep goin.
SIMONE: I know.

(Beat.)

JAMIE: How'll we pick?
SIMONE: Hmm?
JAMIE: How'll we pick which one, which stop?
SIMONE: Jump off. We'll just jump off, see where we land.

(Train sound swells briefly.)

We're just whizzin, aren't we? Flyin through the night.
I like when it goes fast. Like that.
You feel like you're part of the train:
part of this big machinery that's cuttin through space and time
and all the crooked ways left in this earth.
It's like bein free for a second.

(Beat.)

JAMIE: Simone?
SIMONE: Hmm?
JAMIE: Sing me somethin.
SIMONE: What?
JAMIE: A song.
SIMONE: I don't remember the words to anythin.
JAMIE: Make 'em up. I don't care. Just sing to me.
　　　Make me go to sleep.

(After a moment, she sings. Train sound fades out, as she does so.)

SIMONE:
　Sleep on—rocky water.
　Send my baby down.
　Moon come up.
　Turn the world 'round.

　Sleep on—rocky water.
　Thunder in a cloud.

Rest your head upon me.
Hush now, child.

Lay your head upon me.
Hush . . .

(She stops singing. He has fallen asleep.)

It's quite possible we're made of air.
That we're deep-down truly made of air.
That the rest is just stuff to keep us tied to the ground,
to keep us from flyin.

(Lights fade.)

18.

Miranda, Caroline, Tirasol and Selah are smoking cigars amidst a blanket of purple flowers.

MIRANDA: I'm wore out.
CAROLINE: Yeh.
MIRANDA: I'm plain wore out.
TIRASOL: Spirits are hard.
CAROLINE: Yeh. They're hard.
SELAH: Nobody said it'd be easy to get rid of a spirit.
MIRANDA: Smells nice, though.
CAROLINE: Flowers, yeh.
MIRANDA: Flowers and tobacco—their smells just comin up together.
CAROLINE: Rich.
MIRANDA: Yeh.
TIRASOL: Strong.
MIRANDA: Yeh. Like the whole world's gonna bust open with the
    smell.
SELAH: It's been a long time.
MIRANDA: Mmm?
SELAH: Long time since I swept a spirit up and out of here.
    Must've been . . . Some other war.
CAROLINE: . . . Another war.
SELAH:
    Why, I remember Lucy Hawkins, Caroline and I,
    we shouted so hard we couldn't speak for days and days

after that sweepin. Lost our speech.
(To Caroline) You remember that?
CAROLINE: I remember.
SELAH: It was hard, it was.
CAROLINE: Uh-huh.
SELAH: Gettin harder.
CAROLINE: Yeh.
MIRANDA: It's war.
SELAH: More than that.
MIRANDA: Huh?
SELAH:

People don't know how to honor the land no more.
Bad spirits been 'round all the time, sure,
but these hard ones,
that wear you down with their hunger and anger,
these come from a different soil,
a soil that's been scarred, spat on, taken a killin.
This land's become corrupt inside.
Damn wonder everyone's not wore out.

(Beat.)

MIRANDA: Still feels like somethin.
TIRASOL: What you talkin about?
MIRANDA: Don't know. Just feels like somethin's still here.
SELAH: It's the murmurin, child. That's what you feel.
MIRANDA: Don't feel like murmurin. Feels more like—
SELAH:

Ain't just about "feelin," child.
Spirit is vision: fragment and memory reflected in the mind's eye.
You got to see it. Inside you.
It's in the heart where we see things.
It's in the heart where we lay to rest trouble and joy.
Go on, now. Let it come into you.

MIRANDA: . . . Don't see nothin.
SELAH: Look hard. Go on.
MIRANDA: . . . See somethin.
CAROLINE: Yeh?
SELAH: What'd you see, child?
MIRANDA: I see small lights walkin up and down the sky.
TIRASOL: Yeh?

MIRANDA: Catchin hold of the wind. And dancin.
CAROLINE: Mercy.
SELAH: Mercy on the child.

(Light change.)

19.

In the background, a bone yard looking on to a wide sea. In the foreground is Simone. She wears a pale green dress and is barefoot. Jamie's dog tags hang around her neck.

SIMONE:
I got up this mornin and said to myself,
"I'm gonna find me some shoes.
I'm gonna find me some shoes
so I can walk this earth and see where my feet land.
See what my feet see that my head can't."

You need shoes
'cause bare you're just another part of the earth—
not on top of it, not above it—
ain't no way you can own a part of this world if you don't got shoes.

So, I set out. My toes wigglin.
I set out in search of what would find me.
Not long before walkin became too much.

I got on my knees,
rubbed my hands in the ground,
and said to myself, "Find them.
And if you don't find them—
don't look back.
'Cause what is waitin for you
is the footprint of every other mad soul
who lost their wiggle on the search for a bit of stride."

And as I was rubbin, my hands raw with motion,
I found this spot, where there was nothin.
And in this spot, I found myself a piece of cardboard
that had belonged to a bucket of chicken.

I looked at it. Looked at it hard. Took my nose to it.
But it didn't smell no more.
Didn't smell like nothing 'cept the dirt it come from.
I thought, The underneath of the earth must be littered
for miles and miles with pieces of cardboard
from buckets of chicken that have been buried—cast off—
by those that have loved, lost or seen too much
of the earth's ways to believe in them.

*(Reveals Kentucky Fried Chicken box "shoes" that have been off
to one side, unseen, and she sets them before her.)*

I got off my knees.
And as I stood there,
somethin come over me:
and I just took a blade to it,
a sharp blade of grass,
and with it, I cut myself some soles,
some soles to walk this earth,
and strapped them to my feet with a piece of chicken wire
till my feet bled—
bled,
but navigatin the world.

(Simone steps into her "shoes."
*The sound of bagpipes—a hymn—is heard, as if from a
distance. She takes off the dog tags, and sets them aside. She
stands, looking out.*
*The bone yard slowly disappears, until all that can be seen is a
wide, wide sea. The sound of bagpipes swells. Lights slowly fade.)*

END OF PLAY

CAROLINE'S SONG
Words and Music by Caridad Svich

SPIRIT CALL
Words and Music by Caridad Svich

SELAH: Spi-rit, you he-re? CAROLINE: Spi-rit, you he-re?

TIRASOL: Get-a-way, spi-rit. MIRANDA: Get a-way, spi-rit.

SELAH: Spi-rit, you he-re? CAROLINE: Spi-rit, you he-

-re? TIRASOL: Get a-way, spi-rit. MIRANDA: Get a-way,

spi-rit. CAROLINE: Don't wan-na take you up to hea-ven. Don't

wan-na take you up, no sir. Don't wanna send your soul a-tempt-in.

Don't wan-na send your soul no-where. TIRASOL: 'Cause I'm gon-

-na sweep you und -er my feet. I'm gon-na sweep you

off this floor. I'm gon-na sweep you straight to the

de-vil. Ain't gon-na sin 'round this house no more.

SELAH: Oh, Lord. Oh, Lord. ALL: Hey. Uh.

CAROLINE: Fa-ther, can you hear me?

CAROLINE: 'round this house no more. TIRASOL: 'Cause I'm gon-na sweep you

TIRASOL: off this floor now. — I'm gon-na sweep you out of

TIRASOL: sight. I'm gon-na sweep you straight to hell now. — I'm

TIRASOL: gon-na sweep you with all my might. SELAH: Oh, Lord. —

SELAH: — – hear me? Oh, Lord. Hey. Uh.

CAROLINE: Fa-ther, can you hear me? Hey. Uh.

TIRASOL: Fa-ther, can you hear me? Hey. Uh.

MIRANDA: Fa-ther, can you hear me? Hey. Uh.

SELAH: Oh, Lord. Save this house from fal-lin.

CAROLINE: Save this house from fal-lin.

TIRASOL: Save this house from fal-lin.

MIRANDA: Save this house from fal-lin.

ALL: Spi-rit don't you come 'round this house no more.

SELAH: Oh, Lord. –house from fal-lin. — Spirit, don't you come·

CAROLINE: Save this house from fal-lin. — Spirit, don't you come

TIRASOL: Save this house from fal-lin. — Spirit, don't you come

MIRANDA: Save this house from fal-lin. — Spirit, don't you come

ALL: 'round this house . . . . . CAROLINE: Spi-rit, fly a-way.

CAROLINE: Spi-rit, no more. TIRASOL: Spi-rit, – fly a-way.

TIRASOL: Spi-rit, no more. MIRANDA: Spi-rit, – fly a-way.

MIRANDA: — Spi-rit,– SELAH: No more.—

SELAH'S CALL
Words and Music by Caridad Svich

Ai– ah! La-le lai- ah!

Ai– ah! La-le lai . . . —

SIMONE'S LULLABY
Words and Music by Caridad Svich

CARIDAD SVICH is a playwright, songwriter and translator of Cuban, Argentine, Croatian and Spanish descent who was born in Philadelphia. She now lives in Los Angeles, where she is a resident playwright at the Mark Taper Forum and where she previously held an NEA/TCG Theatre Residency Program for Playwrights residency.

Her plays include *Any Place but Here, Pensacola, Prodigal Kiss, 12 Short Prayers for Life When Dying* and *The Archaeology of Dreams.*

Her work has been produced in the U.S. and abroad by The Women's Project & Productions (New York City), INTAR (New York City), Latino Chicago Theater Company, Beyond Baroque Arts Center (California), Theatre Key West Festival and the Traverse Theatre (Edinburgh).

Her awards include a TCG/Pew Observership, a California Arts Council Fellowship, the Rosenthal New Play Prize, a TCG Hispanic Translation Commission, four residencies at the Playwrights' Center PlayLabs (Minnesota) and a Pew/National Theater Translation Commission.

Her play *Gleaning/Rebusca* is published in an anthology of contemporary plays by U.S.-based Hispanic women entitled *Shattering the Myth* (Arte Público press), *Brazo Gitano* is published in *Ollantay Theater Magazine* (December 1999). *Any Place but Here* was circulated through TCG's Plays-in-Process.

She is co-editor of the volume *Conducting a Life: Reflections on the Theatre of Maria Irene Fornes* (Smith & Kraus) and of a forthcoming volume of essays *Theater in Crisis?* Her English-language translations of five plays and thirteen poems by Federico Garcia Lorca are collected in *Federico Garcia Lorca: Impossible Theatre* (Smith & Kraus).

Ms. Svich holds an M.F.A. in playwriting from the University of California–San Diego, and a B.F.A. from the University of North Carolina–Charlotte. She has taught at the Yale School of Drama, Paine's Plough Theatre (London) and the U.S.–Cuba Writers Conference. She is a member of The Dramatists Guild, the Playwrights' Center of Minneapolis, New Georges, The Women's Project & Productions of New York and the RAT Theater Network.

FROM THE U.K.:
A EUROPEAN PERSPECTIVE ON LATINO THEATRE

> Seeing yourself represented is what makes you feel you have
> a place in the world.   —Lisa Kron

In the Spring of 1998, London's Southwark Playhouse presented a series of three Spanish plays: the first was Lorca's *In Five Years Time*, the second Calderón's *The Surgeon of Honour* and the third was José Rivera's *Marisol*. When the *Times'* theatre critic, James Christopher, drew attention to the fact that Rivera's play shouldn't "strictly speaking" be part of the season, as he was actually Puerto Rican, I was left to ponder whether Christopher's placing of Rivera's play "somewhere between Gabriel García Márquez and Tony Kushner" marked an inability or unwillingness to locate the work within the spheres of North or South or whether his categorization of the playwright as Puerto Rican somehow rather conveniently fitted geographically within the North American Kushner and the Latin American García Márquez. *Time Out* found categorizing Rivera equally problematic, locating the L.A.-based Rivera as a "hip Hispanic New Yorker."

These critical responses to *Marisol* served to remind me of an event on Latino theatre held at Edinburgh's Traverse Theatre in 1993, where a reading of Maria Irene Fornes's *Mud* was followed by a public discussion at which numerous audience members expressed dissatisfaction at the choice of the play. As far as they were concerned it was simply not "Hispanic enough." Why wasn't there any singing or dancing in it? It didn't sound like a Hispanic play and it didn't articulate the sort of problems they expected a Hispanic play to concern itself with. Clearly they had come to the Traverse expecting either a tapas bar, a salsa night, *West Side Story* or a mixture of all three, and felt cheated that they had been denied this experience in favor of a short, delicately paced three-hander examining the shifting power relations in a domestic environment that remains decidedly nonspecific.

This view is not unique. A problem I have encountered repeatedly when teaching Latino theatre is the conception of minority identities as single, cohesive units which somehow posit that the "Hispanic" can be defined in dramatic terms. Despite the powerful polycultural influences of Spanish American in the U.S., in Britain the received images of Latinos provided by American popular culture are still those of the deviant "other"—exotic, dangerous, passionate, antagonistic. The popularity of *West Side Story*, *L.A. Law*, *High Chapparal* or any number of exported cultural texts that feature Latino characters, demonstrates the difficulties of conceiving Latino identities beyond clichéd stereotypes.

The performance of the "Latino" by non-Latino actors is perhaps the most conspicuous manifestation of these populist staged spectacles and is clearly personified in the Antonio Banderas phenomenon. All exist in the sphere of what the critic Jean Baudrillard terms "hyperreality"—a realm that recognizes that the fabricated relations between representation and the real (which Baudrillard refers to as "the representational imaginary") no longer exists, because "the real is no longer real, merely signs referring only to themselves." In the words of Linda Hutcheon: "Simulacrum gloats over the body of the diseased referent." Our access to the Latino, always mediated though representation, is therefore filtered through the dominant white Protestant ideological apparatus of North America, which has primarily categorized it as a single performable entity. Each of the plays in this extraordinary anthology decisively questions the dramatic treatment of minority or muted voices as a single monolithic entity. All the work here demonstrates the varied ways in which cultural, political and social priorities are being redefined within the larger parameters of North America.

For British audiences it is perhaps the Los Angeles Riots of 1992, following the acquittal of four police officers accused of grievously assaulting a black man, Rodney King; the Crown Heights Riots, erupting that same year in Brooklyn between the Hasidic and Afro-American communities following a hit and run incident; and the more recent O. J. Simpson trial which have demonstrated both the way in which minorities are expected to accept a single, white, unjust system of justice and, crucially, the ways in which different communities do not share political, social or cultural agendas. Concerns and commitments are multidimensional; demands and objectives differ.

The theatrical languages employed by the writers of this volume challenge and interrogate the cultural baggage that audiences bring to the performance event. The diversity of Latino theatre in the U.S. is reflected in the eclectic choice of texts. While issues of cultural difference, transformation, interpretation, assimilation, separatism and marginality are features of all the pieces, the differing and varied discourses employed by each of the dramatists articulate a plethora of stories which provide a politics of representation inventively "other" to that promoted by the sensationalist film and television products— mostly centered around enterprising gigolos and gang violence— which more readily reach these shores.

Caridad Svich's eloquent essay, "Out of the Fringe: In Defense of Beauty," which accompanies this collection, looks at how the writers in this anthology is representative of a generation of artists "at the intersection of theatre and performance," who have occupied new thematic territories. In her "Writer Speaks," Cherríe Morraga talks of her work as "in dialogue with the Chicano theatre," and while the bilingualism and geographical specificity of *The Hungry Woman: A Mexican Medea,* positions itself within a tradition pioneered by Luis Valdez, its focus on how femininity and womanhood are defined, like in her earlier play, *Shadow of a Man,* clearly destabilizes sexual and gender stereotypes.

Like English writer, Rod Wooden's recent *Medea Media, The Hungry Woman* reworks and relocates Euripides' classic tale as a way of interrogating the politics of such mythologies. Medea's statement to Jasón that their son must not be subject to the model of masculinity that Jasón represents, poses the need for alternative role models. "The man I wish my son to be does not exist . . . must be invented," Medea states, questioning a relationship with inherited customs and traditions on both a social and cultural level. Notions of normality are re-viewed as Medea's position queries a process of indoctrination and initiation which serves to validate the masculine and the white, a world in which it is acceptable "to lie about your race, your class, your origins" and "create a completely unoriginal fiction about yourself." The mechanization of the normal or natural is here communicated as a masculine-orientated reality. Incarceration awaits Medea, evoking an illustrious list of fictional constructs whose defiant pronouncements have led to conspicuous imprisonment; another "mad woman in the attic," to evoke Gilbert and Gubar's term, whose defiance meets with institutional opposition.

Voyeurism, the politics of motherhood, the denigration of the female at the expense of the male, the plundering of cultural artifacts and their exhibition in a culturally dislocated environment are all discussed in a piece that occupies a space recognizing the intertexts— Aztec, Greek, Chicano, Euro-American—on which it comments.

The myth of woman is at the center of a number of the plays here. Like *The Hungry Woman*, Migdalia Cruz's *Fur* exposes the instability of gender categories, exploring the extent to which gender goes beyond impersonation, instinct and performance. Both plays, like Naomi Iizuka's *Skin* and Caridad Svich's *Alchemy of Desire/Dead-Man's Blues*, are concerned with the acting out of femininity and desire, and the politics of the gaze. These plays conspicuously invert dominant discourses of theatrical representation—women are seen in positions that challenge widely held assumptions.

In *Fur*, the imprisoned hirsute Citrona, her keeper Michael, and the woman he employs to watch over her, Nena, are all engaged in the act of reciprocal surveillance in a caged setting, which is both physically real and imaginatively metaphorical. During the course of the play, the female body is reclaimed as a text written by a whole series of socio-cultural factors. Michael sees Citrona and Nena as commodified products, but his attempts to appropriate Citrona are consistently frustrated. He gives her what he thinks she desires but it is never enough, for desire always exceeds the means through which it can be satisfied. Recalling Angela Carter's work with fables, *Fur* questions the acceptable norms and values through which behavior is regulated and enforced. Citrona begins the play as a freakish exoticized being, a voracious witch who stands in opposition to the more angelic Nena. As the play progresses such stereotypes are dismantled. The human and the animal are no longer polarized into opposed binarisms, rather shown to be interdependent. All the characters, as Cruz indicates in her author statement preceding the play, "take turns in being the ideal of physical beauty" but act in "beastly" ways to get the object of their affections to love them. The alluring sexuality that Citrona represents is both destructively and constructively seductive. Power is used and abused by all the characters in the name of desire. As with the Frankenstein myth evoked by Citrona, "sometimes you kill the thing you love most," because it is the only way you can entirely control and possess it.

Naomi Iizuka's *Skin*, which directly acknowledges in its subtitle to be an adaptation of Büchner's *Woyzeck*, is also concerned with female desire. Its world is eerily immediate and quirkily distant. The urban landscape, although Southern Californian unlike José Rivera's New York-based *Marisol*, shares with Rivera's play an evocative ability to present environment as a tangible and at times frightening entity which decisively shapes its inhabitants. As with the characters in Fornes's work, the protagonists of Iizuka's play physically and verbally articulate their pain as they seek to make sense of a society which renders them anonymous, invisible beings. Her bold images and endless locations appear to flaunt logical expectations of what is possible on a stage, and her feverish, highly charged language, reminscent of that created by the French dramatist Bernard-Marie Koltès, evokes the patterns of ordinary speech while retaining a magical, intense, almost dreamlike quality much like Koltès's *Black Battles with Dogs* and *Roberto Zucco*. The play's title and its final image point to its translucent brilliance. The characters themselves are as fragile, vulnerable, protective and resilient as the skin which contains them: all are easily scarred but contain within themselves both the capacity for self-healing and self-destruction.

Like *Skin,* Svich's *Alchemy of Desire/Dead-Man's Blues* evolves within a dramatic and geographical setting which, like that of *Skin*, acknowledges its textual referents. The female chorus evokes both the witches of *Macbeth* and the washerwomen of Lorca's *Yerma*. The play's world, like that of *The House of Bernarda Alba*, is defined by the absence of men and the mourning of the phallus. Simone's husband, Jamie, has died in the last war—a war which could be Vietnam, Iraq or Bosnia—and the iconography of war provides a powerful magnet for the masculinity personified by Jamie. As with the female protagonists of *Blood Wedding* and the historical figures in the opening scene of Caryl Churchill's *Top Girls*, for the women of Svich's play the loss of lovers, husbands and children is a brutal fact of their existence.

As with Rivera's *The Promise*, his dramatic appropriation of *The Dybukk, Alchemy of Desire/Dead-Man's Blues* rewrites cultural myths with a defiantly political agenda. The exorcising of Jamie's ghost artic-ulates a vision of theatre as ritual, a bringing together of communities in religious celebration. As with Martin McDonagh's *The Beauty Queen of Leenane* and Sarah Kane's *Cleansed*, the play is conspicu-ously mythical, subverting reductionist positions in its construction of a space which avoids gravitation toward the mimetic sign. Like Kushner's *Angels in America*, silence becomes part of the texture of the play, as characters reveal and conceal their own relationships to the deceased Jamie. Simone's ability to hallucinate and then exorcise Jamie testifies to theatre as an alternative state which permits the unknowable to be revealed. The sensual world of brambles, blankets of purple flowers, earth, water and fireflies that light up the night provide a twinkling surreal realm at once removed from the cityscape of Kushner's *Angels in America*, but similarly obsessed with issues of identity and the ability of individuals to define themselves through the communities they are obliged to exist in but remain in conflict with.

These communities are never idealized, on the contrary, as in Coco Fusco and Nao Bustamante's *Stuff*, the complex ways in which the self is mapped within cultural, social, economic and political boundaries, and the tension between the role and the real is the subject of constant interrogation. Popular iconography infuses both plays. In *Alchemy of Desire/Dead-Man's Blues,* Simone is brought buckets of Kentucky Fried Chicken. Its odor permeates her house, and the contamination of the space by its pungent smell is perhaps significant of American popular culture's surreptitious infiltration of all layers of the country's consciousness.

In *Stuff*, one of the few pieces seen in Britain to date*, cultural exportation is problematized through an examination of how Hispanic culture is offensively packaged into a single unified entity, a commodity which can be readily consumed by an audience in search of ever more titillating experiences. The play's game show formula offers a menu of the "foreign" where fast food tourism is all too easily available to the indiscernible traveler. The audience's own implication in this process is made tangible as our own act of looking is made conscious. The piece is a stark and uneasy indication of the ways in which we are conditioned to undertake certain responses to the material presented before us. The tourist sex industry and encounters with cultures perceived as "other," which are reduced to spiritual transformations, are placed graphically on display. The Travel Taster Service provides consumption with the minimum of hassle where experiences can be purchased without ever having to travel. The traffic in sexual and cultural exploitation and the linguistic codes that allow both to

---

Stuff was seen at Glasgow's CCA and London's ICA in November 1996. Caridad Svich's *Alchemy of Desire/Dead-Man's Blues* played at the Hackney Empire Studio Theatre in August 1999. Although a number of the writers featured in this anthology have enjoyed residencies at London's Royal Court Theatre, where work like Oliver Mayer's *Ragged Time* was developed, their work has too often been presented solely as rehearsed readings.

exist and indeed flourish are articulated through an interactive format where duplicity and deception are suggestively invoked to allow us to further understand and, as appropriate, intervene in the relationships between representation and reality, the viewer and the viewed, subject and object, and the permissive and the prohibited.

Oliver Mayer's *Ragged Time* also encourages an interrogation of spaces which seem to have passed into popular consciousness. The hard sell of American capitalism is here defined through an all-pervasive bartering where everything, including children, can be bought and sold, if the price is right. The play's title invokes a direct reference to E. L. Doctorow's classic novel, *Ragtime*, and the focus is similarly on those written out of official historical discourses. Here, however, the panoramic emphasis is more defiantly political. Set in 1898, it juggles a series of encounters between two blind black singers (Gary and Ross), a Jewish newspaper seller (Abe), a struggling black prostitute (Freda) and a musically gifted Mexican boy (Ignacio). The conflicts it presents, however, are not simply issues of black versus white. Rather the power of slavery and its legacy ensure a battle of cultural heritages as the diverse characters each grapple for their share of power and "success" as personified by the cult of the celebrity explored in the play.

Here, too, popular culture provides an alluring model. The Yellow Kid and The Sanctimonious Kid are conjured from the newspaper page to offer choreographed routines that frame the interweaving narratives. The repeated recourse to "Yankee Doodle" illustrates the power of its ideological associations to shape the characters' behavior. The politics of the family, the nuclear family's status as a defining metaphor for our societies and oppressive moralities contained and promoted by the family all come into play as the characters' actions are placed within a wider socio-historical context. Our practices of reading is highlighted in the play as the iconographies that determine our sexual, gender and racial practices are made visible to us. In the interplay of the fictional and nonfictional, as in Sergi Belbel's *A.G./V.W. Kaleidoscopes and Lighthouses of Today,* Thomas Bernhard's *Lunch with Ludwig* and Churchill's *Top Girls,* we are repeatedly asked to reevaluate the ways in which history—both political and personal—has been registered and documented from a particular white male viewpoint. Freda's need to look white becomes emblematic of the need to erase difference; a difference that is further articulated through Abe and Gary's tussles. The official discourses of history are contested by the play's comprehension of how contemporary subjectivities are shaped by a complex series of past events.

If the revisioning of the past is the thematic terrain of *Ragged Time*, *Greetings from a Queer Señorita* and *Trash* both turn to a more immediate present in their examinations of the negotiations of identity in climates of cultural and social dislocation. As with *Ragged Time* and Luis Alfaro's *Straight as a Line*, the body becomes the site of a struggle for self-determination, used in different ways to serve white America's economic priorities. Issues of visibility and power, theorized so powerfully in Peggy Phelan's *Unmarked: The Politics of Performance* (London/New York: Routledge, 1993), are here made present through interventions where simplistic politics of assimilation are questioned and refocused. All three plays highlight the artifice of the medium; the performance situated in a context that consciously demonstrates how roles are formed and the multifarious ways in which censorship is perpetuated. Narrative disclosure is accompanied in all three plays by its positioning against the silence that accompanies the manifestation of gay and lesbian desires within the dominant cultural milieu. These plays can be linked to the confessional theatre of such performance artists as Holly Hughes, Tim Miller and Kate Bornstein. Direct address is used here to redefine not only the audience/performer relationships but also as a graphic means of negotiating the relationships between private and public worlds where complicity is both encouraged and problematized.

In *Trash,* Pedro Monge-Rafuls's protagonist José confides in his audience, sharing intimate details of the offense taken at attempts to anglicize his name to Joe, his acknowledgment of Hispanic role models and the abuse suffered by Latinos at the hands of a U.S. economy which relies on illegal labor for social survival. Conflicting histories reflect different ideological positions. José's story allows an alternative to a hegemony of representation by presenting a counter-image that forefronts the identity of the teller.

In the autobiographical *Greetings from a Queer Señorita*, Monica Palacios reinvents herself as Don Juanita, marking both a reappropriation of traditionally masculine territory and a rejection of an ideological agenda which sees her performative capacities defined solely through an ability to play maids. Working outside realist structures, the play's emphasis on performativity (both Latina and lesbian), presents a series of positions by which the subject is, to use Althusser's term, "interpellated" within dominant white, hetero-sexual discourses. The coding of lesbianism in predictable stereo-typical ways is here subverted. Excavating Palacios's own stories, the piece marks a journey from reactive object to decisive subject and, as with *Stuff*, articulates the potential power of humor as an enpower-ing strategy, which can resist appropriation by the male gaze. Standup comedy is used to confront attitudes which confine women to the status of inferior "other."

In *Straight as a Line* "otherness" is primarily explored through the relationship between two Brits, Paulie and his middle-aged mum. Their physical and metaphorical odyssey—the play begins in New York and ends in Las Vegas—allows for reflection on racism and xenophobia; masculinity and its discontents; motherhood and the means through which it is defined and articulated; dependency and desire; and, as in *Trash*, the role of popular culture in constructing our identities. Ann Margaret and Hollywood films, Oprah Winfrey and talk shows, Elizabeth Taylor and idealized TV movies are all used to delineate cultural forms through which the characters con-struct and measure their own behavior. The association of AIDS with death and its visualization as a signifier of impending and morbid-laden doom are here set against a death performed before our inva-sive eyes. The glorious manufactured bodies of the television pro-grams that Paulie and his mother discuss, conceal their vulnerabilities; Paulie's later become brutally displayed. *Straight as a Line*'s narrative of AIDS serves to provide an identity for an illness whose public face has been graphically interwoven with homophobic discourses. As Paulie and his mother navigate their allocated roles, their relationship is defined within ever-shifting dramatic rituals which clearly place all social action and interaction as performance.

The only play within this anthology to be geographically situated within Latin America, Nilo Cruz's *Night Train to Bolina*, shares with *Straight as a Line* an episodic structure which denies a neat bounding politics. Here ideological indoctrination is manifest through the strategies employed to control the two children, Mateo and Clara. The place of violence within that process is made visible through the bruises Mateo has been given. With Clara it is religion that determines how she is expected to conduct herself. She is taught to walk "correctly" and, as with Mateo, is coerced by her family into adhering to a series of superstitious rituals. Escape brings further abuse as the children find themselves trapped within an environment as constrictive as that they left behind. As in *Alchemy of Desire/Dead-Man's Blues* the presence of the dead within the living serves as a potent illustration of our position within the larger institutional frameworks in which we attempt to define our subjectivities. In his author statement before the play, Cruz celebrates the power of the imagination as a means for the children in the play to "transcend the poverties of their existence." As with Maria Irene Fornes's *Mud* and *Enter the Night,* the transformative potential of the imagination serves to grace their lives with a vitality and beauty that is distinctly lacking in those around them.

Like Fornes, Cruz shares an ability to create images that resonate beyond the stage world that engenders them. Like the other playwrights whose work is included in this anthology, he demonstrates the problems inherent in attempting to define a Latino sensibility.

All these pieces, in differing ways examine the parameters of dramatic representation—how it works? Who it's for? Who is performing and where? How societies and performers relate to shared bodies of knowledge? They provide a wonderful indication of the varied theatrical languages of Latina/o writers and performance artists, and make so much of what is reaching the British stages— both mainstream and fringe—seem dated, predictable and unengaged with the multicultural profile of the country's urban centers.

Although Peter Sellars's 1994 production of *The Merchant of Venice* provided London audiences with an indication of the strength of contemporary Latino actors, a Latino presence on British stages has been largely limited to a few fringe productions of plays by José Rivera and Maria Irene Fornes, and visits to the ICA and London International Festival of Theatre (LIFT) by Coco Fusco, Luis Alfaro and Guillermo Gómez-Peña. Even the astounding attention given to Junot Diaz's *Drown* in 1996 failed to acknowledge its place within a wider context of Latino writing or arouse interest in other Latino cultural movements.

Love's Fire: Fresh Numbers by Seven American Playwrights, an Acting Company production directed by Mark Lamos, came to Britain's Barbican Theatre in May and June of 1998 as part of that year's "Inventing America" celebrations. Marketed as "a reflection on love and romance . . . by America's leading contemporary playwrights," the list of writers was conspicuous by its omission of Latino figures. A program bereft of the Latino, once more asks whose America is being invented and why? It poses the question of how long it will be before Britain, and indeed the U.S., provide representational space for some of the bold Latino writing which is collected in this anthology.

Maria M. Delgado
School of English and Drama,
Queen Mary and Westfield College
University of London
December 1999

CARIDAD SVICH is the resident playwright at the Mark Taper Forum in Los Angeles, where she was formerly an NEA/TCG Theatre Residency Program for Playwrights grant recipient. She is co-editor of the volume *Conducting A Life: Reflections on the Theatre of Maria Irene Fornes* (Smith & Kraus, 1999) and her Lorca English-language translations are collected in the forthcoming book *Lorca: Impossible Theatre* (Smith & Kraus). Ms. Svich has taught at the Yale School of Drama, Traverse Theatre (Edinburgh) and Paine's Plough (London), among others.

MARÍA TERESA MARRERO is Assistant Professor of Spanish at the University of North Texas. She is both a scholar and creative writer who has written extensively for anthologies, such as *Negotiating Performance: Gender, Sexuality & Theatricality in Latina/o America* (Duke U.P., 1994) and *Tropicalizations: Transcultural Representations of Latindad* (University Press of New England, 1997), and for such scholarly journals as *Latin American Theatre Review, Gestos, Ollantay* and will be featured soon in *TDR*.

MARIA M. DELGADO teaches in the School of English and Drama at Queen Mary and Westfield College, the University of London. She is editor of *Valle-Inclán Plays: One* (London: Methuen, 1993, 1997); the recent edition of *Contemporary Theatre Review*, entitled "Spanish Theatre 1920–1995: Strategies in Protest and Imagination"; and is co-editor of *In Contact with the Gods?: Directors Talk Theatre* (Manchester University Press, 1996) and *Conducting a Life: Reflections on the Theatre of Maria Irene Fornes* (Smith & Kraus, 1999). She is currently working on a book with Peter Sellars.

Citations

Manifestations of Desires: Roland Barthes, A Lover's Discourse, Fragments, Richard Howard, trans., New York: Hill and Wang, 1978. Straight as a Line: Ana Castillo, Massacre of the Dreams: Essays on Xicanisma, Albuquerque: University of New Mexico Press, 1994; Joni Mitchell, "Last Chance Lost," Turbulent Indigo, Warner Brothers, 1994; Gil Cuadros, "Resurrection," City of God, San Francisco: City Lights Books, 1994. Fur: The Beatles' "Yes It Is" and "Girl," are written by Lennon/McCartney, Sony/ATV Songs LLC Maclen SP publishers, 1965; "Here, There and Everywhere," Lennon/McCartney, 1966. Ragged Time: Robert Hayden, "Aunt Jemima of the Ocean Waves," Collected Poems, Frederick Glaysher, ed., New York: Liveright/W. W. Norton, 1985. Greetings: The Beatles' "I Saw Her Standing There," written by Lennon/McCartney, Gil Music Corporation, Northern Songs LTD publishers, 1964; "Evergreen: The Theme from A Star Is Born," written by Barbra Streisand and Paul H. Williams, Warner Brothers, 1976. The Hungry Woman: Christa Wolf, Medea: A Modern Retelling, New York: Bantam Books/Doubleday, 1998. "From the U.K.": Lisa Kron, from Kate Davey's "Fe/male Impersonation: The Discourse of Camp," p. 231, Critical Theory and Performance, Janelle G. Reinalt and Joseph R. Roach, eds., Ann Arbor: University of Michigan Press, 1992; Jean Baudrillard, Simulations, pp. 1–3, 24–27, Paul Foss, Paul Patton and Philip Beitchman, trans., New York: Semiotext, 1983; Linda Hutcheon, The Politics of Postmodernism, p. 33, London/New York: Routledge, 1989; Sandra Gilbert and Susan Gubar, The Mad Woman in the Attic, New Haven: Yale University Press, 1979.

Photographic credits

Alfaro: Jay Thompson; Bustamante: Sven Wiederholt; Delgado: furnished by the editor; Fusco: Lyle Ashton Harris; M. Cruz: Diana Solis; N. Cruz: Carol Rosegg; Iizuka: furnished by the author; Marrero: furnished by the editor; Mayer: Renard Garr; Monge-Rafuls: Joel Cano; Moraga: furnished by the author; Palacios: Becky Villaseñor; Svich: furnished by the editor.